WORKING I...
NEWCOMER'S...

SECOND EDITION

Employment
EDUCATION
Benefits
Immigration
Citizenship
Rights

EDITED BY WILL SOMERVILLE

The Centre for Economic & Social Inclusion

This book has been produced by the Centre for Economic & Social Inclusion, an independent non-profit organisation dedicated to tackling disadvantage and promoting social justice. *Inclusion* offers research and policy services, tailored consultancy, bespoke and in-house training and running a wide range of conferences and events.

Inclusion also produce the Welfare to Work Handbook, Working in the UK: Newcomer's Handbook and The Young Persons Handbook. More information about these publications, and our other products and services, is available on our website: www.cesi.org.uk

WORKING IN THE UK: NEWCOMER'S HANDBOOK
The guide to rights and guidance in and out of employment for all working age migrants

Edited by Will Somerville
IBSN: 1-870563-74-3
© 2006 Centre for Economic & Social Inclusion

First edition published in 2004

Second edition published 2006 by:
Centre for Economic & Social Inclusion
3rd floor, 89 Albert Embankment, London SE1 7TP

All rights reserved. Paragraphs from this book may be quote, and short extract reproduced without permission, with an appropriate credit, without prior permission. Full page reproduction, copying or transmission may be undertaken only with written permission or in accordance with the Copyright, Designs and Patents Act 1988.

Editor: Will Somerville has edited this book in an independent capacity
Design: www.origin8creative.co.uk
Printing: www.cpd-group.co.uk
Text editor: Ann Watt.

Disclaimer
Every effort has been taken the accuracy of the advice in this handbook. However, we cannot guarantee the information contained is absolutely accurate. This is because guidance is constantly changing. Furthermore, partners can only endorse the contents of their own chapter(s). As far as the authors are aware, all chapters contain correct information at the time of writing.

Contents

About this book	13
Acknowledgement	14
Introduction (Will Somerville)	15

❶ Overview of workers and the immigration system — 24
(Parnesh Sharma, JCWI)

- Can I work in the UK?
- I am from Europe
- I am from outside Europe
- Does my status make a difference?
- Work permits
- Work permit employment
- Permit free employment
- Family
- Students (non-EEA nationals)
- Appeals

❷ Asylum seekers and refugees (James Lee, Refugee Council) — 70

- How to claim asylum
- I am an asylum seeker
- I am a Refugee
- Differences in Scotland and Wales
- Citizenship

3 Refugees and higher education 92
(Council for Assisting Refugee Academics)

- How can I study?
- How can I access financial support?
- University Courses in the UK

4 Benefits (Neil Bateman) 108

- Outline of the benefits system
- Benefits at a glance
- Entitlements at a glance
- Making benefits claims
- At a glance guide to migration and social security
- Glossary
- Jobseeker's Allowance
- Income Support
- Pension Credit
- Benefits for ill-health and disability
- Child Benefit
- Help with paying your rent, Council Tax and other housing costs
- Working Tax Credit
- Child Tax Credit
- Social Fund
- Benefit decisions and appeals
- Benefit and tax credits if you are in work

5 Training and education to help find work (Sean Moley, *Inclusion*) 192

- Work Based Learning for Adults (WBLA) and Training for Work (TfW)
- Programme Centres
- Learn Direct
- Entry to Employment (e2e)
- Education Maintenance Allowance (EMS)
- The Get Ready For Work Programme (Scotland only)
- Skillseekers (Scotland only)
- Apprenticeships
- The Employer Training Pilots (ETPs) and the National Employer Training Programme (NETP)
- Qualifications

6 Employment programmes (Bee Brooke and Alex Doyle, *Inclusion*) 220

- Work Focused Interviews
- New Deal for Young People
- New Deal for Musicians
- New Deal for 25 Plus
- New Deal for 50 Plus
- New Deal for Lone Parents and the New Deal for Partners
- New Deal for Disabled People
- Action Teams for Jobs
- Employment Zones
- Pathways to Work
- Jobseeker Mandatory Activity
- Progress2Work
- LinkUP
- Building on New Deal

WORKING IN THE UK: NEWCOMER'S HANDBOOK *2ND EDITION*

7. How can I improve my English? (Helen Sunderland, LLU+) — 284
- What is ESOL and where can I fund ESOL courses?
- What is language support?
- Translation assistance for people whose first language is not English
- ESOL in Scotland (Rob Whelton and Philomena De Lima, Policy Web)

8. Finding and starting work (Beryl Randall, Employability Forum) — 294
- Finding work
- Starting work

9. Documentation (Will Somerville) — 318
- Background and forthcoming changes
- Exceptional Leave to Remain and varying leave
- Glossary of documentation terms
- Proof of the right to work

10. Recognition of qualifications (Will Somerville) — 326
- NARIC
- Professional body exemptions and membership
- Portfolios, APEL and recognition of trade experience
- Four key tips for qualifications on CVs and application forms

11. Volunteering, work experience, placements and mentoring — 336
(Beryl Randall, Employability Forum)
- Volunteering
- Mentoring
- Employment Placements
- Work Trials
- Travel to Interview scheme
- Advice for refugee and migrant community organisations

UK work culture (Beryl Randall, Employability Forum)   **362**

    National Insurance

    Finding my tax code

    Bank Accounts

    Pay slips

    Driving licences

    Car insurance

 Employment Rights (Alison Balchin, TUC)   **370**

    Who can work in Britain?

    What are my rights at work?

    Legal rights

    Rights for working parents

    What happens when something goes wrong?

    Discrimination

    Health and Safety

    Bullying and harassment

    Redundancy and dismissal

    Rights of specific groups of workers

 Racial Discrimination (Ranjit Singh Rana with Graham O'Neill, CRE)   **424**

    What is racial discrimination?

    Key issues for newcomers

    Unlawful racial discrimination

    Exceptions to unlawful racial discrimination

    Making a complaint of racial discrimination

    Evidence in a case of racial discrimination

    The Commission for Racial Equality

15 Maternity Rights and Benefits (Liz Carney)   **466**
     Rights and benefits
     Sex discrimination and work

16 Renting in the private sector (Slickston De Alyn)   **480**
     Tenancy agreement
     Different types of tenancy
     The landlord's general responsibilities

17 Employment Tribunals   **488**
(Amar Dhudwar, Working Lives Research Institute)
     The Employment tribunal system
     What kind of claims can I bring?
     'Types' of worker
     Discrimination
     Discrimination law
     Types of unlawful discrimination
     Equal pay
     Unfair dismissal
     Proving Discrimination
     How do I make a claim to an employment tribunal?
     How do I appeal to the employment appeal tribunal?

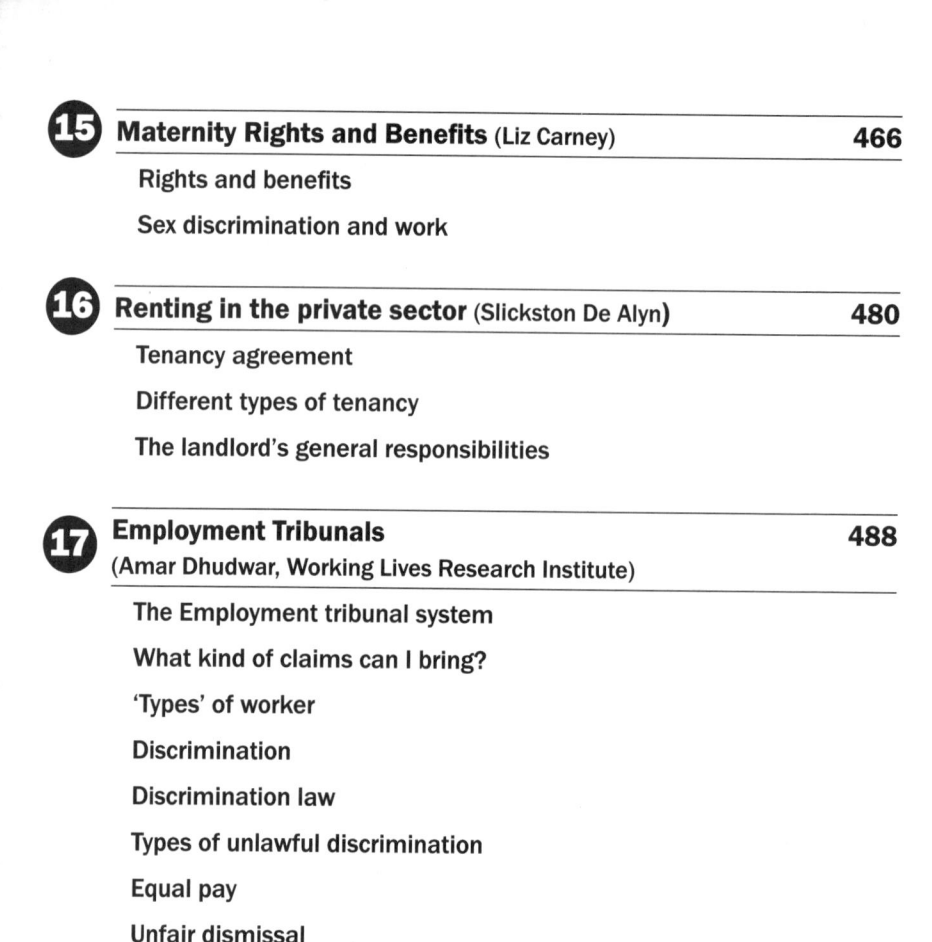

WORKING IN THE UK: NEWCOMER'S HANDBOOK *2ND EDITION*

18. How can I send money to another country? 534
(Andrea Winkelmann-Gleed, London Metropolitan University)

- What are remittances?
- How can you send remittances?
- Choosing a service
- How do I choose a provider?
- How much will it cost?
- How can I complain if transfers go wrong?

19. How do I become a UK citizen? (Chris Taylor, NIACE) 550

- What are the benefits of having UK citizenship?
- How do I become naturalised?
- How long do I have to be in the UK before applying?
- What is the citizenship test?
- The citizenship ceremony

20. Further information for advisers (Gavan Curley and STAR) 556

- A to Z of common issues and queries and how to tackle them
- A to Z of organisations

21. Benefit Rates Table 2006-07 632

22. Biographies 638

23. Abbreviations 648

24. Index 656

About this book

The *Working in the UK: Newcomer's Handbook* draws on the expertise of leading organisations engaged in the fields of work and of newcomers. It is aimed at advisers, representatives, advocates and other parties interested in ensuring that working age migrants are aware of their rights and of the help that is available in and out of work.

This handbook concentrates on migrants and work. The first edition of this handbook was written in co-operation with the Joint Council for the Welfare of Immigrants (JCWI) and the Trades Union Congress (TUC) and was intended as a follow up to the joint JCWI and TUC guide on migrant workers. In preparation for the first edition, the editor carried out 50 phone interviews with Migrant and Refugee Community Organisations, asking what the key issues were and how the handbook could be usefully structured.

For this edition, an email survey was conducted of those who purchased the first edition (over 2,000 individuals and organisations) to ask for their feedback. The survey was also sent to key advice and advocacy stakeholders. As a result of the consultation the handbook has incorporated a number of new issues raised by frontline staff and has gained immeasurably from the expertise and input of partners.

The content of the handbook has also been significantly broadened with two specific discrimination sections (on gender and race), a separate section on refugees and asylum seekers, and a new section on employment tribunals. There are also new sections on renting in the private sector, UK work culture and citizenship.

A number of sections have also been expanded, such as the sections on English language and on recognition of qualifications. Finally, the further information section – previously placed on an accompanying CD-ROM – was found to be little used, so a new 'Further Information for Advisers' section has been included in the text of the handbook.

Disclaimer: This handbook has been written by experts and is correct at the time of writing to the best of our knowledge. However, legislation and policy change quickly in this area and we cannot be held responsible for any errors in the text.

WORKING IN THE UK:
NEWCOMER'S HANDBOOK
SECOND EDITION

Acknowledgements

As always, many people have contributed a great deal of time and effort to the preparation of this handbook. Particular debts are acknowledged below.

All the partners in the process have given both time and effort to making this handbook a reality. The majority of partners have done so without receiving any financial or material reward.

In addition to the chapter partners particular thanks also go to a number of individuals who helped quality assure and check the text, again without material benefit. These individuals also provided expert advice and assistance. They include:

Jane Caple from Citizens Advice for her help in checking the renting in the private sector section

Rebecca Crosby and **Shelly Perrera** from the CRE for their work on the racial discrimination section

Gill Green from the Audit Commission for her excellent advice and suggestions

Kelsey Froehlich for her contribution to the volunteering, mentoring and placements section

Jane Mansour of Work Directions for her help in checking the employment programmes section

Sonia McKay of the Working Lives Research Institute for her assistance in checking the employment tribunals section

Terry Patterson of Manchester Advice for checking the benefits and tax credits material

The Refugee Advice and Guidance Unit for their help with the recognition of qualification section

Lucia Webster for her advice on Credit Unions, found in the remittances section

Finally, **Nicola Smith** and **Ann Watt** deserve particular mention. Nicola managed the project at *Inclusion* and Ann Watt edited the text of the handbook.

Introduction
Will Somerville

This book draws on the expertise of leading organisations engaged in the fields of work and of newcomers. It is aimed at advisers, trade union representatives, welfare advocates, officials, community activists and other parties interested in ensuring that migrants are aware of their legal rights and of the help that is available to them in and out of work.

The handbook takes account of all recent legislative and policy changes, including the recent changes to work permits, changes to the asylum system and EU enlargement.

The first edition of the handbook established itself as the leading introductory guide in this area of immigration, welfare, and work. This edition expands the scope of the book, including sections specifically on asylum seekers and refugees, discrimination law, grievance and dismissal procedures, and citizenship. Furthermore, the new handbook is now referenced.

The following chapters should not be read as a full and comprehensive statement on immigration, citizenship and employment law and are intended as guides to the range of issues involved. Primary sources of information should be consulted for more detailed information, and these are accessible on the web. Where possible we have referenced our advice but if further advice is needed, you should go to one of the recommended organisations, or consult a solicitor.

This handbook concentrates on newcomers (migrants) and work. The organisations who have contributed to this handbook also produce a range of other guidance and have useful and informative websites. For information that doesn't address migrants and work, publications[1] produced by partner organisations and partner websites may be more appropriate.

Using this handbook

The book has been organised according to areas where you might have a particular question. In summary, we have tried to answer the following key questions:

- Can I work in the UK?
- Does my immigration status make a difference to working in the UK?
- Can I stay in the UK?
- What if I am applying for another visa?
- What if I am an asylum seeker?
- What if I am a refugee?
- How do I find work in the UK?
- How do I know if I am working legally?
- What do I need to know to start work?
- What do I need to know about working in the UK?
- How can I access English language support?
- How can I get my qualifications recognised?
- How can I access training to help me find work?
- How can I get help through the New Deal?
- How can I get help through other employment programmes?
- What are my rights in work?

[1] For example, *Inclusion* publishes the Welfare to Work handbook; the TUC publishes a range of guidance relating to employment rights; JCWI publishes the Immigration, Nationality and Refugee Law Handbook; CARA publishes Higher Education Pathways: A Handbook for the Refugee Community; and the Refugee Council publishes the Information Source.

WORKING IN THE UK: NEWCOMER'S HANDBOOK *2ND EDITION*

- What if I work for an agency?
- What happens when something goes wrong?
- What if I am discriminated against because of my race?
- What if I am discriminated against because of my gender?
- How do I take action against an employer?
- How do I get work experience?
- How can I access financial support outside work?
- What is a Work Focused Interview?
- How can I access financial assistance between benefits and a job?
- How can I access financial support to live?
- How can I access financial support in-work?
- How can I send money to another country?
- How do I become a UK citizen?
- Where can I find out more?

Newcomers to the UK are subject to a range of immigration statuses. The different statuses include students, people in permit-free employment, people requiring work permits, EEA Nationals, EEA Nationals of the new accession states (usually referred to as A8 nationals) and asylum seekers and refugees. Immigration statuses have different restrictions and requirements on work, we provide an overview and introduction to the detail.

Financial assistance and benefits are available to newcomers out of work, depending on the restrictions of the leave you have been granted in Britain (the 'terms and conditions' of your status). They include Jobseeker's Allowance, Income Support, Pension Credit, educational benefits, benefits for ill-health and disability, help with rent and council tax, and the social fund. We provide a comprehensive introduction to benefit entitlement for migrants.

Benefits often act as the 'gateway' to a range of other support that can help newcomers into work. This help includes a range of employment programmes that newcomers can access to help them find work, such as the New Deal and a range of geographic employment programmes including Action Teams and Employment Zones. In addition to employment programmes, benefits often act as the gateway to work-based learning, and modern apprenticeships. Some of this support is mandatory if you are receiving certain benefits (such as work focused interviews) and some is voluntary (such as the New Deal for Lone Parents).

Newcomers can access support without being on a particular benefit (particularly in terms of accessing education and training provision). Newcomers can also undertake activities that are likely to improve the prospects of getting work. This includes volunteering, mentoring, employment placements and work experience.

Newcomers to the UK may find the culture of UK workplaces alien or that they lack awareness of processes and regulations. We provide advice and guidance on the recruitment process and on the practicalities of the UK workplace. The handbook also examines at length the rights of newcomers within the workplace, including what documentation is required, the relevant employment rights, guidance on race and gender discrimination, and the process of taking a complaint through an employment tribunal.

Newcomers may wish to continue working and living in the UK. This handbook provides advice on switching visas, staying in the UK, and on becoming a British citizen.

Policy

This handbook is not concerned with Government policy. It is a statement of legal entitlement and, in places, a record of good practices and standards. However, there have been significant changes in immigration policy and the immigration system in recent years and both practitioners and policymakers should be aware of those changes. The ongoing change to the economic migration system with the introduction of a points-based approach is a good example of this.

A number of the partners involved in this handbook have policy expertise and describe recent changes in the policy and legislative framework in published papers or on their websites. For those interested in recent policy, a useful introduction is 'Success and Failure under Labour: Problems of Priority and Performance in Migration Policy, IRP Working Paper 3' available at www.jcwi.org.uk.

Terminology and definitions

This handbook covers all newcomers to the UK. However, there is a range of complex terms, definitions, and concepts which are employed across the handbook. These come from different disciplines (such as immigration law, welfare and benefit terminology or employment law).

Glossary of terms used in this handbook

It is important that readers are familiar with this often complex terminology. This glossary is to introduce the reader to some key terms, they are not the only technical terms used in the handbook and other specialised terms will be defined throughout.

Newcomers

Throughout this book, we refer to newcomers as a neutral term that covers all people new to the UK. Newcomers include all new migrants – from students and migrant workers, through those joining families, to those seeking asylum.

Status and leave

Immigration status refers to the type of permission or leave you are granted when entering the UK. The type of status granted depends on your reasons for wanting to enter or remain in the UK.

To seek leave is to apply for permission to enter the UK (before your travel or when you arrive) or permission to remain in the UK (if you are already in the UK and wish to stay longer than the period for which you were allowed to enter). The following are the general types of leave or status:

- **Indefinite Leave to Enter or Remain** is permission to stay in the UK permanently, typically granted for people who are seeking to settle.
- **Limited Leave to Enter or Remain** is permission to enter or remain in the UK for a specified and temporary time period. This type of leave is granted to those coming to the UK as tourists, visitors, students, and workers – anyone coming for a temporary period of time.
- **Humanitarian Protection and Discretionary Leave** are types of leave which may be granted to those who can demonstrate that they have protection needs.
- **Temporary Admission** is not an official immigration status in the UK (typically asylum seekers).

Refugees and asylum seekers

A refugee is someone whom the Home Office has decided falls within the 1951 Convention definition of a refugee and who is granted asylum. Refugees were automatically given Indefinite Leave to Remain (ILR) in the UK. However, since August 2005 this is reviewed after 5 years.

An asylum seeker is someone who has come to the UK, and formally applied for recognition as a refugee under the 1951 Convention and is awaiting a decision.

Person Subject to Immigration Control

A *Person Subject to Immigration Control (PSIC)* covers people with certain leaves and statuses, including:

- people who have claimed or been refused asylum
- people whose stay in the UK is subject to a written maintenance undertaking and who have been in the UK for less than five years
- people whose stay in the UK is on condition that they don't have recourse to 'public funds'
- people who have appealed against a decision refusing them leave.

People who have refugee status, Exceptional Leave to Remain, Humanitarian Protection, Discretionary Leave or Indefinite Leave to Remain are not PSIC.

Public funds

Public funds are defined as help with provision of housing and a number of benefits, including Child Benefit, Attendance Allowance, Disability Living Allowance, Income Support, income-based Jobseeker's Allowance, Housing Benefit, Council Tax Benefit, Carer's Allowance, Pension Credit, Severe Disablement Allowance (which is not available after April 2001) and the Social Fund.

Europe

The member countries of the European Union (EU) are the UK, France, Spain, Portugal, Italy, Netherlands, Belgium, Luxembourg, Germany, Austria, Greece, Sweden, Denmark, Finland, and Ireland, Hungary, Czech Republic, Slovakia, Slovenia, Poland, Latvia, Lithuania, Estonia, Malta and Cyprus. EU nationals must have the right to reside in the UK in order to qualify for means tested benefits. Nationals of the new accession states are often referred to as A8 nationals. The A8 countries are Hungary, Poland, Estonia, Latvia, Lithuania, Czech Republic, Slovakia and Slovenia. Malta and Cyprus are the two other accession states. The European Economic Area (EEA) is all the EU states plus Norway, Liechtenstein and Iceland. Nationals of Switzerland are treated as EEA nationals for benefit purposes. The European Convention on Social and Medical Assistance (ECSMA) applies to nationals of EEA countries and Ukraine, Romania and Turkey. EU Agreements cover nationals of Algeria, Slovenia, Tunisia & Turkey and give them the same rights as EU nationals who are working and/or have lawfully worked in the UK.

Right to reside

This is automatically acquired if you become a British or Irish Citizen or if you have the right of abode in the UK. It is also gained by people with leave to remain in the UK or a right under European law to reside in the UK, including students, self-employed people, workers and retired workers. The right is not lost by having to claim means-tested benefits for short periods. The government has stated that A8 workers acquire the right to reside after 12 months as a registered worker.

EC Directive 2004/38, in force from 30th April 2006, gives a right to reside for the first three months after entry provided that you do not become an 'unreasonable burden' on the means-tested benefits system.

Ordinarily resident and habitually resident

Ordinarily resident can apply from the first day of arrival in the UK and for any purpose. Habitually resident applies to people of any nationality. To be habitually resident you must be in the UK or the Common Travel Area (Isle of Man, Channel Islands and Ireland) for 'an appreciable period of time'. There is no fixed period which qualifies for being habitually resident. It does not apply to EEA nationals who are workers or to EEA nationals who have lived in UK and return from another EEA state.

Overview of workers and the immigration system

Parnesh Sharma, Joint Council for the Welfare of Immigrants

Can I work in the UK?

A brief answer is that it generally depends on two main issues: whether you are from Europe and the type of employment you want to do. Answering the following questions will help clarify your position:

- Are you from Europe?
- Are you from outside Europe?

If you are from outside Europe, then the type of work you want to do may fall into either of two categories:

- Permit-Free Employment (work for which you do not need a permit)
- Work Permit Employment (work for which you require a permit)

The Home Office has a specific website for those wanting to come to the UK for work or who are already working in the UK: www.workingintheuk.gov.uk

Application forms, with instructions and guidance notes, can be downloaded from the above website. The site also contains a great deal of useful information on various programmes under which non-UK nationals can work or apply to work in the UK.

If you are from *outside Europe* you may also require an 'entry clearance' or 'visa' before you travel to the UK. You can find out online exactly what you require by checking the UK Visas website: www.ukvisas.gov.uk

UK Visas is a joint unit of the Home Office and the Foreign and Commonwealth Office.

Important: It is your responsibility to ensure that you meet all the requirements and have the proper documentation (such as visas or work permits) before you travel to the UK for work.

I am from Europe

If you are a national of any of the member states of the European Union (EU) or a national of Iceland, Liechtenstein or Norway, which together comprise the European Economic Area (EEA), or a national of Switzerland:[1]

- You do NOT need permission (work permit) to work in the UK
- You have full free rights of movement in the UK

Please note that there are special provisions for nationals of the **A8 Member States**, namely, the requirement to register when working in the UK (see below).

If you require further details, or if the section below does not address your question, please consult Guidance Notes – INF 18 published by UK Visas, and available on their website at: www.ukvisas.gov.uk

The member states of the EEA include the following countries:

- Austria
- Belgium
- Cyprus
- Czech Republic
- Denmark
- Estonia
- Finland
- France
- Germany
- Greece
- Hungary
- Iceland
- Ireland
- Italy
- Latvia
- Liechtenstein
- Lithuania
- Luxembourg
- Malta
- Netherlands
- Norway
- Poland
- Portugal
- Slovakia
- Slovenia
- Spain
- Sweden

I am a national of Malta or Cyprus

- You have full free rights of movement in the UK
- You do NOT have to register
- You do NOT need a work permit to work in the UK

I am a national of one of the A8 Member States of the EEA

The Accession or New Member States of the EEA, which joined the EEA in May 2004 and for which special provisions apply, are commonly referred to as 'A8 Member States.'

The A8 Member States are:

- Poland
- Lithuania
- Estonia
- Latvia
- Slovenia
- Slovakia
- Hungary
- Czech Republic

If you are a national of an A8 Member State:

- You are free to enter the UK
- You are free to seek employment in the UK
- You do NOT need a work permit to work in the UK
- You MUST register as per the 'Worker Registration Scheme' once you start your job

What is the 'Worker Registration Scheme'?

Since May 2004 nationals of the A8 Member States are subject to the 'Accession State Worker Registration Scheme'.

If you are a national of an A8 Member State, and you intend to work for more than one month in the UK, then you must register.

The requirement to register applies to ALL nationals of the A8 Member States.

You should register as soon as you start a new job.

The application form can be downloaded from the Home Office website: www.workingintheuk.gov.uk/working_in_the_uk/en/homepage/schemes_and_programmes/worker_registration.html

Or, if you wish, you can order application forms and guidance notes by telephone: 08705 210 224.

You should complete the application (Form WRS) giving your name, address, date of birth, nationality and your employment details.

A one-time fee of £70.00 MUST be paid at time of application.

If you change jobs you must apply for a new registration (on Form WRS) so that you can legally work for your new employer.

You do NOT have to pay a fee for this new application.

You can have more than one job but must register each job (if you have two jobs, then you must register both jobs).

Once you have been working legally in the UK for 12 months without a break (you are entitled to vacations that are part of your employment contract) you will have full rights of free movement and will no longer need to register on the Worker Registration scheme.

You can apply for a residence permit confirming your right to live and work in the UK.

Information leaflets on the Worker Registration Scheme are available in your language (i.e. the language of each of the A8 Member States) and can be downloaded from: www.workingintheuk.gov.uk/working_in_the_uk/en/homepage/schemes_and_programmes/worker_registration.html

How do I apply to register under this scheme?

A complete application will consist of ALL of the following:

- Form WRS (the actual application form)
- A letter from your employer confirming your employment and the date you started working
- Two passport-size photographs

- Your original passport or ID document
- Payment of £70

The completed application should be sent by registered mail to:

Worker Registration Team
Home Office
Walsall Road
Cannock WS11 0JA

If your application is successful you will receive a registration card (and your passport) by return mail.

I am from outside Europe

I am from outside Europe (but am presently in the UK)

If you are already in the UK, and are not a national of a member state of the EEA, you should check your status before you consider working.

Not everyone who comes to the UK is allowed to work.

How do I check my status?

The type of status that you were granted when you first entered the UK is stamped in your passport. It is very difficult to change your status from inside the UK. To do this you may have to leave the UK and apply for Entry Clearance at a British High Commission or Embassy overseas.

The following Home Office website gives examples of the various types of passport stamps:
www.workingintheuk.gov.uk/ind/en/home/0/preventing_illegal/uk_passport_stamps.htlm

If you are still unsure about your immigration status then contact the Immigration and Nationality Enquiry Bureau by telephone at: 0870 606 7766

The following link gives information on how to contact the Home Office by regular mail or email: www.workingintheuk.gov.uk/working_in_the_uk/en/homepage/contact_us.html

Note: if you do not have permission to be in the UK, or your status has expired and you are out of status, it is strongly recommended that you seek specialist advice. There are very serious consequences for violating immigration law. You may be arrested, detained, criminally prosecuted and/or deported. This book provides contact details of various agencies from which you can seek advice.

In-Between Visas

Immigration law automatically extends the leave of a person who has applied for an extension but has not yet received an answer.[2]

The status you were given when you came to the UK is automatically extended as long as you applied for the extension before the expiry of your present status.

For example, if you were given leave or status as a permit-free worker, you can continue to work in that specific job even though your status has expired, if you meet the following conditions:

- You applied for an extension before the expiration of your leave
- You have not yet received an answer to your application.

Change of status (or changing your status once you are in the UK)

In some very limited cases you may be permitted to change status and apply for a work permit to work in the UK.

You may apply to change status if you were given leave to enter the UK as any of the following:

- Student
- Student nurse
- Postgraduate doctor or dentist

- Working holidaymaker
- Sector-based scheme permit holder

Note: Only your prospective employer can apply for a work permit on your behalf. You cannot apply for a work permit yourself.

You can continue to work within the terms of your existing status or entry (for example, as a working holidaymaker) while the application for a work permit is processed. The application to change status must be made before the expiry of your existing status.

Further information on how to apply to change your status and the conditions which you must satisfy are outlined in detail on the Working in the UK website at:

www.workingintheuk.gov.uk/working_in_the_uk/en/homepage/your_status/already_in_the_uk/change_status.html

I am from outside Europe (and want to come to the UK for work)

You may need a visa *before* you travel to the UK.

You may need a work permit *before* you travel to the UK.

You may need both a visa and a work permit before travel to the UK.

Whether you need a visa or work permit or both will depend mainly on any one or all of the following:

- Your nationality
- The work programme for which you wish to enter the UK
- The duration of your stay

Note: It is your responsibility to make sure that you meet all the requirements before travelling to the UK.

What is a visa?

A visa is a document, issued by UK authorities and placed in your passport, if you meet the requirements to enter the UK. Visa applications are processed by 'UK Visas' at British embassies and consulates overseas.

You can find out if you require a visa to travel to the UK by completing a simple online form at UK Visas:
www.ukvisas.gov.uk

In a few seconds the above site will tell you exactly what you need before you travel to the UK. Before you apply for a visa it is important to do some basic research. Read about the various work programmes to see what best suits your needs.

Ask yourself the following questions:

- Why do I want to come to the UK?
- What type of work do I want to do?

Information on the various work programmes is available at the following website: www.workingintheUK.gov.uk

What is a work permit?

A work permit is a legal authorisation to work in the UK and is issued to a specific person for a specific job and employer. A work permit is issued to an overseas national (from a non-EEA country) giving them the legal right to work in the UK. You cannot apply for a work permit; it has to be obtained for you by a UK employer who wants to employ you.

For details see the section on Work Permits on page 34.

Does my status make a difference?

What is status?

Immigration 'status' generally refers to the type of permission or leave you are granted when entering the UK. The type of status depends on your reasons for wanting to enter the UK.

To seek leave is to apply for permission to enter the UK (before you travel or when you arrive) or permission to remain in the UK (if you are already in the UK and wish to stay longer than the period for which you were allowed to enter).

An entry clearance officer (at a British diplomatic post overseas), a UK Immigration Officer (at a port of entry) or the Immigration and Nationality Directorate (if you are already in the UK) will consider your application and your reasons for wanting to enter or remain in the UK, and decide if you meet the legal requirements.

How do I check my status?

The type of status that you were granted when you first entered the UK is noted in your passport. It is very difficult to change your status from inside the UK. To do this you may have to leave the UK, return to your country and apply for Entry Clearance at a British High Commission or Embassy.

The following Home Office website gives examples of the various types of passport stamps:
www.workingintheuk.gov.uk/ind/en/home/0/preventing_illegal/uk_passport_stamps.html

If you are still unsure about your immigration status then contact the Immigration and Nationality Enquiry Bureau by telephone at: 0870 606 7766

The following link gives information on how to contact the Home Office by regular mail or email:
www.workingintheuk.gov.uk/working_in_the_uk/en/homepage/contact_us.html

Note: if you do not have permission to be in the UK, or your status has expired and you are out of status, it is strongly recommended that you seek specialist advice. There are very serious consequences for violating immigration law. You may be arrested, detained, criminally prosecuted and/or deported. This book provides contact details of various agencies from which you can seek advice.

Change of status (or changing your status once you are in the UK)

In some very limited cases you may be permitted to change status and apply for a work permit to work in the UK.

You may apply to change status if you were given leave to enter the UK as any of the following:

- Student
- Student nurse
- Postgraduate doctor or dentist
- Working holidaymaker
- Sector-based scheme permit holder

Note: Only your prospective employer can apply for a work permit on your behalf. You cannot apply for a work permit yourself.

You can continue to work within the terms of your existing status or entry (for example, as a working holidaymaker) while the application for a work permit is processed. The application to change status must be made before the expiry of your existing status.

Further information on how to apply to change your status and the conditions which you must satisfy are outlined in detail on the Working in the UK website at.
www.workingintheuk.gov.uk/working_in_the_uk/en/homepage/your_status/already_in_the_uk/change_status.html

Work permits[3]

Any non-EEA national seeking to enter or remain in the UK for employment will normally require a work permit. A work permit is a legal authorisation to work in the UK and is issued to a specific person for a specific job and employer.

In general employment in the UK can be divided into two categories:

- Work Permit Employment (where a work permit is required)
- Permit-Free Employment (where a work permit is NOT required)

If you require further details, or if the section below does not address your question, please consult Guidance Notes – INF 13 published by UK Visas, and available on their website at: www.ukvisas.gov.uk

How do I get a work permit?

You cannot apply directly for a work permit. An employer in the UK who wants to employ you must apply for a work permit for you.

More information, advice, and application forms are available online at: www.workingintheuk.gov.uk

Can I transfer my work permit?

Since work permits are issued to a specific person for a specific job you cannot transfer work permits.

I am a family member of a work permit holder

You do not need a work permit if you are a dependant (spouse, partner, or child) of a work permit holder. You are free to work in the UK (unless you have had restrictions placed in your passport).

How will I know if my employment requires a work permit?

If you are a non-EEA national you should assume that you need a work permit unless you are certain that the work you wish to do is permit-free work. It is your responsibility to find out exactly what you require before you apply for a visa or travel to the UK.

It is essential to do your research. Good places to start are the 'UK Visas' and 'Working in the UK' websites:
www.ukvisas.gov.uk
www.workingintheUK.gov.uk

Taking a few minutes to do some basic research will help make your journey and/or stay in the UK a problem-free and enjoyable experience.

Employment is a complex area because there are so many types of work, and the demand or need for certain types of work is always changing. For example, if there is a great demand for a certain type of job, and there are not enough resident workers to fill the vacancies, then the requirement for a work permit may be changed. There are also many rules about who can and cannot work in the UK, and it is your responsibility to know what is required

Work permit employment[4]

What is this?

Work Permit employment means that you need special permission (in the form of a work permit) to work in the UK.

You can find further details in the UK Visas publication, Guidance Notes – INF 13, available online at: www.ukvisas.gov.uk

You should obtain the work permit before you travel to the UK. Your employer in the UK is responsible for arranging a work permit for you.

There are six types of work permits:

1. Business and Commercial
This allows UK employers to hire people from overseas for jobs that they have not been able to fill with an EEA national.

2. Sportspeople and Entertainers
This allows UK employers to employ established sportspeople, entertainers, cultural artists and technical and support people from outside the EEA.

3. Internships
This allows students from outside the EEA, studying for a first or higher degree, to undertake an internship with a UK employer.

4. GATS (Global Agreement on Trade in Services)
This allows employees of a company, based outside the European Union, to work in the UK on a service contract awarded to their employer by a UK based organisation.

5. Sector Based Scheme (SBS)
This scheme allows workers from outside the EEA to work in low-skilled jobs for up to 12 months in the UK. You should check www.workingintheuk.gov.uk website for the most current information on this programme as it is under review and changes have been made. At present you can only work in the 'food processing sector'. The programme is due to end permanently in December 2006.

6. Training and Work Experience Scheme (TWES)
This scheme allows non-EEA nationals to work where the purpose is to gain work experience or to do work-based training or to get a professional or specialist qualification.

In all the above instances your UK employer is responsible for obtaining a work permit for you should the employer wish to employ you.

If the UK employer is recruiting in your country, for example under the Sector Based Scheme, the employer will arrange a work permit for you. Then you must apply for a visa (if you are a national who requires a visa) and submit all the proper documents (including proof of your employment and work permit) with your application.

For more details on these various programmes consult the UK Visas website:
www.ukvisas.gov.uk

In particular, consult Guidance Notes – INF 13 published by UK Visas, which explains what you need to do if you want to come to the UK to engage in work permit employment.

The application fee for a work permit is currently £153.00. The person or employer making the application is responsible for making the payment.

Dependants of Work Permit holders

If you are in the UK on a work permit then your spouse, partner and children under 18 can join you if:

- They have a visa for the purpose
- You can support them without need for public funds

For this purpose your dependants must obtain a visa even if they are of a nationality not requiring visas.

Settlement (in the UK) of Work Permit holders[5]

You may apply to live in the UK if you have lived in the UK, as a work permit holder, for a continuous period of 4 years, and:

- your employer certifies that you are still needed for employment for which you hold the work permit
- you meet all the requirements for residency as detailed in paragraph 134 of the Immigration Rules, Part 5:
www.ind.homeoffice.gov.uk/ind/en/home/laws___policy/immigration_rules/part_5/section_1.html

Permit-free employment

What is this?

Permit-free employment is work for which you do not need a work permit.

If you require further details, or if the section below does not address your question, please consult Guidance Notes – INF 14 published by UK Visas, and available on their website at: www.ukvisas.gov.uk

Permit-free employment includes the following:

- Ministers of religion, missionaries or members of religious orders
- Sole representatives of overseas companies in the UK
- Representatives of overseas newspapers, news agencies and broadcasting organisations
- Airport-based operational ground staff of overseas-owned airlines
- Postgraduate doctors and dentists (for training purposes) including those attending Professional and Linguistic Assessment Board (PLAB) tests
- Teachers and language assistants coming to the UK under approved exchange schemes
- Seasonal agricultural workers
- Writers, composers and artists
- Overseas government employees
- Science and engineering graduates
- Overseas domestic workers
- Au pairs
- Working holidaymakers
- Investors
- Business people – setting up a business
- Innovators
- People on the Highly Skilled Migrant Programme

Minister of religion (missionary, or member of religious order)

What is this?
A minister of religion is a religious worker whose main duty is to lead a congregation in prayer and preach about religious beliefs.

What are the requirements?
You must have been working for at least one year during the last five years as a minister of religion. If your faith requires ordination before entry to the ministry, then you must have been ordained for at least one year (full-time) or two years (part-time) training for the ministry.

If English is not your first language or you have not been educated in an English-speaking country, then you must provide proof of having achieved at least Level 4 (spoken English) in IELTS (International English Language Testing System).

If you are a missionary, then you must have worked or been trained as a missionary and are being sent to the UK by an overseas organisation. If you are a member of a religious order, then you must be coming to the UK to live in a community funded by your religious order. If you plan to teach then you can only teach at an establishment funded by your religious order.

You will need a visa (if you are a visa national). You do not need a work permit.

You must intend to work full-time as described above. You must be able to support yourself and your dependants without need for public funds (such as welfare or housing benefits).

You will need a letter from your employer with details of your employment. You must provide proof of your qualifications.

You should provide a contract of employment (if one has been issued to you by your employer).

Restrictions under this category

You cannot work in any other occupation.

Extension of your stay

If you are still working as a minister and your congregation still needs you, then you can apply for an extension providing that you are able to support yourself without need for public funds.

Sole Representative of an overseas firm

What is this?

A senior non-shareholder employee, directly employed by the firm, with full decision-making authority coming to the UK to represent that company.

What are the requirements?

- You must be the sole representative of the company.
- You must be able to support yourself without public funds.
- You will need a visa.

Restrictions

You cannot work in any other employment.

Extension of stay

Initial entry will be for 12 months but you can apply to extend your stay for up to a maximum of three years.

Representative of an overseas newspaper or news agency

What is this?

Media representatives are employees of news gathering organisations who are assigned to the UK on a long-term salaried basis. They include correspondents, producers, cameramen and reporters.

What are the requirements?
- You must be employed by that organisation outside the UK.
- You are being posted to the UK on a long-term basis by your employer.
- You must be able to support yourself without public funds.

Restrictions
You cannot work in any other occupation.

Extensions
Initial entry will be for 12 months but you can apply to extend your stay for up to a maximum of three years.

Airport-based operational ground staff of overseas-owned airlines

What is this?
This allows transferred senior staff members of overseas-owned airlines, which operate services to and from the UK, to work at an international airport.

What are the requirements?
- You must be employed by an overseas-owned airline at a senior level (station manager, security manager or technical manager).
- You must intend to work full-time for the airline.
- You must be able to support yourself without public funds.

Restrictions
You cannot work in any other occupation.

Postgraduate doctors and dentists – for training purposes

What is this?

Overseas doctors and dentists are allowed to enter the UK to continue their training. It is important to note that this category is for trainees only, not for those wanting to work as a doctor or dentist.

There are various levels of qualifications and training and you should consult the Working in the UK website for further details: www.workingintheuk.gov.uk

Note: The rules for postgraduate doctors and dentists changed on 30 March 2006. Posts are considered as employment posts for immigration purposes and internationally qualified graduates who have not been trained in UK medical schools will now be considered for training positions only if employers are unable to fill those positions with UK trained graduates.[6]

What are the requirements?

- You must have a letter from the Dean of the UK school where you will do your training.
- The letter should outline your training programme.
- You must be able to live in the UK without public funds.
- You must intend to leave the UK at the end of your training.

Restrictions

Your work will be restricted to what is outlined in your training programme.

Extensions

You will be granted entry for the length of time of your training programme up to 26 months or longer. Extensions of up to three years at a time may be granted

Upon completion of your training programme you can apply to switch categories (providing you meet all the requirements) to any of the following:

- Work permit holder
- Highly skilled migrant
- Business person
- Innovator

Note: The rules for postgraduate doctors and dentists have recently changed and therefore the rules around extensions have also changed. For those currently in post, and who apply before 31 December 2006, the 'old' rules should still apply.[7]

Teachers and language assistants (on approved exchange schemes)

What is this?

You must be coming to the UK to work in an approved exchange programme (as a teacher or language assistant). The organisation which arranged your exchange will issue a 'certificate of appointment' outlining details of your work. You must present this certificate with your visa application.

What are the requirements?

- You must intend to leave the UK at the end of the approved exchange.
- You cannot work in any other occupation.
- You must be able to support yourself without public funds.

Seasonal Agricultural Workers Scheme (SAWS)[8]

What is this?

The scheme allows workers from outside the European Economic Area (EEA) to enter the United Kingdom to do seasonal agricultural work for farmers and growers. This work is low-skilled and includes planting and gathering crops, on-farm processing and packing of crops and handling livestock.

What are the requirements?

- You must be 18 or over and in full-time education abroad.
- You must have a valid Home Office card issued by the operator of the scheme where you will be working.
- You must leave the UK at the end of your stay.
- You cannot work in any other occupation.
- You must be able to support yourself without public funds.

Additional Information

There is no limit on the number of times you can work under this scheme as long as you meet the requirements, and it is at least three months since your last stay in the UK.

The SAWS programme is run by operators who have been approved by the Home Office. You can find out more about how to work under this programme by contacting the operator or your university of college (either the student union or campus employment office). If you are hired the operator will provide you with an information package. You will also receive a work card (similar to a work permit).

You must apply for a visa before you travel to the UK.

Note: The SAWS scheme will be in operation until 2010.

Writers, composers, and artists

What is this?

Authors, essayists, playwrights, poets, composers of original music (not performing someone else's work) painters, sculptors, photographers of international repute, and cartoonists and illustrators whose work has been published or exhibited for its artistic merit.

What are the requirements?

- You must have built a reputation outside the UK.
- You must be mainly involved in producing original work.
- You must intend to work only as a writer, composer, or artist.

- You must earn your income only as a writer, composer, or artist and be able to support yourself and dependants on that income (in the past one year and in the future).

Restrictions

You cannot work in any other occupation except your field of artistic work.

Overseas government employees

What is this?

Someone employed by an overseas government, the United Nations or other international organisation of which the UK is a member.

What are the requirements?

- You must provide a letter confirming you are an overseas government employee.
- You must intend to work full-time for the government or organisation.
- You must be able to support yourself without public funds.

Restrictions

You cannot work in any other occupation.

Extensions

Initial entry will be for 12 months. You can apply to extend your stay for a maximum of three years.

Overseas domestic workers[9]

What is this?

Persons employed in private households providing personal services to do with the running of the employer's household, such as servants, nannies, gardeners, or cooks.

What are the requirements?

If you require further details, or if the section below does not address your question, please consult Guidance Notes – INF 17 published by UK Visas, and available on their website at: www.ukvisas.gov.uk

In general you must be coming to the UK with your employer, and you must intend to work for your employer.

You will need a visa.

Restrictions

You cannot work in any other occupation.

Extensions

You should consult Guidance Notes – INF 17 about extensions as whether you can extend or not depends on the intentions of your employer.

Science and Engineering Graduates Scheme (SEGS)

What is this?

This scheme allows overseas graduates of UK schools to remain in the UK for 12 months after graduating to further their career.

What are the requirements?

- You must have graduated from a UK institution with a Bachelor's, Master's, or Ph.D. degree in an approved subject.
- You must intend to work during your 12 month grant of stay.
- You must support yourself without public funds.
- You must intend to leave upon completion of your work period.

Restrictions

There are no restrictions on the type of work you can do.

Extensions

You can only stay in the UK for 12 months under this scheme but you can switch into another employment category if you meet the requirements.

You may also switch to the Fresh Talent scheme in Scotland. However, if you do so you can only be on the scheme for one year rather than two years. See page 53 for further information on Fresh Talent.

Additional Information

To find out if your degree is in an approved subject go to www.workingintheuk.gov.uk and click on 'SEGS' in the left column of the website, where the various programmes and schemes are listed.

Note: The Immigration rules recently changed in regard to the SEGS. All Master's and PhD students will now be allowed to apply for 12 months' work in the UK after completing their studies regardless of the subject studied.[10]

Au pair[11]

What is this?

Au pair placements are intended to assist young people who wish to reside in the UK to learn English. As an au pair you are required to live with an English-speaking family and work in their home, generally looking after children, for up to 5 hours per day. In return you will be paid a reasonable allowance for the work and get two free days off work per week.

If you require further details, or if the section below does not address your question, please consult Guidance Notes – INF 16 published by UK Visas, and available on their website at: www.ukvisas.gov.uk

What are the requirements?

To be au pair you must meet ALL of the following requirements:

- The au pair placement must be arranged before you arrive in the UK.
- You must be between the ages of 17 and 27.
- You must be unmarried, have no civil partner and no dependants.
- Your main purpose is to study English.
- You must live with an English-speaking family during your stay in the UK.
- The living arrangement must provide you with enough time to study.
- You must be a national of one of the following countries:
    - Andorra
    - Bosnia-Herzegovina
    - Bulgaria
    - Croatia
    - The Faroes
    - Greenland
    - Macedonia
    - Monaco
    - Romania
    - San Marino
    - Turkey

- You must have a visa before you travel to the UK (if you are a national of a country for whom visas are required)

Note: If you are a non-visa national or you do not require entry clearance, you will have to satisfy an immigration officer that you qualify for entry as an au pair. If so, you will be granted six months' entry. If you wish to continue working as an au pair for longer than the initial six months, you must apply for an extension before your current leave expires.

To find out exactly what you need before you travel to the UK, check the UK Visas website and complete the online form: www.ukvisas.gov.uk

Restrictions
- You cannot stay for longer than two years as an au pair.
- You must leave the UK at the end of the two-year term.
- You cannot receive public benefits (i.e. welfare).

Extension of your stay
If you were allowed to enter the UK, as an au pair, for a period of less than two years, then you can apply to extend your stay.

Additional Information
If you wish, you may change your au pair placement to another family.

Working holidaymaker

What is this?
This programme allows Commonwealth citizens to enter the UK for work and travel for a maximum period of two years, where the primary objective of the travel is to holiday.

If you require further details, or if the section below does not address your question, please consult Guidance Notes – INF 15 published by UK Visas, and available on their website at: www.ukvisas.gov.uk

What are the requirements?
- You must be a Commonwealth citizen, a British Dependent Territories Citizen, a British Overseas citizen or a British National (Overseas).
- You must have a valid UK visa before you arrive in the UK.
- You must be aged 17 to 30 years of age (inclusive).
- You may take employment as part of your holiday for no more than 12 months during your stay.
- If you are married then your spouse must also meet all the requirements of this category, and you both must take the working holiday together.

- If you have dependent children none should be five years of age or over, or who will be five before you complete your holiday.
- You must be able to pay at least the costs of your onward journey.
- You must be able to support yourself without need for public funds.
- You must intend to leave the UK at the end of your holiday.

To find out exactly what you need before you travel to the UK consult the UK Visas website and complete the online form:
www.ukvisas.gov.uk

Restrictions under this category

You can do most types of work, including voluntary work, but not engage in business, or provide services as a professional sportsperson.

Extension of your stay

No extensions of stay are allowed under this category.

Additional Information

You may be eligible to switch to work permit employment after 12 months in the UK if your occupation is on the list of designated shortage occupations.

You may also switch to Innovators or Highly Skilled Migrant Programme.

For details go to:
www.workingintheUK.gov.uk

Investors

The requirements under this programme are lengthy and very specific and you should consider specialist advice.

If you require further details, or if the section below does not address your question, please consult Guidance Notes – INF 13 published by UK Visas, and available on their website at:
www.ukvisas.gov.uk

In general:

To qualify as an investor you must have at least £1 million under your control. You must invest not less than £750,000 of this in an acceptable form of investment and you must meet the following requirements:

- You must intend to make the UK your main home.
- You must have an acceptable plan of investment.
- You can be self-employed but cannot work as an employee.
- You must be able to support yourself without public funds.

You do not need a work permit. You do need a visa.

After living in the UK for four years under this category you can apply for permanent residence.

Business person – Setting up a business in the UK

The requirements under this programme are lengthy and very specific and you should consider specialist advice.

If you require further details, or if the section below does not address your question, please consult Guidance Notes – INF 10 published by UK Visas, and available on their website at: www.ukvisas.gov.uk

In general:

To qualify as a business person you must have at least £200,000 of your own money for investment in the business, and:

- You must have a detailed and sound business plan
- You must be actively involved in the management of the business
- The business must provide you with an income
- You cannot access public funds

You do not need a work permit. You do need a visa.

If you meet the requirements you will be granted entry for 12 months. You can apply for an extension of your stay for up to another three years.

Innovators

The requirements under this programme are lengthy and very specific and you should consider specialist advice.

You should thoroughly review the requirements as detailed in Innovators: Guide for Applicants published by 'Working in the UK' and available on their website:
www.workingintheuk.gov.uk

In general:

Innovators are entrepreneurs with new and creative ideas, who want to set up business in the UK, which will result in exceptional economic benefits for the UK.

Highly Skilled Migrant Programme (HSMP)

The requirements under this programme are lengthy and very specific, and you should consider specialist advice.

You should thoroughly review the requirements as detailed by 'Working in the UK' and available on their website:
www.workingintheuk.gov.uk

Application forms and guidelines can be downloaded from the above site.

In general:

This programme is for highly skilled and exceptionally qualified and talented people who wish to come to the UK. You can apply to stay permanently after you have been in the UK for a period of four years under this programme.

Note: From 3 April 2006, the HSMP initially accepts migrants for a period of 24 months. After 24 months the situation is reviewed and an extension of three years can be granted. Therefore, if you want to apply to stay permanently in the UK, the period of residence is five years (and you apply near the end of five years' residence).

Fresh Talent[12], Rob Whelton and Philomena De Lima, Policy Web

Overview

The Fresh Talent Initiative forms part of the Scottish Executive's response to the demographic challenge of Scotland's ageing and declining population. The aim of Fresh Talent is to attract young, highly skilled people to live and work in Scotland.

One strand of activity is the 'Fresh Talent: Working in Scotland' scheme (FT:WISS). This scheme enables nationals of countries outside the EEA who have graduated from a Scottish university or college to apply to remain in Scotland for up to two years without the need for a work permit (EEA nationals do not require a permit to live or work in any part of the UK).

What are the criteria for joining Fresh Talent?

The FT:WISS is open to anyone who is a national of a country outside the European Economic Area (EEA)[13] who completes a Higher National Diploma (HND), UK-recognised first degree, Master's, or PhD at a Scottish Institute of Higher or Further Education, and who lived in Scotland whilst studying. You must apply within one year of graduation.

If your course was sponsored (e.g. by your government or an international scholarship agency) you must obtain written permission from them before applying.

How do I apply?

You must use a FLR (FT:WISS) form, available from the Home Office[14] or on the website www.scotlandistheplace.com. There is an application charge (currently £335 for postal applications).

You must submit a genuine HND or degree certificate[15] when making your application

You can apply in a number of ways:

- From outside the UK
- From within the UK if you have leave to remain (as a student)
- From within the UK if you have graduated under the Science and Engineering Graduates Scheme (SEGS). If you are on any scheme other than SEGS you cannot switch to the FT:WISS Scheme

If your application is refused, appeals are governed by Chapter 12 of the Immigration Directorate's Instructions in the same way as other immigration matters (see page 65).

How long can I stay?

The FT:WISS allows you to remain in Scotland for up to two years.[16]

If you switch to FT:WISS from SEGS (see above) the one year period of leave granted under that scheme will be deducted from the two years.[17]

The two years' leave granted under FT:WISS does not count towards the qualifying period for settlement in the UK.

If you wish to stay for a longer period of time you will need to change to a different scheme before your two years' period of leave ends. You may apply to the following schemes:

- Work permit. In common with some other schemes such as SEGS, you can do this without the need to leave the UK (see page 34)
- The Highly Skilled Migrant Programme (see page 52)
- As a business person (see page 51)
- As an Innovator (see page 52)

There are some schemes that you can not switch to from the FT:WISS scheme, including:

- Retired Person of Independent Means
- Investor
- Seasonal Agricultural Workers Scheme (SAWS)
- Sector Based Schemes (SBS)

Can I bring family members?

Under the scheme your dependants (see page 121 for definition) may stay in Scotland with you so long as they meet the immigration rules. However, you must be able to support them without recourse to public funds.

Family members will be admitted to the UK on the same terms as would be the dependants of work permit holders (see page 37). These rules allow your spouse or partner to seek employment anywhere in the UK. There is no restriction requiring them to work in Scotland.

What kind of work can I do, and where can I work?

Under the scheme you are free to look for and take on any kind of employment, including paid or unpaid work, or self-employment. You do not need to have an offer of employment before joining the scheme, nor do you have to work in a field related to your studies.

Entry to the scheme is dependent upon your intention to work in Scotland. If it is discovered by immigration officials (e.g. when you are returning from a trip outside the UK) that you are working in a part of the UK other than Scotland, your place on the scheme is liable to be revoked.

If I wish to study in Scotland, can I get financial assistance?

Under the Fresh Talent Initiative, a new scholarship programme – the Scottish International Scholarship Programme – has been created. For the 2006-07 year, there are a total of 22 places available.

You can apply only if you are a national of China, India, Australia, South Africa, New Zealand or Singapore. For more information, see www.scotlandscholarship.com

Funding has also been allocated to facilitate the creation of approximately 20 work placements with 'Scottish Networks International'.[18] This organisation aims to recruit overseas graduates of the highest possible calibre and to arrange work placements with suitable businesses in Scotland.

A number of Further and Higher Education Institutions have been granted funding under the Fresh Talent 'Challenge Fund'. This has been used to support a wide range of projects including advice services and seminars, work experience and placements, social activities, and support for families of international students. Provision varies significantly between institutions. For more details you should contact the institutions directly – see the list of participating institutions at the end of this chapter.

Outside these schemes financial assistance is not available. Under the criteria for joining the FT:WISS, you must be able to support yourself without recourse to public funds.

The Relocation Advisory Service

The Relocation Advisory Service was established under the Fresh Talent Initiative and aims to be a 'one stop shop'. It should be able to answer questions relating to your move to Scotland, including work permits, accommodation, and becoming a student. They can advise you on how to find employment but will not be able to find you a job. The service can be contacted in a number of ways:

Relocation Advisory Service
Scottish Executive
3rd Floor, Meridian Court
5 Cadogan Street
Glasgow G2 6AT

Phone (from UK): 0845 602 0297
Phone (overseas): +44 141 248 2808
info@scotlandistheplace.com
(Please note that replies to email enquiries may take 20 working days)

www.scotlandistheplace.com

List of institutions participating in 'Challenge Fund' projects
- University of Aberdeen
- Robert Gordon University
- Aberdeen College
- University of Abertay
- University of Dundee
- Dundee College
- University of Edinburgh
- Edinburgh College of Art
- Glasgow School of Art
- Telford College Edinburgh
- University of Glasgow
- James Watt College
- Moray College
- University of St Andrews
- University of Stirling
- University of Strathclyde
- University of Paisley
- Glasgow Caledonian University
- Bell College
- UHI Millennium Institution (Environmental Research Institution)

Family

Family members or dependants of permit-free workers[19]

Unless specifically restricted – as in the case of au pairs or seasonal agricultural workers – your dependants (spouse, partner or children under 18) can join you in the UK if:

- they have a visa for this purpose
- you can support them without need for public funds

Students (non-EEA nationals)

I want to come to the UK as a student

For details on how to qualify for entry as a student please consult Guidance Notes – INF 5 published by UK Visas, and available on their website at: www.ukvisas.gov.uk

In general:

You must be accepted at a recognised/approved educational institution.

You must show that you are going to follow:

- a recognised full-time degree course
- a course which involves at least 15 hours of daytime study each week
- a full-time course at an independent fee-paying school

You must be able to support yourself without working or assistance from public funds.

You must intend to leave the UK upon completion of your studies.

You will need a visa if you are a visa-national.

If you are a non-visa national you will also need a visa if your course is for longer than six months.

If you are unsure whether you qualify for entry as a student, you should apply for a visa at your nearest British diplomatic post.

Can I apply to extend my stay as a student?

If you entered the UK on a student visa you can apply to extend your stay.

Application forms and guidelines are available online at the Immigration and Nationality Directorate website: www.ind.homeoffice.gov.uk

If you entered the UK for a short course (6 months or less) and you wish to take another short course, the maximum time you can stay in the UK is two years (as long as you continue to be enrolled in short courses).

For a course at degree level or higher you can stay for the duration of your study, and apply to extend your stay for the period you are studying.

Can I work while I am a student?

You can do part-time or holiday work, but you cannot:

- work for more than 20 hours a week during term unless the placement or work is part of your programme of study
- engage in business, be self-employed, a sportsperson or entertainer
- work full-time in a permanent job

If your course is for six months or less you cannot work unless you were given permission, before you came to the UK, and this is noted in your visa.

There are two types of stamp in your passport:

- if you have a restriction you are allowed to work
- if you have a prohibition you are not allowed to work

Restriction

A restriction will typically look like either of the stamps below. You are allowed to work with a restriction (within the 20 hour limit).

> No recourse to public funds
> Work (and any changes) must be authorised

Or

> Leave to enter/remain in the United Kingdom on condition that the holder maintains and accommodates herself and any dependants without recourse to public funds and does not enter or change employment paid or unpaid without the consent of the Secretary of State for Employment and does not engage in business or profession without the consent of the Secretary of State for the Home Department is hereby given for/until (specified time)

Prohibition

A prohibition will typically look like the stamps below. You are not allowed to work if you have such a stamp.

> No work or recourse to public funds

Or

> Leave to enter/remain in the United Kingdom on condition that the holder maintains and accommodates himself and any dependants without recourse to public funds, does not enter employment paid or unpaid and does not engage in any business or profession, is hereby given for/until (specified time)

For further details on working while a student please consult Guidance Notes – INF 5 published by UK Visas, and available on their website at: www.ukvisas.gov.uk

Can I switch from student visa to work permit when I am in the UK?

You may be able to switch if you meet the following conditions:

- You have completed a recognised degree programme
- You have a valid work permit for employment
- You have the written permission of any government or agency sponsoring you
- You have not broken any immigration laws

If you have leave to remain as a student you may switch to the Fresh Talent scheme (see page 53).

Family Members or dependants of students

Can my wife, husband, partner or children join me in the UK?

Your spouse, civil partner or any children under the age of 18 can join you in the UK for the duration of your studies. They must have visas. You must be able to support them without the need for public funds.

Can my husband, wife or civil partner work in the UK?[20]

If you have permission to stay in the UK for 12 months or more, your spouse or civil partner will be allowed to work.

Passport stamps or stickers

Stamps or stickers (typically placed in your passport) that show your wife or husband is allowed to work:

> Leave to enter for/until (specified time)
> No recourse to public funds

Or

> Leave to enter/remain in the United Kingdom on condition that the holder maintains and accommodates herself and any dependants without recourse to public funds is hereby given for/until (specified time)

Stamps or stickers (typically placed in your passport) that show your wife or husband is prohibited from working:

> Leave to enter for/until (specified time)
> No work or recourse to public funds

Or

> Leave to enter/remain in the United Kingdom on condition that the holder maintains and accommodates himself and any dependants without recourse to public funds, does not enter employment paid or unpaid and does not engage in any business or profession is hereby given for/until (specified time)

Nurses and midwives –
Overseas Nurses Programme (ONP)

The rules and procedures governing entry to the UK under this programme are strict and complex.

Under the Overseas Nurses Programme (ONP) all overseas-qualified nurses must register with the Nursing and Midwifery Council of the UK (NMC), the regulatory body for nurses and midwives practising in the UK. The NMC will assess your qualifications and decide if you are eligible for admission to the Overseas Nurses Programme (ONP).

The NMC has published a detailed 28-page booklet for overseas nurses available on its website: www.nmc-uk.org

Your first step should be a thorough review of exactly what is required for an overseas-qualified nurse to work in the UK.

How can I come to the UK as a nurse or midwife?

You must first have your qualifications assessed by the NMC.

You must have confirmation from the NMC that you are eligible:

- for admission to the Overseas Nurses Programme, or
- to undertake a period of supervised practice, or
- to undertake a programme leading to registration as a midwife

You will need a visa before you travel to the UK.

You will not need a work permit during your learning period in the UK.

You will need a work permit if you work as a nurse in the UK.

Concessions for irregular residents or long-term residents without status or overstayers[21]

There is no provision in the Immigration Rules to grant residence, or Indefinite Leave to Remain, solely on the basis that someone has been in the UK for a long period of time. However, this is done on a case by case basis and is purely discretionary.

You should seek specialist advice if you feel that you may qualify under this policy for Indefinite Leave to Remain in the UK.

In general, this policy applies to:

- All foreign nationals
- All EEA nationals

Where a person has had:

- up to 10 years or more of continuous *lawful* residence

or

- 14 years of continuous residence of *any legality* (including overstayers or those with no status)

Indefinite Leave to Remain will normally be granted, unless:

- you have a criminal record (except minor non-custodial offences)

or

- you have deliberately and blatantly evaded immigration controls, for example, by using forged documents, absconding, or entering into a marriage of convenience

If you feel you may qualify, it is recommended that you seek specialist advice because of the potential consequences it may have for you, particularly if you have been in the UK for a long time and have established a life, business, or family here.

Child concessions

While there is no provision within the Immigration Rules for a person (whether child or adult) to be granted Indefinite Leave to Remain (ILR) solely on the length of her or his residence, there is a policy 'concession' that operates outside the Immigration Rules which can be used by a child's or family's immigration lawyer to argue that ILR should be granted to the family in individual circumstances.

It should be noted that because the concession outlined below is not incorporated into the Immigration Rules, it is 'discretionary' – that is, the Home Office will consider each case to which the concession applies 'on its merits'. A full discussion should be had with the child's or family's immigration lawyer where the concession appears to apply in order that all the 'merits' of the case can be fully considered prior to contact with the Home Office. The Home Office have suggested that it is not possible to make a formal 'application' under this concession but immigration lawyers have successfully applied to regularise a family's immigration status quoting the concession. The Home Office have stated that where it is decided not to proceed with 'enforcement action' (deportation or removal) because of the concession, consideration will be given to regularising the stay of the family and that they will not be left in limbo.

The Seven year concession

The 'seven year concession' applies to families with a dependent child (under 18) or children living with them who have been living in the UK 'continuously' for 7 or more years. In such cases the Immigration and Natronality Directorate (IND) accepts that 'enforced deportation or removal will not normally be appropriate' as the ties established by children over this period will 'outweigh other considerations and it is right and fair that the family should be allowed to stay here'.[22] There is no requirement that the children should have been born in the UK.

It should be noted that contrary to other policies in relation to applications made by children, the policy is applied only where there is a child aged under 18 at the time the case is considered by the Home Office rather than the date the application is made.

As the concession relates to the length of residence of the child, the immigration status of the parent should not matter even, for example, where removal directions have been set or a deportation order signed.

Exceptions to this concession include where there has been a flagrant abuse of the immigration law or where the parent has been convicted of a serious criminal offence which outweighs the compassionate circumstances of the case, including the length of residence of the child.

Appeals

Generally, you have a statutory right of appeal against immigration decisions provided:

- that your application falls within the Immigration Rules
- that you have made a valid application on the appropriate form
- that you have made your application within any required time limit and in certain other cases

Exceptions

You do not have a right of appeal if you are:

- refused entry to come to the UK as a visitor, unless your application relates to an application for entry clearance as a family visitor
- refused entry to come as a student on a short course of six months or less, or as a 'prospective student' wishing to enter the UK in order to arrange your studies, or as the dependent family member of such a person

Note: Even where there is no specific right of appeal under the immigration laws, there are rare cases where it may be possible to apply to the High Court for 'judicial review' or under the Human Rights Act. You will need to seek expert legal advice as to whether this is possible as you will need to deal with it promptly.

Reasons for refusal

If your application is refused, the Notice of Refusal will tell you the reasons for refusal. It will also state whether or not you have a right to appeal against the decision and the time limit within which you must submit your appeal. If so, a copy of the Notice of Appeal should be attached to the Notice of Refusal.

How to appeal

You will have to complete a Notice of Appeal form within the relevant time limits. The Notice of Appeal should be enclosed with the Notice refusing your application.

There are three basic types of form for appealing against a Home Office or entry clearance decision:

- Form 1 is used for cases where you are appealing from the UK
- Form 2 is used where you are conducting your appeal from outside the UK (other than for family visit appeals)
- Form 3 is used for family visit appeals only (which will also be conducted from outside the UK)

How do I complete the Notice of Appeal?

The Notice of Appeal must be completed in English. The most important thing is that the form is completed and sent off in accordance with the strict time limits.

Time limits

There are strict time limits and if you submit your appeal after the limits, you are likely to lose your right of appeal:

- For Overseas Refusals the time limit is 28 days
- For UK Refusals the time limit is 10 days

The time limit for lodging your appeal will be stated in the refusal notice.

Note: The decision will be presumed to have been received by you:

- two days after it was sent, if you are in the UK

or

- 28 days after it was sent, if you are appealing from outside the UK (unless the contrary is proved)

The Notice of Appeal must actually be received by the Home Office or entry clearance officer within that period, not just sent within the period. When calculating the 10 day period, weekends and bank holidays are not taken into account. However, the 28 day period is calculated as 28 calendar days.

Also note that in immigration cases (particularly overseas cases), it can be several months after you have sent your Notice of Appeal before the appeal papers are received by you or your representative.

Tips

The form asks whether you have a representative to help you with your appeal. If you have a legal representative, you should enter their details in this section.

The form asks you to give the grounds on which you are appealing. If you are appealing against an immigration decision, you should:

- put in as your grounds of appeal
    - that the Appellant meets the requirements of the Immigration Rules
    - that the decision is contrary to the evidence and does not take all relevant circumstances into account
- ensure that you complete the form fully and carefully and most particularly the Declaration part of the form
- print your full name and ensure that you or your representative sign and date the form. If the form is not signed, it will not be valid.

The Notice of Refusal will tell you where to send the Notice of Appeal. Ensure you send it to the correct address.[23] Notices of Appeal may be sent by post (use registered or recorded delivery post if possible and keep the posting slip as evidence) but make sure you keep a copy of the Notice of Appeal for your own records.

With the Notice of Appeal you should enclose a copy of the decision against which you are appealing.

Where does the appeal take place?

In all cases, the appeal will take place in the UK, even if you yourself are not in the UK. The courts dealing with appeals against immigration and asylum decisions are part of the Immigration Appellate Authority. The courts sit in a number of different locations in the UK.

Do I need a legal representative to act for me in my appeal?

In all immigration and asylum appeals, you will have a much better chance if you are represented by a competent and experienced legal representative.

Endnotes

[1] Immigration (European Economic Area) Regulations 2000 or Commission Regulation 1251/70

[2] Immigration Act 1971 s 3(c)

[3] Immigration Rules Part 5 s 1
www.ind.homeoffice.gov.uk/ind/en/home/laws_policy/immigration_rules/part_5/section_1.html

[4] www.workingintheuk.gov.uk/working_in_the_uk/en/homepage/work_permits/applying_for_a_work.html

[5] Immigration Rules Part 5 section 1

[6] Statement of Changes in Immigration Rules 13 March 2006 HC 974 and 30 March 2006 HC 1016

[7] See British Medical Association (BMA) website for more detail. For example http://www.bma.org.uk/ap.nsf/Content/IMGHomeOffice

[8] www.workingintheuk.gov.uk/working_in_the_uk/en/homepage/work_permits/saws.html

[9] www.workingintheuk.gov.uk/working_in_the_uk/en/homepage/schemes_and_programmes/domestics_workers.html

[10] Statement of Changes in Immigration Rules 13 March 2006 HC 974 and 30 March 2006 HC 1016

[11] www.workingintheuk.gov.uk/working_in_the_uk/en/homepage/schemes_and_programmes/au_pairs.html

[12] The following were used as references throughout the Fresh Talent section. Commission for Racial Equality (2005) Broadening Our Horizons Summary Report at www.cre.gov.uk; 'FLR (FT:WISS) Form Version 09/2005' <http://www.ind.homeoffice.gov.uk/ind/en/home/applying/application_form.Maincontent.0130.file.tmp/FT%20WISS%20Form.pdf> (05 February 2006); 'Fresh Talent: Working in Scotland scheme' <http://www.workingintheuk.gov.uk/working_in_the_uk/en/homepage/schemes_and_programmes/fresh_talent__working.html> (05 February 2006); 'The Fresh Talent: Working in Scotland scheme Policy Index' <http://www.ind.homeoffice.gov.uk/ind/en/home/laws___policy/policy_instructions/table_of_contents/chapter_5.Maincontent.0028.file.tmp/ch5sect14.pdf> (05 February 2006); 'A Place to Live and Work: Introduction' <http://www.scotland.gov.uk/Topics/Government/Promoting-Scotland/18738/14640> (05 February 2006); 'Helping Overseas Students Work in Scotland' <http://www.scotland.gov.uk/News/Releases/2004/12/09100921> (05 February 2006); 'New Fresh Talent Challenge Fund' <http://www.scotland.gov.uk/News/Releases/2005/04/06123057> (05 February 2006); 'Statement of Changes in Immigration Rules HC 104 15 June 2005' <http://www.ind.homeoffice.gov.uk/ind/en/home/laws_policy/immigration_rules/statement_of_changes15.html> (14 February 2006)

[13] The EEA comprises all 25 EU Member States plus Iceland, Liechtenstein, and Norway

[14] The form can be downloaded from: http://www.ind.homeoffice.gov.uk/ind/en/home/applying/application_form.Maincontent.0130.file.tmp/FT%20WISS%20Form.pdf

[15] Immigration and Nationality Instructions Chapter 5 (Academic Qualification: General Requirements, para 3)

[16] Immigration Rules HC104, paragraph 96

[17] Immigration Rules HC104, paragraph 143A (viii) (b)

[18] See www.scottishini.org for further information

[19] Immigration Rules Part 4 & 5 paragraph 194-199

[20] Immigration Rules Part 3 paragraph 77

[21] Immigration and Nationality Directorate Instructions Chapter 18

[22] See House of Commons written answers, 24 February 1999, column 310

[23] If it is an overseas appeal against refusal of entry clearance, it must be sent to the Entry Clearance Officer at the British Embassy, Consulate or High Commission where your application was made. If you are in the UK, the Notice of Appeal must be sent to the Home Office in Croydon or the Chief Immigration Officer at the port or airport where the refusal decision was made

2 Asylum seekers and refugees[1]

James Lee, Refugee Council

How to claim asylum

Asylum seekers

An asylum seeker is a person who has left their country of origin, applied for recognition as a refugee in another country, and is awaiting a decision on their asylum claim.

An asylum claim is made under the 1951 UN Convention Relating to the Status of Refugees (the Refugee Convention).[2] The claim is considered by the Home Office to see if it satisfies the criteria set out in the Convention for being a refugee.[3]

If it is decided that your asylum claim does not meet the criteria fully but that protection is still needed, you can be given Humanitarian Protection or Discretionary Leave to Remain.[4]

Applications for asylum should be made as soon as possible at either:

- the port of entry upon arrival in the UK
- one of the designated Home Office Asylum Screening Units (ASU) in Croydon or Liverpool.

After this, you will be issued with an Application Registration Card (ARC) which is both a form of identification and the means by which you receive financial support.

What support is available

While your claim for asylum is being considered, you can access support provided by the National Asylum Support Service (NASS) which is part of the Home Office. Support falls into two main types:

- subsistence (subs only) – if you do not need NASS accommodation, you can apply for a weekly amount which you collect at your local post office through your ARC card
- subsistence and accommodation (both) – if you ask NASS for accommodation and subsistence, you will not have a choice as to where you live unless you have a connection to a particular area (ie family)

NASS support is given while your asylum claim is ongoing. When it finishes, Section 4 ('Hard Case') support is available.[5] The main differences are that Section 4:

- replaces cash payments with vouchers of a lower value
- provides accommodation and vouchers together
- is usually dependent on signing up for the Voluntary Assisted Return and Reintegration Programme when an asylum claim has been refused

There are a number of agencies around the UK that have a One Stop Service (OSS) that can help with your support. They offer free independent and confidential advice about NASS and can be found at: http://www.refugeecouncil.org.uk/contact/ukandaddresses.htm[6]

If you are under 18 and have arrived on your own as an unaccompanied minor, local authority social services will support you. See http://www.refugeecouncil.org.uk/refugeecouncil/what/what002.htm[7] for further details.

As an unaccompanied minor, you may well be given leave to remain in the UK until your 18th birthday. This is usually called Discretionary Leave to Remain. Before you turn 18, you should take legal advice about applying for this leave to be extended.

If you are over 16 and have Discretionary Leave, or are applying for it to be extended, you are fully entitled to access the employment, education, and other mainstream benefits outlined in the sections for refugees below.[8]

I am an asylum seeker

Can I work?

In July 2002, the government withdrew a policy concession that allowed asylum seekers to work if, after six months, they had not received an initial decision on their claim. Now you cannot work for money, or payment in kind (that is, where you are given board and lodging) unless you have received permission from the Home Office.

You can apply for permission to work if:

- you waited more than 12 months for an initial decision by the Home Office on your asylum claim[9]
- the delay in the Home Office's decision was not your fault
- your claim for asylum is ongoing, even if it is now at the appeal stage

Applications should be made by post to the Asylum Casework Directorate at the following address: Lunar House, 40 Wellesley Road, Croydon, Surrey, CR9 2BY

In the letter you must state:

- your Home Office reference number
- that you are requesting permission to work on the basis that your application for asylum is or has been outstanding for over 12 months without a decision

If successful, the asylum casework team dealing with your claim will respond in writing confirming that you have permission to work. They will also give details of where to go for a new Application Registration Card (ARC). Your ARC will need to be changed so as to show that employment is permitted.[10] See 'Finding and Starting Work' on page 294 for information relating to employment. Permission to work will be shown on your Application Registration Card (ARC).

If your application is refused, you will need to get legal advice on other ways of challenging the negative decision if you want to pursue it further.

If you do not have permission to work then volunteering opportunities are open to you and can offer many significant benefits, including:

- constructive use of time and building self confidence
- exposure to the UK working environment
- references for future employment if you are granted permission to work
- improving your English language proficiency
- building bridges with the local community

Further information about volunteering can be found on page 336.

How can I access training?

Training courses help develop vocational (work-related) skills. Some training will require permission to work (for example, New Deal, Modern Apprenticeships), but there are a number of other training opportunities available if you cannot work.

Many vocational courses in Further Education colleges will be free for asylum seekers on NASS support. Even when charges are made, it is always advisable to approach the college directly and ask them to waive fees. Colleges can do so if they think you are a strong student, or where it fits in with their widening participation strategy.

You are also able to enrol on job-related (vocational) training which has a work placement, provided the work part is unpaid.[11] Where the training includes a 'training allowance', you must inform NASS before you start the course as you may need to have the conditions of your temporary admission to the UK amended and the level of your support reassessed.[12]

There are many opportunities, mainly through Further Education colleges, for asylum seekers receiving NASS support to do vocational courses beyond basic English for Speakers of Other Languages (ESOL) courses and IT (free of charge). You may need permission to work to access some types of training because of funding restrictions. It is always best to speak with the training provider directly to ask about eligibility and fee concessions. See page 192 on adult education and training for further information.

How can I get language help?[13]

Courses in English for Speakers of Other Languages (ESOL) are widely available and mostly free, although there may be charges for certain specialist or more advanced courses. The biggest providers are Further Education (FE) colleges. Each college will have a main site where you can register but they may well run ESOL courses at other venues as well.

There is a range of ESOL courses that you can take. Some cover general English communication; others can have a specific focus (for example, ESOL for women, healthcare, writing, etc).

Many voluntary organisations also run ESOL courses but these are unlikely to be accredited. However, they are often specifically for asylum seekers and may even offer one-to-one language support at home. Your local One Stop Service (OSS) will have more information about ESOL courses and projects in your area.

If you want to learn English for a specific purpose, such as to retrain as a doctor or to study at university, then an English as a Foreign Language (EFL) qualification may be necessary. EFL provision is expensive and aimed mainly at international students coming to study in the UK. Funding is not usually available to people claiming asylum. You will need to pay registration fees and examination costs as well.

For further details on English language learning, see the 'How can I improve my English?' section on page 284.

How can I study?

There are many courses freely available at Further Education colleges to asylum seekers who are receiving support. To qualify for a fee waiver you will need to show the college:

- your Application Registration Card (ARC)
- evidence of NASS support (i.e. Post Office receipt for last payment)

There are some instances when charges will be made for courses:

- for some advanced level courses and specialist short-term courses
- for higher level qualifications (i.e. level 3 and above), including foundation degrees
- to people on Section 4 support or whose asylum claim has been refused and are unsupported

You will usually have to pay the international student rate for full-time courses and part-time higher level courses. However, it is always worth approaching the admissions tutor of the relevant department or school as universities and colleges have the discretion to charge home student fees, or to waive them completely. Universities are generally very keen to meet students with academic potential and you should make use of this.

Note: Each school or department will have an admissions officer for undergraduate and postgraduate study. It is advisable to approach them directly.

There are also additional costs you need to consider:

- registration and examination – you should not have to pay if the course is free, but always check with the college before enrolling
- books and other materials – each college will have its own library, but there may be core text books which are useful to buy; you also need to budget for paper, files, stationery
- transport – colleges run courses in a range of venues, in addition to the main site, which may be closer to where you live

See the section 'How can I study?' on page 92 for more details.

What if I am a family member of an asylum seeker?

If your partner is the main NASS applicant you are entitled to claim NASS support in your own right. Get in touch with your nearest OSS for further information.

If you are dependent on someone else's asylum claim you cannot apply for permission to work. Only main applicants can do so if they meet the criteria (see 'Can I work' section above). If granted, the permission does not cover any dependants of the asylum seeker.

If you are aged between 16 and 18, then you should be able to continue in full-time education subject to the criteria outlined above.[14]

I am a refugee

A refugee is a legal term for someone who, following their claim for asylum in the UK, has met the criteria laid out in Article 1 of the 1951 Refugee Convention.[15] This defines a refugee as a person who:

- is outside his/her country of nationality or habitual residence
- has a well-founded fear of persecution for reasons of race, religion, nationality, political opinion, or membership in a particular social group
- is unable or unwilling to avail himself/herself of the protection of that country, or to return there, for fear of persecution

In the past, refugee status meant you had Indefinite Leave to Remain in the UK. However, from 30 August 2005 you will be given 5 years' leave to remain before having your case reviewed.[16]

If you do not meet the criteria of the Refugee Convention you may qualify either for 'Humanitarian Protection' or 'Discretionary Leave'. There is little difference in terms of access to mainstream services and employment rights between refugee status, Humanitarian Protection and Discretionary Leave to Remain.[17]

In addition to leave to remain following a claim for asylum in the UK, there have been two recent developments resulting in Indefinite Leave to Remain (ILR) being awarded. These are as follows:

- The Gateway Protection Programme is the UK's new resettlement programme. The first refugees on this resettlement programme arrived in Sheffield in March 2004. Working in partnership with the Office of the United Nations High Commissioner for Refugees (UNHCR), the UK intends to resettle an annual quota of refugees each of whom will have Indefinite Leave to Remain.[18]
- Family Indefinite Leave-to-Remain Exercise (Family Amnesty) was initiated by the Home Office to clear the backlog of asylum claims made before 2 October 2000. Those qualifying will receive Indefinite Leave to Remain. The amnesty application process is not time limited, nor is it dependent on your still having an ongoing asylum claim. The basic criteria are that you:
    1. made an initial claim for asylum before 2 October 2000
    2. had at least one dependant aged under 18 (other than a spouse) in the UK on 2 October 2000 or 24 October 2003.[19]

Applications should be made to IND Casework, Home Office, PO Box 1541, Croydon, CR9 2YS. You should include your name, date of birth, Home Office reference number, and details of why you think you are eligible.

What happens at the end of process?

If you get a positive decision on your asylum application, you should receive three pieces of correspondence:

- a letter from the Home Office confirming their decision on your asylum and leave to remain
- a letter from NASS noting that you have your positive decision and detailing when your NASS support will finish
- a NASS 35 document that will have your photograph on it and give details of the support you have received from NASS

If you have been receiving NASS support, you will only have 28 days from the date of your Home Office letter until it finishes.

Can I work?

If you have received a positive decision from the Home Office on your asylum claim, you have full employment rights and are legally protected from discrimination.[20] This means that you can get a paid job, set up your own business or receive benefits such as Jobseeker's Allowance (see 'What support is available?' below).

Permission to work is given from the date of the Home Office letter confirming your leave to remain. If you are receiving NASS support, then 28 days are given from the date of the Home Office letter before it finishes. During this time you are able to start work but must inform NASS if you get a job.

You will need to show a potential employer documents proving that you have permission to work. These can include:

- your Immigration Status Document (ISD) confirming your leave to remain and your status
- your Application Registration Card (if you are claiming asylum but have permission to work)

Both of these documents will state that employment is permitted. Employers are legally obliged to check and keep a copy of these documents.[21] They also have to make sure that any photographs on the documents are of you and that dates of birth are consistent with how old you look.[22]

Can refugees work in Europe?

If you want to work outside the UK, then you will need to contact the relevant national embassy or consulate to find out about their visa requirements.

Until you have British Citizenship, you will still be considered as a national of your country of origin. Therefore, you will also need to apply to the Home Office for:

- a UN Convention Travel Document (CTD) or 'blue document' if you have refugee status

WORKING IN THE UK: NEWCOMER'S HANDBOOK *2ND EDITION*

- a certificate of identity or 'brown document' if you have Humanitarian Protection, Indefinite, Discretionary or Exceptional Leave to Remain and do not have a current passport recognised by the authorities of your nationality

Application forms for these documents can be obtained by writing to:

Travel Document Section, Immigration and Nationality Directorate, Block C, Whitgift Centre, Wellesley Road, Croydon, CR9 1AT.[23]

What support is available?

You can register at your local Jobcentre Plus office and apply for welfare benefits such as Income Support or Jobseeker's Allowance (JSA). These are paid if you do not have a job, or are on a low income. See the 'Social Security Benefits and Tax Credits' chapter on page 108 for further details.

If you have not received the NASS 35 document you can still register for JSA by presenting the Home Office status letter and NASS termination letter.[24] The Jobcentre Plus advisers are able to request details from NASS.[25]

If you have been given refugee status, then you are also entitled to an Income Support (IS) backpayment and need to apply for it within 4 weeks of a positive decision.[26] It is best to register for the payment at the Jobcentre Plus as soon as you receive the Home Office letter confirming your position as a refugee.

Note: The backpayment will be changed into a loan under current law

The Government is intending to replace the backdated payment with a Refugee Integration Loan.[27] This is likely to be introduced in Spring 2006, but at the time of writing no specific date or amount has been finalised.

National Insurance Numbers

A National Insurance Number (or NINO) is a personal number

- to record a person's National Insurance (NI) contributions and credited contributions
- as a reference number for the whole social security system

The Home Office intends to issue NINOs with each positive decision letter confirming refugee status or other forms of leave to remain following a claim for asylum. However, this is dependent on your having requested a NINO at the time of claiming asylum.

If you do not receive a NINO with your positive decision letter then you should contact your local Job Centre. They will arrange an interview to apply for a NINO.

You will need to bring proof of identification and permission to work to the NINO interview. This can be your positive decision letter from the Home Office or NASS 35. If you are still claiming asylum, you should take your Application Registration Card or another Home Office document stating that employment is allowed.[28]

It is important to note that you do not need a National Insurance Number (NINO) to get a paid job; nor is a NINO proof that you have permission to work. If you do start work without a NINO, you should apply for one soon afterwards at your local Jobcentre Plus with supporting documents from your employer.

What help will I receive during the 28 days?

At present, there is no national structure for helping you to move from NASS to mainstream support, unless you live in certain specified areas (see below under SUNRISE). Your nearest refugee agency's One Stop Service will be able to provide you with information on where to register for benefits, housing, etc.

SUNRISE

The government launched pilots of its SUNRISE initiative in late 2005 in four pilot areas. SUNRISE will be operated by local authority asylum teams and refugee agencies and support will last for an anticipated period of 12 months.

- West London and Croydon by Refugee Arrivals Project from 17 October 2005
- Glasgow by the Scottish Refugee Council from 17 October 2005
- Leeds and Sheffield by the Leeds and Sheffield Local Authority Asylum Teams and the Refugee Council from 31 October 2005
- Manchester by Refugee Action from 31 October 2005

The aim is for SUNRISE to help people who have received refugee status, Humanitarian Protection and Discretionary Leave to Remain with 'housing, health and child education needs and ensure that mainstream benefits and employment advice is accessed.'[29] If you live in one of the pilot areas, you should receive contact details for SUNRISE with your Home Office status letter.

Where do I go for advice once the 28 days finishes?

The main organisation providing free, independent and confidential advice on a range of issues, including housing, employment, discrimination and benefits, is the Citizens Advice Bureau (CAB). You can find out where their nearest offices are at http://www.citizensadvice.org.uk/ [30]

What if I am a family member of a refugee?

When the main applicant on an asylum claim receives a positive decision, this covers all dependants on the same claim. For example:

A family of five with three children aged 10, 12 and 17 made a claim for asylum with the wife being the main applicant on the claim. Her husband and three children were dependants on the same claim. If the wife receives a positive decision and is given refugee status, Humanitarian Protection or Discretionary leave, this also covers the rest of the family. It means that the husband and eldest child have full employment rights and access to welfare benefits along with the main applicant. The same criteria for accessing work, training, etc., would apply to each family member.

If you receive Refugee Status and have pre-existing family[31] either outside or inside the UK but who were not dependants on your asylum claim, you can apply for a family reunion. If successful, it means that the other family members are given the same status as you. As a result they get full access to the same rights and entitlements.

If you have Humanitarian Protection or Discretionary Leave to Remain, family reunion is considered once Indefinite Leave to Remain has been granted (usually after 3 and 6 years respectively).

Each member of the family will be given their own status letter confirming their leave to remain in the UK. This can then be presented to employers, Jobcentre Plus, Further and Higher Education Institutions, etc.

How can I access training?

Once you have permission to work, you can access work-based learning and other vocational training. You may also need some pre-vocational training to strengthen your English language or jobseeking skills.

Jobcentre Plus have a number of support services for people looking for work. For example, if you are a single parent in the UK, then there is the Lone Parent Initiative to help with getting a job (see sections on training and education and English language support on pages 192 and 284).

If you want to retrain in a particular job or profession (eg health, law, teaching), it is best to contact the appropriate professional body. Your overseas qualifications and experience may provide exemptions from exams, but it is likely that you will need to do additional training in the UK. This may also include gaining an English as a Foreign Language (EFL) qualification.

How can I get language help?

As noted above, it is important to be aware of the language requirements for training and employment opportunities. It might be that you need to take a general ESOL course to improve your English, in which case you should register at your local FE college.

If you want to learn English for a specific purpose, such as retraining as a doctor or to study at university, then an EFL qualification may be necessary. The most recognised of these is the International English Language Testing System (IELTS). IELTS preparation courses are generally run by private language providers, including universities.[32] Some FE colleges have funded courses but these are not common and you may still need to pay registration fees and examination costs.

For more information on IELTS, see the section 'English Language requirements' on page 95. For more information on ESOL generally see page 284.

How do I get my professional qualifications recognised?

Many refugees have professional qualifications from outside the UK. It can be deeply frustrating when these are not recognised, or considered to be the equivalent of a lower level UK qualification. This may mean having to retrain just to get the necessary paperwork.

The National Recognition Information Centre (NARIC) can tell you how qualifications gained overseas relate to those in the UK. Contacting them is the first step to knowing what further qualifications and training you may need to undertake (See 'Recognition of qualifications' section on page 326).

Student and guidance services at FE colleges and universities usually have access to NARIC. If you are currently registered as a student or are considering enrolling on a course, they should be able to go through the NARIC process with you free of charge.

Once you have received information from NARIC, you need to think about the following:

- time – how long it will take to retrain to continue working in the same profession in the UK?
- cost – how much does it cost to study for and take examinations, along with any charges for joining professional associations?

- work experience – you will often have to complete a period of work experience before you qualify for a particular profession. This may not necessarily be paid and competition for places can be high
- transferable skills – you will have a range of skills that are appropriate for a variety of jobs. www.prospects.ac.uk[33] is a useful resource for looking at what kind of jobs might suit you

If your qualifications are not recognised in the UK, there are ways of making your work experience count. Some colleges and universities run courses on the Assessment of Prior Experiential Learning (APEL). These can give accreditation for previous experience gained. You will then be able to use this when applying for further courses or applying for jobs. The Refugee Assessment and Guidance Unit (RAGU) run APEL courses in London specifically for refugees and asylum seekers.[34]

Many universities also have provision for accrediting previous learning (APL) and experience within related degrees. You should contact the admissions tutor for the department where you wish to study and discuss your previous experience with them. Universities operate their own admissions systems and can be flexible if they think someone has the potential to be a successful student. For further information see 'How can I study' in the 'Refugees and Higher Education' on page 92.

Differences in Scotland and Wales

There are no statutory differences but there are variations in attitudes particularly towards asylum seekers in Scotland. In general, they can be summarised as:

- There are more opportunities in further education in Scotland, including colleges exercising wider discretion for asylum seekers wishing to access vocational training, Higher National Certificates and Diplomas.
- The Scottish Executive funds integration initiatives for asylum seekers that seek to prepare people for the workplace though work shadowing.[35]
- As an asylum seeker, you can access training and register with the General Teaching Council for Scotland which qualifies you to teach once you receive a positive decision or permission to work.[36]

Citizenship

If you have Indefinite Leave to Remain in the UK, you can apply for British citizenship one year after the leave was given and after living continuously in the UK for five years.

If you receive citizenship you will be able to travel freely within the European Union, accessing European Constitutional rights such as being able to work and study in other EU countries.

For a fuller explanation see 'How do I become a UK citizen?' on page 550.

Asylum and immigration status and definition[37]

Status	Definition
Asylum Seeker	Someone who has come to the UK, and formally applied for recognition as a refugee under the 1951 Convention and is awaiting a decision
Refugee Status	Someone whom the Home Office has decided falls within the 1951 Convention definition of a refugee and is granted asylum. They used to be automatically given Indefinite Leave to Remain (ILR) in the UK. However, since August 2005 Refugee Status is reviewed after 5 years and, if successful, will lead to ILR
Humanitarian Protection (HP)	HP is granted when the Home Office believes the claim for asylum falls outside the strict terms of the 1951 Convention, but comes within the scope of Article 3 of the European Convention for Human Rights (ECHR). HP is now granted for up to 5 years (as of 30 August 2005), after which you can apply for ILR
Discretionary Leave (DL)	DL can be granted for up to 3 years after which time you can apply for a further extension. You can apply for ILR after 6 years of DL
Exceptional Leave to Remain (ELR)	Temporary status for asylum seekers who do not meet the strict criteria of the 1951 Convention yet still require protection. Previously granted ELR for up to 4 years until April 2003 when replaced by HP and DL
Indefinite Leave to Remain (ILR)	Some people receive ILR without receiving Refugee Status such as during Home Office amnesty schemes or certain participants in the Gateway Protection Programme
Failed Asylum Seeker	Someone who has received a 'negative decision' upon their asylum claim and exhausted all appeal rights

Asylum and immigration status and entitlements

Status	Work Permission	Training	Further Education	Higher Education
Asylum Seeker	No in general but exceptions if applied before 7/02 or initial decision on asylum claim is outstanding after 12 months	Eligible for certain training courses. Needs permission to work if work-based learning. Can access training with work placement if unpaid	Home student eligibility and fee concessions if NASS supported. Liable for international students' fees for some higher level courses	International student fees although university has discretion to waive or charge home student fees. Not eligible for learner support funds
Refugee Status	Yes	Yes	Home student and fully eligible for student support	Home Student fees and fully eligible for learner support funds
Humanitarian Protection (HP) Discretionary Leave (DL) Exceptional Leave to Remain (ELR) Indefinite Leave to Remain (ILR)	Yes	Yes	As refugee status, but eligible for learner support funds after being ordinarily resident for 3 years at the start of the course	As refugee status, but eligible for learner support funds after being ordinarily resident for 3 years at the start of the course
Failed Asylum Seeker	No	International student fees	International student fees	International student fees

Endnotes

[1] The table at the end of this chapter provides an overview of the rights and entitlements to employment and training for refugees and asylum seekers. Please note that this is an outline guide only and you should refer to the relevant parts of this chapter

[2] Asylum and Immigration Appeals Act 1994 s 1

[3] Further details on the asylum process can be found at http://www.refugeecouncil.org.uk/downloads/info_for_clients/applying_asylum/English_May2005.pdf, last searched 8 February 2006

[4] See the section below under 'I am a refugee' on page 76 for further details. Table 1 at the end of this chapter also gives an overview of the various decisions that can follow a claim for asylum in the UK

[5] Immigration and Asylum Act 1999 s 4. Section 4 is mainly used to provide support for people whose asylum claims have been refused. There are certain criteria for applying and support is not given automatically. Please see http://www.ind.homeoffice.gov.uk/ind/en/home/applying/national_asylum_support/how_to_apply.html, last searched 17 February 2006. There may be people with ongoing asylum claims receiving Section 4 support. This sometimes happens if an asylum appeal has been submitted out of time, or where a Statutory Review is outstanding

[6] Last searched on 10 February 2006

[7] Last searched on 10 February 2006

[8] Letter from the Office of the Deputy Prime Minister to the Chief Executives and Housing Directors of all English local housing authorities, 25 March 2003

[9] This follows the European Directive 2003/9/EC which came into force on 5 February 2005. Further details can be found at http://www.ind.homeoffice.gov.uk/ind/en/home/laws___policy/immigration_rules/statement_of_changes11.html?, last searched 8 February 2006

[10] This information relating to asylum seekers applying for permission to work was received through personal correspondence with the Director's Office, NASS, 26 January 2006 and 7 February 2006. If you experience difficulties getting your ARC changed, please contact your nearest One Stop Service

[11] Unpaid means that only 'reasonable expenses' can be given (for example, for lunch or travel) and excludes payment in kind (such as board and lodging)

[12] The NASS Policy Bulletin 72 outlines their position further and can be found at http://www.ind.homeoffice.gov.uk/ind/en/home/applying/national_asylum_support/stakeholders/policy_bulletin.Maincontent.0048.file.tmp/Policy%20Bulletin%2072v2[1].pdf , last searched 8 February 2006 Further clarification was provided through email correspondence by NASS CIAU, Policy on 28 April 2006 and the statement is reproduced here in full

'The Home Office is keen for asylum seekers to do voluntary work whilst their claim for asylum is under consideration. This work must not amount to paid or unpaid employment, but travelling costs and food expenses may be met, provided this is not at a flat rate. Asylum seekers undertaking voluntary work may wish to inform NASS of this to avoid any misunderstandings with regard to 'work', 'pay', 'expenses' and 'support'

Supported asylum seekers can be accepted by a college on to a vocational course which includes an unpaid 'work placement' (where this is part of the course and is not paid employment). Again they may wish to inform NASS of their intentions to avoid any misunderstandings with regard to 'work', 'pay', 'expenses' and 'support'. If a course including a work placement provides a training allowance, supported asylum seekers may need to have the conditions attached to their temporary admission amended. They will also need to inform NASS and submit details of the allowance received so that their support can be reassessed. The provision of travelling expenses and/or food costs will not be taken into account by NASS

[13] Help with English is dealt with more fully in the section 'How can I improve my English?' on page 284

[14] A child of an asylum seeking family can usually stay on at the same school after Year 11. However, there are sometimes difficulties if they move to a new learning provider. In general, they should still qualify for free full-time study and your nearest OSS will be able help if any problems arise

[15] The Convention Relating to the Status of Refugees 1951 Article 1. This was amended by the Protocol Relating to the Status of Refugees 1967 to include people who become refugees after 1 January 1951. http://www.unhcr.org/cgi-bin/texis/vtx/protect/opendoc.pdf?tbl=PROTECTION&id=3b66c2aa10, last searched 8 February 2006

[16] Written Ministerial Statement in the House of Commons on 19 July 2005 by Tony McNulty MP, Minister for Immigration, Citizenship and Nationality http://www.publications.parliament.uk/pa/cm200506/cmhansrd/cm050719/wmstext/50719m05.htm#50719m05.html_sbhd0, last searched February 2006

[17] Further information can be found at http://www.refugeecouncil.org.uk/infocentre/asylumlaw/seeking_asylum.htm, last searched 8 February 2006

[18] Further information on the Programme can be found at http://www.refugeecouncil.org.uk/publications/pub014.htm, last searched 8 February 2006

[19] Inter Agency Co-ordination Team Policy Briefing No.26, 9 February 2006

[20] See 'Employment Rights' and 'Racial Discrimination' sections on pages 370 and 424

[21] Immigration and Asylum Act 1996 s 8(2)(a)(b)

[22] The Immigration (Restrictions on Employment) Order 2004 s4(4)(a)(b)

[23] For further information on application criteria, costs, etc., for travel documents, please see http://www.ind.homeoffice.gov.uk/ind/en/home/applying/travel_documents.html?, last searched 10 February 2006

[24] Written correspondence with Special Groups and Initiatives Team, Department for Work and Pensions 21 December 2005

[25] Further information can be found at http://www.refugeecouncil.org.uk/downloads/info_for_clients/nass35/english.pdf, last searched on 10 February 2006

[26] NASS support is set at 30% less than IS. When you are recognised as a refugee, the 30% you have missed out on during your asylum claim is paid back. The Immigration, Asylum and Nationality Act 2006 replaces the backdated payments with a Refugee Integration Loan

[27] Asylum and Immigration (Treatment of Claimants, etc.) Act 2004 s13

[28] The following link outlines the range of documents that can be used: http://www.dwp.gov.uk/publications/dwp/2003/gl25_oct.pdf, last searched on 10 February 2006

[29] For further details, please see http://www.ind.homeoffice.gov.uk/ind/en/home/laws_policy/refugee_integration0/sunrise_strategic0.html, last searched 8 February 2006

[30] Last searched on 10 February 2006

[31] 'Pre-existing family' means spouse, or civil partner and minor children who formed part of the family unit before the main applicant fled to seek asylum in the UK. For further information, please see http://www.ind.homeoffice.gov.uk/ind/en/home/laws_policy/policy_instructions/apis/refugee_leave.html, last searched 8 February 2006

[32] The University and Colleges Admissions Services (UCAS) state that certain ESOL qualifications may be acceptable as evidence of proficiency in English. See http://www.ucas.com/studyuk/englang.html, last searched 17 February 2006

[33] Last searched on 10 February 2006

[34] For further information, please go to http://www.londonmet.ac.uk/ragu, last searched on 10 February 2006

[35] http://www.scottishexecutive.gov.uk/Topics/People/Equality/Refugees-asylum/support#a3, last searched 10 February 2006

[36] http://www.bridgesprogrammes.org.uk/29862.html, last searched on 10 February 2006

[37] Further information can be found at http://www.refugeecouncil.org.uk/downloads/info_for_clients/positive_dec/english.pdf, last searched 10 February 2006

3 Refugees and higher education[1]

Council for Assisting Refugee Academics

How can I study?

This section covers the following:

- Plan in advance
- Educational Entitlement
- Student Support Funds
- Relocating for your degree
- Prerequisites for beginning a course

Plan in advance

There are many organisations in the UK that help refugees and asylum seekers by providing specialist advice on higher education.[2] Generally speaking, the earlier you start researching and applying for courses, the better. By applying early, you have a better chance of gaining a place on a course and a much better chance of securing the funding you need to enrol. In general, a good rule of thumb is to apply almost a full year in advance of your desired start date. Most undergraduate courses start in the autumn, but many postgraduate courses have flexible start dates and accept applications throughout the year.

Educational entitlement

If you have refugee status, Indefinite Leave to Remain (ILR), Exceptional Leave to Enter or Remain (ELE/R), Humanitarian Protection (HP) or Discretionary Leave (DL) to remain in the UK, your entitlements are as follows:

- If you have refugee status, you have the same rights to further and higher education as UK citizens. You will be granted home fees status and you will automatically be eligible to apply for Student Support funds,[3] including loans and grants. In addition, Further Education providers have some discretion to waive or reduce fees for refugees.
- If you have ELR, HP, DL or ILR, you will be charged home student fees, but you will only be eligible for Student Support funds after three years of residence in the UK.

Note

- If you have already started studying and are paying overseas student rates, you should be charged as a home student if and when the next payment is due.
- Dependants – the spouse and children of those with the above status have the same entitlements as their spouse or parent.

Student Support funds

Student Support is statutory funding available from your local funding agency.

If you have refugee status, or you are the spouse or child of someone who has refugee status, you will be eligible for Student Support to help with your fees and living costs if you are studying for a first degree or certain other degree-level courses.

See section 2 on Statutory funding on page 96 for more information.

Relocating for your degree

You may believe that the best course for you is at a university that is at a significant distance from your home. You therefore may wish to relocate for your degree. However, at the time of going to press, you are unlikely to be eligible to apply for local authority housing if you relocate. The Asylum and Immigration Act 2004 establishes a local connection between successful asylum applicants and the local authority to which they are dispersed.[4] This will affect you if you are currently living in council accommodation and plan to continue to do so as a student. Unfortunately, this provision means that you will probably find it difficult to be re-housed by another local authority.[5]

Prerequisites for beginning a course

Educational requirements

Each course will have its own entrance requirements, which will usually be based on UK secondary school exams. However, you should not allow a lack of educational experience in the UK to deter you from applying for university courses. Information on the entry requirements for each course can be found in the university's prospectus (which describes all the courses on offer). For undergraduate degree courses, there is a tariff point system that is allocated to different UK qualifications. However, if you were educated outside the UK, your qualifications will be assessed individually. Each institution you apply to will decide whether your qualifications meet the requirements for its courses.[6] The admissions tutor for each course will assess your UCAS application form[7] to make sure that you meet the entry requirements. You can have your existing qualifications reviewed by UK NARIC or an organisation that subscribes to UK NARIC's membership service.[8] See page 326 for more information on 'qualification recognition'.

Access and Foundation courses

If you do not have the required qualifications for the course you have chosen, you may need to consider an Access or a Foundation course.[9] These preparatory courses are designed to provide you with the level of knowledge you need prior to continuing your education at the next level. Access and Foundation courses are often offered by universities and you may be able to secure a grant to attend such a course.

Mature students

If you are a mature student (usually defined as over 21 years of age for those embarking on a first degree), the university will consider other elements, including your qualifications, employment, interests, motivation, and other life experience. APEL courses may also count towards entry requirements.[10]

English language requirements

In order to secure a place at a university, you will need to possess a high standard of English. If English is not your first language, you will probably need a qualification in English or be asked to take an English language exam. A list of acceptable English language qualifications is provided by UCAS.[11] For general information on English language learning and ESOL, see page 284.

Many institutions and professional bodies use the International English Language Testing System (IELTS). This exam tests your reading, writing, speaking and listening skills and each section is scored separately. The exam is difficult and it is not unusual for candidates to sit the exam more than once to achieve their desired result. Many organisations offer preparation courses for the IELTS and there are plenty of study groups available for those who are preparing to sit the exam. A large number of these courses and groups are free and many are aimed specifically at refugees and asylum seekers. Universities often offer pre-sessional intensive English language courses to assist students who are preparing to start a course. Many Higher Education Institutes (HEIs) also provide courses on using English for Academic Purposes. See page 284 for more information on ESOL.

How can I access financial support?

This section covers the following:

- The importance of planning in advance
- Statutory funding
- Other sources of funding

The importance of planning in advance

Financing a degree, particularly a postgraduate degree, requires a great deal of advance planning. It is important to secure adequate funding for both fees and maintenance (living expenses) before enrolling on a course. There is significant competition for financial assistance, so it is best to begin your search for funding at least a year before starting a course. You should begin to research funding at the same time as you begin to research courses.

Statutory funding

There will be different types of funding available to you, depending on your immigration status, whether you undertake an undergraduate or postgraduate course, and your mode of study. Most of the statutory (government) support available is aimed at students undertaking undergraduate degrees. However, a number of scholarships are aimed at postgraduates. These distinctions are covered in the sections below.

Student Support funds

Student Support is statutory funding available from your local funding agency. This support is aimed primarily at students undertaking first degrees and a small number of other degrees.[12] It includes assistance with fees and the provision of grants and loans to help students meet the costs of their tuition fees and living expenses. There are also grants available for childcare and other specific needs.

The bodies that administer student support are:

- Local Education Authorities (LEAs)[13] for England and Wales
- Student Awards Agency for Scotland (SAAS)[14] for Scotland
- Education and Library Boards (ELBs)[15] for Northern Ireland

If you are planning to enrol on a course that entitles you to student support, you should request an application form from the relevant agency and submit your application for support funds well in advance.

Eligibility

Depending on your status, you may have a waiting period before you are eligible for student support funds.[16] If you are a refugee, you are eligible from the moment you receive refugee status. However, if you have another form of leave to remain, you will be eligible only after three years' residence in the UK.

Part-time students are eligible for some assistance depending on their circumstances. You should check with the appropriate agency listed at the beginning of this section. Asylum seekers are not eligible for student support funds, except in rare circumstances, such as when young asylum seekers are being cared for by their local authority. For more details refer to the UKCOSA guidance note on studying and asylum.[17]

Types of support

Loans

The student loan is a low-interest loan intended to support student maintenance costs, such as accommodation, food, travel, etc. The amount for which you are entitled to apply changes each year, and depends on the income of yourself and your family, where you plan to study and the course that you intend to take. You do not have to apply for the maximum amount. The Student Loans Company (SLC) administers this loans scheme.[18]

Grants

A grant is a type of financial assistance that does not have to be repaid. Depending on a student's need, grants may cover course fees, maintenance for dependants and special allowances for certain groups (e.g. student parents and people with disabilities). Most of this support is means-tested, i.e. it will take into account any income you have and then determine how great your need for financial assistance is. The amounts and types of support packages that are available change annually. Each awarding agency listed above provides information on funding.

Access to Learning Fund

An additional source of funding for students facing financial difficulties is the 'Access to Learning Fund'. Awards from this fund are non-repayable grants. The purpose of the fund is to provide additional financial assistance to priority groups, students with financial emergencies and students who are considering abandoning their studies due to financial hardship. These funds are open to both full-time and part-time students and postgraduates.

Priority groups for assistance include students with children (particularly lone parents), mature students with existing financial commitments and students from low-income families. This fund is administered directly by HEIs (Higher Education Institutes), so you will need to contact the student services department at your university to receive information on this fund.

Regional differences

Students in Wales may apply for funding via the Financial Contingency Funds (FCFs) scheme.[19] Students in Northern Ireland can apply for Support Funds.[20] For students in Scotland, there are Hardship Funds[21] available. Citizens of the EU (excluding UK nationals), who are resident in Scotland for purposes other than education, can also apply to the Student Awards Agency for Scotland (SAAS) and are eligible to have their college or university tuition fees paid for them. For more information visit www.student-support-SAAS.gov.uk or contact SAAS:

The Student Awards Agency for Scotland
Gyleview House
3 Redheughs Rigg
EDINBURGH
EH12 9HH

Tel: 0845 111 1711

In all cases, you should request information on funding from the student services department at your university.

Other sources of funding

The Education UK website provides a search facility for scholarships, bursaries and awards available.[22] The British Council's website also provides a comprehensive list and links to sources of funding for education in the UK.[23] The CARA handbook contains a directory of organisations that provide funding to refugees and asylum seekers for higher education in the UK.

Below is a short description of the different categories of funding available.

University funds

Your university may have funds that it provides to students in the form of scholarships or bursaries. In some cases, you will apply for funds at the same time as you apply for your place on the course. You should check with the student finance/fees office at your university and also with your academic department to find out if there are funds for which you are eligible to apply.

Career Development Loans

The Career Development Loan (CDL) is a loan that is offered to fund up to two years of vocational training or education (it can be one additional year if a practical work experience placement is part of the course). For those who do not qualify for student support, a CDL may be an alternative. A CDL is a commercial bank loan, so the rate of interest is higher than student loans. This is difficult to acquire but you should not be deterred from applying nonetheless. Whilst your loan application is under review, you should continue to look for funding elsewhere, in case your application for a CDL is unsuccessful.

Research councils

The main form of statutory funding for postgraduate study is via the various research councils listed below:

- Biotechnology and Biological Sciences Research Council (BBSRC) www.bbsrc.ac.uk

- Engineering and Physical Sciences Research Council (EPSRC) www.epsrc.ac.uk
- Economic and Social Research Council (ESRC) www.esrc.ac.uk
- Medical Research Council (MRC) www.mrc.ac.uk
- Natural Environment Research Council (NERC) www.nerc.ac.uk
- Particle Physics and Astronomy Research Council (PPARC) www.pparc.ac.uk
- Arts and Humanities Research Board (AHRB) www.ahrb.ac.uk
- Council for the Central Laboratory of the Research Councils www.cclrc.ac.uk

The awards offered by research councils are highly competitive and usually require either a 2:1 degree from a UK university or an equivalent qualification. The awards normally cover fees and a portion of maintenance costs and other expenses. Selection is based on both a quota system and on merit.

If you would like to be considered for funding, you should contact the university to which you have applied. You do not apply directly to the research councils as universities submit the application to the appropriate council or board on behalf of the student.

Trusts

There are a number of private, non-governmental trusts (also called foundations) and charities that offer financial assistance to students. Each trust has its own set of criteria that govern whom it can help and what type of assistance it can offer. The important thing to remember is to apply only to those trusts which clearly state that they help individual students, and to make sure that you check whether you fulfil all the other relevant criteria. Some trusts were established to help members of a particular local community. It may be worth investigating whether such trusts exist in your area.

A visit to your local public library is a good place to start researching trusts. The library will have a copy of useful publications and may subscribe to FunderFinder, a database of funding resources. The

Educational Grants Advisory Service (EGAS) also maintains a database of trusts and will provide you with a free assessment of your eligibility for these trusts. EGAS also provides guidance on other aspects of funding. Apply to a number of trusts, as this will increase your chances of receiving funding.

How to apply to a trust

Before you apply, find out whether there is a deadline for applications. Applications should always be in the form of a written request. Some trusts have an application form. This should be filled in carefully and all the questions answered in full, giving as much detail as you can. Most charities are only able to help a very small number of the people who apply to them. Therefore it is essential that you make a strong case.

Always send a covering letter introducing yourself and outlining what you need and the amount that you are seeking.[24] It usually helps to detail your income and expenditure. It is not a good idea to exaggerate your financial problems. Trusts are less likely to help if they feel you need far more than they or any other trust you have applied to can offer. Trusts will be familiar with the costs associated with degrees and will be able to determine whether you have costed your studies accurately.

You should enclose a Curriculum Vitae (CV) with your application. Postgraduate degree students should also send a summary of their research proposal or thesis. It is essential that you include the names and full contact details of referees or written references with your application. These should be from a tutor, teacher or someone who knows you well.

Finally, you should not assume that because you meet the eligibility requirements for a trust you will automatically receive funding. Most trusts receive more applications than they can fund, so many applications will be unsuccessful.

Other sponsors

Some fields, such as science and technology, will receive funding from sponsors such as industrial and commercial companies. This type of funding is normally made available directly through university departments. Information about such funding will often be available on departmental notice boards in the university.

University courses in the UK

This section covers the following:

- Types of university degrees
- Choosing your mode of study
- How to research courses that interest you
- The admissions process

The higher education system in the UK varies between Scotland, England and Wales and Northern Ireland.[25] Higher Education Institutions (HEIs) in the UK include universities, university-sector colleges, colleges of higher education and institutes of higher education. HEIs provide courses that normally lead to a degree or equivalent qualification.

Types of university degrees

(a) Undergraduate (First) degrees

These are traditionally bachelor's degrees which cover subjects in the arts and sciences and require three to four years to complete on a full-time basis. There are also Higher National Diplomas (HNDs), Higher National Certificates (HNCs) and the Diploma in Higher Education (DipHE), which take one or two years to finish. Finally, Foundation degrees are vocational higher education qualifications that take two years to complete.[26]

Undergraduate degrees are structured in a variety of ways.[27]

- A single-subject degree is a degree that focuses on a sole subject for the entire course.
- A joint degree is a degree that combines elements of two single-subject degrees.
- A modular/combined degree is a multi-disciplinary or inter-disciplinary degree that combines elements of various degree programmes.

- A sandwich course is a course that offers a period of practical training 'sandwiched' between years of academic coursework.

(b) Postgraduate degrees

These range from Postgraduate Certificates (PGCert/Diplomas /PGDip) to master's degrees such as Master of Arts (MA) and doctorates (conferring PhD/DPhil status). The length of time required to complete a postgraduate course can vary from nine months to six years, depending on the course and the mode of study (full-time versus part-time; research versus taught).

There are various types of master's degrees, including the MA (Master of Arts) and the MSc (Master of Science). An MPhil is a type of master's degree normally used as a stepping-stone to a PhD/DPhil. The DPhil and PhD degrees (both terms equate to a Doctor of Philosophy) are at the upper end of the higher education spectrum. A PhD can take as few as three years on a full-time basis or as many as six on a part-time basis.

Postgraduate courses are divided into taught and research courses:

- Taught (one to two years full-time) – taught courses comprise various types of instruction and exams (e.g. seminars and tutorials) and often include a piece of research or a dissertation that the student completes at the end of the course.
- Research (usually two years full-time for a master's, three for a doctorate) – research courses offer a student the opportunity to research a topic in depth and present this work in a thesis or dissertation.

Usually, DPhil/PhD students will have completed a master's degree already. However, some disciplines allow you to be accepted directly onto a DPhil/PhD.

Modes of study

There are several ways in which you can pursue your degree: full-time, part-time or via distance learning. If you study part-time and you are claiming social welfare benefits, these are unlikely to be affected.[28]

Another option is to study via distance learning. The Open University (OU) is the largest provider of distance learning opportunities, including pre-undergraduate, undergraduate, postgraduate and professional development courses.[29]

According to Universities UK, 'The UK does not have an official system of university rankings. The UK HE sector is very diverse and this makes any rankings difficult and subjective'.[30] The Quality Assurance Agency for Higher Education produces an independent academic review of UK universities.[31] In addition, the Higher Education Funding Council for England produces university performance indicators for teaching and research in the UK.[32] The Guardian and Sunday Times newspapers and the Times Higher Education Supplement also review universities, and such reviews can help you compare and contrast the sometimes overwhelming number of courses on offer within a discipline.

How to research courses that interest you

It is important to begin researching your course well in advance of your desired start date. The Universities and Colleges Admissions Service (UCAS) provide information on undergraduate courses.[33] For postgraduate courses, 'Prospects' is a website that offers an overview of many of the courses available.[34] However, for detailed information on courses you will need to request a prospectus from the admissions office at the relevant HEI.

You should also consider how the university as a whole matches up with your personal preferences. You may want to consider:

- the costs of fees and living expenses and the availability of funds offered by the university
- the quality of the facilities – academic (e.g. libraries and computer facilities), leisure and social facilities)
- the prestige of the institution and department (see advice on rankings below)
- the quality of career advice facilities and other support services
- the location and type of campus (rural or urban, traditional or modern)

You should consider whether or not the institution and department you have chosen are well respected in your field. This is important because many employers will value a degree more highly if it has been awarded by a university with a solid reputation in that field. This is not to say that you should only consider elite institutions. Some institutions may not be at the top of the league tables overall, but they may have a strong reputation in certain disciplines and have many contacts with potential employers.

The admissions process

(a) Undergraduate applications

Full-time courses: Apply for undergraduate courses through UCAS.[35] Applications are accepted from 1 September to 15 January each year and some closing dates are as early as mid-October the year before the course starts. For guidance on how to apply through UCAS, or on choosing the right course and college or pre-university course in the Further Education sector, please refer to the UKCOSA guidance notes.[36]

Part-time courses: Apply directly to the university or college if you wish to undertake a course on a part-time basis. Each institution will have a separate application form that you will need to complete.

(b) Postgraduate applications

Apply for postgraduate courses directly through the university. Although there is no central clearing house, a list of many of the courses can be found at Prospects, the official website for graduates. A number of universities now take online applications via the Prospects site.

Closing dates vary, but it is advisable to apply early, as spaces on some courses will be filled quickly. Some institutions may require applications a year in advance. Also bear in mind that if you apply well in advance of the start date, you will also have a greater chance of securing funding. Prospects provides a proposed timetable for applying for a postgraduate course.[37] Also remember that some institutions may have an application fee. For more guidance on postgraduate study, refer to the UKCOSA guidance note on Postgraduate study in the UK.[38]

Endnotes

[1] The following is adapted from Higher Education Pathways: A Handbook for the Refugee Community in the UK, Council for Assisting Refugee Academics (CARA), 2005. For further information on CARA and the guidance, see the Further Information section

[2] See CARA handbook and website: http://www.academic-refugees.org

[3] Student Support is statutory funding available from your local funding agency. See section 'How can I access financial support?', p. 95

[4] For further information on The Asylum and Immigration Act 2004, please see http://www.refugeecouncil.org.uk/infocentre/asylumlaw/proposals_2003/2004_act.htm, last searched 10th January 2006

[5] For further information about rehousing and local authorities, please see http://www.odpm.gov.uk/index.asp?id=1155855, last searched 7th February 2006

[6] See Universities and Colleges Admissions Service (UCAS), www.ucas.com/studyuk/what.html#1. Go to course search and entry profiles. Last searched 6th February 2006

[7] See www.ucas.ac.uk, last searched 3rd February 2006. For more details on the application process for students in higher education in the UK, please see section 'University Courses in the UK'

[8] See http://www.naric.org.uk/, last searched 3rd February 2006

[9] For information on the types of Access and Foundation courses available, please see http://www.ucas.com/access/index.html, last searched 3rd February 2006

[10] For further information, see http://www.ucas.ac.uk/candq/apl/, last searched 30th January 2006

[11] See http://www.ucas.com/studyuk/englang.html, last searched 26th January 2006

[12] For more information, see Prince, B., Rutter, J. and Kerrigan, M., Handbook on education for refugees in the UK, RETAS, 2004

[13] See http://www.dfes.gov.uk/localauthorities, last searched 3rd February 2006

[14] See http://www.student-support-saas.gov.uk, last searched 7th February 2006

[15] See http://www.education-support.org.uk/students, last searched 7th February 2006

[16] For further information on Student Support funds, please see http://www.education-action.org/retas.asp_ai=advice&subcat=9.htm, last searched 31st January 2006

[17] For UKCOSA guidance notes, please see http://www.ukcosa.org.uk/images/asylum.pdf, last searched 31st January 2006

[18] See http://www.slc.co.uk/index.html for details, last searched 1st February 2006

[19] See http://www.adviceguide.org.uk/wales/family_parent/education/financial_help_for_students_wales, last searched 31st January 2006

[20] See http://www.education-support.org.uk/students, last searched 7th February 2006

[21] See http://www.adviceguide.org.uk/scotland/family_parent/education_scotland/the_hardship_fund_scotland.htm, last searched 7th February 2006

[22] See http://www.educationuk.org/scholarships, last searched 7th February 2006

[23] See http://www.britishcouncil.org/learning-funding-your-studies.htm, last searched 2nd February 2006

[24] The CARA handbook contains a model letter for applications to trusts, See Part 1, Step 4, "Funding your course, in Higher Education Pathways: A handbook for the refugee community in the UK, Council for Assisting Refugee Academics (CARA), 2005, p. 43

[25] For details of these differences, see http://www.britishcouncil.org/learning-uk-education-systems-school-education.htm, last searched 1st February 2006

[26] For further information on HNDs, HNCs, DipHEs and foundation degrees, please see www.aimhigher.ac.uk, last searched 4th February 2006

[27] The structures are covered in greater depth in Prince B., Rutter, J., Kerrigan, M., Handbook on education for refugees in the UK, RETAS, 2004

[28] For more information, please see www.jobcentreplus.gov.uk, last searched 1st February 2006

[29] See www.open.ac.uk, last searched 2nd February 2006

[30] See www.universitiesuk.ac.uk/faqs/, last searched 25th January 2006

[31] For further information on the Quality Assurance Agency for Higher Education (QAA), please see www.qaa.ac.uk, last searched 3rd February 2006

[32] Performance indicators can be viewed at www.hefce.ac.uk/learning/PerfInd/, last searched 25th January 2006

[33] See http://www.ucas.co.uk, last searched 31st January 2006

[34] See http://www.prospects.co.uk/home.asp, last searched 26th January 2006

[35] For information on the application process, see http://www.ucas.co.uk, last searched 31st January 2006

[36] Available at http://www.ukcosa.org.uk, last searched 7th February 2006

[37] http://www.prospects.ac.uk/cms/ShowPage/Home_page/Why_do_postgrad_study_/Timetable_for_applications_in_the_UK/p!empjbi;DE0Aw$, last searched 7th February 2006

[38] http://www.ukcosa.org.uk, last searched 6th February 2006

4 Social security benefits and Tax Credits

Neil Bateman

Introduction

This part of the book explains the main benefits which are available to people. Some benefits are paid if you are out of work, others if you meet certain conditions (for example if you have a child) and some also have a means test which looks at your personal circumstances, income and capital.

Most social security benefits are administered by the Department for Work and Pensions (DWP) through three separate services – Jobcentre Plus, the Pensions Service and the Disability and Carers Service. Two benefits – Housing Benefit and Council Tax Benefit – are administered by local authorities (LAs), while Child Tax Credit and Working Tax Credit are administered by Her Majesty's Revenue and Customs (HMRC). Each benefit and Tax Credit has its own rules of entitlement.

The information in this section gives a general overview of entitlement. It is a complex subject, there are many exceptions to rules and your circumstances may not fit the rules precisely. It is therefore important to obtain advice from a reputable, independent advice agency.

If you are a newcomer to the United Kingdom (UK), you may find that you are refused benefits because you need permission from the Home Office Immigration and Nationality Directorate to be in the United Kingdom (you are a 'Person Subject to Immigration Control') or because, even if you are allowed to enter and remain in the UK, benefit officials do not accept that you have a 'right to reside' in the UK, or you are not 'habitually resident' and your benefit claim has been refused. There is a right to appeal to an independent tribunal if you are refused a benefit, and you should get help from an independent advice agency if this happens to you. Appeals have a good chance of success, especially if you have someone to represent you.

If you are subject to immigration control and as part of your permission to stay in the United Kingdom you are not allowed to claim 'public funds', you must get independent advice before even enquiring about your benefits at a social security or local authority office.

Outline of the benefits system

The UK's social security benefits system is a mix of different types of benefits each with different rules. There are contributory benefits with entitlement based on National Insurance records, non-contributory benefits with entitlement based on meeting certain rules of eligibility (neither your income, capital nor your National Insurance record usually matters) and also means-tested benefits with entitlement based on detailed eligibility criteria and rules about income and capital. There are also benefits for employees which are administered by employers (i.e. Statutory Sick Pay and Statutory Maternity, Paternity and Adoption Pay).

Tax Credits are a form of income maintenance based on a mix of social security and income tax rules.

Finally, there is a range of education benefits that are administered by the government's Department for Education and Skills and by local authorities, and health benefits, administered on behalf of the National Health Service, which can help towards the cost of certain health related costs such as prescriptions. In Wales, Scotland and Northern Ireland, the administrative arrangements for these are slightly different.

Some benefits are designed to fit with others, so it is best to view the social security system as a jigsaw with interlocking pieces because entitlement to one benefit can sometimes be based on entitlement to another benefit. This is done so that particular groups can receive additional help – for example, people with children or people with a disability – and is commonly referred to as 'passporting'.

Benefits at a glance

Contributory benefits	Non-contributory benefits	Means tested benefits and tax credits	Employee benefits
Retirement Pension ■ ▲ ❖	Disability Living Allowance	Income Support	Statutory Sick Pay ◗
Incapacity Benefit ■ ▲ ❖	Attendance Allowance	Jobseeker's Allowance ■	Statutory Maternity Pay ◗
Jobseeker's Allowance ■ ❖	Child Benefit	State Pension Credit	Statutory Paternity Pay ◗
Maternity Allowance ❖	Industrial benefits	Child Tax Credit	Statutory Adoption Pay ◗
Bereavement Allowance ❖	War pensions	Working Tax Credit	
Widowed Parent's Allowance ▲ ❖	Carer's Allowance ▲ ❖	Housing Benefit	
	Incapacity Benefit (non contributory)/ Severe Disablement Allowance ■ ▲ ❖	Council Tax Benefit	
		Health benefits	
		Social Fund	
		Education benefits	

- ■ – There are both contributory and non-contributory versions of these.
- ▲ – There are Child Dependency Additions to these benefits, but only for people receiving them before 7th April 2003. Claims made after this date will be treated as a claim for Child Tax Credit.
- ❖ – These benefits are covered by the overlapping benefits rules. These mean that you can only receive the higher of whichever one you qualify for.
- ◗ – You can only receive one of these at one time.

Entitlements at a glance

The following list gives some broad indications of the various benefits for different groups of people. People often receive a combination of benefits and may be unclear about which benefits they receive. You must meet the conditions of entitlement for each benefit/tax credit, so this chart does not mean that you qualify for each benefit under the category you fit in.

Older people (aged 60+)	Sickness or disability	Carers
Retirement Pension	Statutory Sick Pay or Incapacity Benefit	Carer's Allowance
Attendance Allowance and/or Disability Living Allowance	Disability Living Allowance	Income Support
		Child Tax Credit
State Pension Credit	Income Support	Housing Benefit
Housing Benefit	Housing Benefit	Council Tax Benefit
Council Tax Benefit	Council Tax Benefit	Health benefits
Carer's Allowance	Industrial injury benefits	Education benefits
Bereavement Allowance	War pension or Armed Forces Compensation Scheme	
Health benefits		
Education benefits	Child Tax Credit	
Winter Fuel Payment	Working Tax Credit	
	Health benefits	
	Education benefits	

Unemployed or part time work (less than 16 hrs pw)	Full time work (more than 16 hrs pw)	People with children	Bereavement
Jobseeker's Allowance	Working Tax Credit	Child Benefit	Bereavement Allowance/ Widow's Pension
Income Support (if not required to be available for work and to sign on for example, lone parents)	Child Tax Credit	Child Tax Credit	
	Housing Benefit	Working Tax Credit	Widowed Parent's Allowance/ Widowed Mother's Allowance
	Council Tax Benefit	Education benefits	
	Health benefits	Health benefits	
Child Tax Credit	Education benefits	All other benefits	Bereavement Payment
Housing Benefit			
Council Tax Benefit			Income Support
			Housing Benefit
Health benefits			Council Tax Benefit
Education benefits			Child Tax Credit
			Working Tax Credit

Making benefit claims

You can make claims for some benefits by using claims forms which are available from social security offices or the DWP website www.dwp.gov.uk. Tax credits can also be claimed by using the form on HM Revenue and Customs website www.hmrc.gov.uk. Alternatively, you can start the claim by making a phone call to the relevant organisation.

For certain benefits – Jobseeker's Allowance, Income Support and Incapacity Benefit – you start the claim by phoning your local Jobcentre Plus office. Make sure that your claim is dated from your first call.

When you make a benefit claim you are required to do one of the following:

- Provide your National Insurance Number
- Provide information to enable your National Insurance Number to be located
- Apply for a National Insurance Number[1]

There can be delays in obtaining a National Insurance Number and if this holds up your benefit claim, you should ask for an interim payment to be made of the benefit you have claimed.[2] If this is refused, seek independent advice.

Interpreters

If you require an interpreter because your first language is not English, DWP policy [3] is to provide an interpreter where they need to communicate with you or to arrange an interpreter if you ask them to do so. For example, this is set out in the Jobcentre Plus statement of customer service standards.[4]

They must not send you away to find an interpreter but they can allow you to use your own interpreter who is over the age of sixteen if you prefer. They can pay the cost of your own interpreter, unless it is a friend or family member in which case, only travel expenses may be paid. If there is an immediate need for an interpreter, they should use a telephone interpreting service. HM Revenue and Customs have similar policies, but local authorities will have policies and practices which vary. However, it is widely accepted as being best practice that an interpreter is found and paid for you by the public body you are dealing with.

For information on help with English, ESOL and for translation assistance, please see the ESOL section on page 284.

Benefits for people from abroad

There are rules which mean that people who have recently arrived in the UK (of any nationality) or who are foreign nationals, may have restricted rights to social security benefits. Some foreign nationals who require 'leave' to remain in the UK may find that they are not entitled to benefits or tax credits (though there are exceptions), and people from European

Economic Area (EEA) countries, while they don't require leave to remain in the UK and are not subject to immigration control, can find that their benefit rights are restricted. People from EEA countries may also be able to use European Community law to challenge refusals of benefits. UK nationals who have recently arrived may also find that they face difficulties claiming some benefits.

The following chart is an at a glance guide to who may receive different benefits. See the glossary on page 117 for what the different terms and categories mean.

At a glance guide to migration and social security

	Income Support, Pension Credit, Housing & Council Tax Benefits	Jobseeker's Allowance (contributory)	Income based Jobseeker's Allowance	Child Benefit	Incapacity Benefit (contributory)	Retirement Pension	Bereavement benefits	DLA/AA/ Carer's Allowance	Benefits for work related disease or disability	Statutory Sick, Maternity, Adoption or Paternity Pay	Maternity Allowance	Child Tax Credit & Working Tax Credit
Person Subject to Immigration Control (PSIC)	✗	✓	✗	✗	✓	✓	✓	✗	✓	✓	✓	✗
PSIC but is a national of a state which has signed ECSMA & lawfully present in UK	✓	✓	✗	✗	✗	✓	✗	✗	✓	✓	✓	✓
National of state with a Reciprocal Agreement with the UK	✗	✓ (if included in agreement and habitually resident)	✗	✓ (if included in agreement and habitually resident)	✓ (if included in agreement)	✓ (if included in agreement)	✓ (if included in agreement)	✓ (if included in agreement)	✓ (if included in agreement)	✓ (if included in agreement)	✓ (if included in agreement)	✓ (if included in agreement)
EEA worker & family	✓ (Exempt)	✓	✓ (Exempt)	✓	✓	✓	✓	✓	✓	✓	✓	✓
EEA service provider or recipient	✓ (if habitually resident in UK/Eire)	✓	✓ (if habitually resident in UK/Eire)	✓	✓	✓	✓	✓	✓	✓	✓	✓

At a glance guide to migration and social security (continued)

	Income Support, Pension Credit, Housing & Council Tax Benefits	Jobseeker's Allowance	Income based Jobseeker's Allowance	Child Benefit	Incapacity Benefit (contributory)	Retirement Pension	Bereavement benefits	DLA/AA/ Carer's Allowance	Benefits for work related disease or disability	Statutory Sick, Maternity, Adoption or Paternity Pay	Maternity Allowance	Child Tax Credit & Working Tax Credit
National of a state with an EU agreement who is lawfully working (not all agreements allow access to public funds)	✗	✓	✓	✓	✓	✓	✓	✓	✓	✓	✓	✓
National of an A8 state	✓ (if a registered worker for over 12 months or not required to register or has the right to reside in UK)	✓	✓ (if a registered worker for over 12 months or if not required to register or has the right to reside)	✓ (Must have right to reside)	✓	✓	✓	✓	✓	✓	✓	✓
Any nationality not ordinarily resident in UK and not in any other category	✗	✓	✓ (but see below)	✓ (Must have right to reside)	✓	✓	✓	✗ (There is also a 6 months residence rule)	✓	✓	✓	✗
Any nationality not habitually resident in UK or Ireland	✗	✓	✗	✓ (Must have right to reside)	✓	✓	✓	✓ (6 months residence rule)	✓	✓	✓	✓ (Must have right to reside)
British Citizen with right of abode in UK	✓	✓ (if habitually resident)	✓ (if habitually resident)	✓	✓	✓	✓	✓	✓	✓	✓	

WORKING IN THE UK: NEWCOMER'S HANDBOOK *2ND EDITION*

Glossary

Various technical terms are used to describe the status of newcomers and these have implications for the benefits they may be able to receive.

People Subject to Immigration Control

Nationals of countries in the European Economic Area are not people subject to immigration control because all such nationals have the right to move freely between EEA countries. Section 115 Immigration and Asylum Act 1999 defines who is subject to Immigration Control and it covers people who require 'leave' (i.e. permission granted by the Immigration Service) to enter or stay in the UK. The category includes:

- people who have claimed or been refused asylum
- people whose stay in UK is subject to a written maintenance undertaking (also known as a 'sponsorship') and have been in the UK for less than five years
- people whose stay in UK is on condition that they don't have recourse to 'public funds'
- people who have appealed against a decision refusing them leave. In limited circumstances some may be able to get Income Support under the Urgent Case Payment rules

The following people are not PSIC for social security purposes:

- people who have refugee status, Exceptional Leave to Remain, Humanitarian Protection, Discretionary Leave or Indefinite Leave to Remain
- people granted refugee status may be able to receive backdated payments of Child Benefit, Income Support, tax credits, Pension Credit, Housing Benefit and/or Council Tax Benefit if they apply within 28 days of being notified about the award of refugee status provided that they were entitled in the past. However, the government intends to remove this sometime in 2006

Public Funds

These are: help with provision of housing under homelessness legislation, or local authority allocation procedures, and the following benefits:

- Child Benefit
- Child Tax Credit
- Working Tax Credit
- Attendance Allowance
- Disability Living Allowance
- Income Support
- Income-based Jobseeker's Allowance
- Housing Benefit
- Council Tax Benefit
- Carer's Allowance
- Pension Credit
- Severe Disablement Allowance (which is not available after April 2001 for new claims)
- The Social Fund

EU

The European Union. Members are:

- UK
- France
- Spain
- Portugal
- Italy
- Netherlands
- Belgium
- Luxembourg
- Germany
- Austria
- Greece
- Sweden
- Denmark
- Finland
- Republic of Ireland
- Hungary
- Czech Republic
- Slovakia
- Slovenia
- Poland
- Latvia
- Lithuania
- Estonia
- Malta
- Cyprus

EEA

European Economic Area. This is all the EU states plus Norway, Liechtenstein and Iceland. Nationals of Switzerland are treated as EEA nationals for social security purposes.

A8 nationals

This is the term to describe people who are nationals of eight of the ten countries which joined the EU in May 2004 and who face restrictions on their right to receive certain benefits. Cyprus and Malta are not included, but the following eight are: Hungary, Poland, Estonia, Latvia, Lithuania, Czech Republic, Slovakia and Slovenia. To qualify for benefits, A8 nationals who are employed must register with the Home Office as part of the 'Worker Registration Scheme' for the first 12 months of being employed. A8 nationals have full EEA worker's rights – see the at a glance guide. A8 nationals from Czech Republic, Hungary, Latvia, Malta, Poland and Slovakia may be able to use the ECSMA (see below) to receive benefits and have access to contributory benefits not affected by the Habitual Residence Test (see below). Note that not all the A8 countries have signed or ratified ECSMA. When registered, A8 workers can claim Child Benefit, Tax Credits and Housing Benefit provided that they are still employed (breaks of up to 30 days are allowed in this time). After 12 months' registration A8 nationals have the same benefit rights as anyone else.

ECSMA

European Convention on Social and Medical Assistance which requires signatory countries to provide assistance and cash help to nationals who are without sufficient resources and on the same basis as their own nationals. ECSMA applies to nationals of EEA countries, Turkey and Croatia.

Reciprocal Agreements

Agreements between the UK and 33 countries which allow for various benefits to be claimed by nationals in the UK or in the other signatory's country.[5] You may also aggregate any National Insurance contributions made in each country, thus enabling you to claim benefits in the UK based on your past foreign contributions. These are in addition to any right under European law.

EEA worker

People from EEA countries who are working or who have undertaken some form of 'genuine and effective' economic work, even for a few hours each week[6] or who are doing vocational training after working. A broad interpretation should be given. If you are looking for work, the government's view is that you must have previously worked in the UK in order to have full rights; however, this may be challenged using European caselaw.[7] The rules about EEA workers also cover family members who are dependent on the worker. The law on this is in EC Regulations 1612/68, 1251/70 and Directives 68/360 & 73/148. This category can now also include people from non-EEA states who are lawfully present and have worked in two or more EEA states.[8]

EEA service provider or recipient

This includes self-employed people and people who provide or receive commercial services, and their family members. European law generally gives such people the right to claim benefits in other EU countries as they should have the same tax and social advantages as nationals in those countries.[9]

Retired and 'incapacitated' workers from the EEA and their families

Some people and their dependent family members from EEA countries who have worked in the UK may be entitled to benefits under rules for retired or incapacitated workers.[10]

Right to reside

This is acquired by: British Citizens or anyone with the right of abode in the UK, Irish citizens, people with leave to remain in the UK, or with a right under European law to reside in the UK for example, students, self-employed people, workers or retired workers. The right is not lost by having to claim means tested benefits for short periods. The government view is that A8 workers acquire the right to reside after 12 months as a registered worker, although this approach may be open to legal challenge. The law about right to reside and benefits is still developing and there are several test cases which at the time of writing are expected to continue for some considerable time, until interpretation of the law in this area is settled.

A new EC Directive about residence[11], in force from 30th April 2006, gives a right to reside to EEA (and Swiss) nationals and their family members for the first three months after entry provided that they do not become an 'unreasonable burden' on the means tested benefits system.[12] Work seekers who are nationals of EEA countries (and their family members) have a right to reside for up to six months provided that they do not become an unreasonable burden on the means tested benefits system. This time limit can be extended if you can show that you are both genuinely seeking work and have a reasonable chance of being offered a job. If you are such a work seeker (or the family member of one) you are entitled to income-based Jobseeker's Allowance (provided that you are also habitually resident – see page 122) and also to Housing and Council Tax Benefit if you receive income-based Jobseeker's Allowance.[13] However, other rules apply to A8 nationals (see page 124).

After three months, you will also have a right to reside right under EC law if you are:

- a worker (including those unable to work temporarily because of illness, or training, or who are unemployed and have made a claim at Jobcentre Plus)
- self-employed (including those unable to work temporarily because of illness or training, or who are unemployed and have made a claim at Jobcentre Plus)
- a self-sufficient person who is economically inactive
- a student able to support yourself when your course starts
- a family member of any of the above people (including children up to age of 21 of the above or their partner, and adult dependants who are members of the household)

Under the Directive, there is a right of permanent residence for EC nationals who have lived legally in the UK for at least five years.[14]

At the time of writing it is not known how the UK government will reflect this EC legislation in domestic law. The Directive may be used to argue successfully at an Appeal Tribunal for benefits to be paid when you have been refused on right to reside or habitual residence grounds.

EU Agreements

These cover nationals of Algeria, Slovenia, Tunisia and Turkey and give them the same rights as EU nationals who are working and/or have lawfully worked in the UK (the question about whether or not asylum seekers are included is before the Courts). There are also 72 countries in Africa, The Caribbean and Pacific which have signed the Cotonou Agreement which enables nationals of these states to access benefits and other services.

British Citizen with Right of Abode

Only applies to full British Citizens (e.g. not British Overseas Citizens or British Dependent Territories Citizens).[15]

Ordinarily resident

Can apply from your first day of arrival in UK and for any purpose provided that it is 'established provided only it is adopted voluntarily and for a settled purpose'.[16]

Habitually resident

Applies to people of any nationality. You must have been in UK or the Common Travel Area (Isle of Man, Channel Islands and Ireland), for 'an appreciable period of time' but there is no fixed period which qualifies.

Many other factors are relevant – ability to return, family, possessions, friends, social contacts, work in the UK, etc.[17] It does not apply to EEA nationals who are workers nor to EEA nationals who have lived in UK and return from another EEA state.[18]

What does 'habitually resident' mean?

The Habitual Residence Test (HRT) affects Income Support (IS), income-based Jobseeker's Allowance (ibJSA), Pension Credit (PC), Housing Benefit (HB) and Council Tax Benefit (CTB). It also applies to the right to obtain public sector housing. There is no fixed period required in order to become habitually resident (though many benefits officials appear to erroneously use a three month period) and it is possible to be habitually resident after a very short period of being in the UK provided that one has a 'settled intention to remain' and have been in the Common Travel Area for 'an appreciable period'.[19] Unless you are exempt from the Habitual Residence Test, you must first be assessed as having a Right to Reside (see page 120). If you do not have a Right to Reside, you will be viewed as not being habitually resident.

The HRT applies to people of any nationality (including British Citizens) who are not habitually resident in the Common Travel Area (see page 122). As well as being habitually resident, people must also first have a 'right to reside' in the Common Travel Area.

It is DWP policy (though this is not in the law) that anyone who has been resident in the UK for at least two years will be accepted as passing the Habitual Residence Test unless immigration law specifically excludes them.[20] Even if the benefit authorities decide that you are not habitually resident when you make a claim, provided that you have a firm and settled intention to remain, they can decide that you will be habitually resident at a future date which means that you should not need to make a new claim for the benefit if this will be within three months.[21] However, it remains to be seen whether or not benefit Decision Makers will adhere to this new rule.

Exemptions from the Habitual Residence Test

Some people are exempt from the HRT:

- workers from the EEA and their family members. This should include workers who become temporarily unemployed or unable to work because of illness or disability[22]
- EEA nationals who have a right to reside in the UK under European law, for example people who are self sufficient or who run a business (seek advice)

- Refugees and people granted Exceptional Leave to Remain, Humanitarian Protection or Discretionary Leave
- People who have been deported or made to leave the country where they were living
- People who had to leave Montserrat after 1st November 1995 because of the volcanic eruption
- People from the A8 states who have been registered as workers and claim in-work benefits or have worked for 12 uninterrupted months as a registered worker[23]

The HRT is most likely to affect people who are new to the UK or who have been living abroad for a very long time. The European Court of Justice has also held that people who work in the UK, move to another EU country and then return to the UK to seek work should not fail the Habitual Residence Test.[24]

In some cases, an 'appreciable period' can start on the first day you arrive in the UK – it all depends what evidence you have of your links with and intention to remain in the UK for a length of time.[25] It is helpful to produce evidence about things such as family and friends in the UK, property, bank accounts, employment, family links, registration with schools, colleges and doctors, bringing possessions to the UK, etc. If you are turned down under the HRT, you should not only seek independent advice and appeal, but also continue to make a new benefit claim each week because this not only means that you are showing evidence of a settled intention but at some point, because of the passage of time, you will become habitually resident.

A8 Nationals

Rules introduced in 2004 mean that there are restrictions for A8 nationals and these are part of the transitional arrangements for these countries joining the European Union.

The government's view is that, in order to qualify for means tested benefits if they are not working, A8 nationals will need to have been registered as workers in the UK for at least 12 months and so be deemed to have a right to reside in the UK. However, it may be possible to use European law to argue that this restriction is unlawful, so you should seek independent advice if you are from an A8 country and have worked for less than 12 months. Interpretation of the law in this area is uncertain.

To register as a worker, you must apply within a month of starting work and pay a £50 fee. The registration only allows you to work for a named employer and it becomes invalid if your employment for that employer ends. Provided that you start work with a new employer and register within 30 days, you do not have to re-do your 12 months registration. You are also allowed breaks of up to 30 days, including being abroad.[26] Once registered, you may receive certain in-work benefits such as Tax Credits, Child Benefit, Council Tax Benefit and Housing Benefit.

If you lose your job during the 12 month registration period (or if you are not required to register and you make a claim) you will only be allowed to remain in the UK if you are self-sufficient – however, this interpretation of the law may be open to legal challenge.

Certain people do not have to be registered – these include self-employed people who are trading, students and people who were legally employed in the UK on 30th April 2004. If you fall into one of these categories, you will have a right to reside.

Destitution

If you have any special needs, a disability or a health problem and if you are destitute because you have been told you are not habitually resident, you may be able to receive help from a local authority using their powers under Section 21 National Assistance Act 1948 if you have special needs. If you have children, you may also get assistance from a local authority because of their duties to support families under Section 17 Children Act 1989 (and the equivalent law in Scotland and Northern Ireland). Local authorities may also be able to help under Section 2 Local Government Act 2000 (and the equivalent law in Scotland and Northern Ireland) – seek independent advice if you are left without any money or accommodation.

EEA workers

People who are not from the A8 states but who are from other EEA countries can qualify as workers, and so be exempted from the HRT if they have worked in the UK even if just for a very short period and part time. You will normally need to have worked at some stage in the UK to qualify as a worker.[27]

Couples

If you are one of a couple (including unmarried men and women who live together as a couple and gay and lesbian couples who live together as a couple) and you have no residence or immigration restrictions but your partner has a different residence or immigration status, the person who is not a Person Subject to Immigration Control should claim benefits. If you qualify for means tested benefits, you will be paid the same amount as a single person[28] but if you qualify for tax credits, you will be paid the same as a couple.[29] However, if your partner has a 'public funds' restriction on their stay in the UK, you must obtain independent advice before making a claim for a benefit or tax credit because it may affect their right to remain in the UK.

If your partner is not habitually resident or does not have the right to reside, the one who does have the right to reside or who is habitually resident should claim the benefits and you will be paid the same amount as a couple.

Reciprocal Agreements [30]

Some people who otherwise face restrictions obtaining benefit may be able to qualify by using a reciprocal agreement. These usually allow for periods of residence and national insurance contributions in one country to be used in another. Each agreement is different and covers different benefits.

Benefits covered in conventions with EU/EEA member and non-member states

State	Retirement pension	Bereavement benefits	Guardian's allowance	Incapacity benefit (short-term)	Incapacity benefit (long-term)	Jobseeker's allowance	Maternity allowance	Disablement benefit	Industrial injuries benefits	Child benefit	Attendance allowance	Disability living allowance	Carer's allowance
Austria	✓	✓	✓	✓	✓	✓	✓	✓	✓	✓	-	-	-
Barbados	✓	✓	✓	✓	✓	✓	✓	✓	✓	✓	-	-	-
Bermuda	✓	✓	-	-	-	-	-	✓	✓	-	-	-	-
Belgium	✓	✓	✓	✓	✓	✓	✓	✓	✓	✓	-	-	-
Canada	✓	-	-	✓	-	✓	-	-	-	✓	-	-	-
Cyprus	✓	✓	✓	✓	✓	✓	✓	✓	✓	-	✓	-	-
Denmark	-	✓	-	✓	✓	✓	✓	✓	✓	✓	-	-	-
Finland	✓	✓	-	✓	✓	✓	✓	✓	✓	✓	-	-	-
France	✓	✓	-	✓	✓	✓	✓	✓	✓	✓	-	-	-
Germany	-	✓	✓	✓	✓	✓	✓	✓	✓	✓	✓	✓	-
Guernsey	✓	✓	✓	✓	✓	✓	✓	✓	✓	✓	✓	-	-
Iceland	✓	✓	✓	✓	✓	✓	✓	✓	✓	-	-	-	-
Ireland	✓	✓	✓	✓	✓	✓	✓	✓	✓	-	-	-	-
Isle of Man	✓	✓	✓	✓	✓	✓	✓	✓	✓	✓	-	✓	✓
Israel	✓	✓	✓	✓	✓	-	✓	✓	✓	✓	-	-	-

Benefits covered in conventions with EU/EEA member and non-member states (continued)

State	Retirement pension	Bereavement benefits	Guardian's allowance	Incapacity benefit (short-term)	Incapacity benefit (long-term)	Jobseeker's allowance	Maternity allowance	Disablement benefit	Industrial injuries benefits	Child benefit	Attendance allowance	Disability living allowance	Carer's allowance
Italy	✓	✓	✓	✓	✓	✓	✓	✓	✓	-	-	-	-
Jamaica	✓	✓	✓	-	✓	-	-	✓	✓	-	-	-	-
Jersey	✓	✓	✓	✓	✓	-	✓	✓	✓	✓	✓	✓	-
Malta	✓	✓	✓	✓	✓	✓	-	✓	✓	-	-	-	-
Mauritius	✓	✓	✓	-	-	-	-	✓	✓	✓	-	-	-
New Zealand	✓	✓	✓	✓	✓	✓	-	✓	-	✓	-	-	-
Luxembourg	✓	✓	✓	✓	✓	✓	✓	✓	✓	-	-	-	-
Netherlands	✓	✓	✓	✓	✓	✓	✓	✓	✓	✓	-	-	-
Norway	✓	✓	✓	✓	✓	✓	✓	✓	✓	✓	-	-	-
Philippines	✓	✓	-	-	-	-	-	✓	✓	-	✓	-	-
Portugal	✓	✓	✓	✓	✓	✓	✓	✓	✓	✓	-	-	-
Spain	✓	✓	✓	✓	✓	✓	✓	✓	✓	✓	-	-	-
Sweden	✓	✓	✓	✓	✓	✓	✓	✓	✓	✓	-	-	-
*Switzerland	✓	✓	✓	✓	✓	-	-	✓	✓	-	-	-	-
Turkey	✓	✓	✓	✓	✓	-	-	✓	-	-	-	-	-
USA	✓	✓	✓	✓	✓	-	-	✓	-	-	-	-	-
**Yugoslavia	✓	✓	-	✓	✓	✓	✓	✓	✓	✓	-	-	-

WORKING IN THE UK: NEWCOMER'S HANDBOOK *2ND EDITION*

There is no agreement with Greece or Liechtenstein. The agreement with Gibraltar provides that, except for Child Benefit, the United Kingdom and Gibraltar are treated as separate European Economic Area countries. Although Northern Ireland is part of the United Kingdom, there is an agreement between Great Britain and Northern Ireland. This is because benefits in Northern Ireland and Great Britain are separate and administered under different social security legislation.

*From June 2002 an agreement with Switzerland allows Swiss nationals the right to rely on EC social security provisions, such as Regulation 1408/71 as if they were EEA nationals.

The agreement with Australia was terminated in April 2002.

**Following the break-up of Yugoslavia the reciprocal agreement between the United Kingdom and Yugoslavia should be treated as separate agreements between the United Kingdom and the residue of the former republic: Serbia and Montenegro, Bosnia-Herzegovina, Croatia, the Former Yugoslav Republic of Macedonia, and Slovenia.

Jobseeker's Allowance (JSA)

Jobseeker's Allowance (JSA) is a social security benefit for people who are unemployed.

There are two types of JSA:

- contribution-based JSA
- income-based JSA

There are four main differences between these two types:

- income-based JSA is means-tested and contribution-based JSA is not
- receipt of contribution-based JSA depends on having paid enough National Insurance (NI) contributions during the last two complete tax years
- contribution-based JSA is paid for a maximum of 182 days
- you can only claim contribution-based JSA for yourself

Eligibility

The following conditions are common to both types of JSA, which you must prove you meet each time you sign on:

- you are aged between 18 and pension age (if you are under 18, seek independent advice)
- you are out of work or working less than 16 hours per week
- you are available to do work for at least 40 hours a week and specify the days of the week that you are available and the hours you can work each day
- you have agreed a Jobseeker's Agreement with Jobcentre Plus which sets out what actions you will take to find work
- you 'sign on' at the Jobcentre Plus office at least once a fortnight (people living more than an hour's travel time from a Jobcentre Plus office may sign on by post)
- you are actively seeking work – you must take at least three steps a week to find work
- you are capable of work (which means you do not have an illness or disability which makes you incapable of work)
- you are not in full-time education[31]

As a newcomer, you are required to meet further conditions – you are eligible for contribution-based JSA if you have paid enough National Insurance contributions and you are:

- a Person Subject to Immigration Control (PSIC)[32] (but you will need to meet National Insurance contribution conditions which will be difficult if you do not have permission to work and may reveal that you have worked without permission)
- a national of a state with a Reciprocal Agreement with the UK which includes JSA (i.e. you may be able to use your equivalent of National Insurance contributions paid in the other country towards entitlement in the UK)
- a person who has Indefinite Leave to Remain, Exceptional Leave to Remain, Discretionary Leave or Humanitarian Protection

- an EEA worker and dependant
- an EEA service provider or recipient
- a British Citizen with the right of abode in UK
- a national of a state with an EU agreement who is working lawfully

You are not eligible for Income-based JSA if:

- you are a Person Subject to Immigration Control (PSIC)[33] unless you are a national of a state which has signed ECSMA and you are lawfully present in UK
- you are not habitually resident in the Common Travel Area
- you are a national of an A8 country and have been registered as a worker in the UK for less than a year (seek independent advice as this is disputable)

Other rules

You can be available to take work for less than 40 hours a week if:

- you have caring responsibilities for someone with a disability or health problem
- you have been laid off or have had your work hours temporarily reduced by your employer ('short-time')
- you have a part-time job
- you are on jury service
- you are a justice of the peace, member of a tribunal or are serving a community order service
- you are a witness in court proceedings[34]

These are certain circumstances where you are able to place additional restrictions on your jobsearch. For example, up to 13 weeks after the beginning of your claim, you may be allowed to search solely for your usual occupation and level of pay, and refuse other job offers. This is, of course, dependent on your having a usual occupation and level of pay. This is known as the permitted period, after which you must be available for a wider range of work. These arrangements must always be agreed with your local Jobcentre Plus office. You can also refuse to be available for or to apply for certain jobs if the work would not fit with a sincerely held conscientious or religious belief and provided that you still have reasonable prospects of finding work.[35] You can also place reasonable restrictions on the type of work you will do because of your physical or mental condition.[36]

After 13 weeks, you may be able to keep restrictions on jobsearch, for example pay, up to a maximum of 6 months from the beginning of your claim.[37]

Short periods of sickness when claiming JSA

You will be able to remain in receipt of JSA for up to two weeks during short periods of illness. You will be required to fill out a form declaring that you are unfit for work.[38]

Suspensions

If an adviser believes that there is doubt about your jobseeking activity, your benefit will be suspended immediately. The main exception to this is if you can prove good cause for your behaviour or appearance through mental illness or a drink or drug-related condition. In this situation, you will have to substantiate that you have a known problem.

If you are not receiving any money, you should immediately appeal and also apply for a hardship payment. If you are told that you cannot do so because your claim has been terminated, you should then ask to make a new claim for JSA.

Penalties

You can be sanctioned from JSA for up to six months if you are shown to be unwilling to accept work or if it is felt that you lost your last job because of 'misconduct' or because you left 'voluntarily without just cause'.[39]

If you are sanctioned you should obtain independent advice and submit an appeal.

Couples

If you are one of a couple (including unmarried men and women who live together as a couple and gay and lesbian couples who live together as a couple), you will both have to make a joint claim for income-based JSA if you are not looking after children and at least one of you was born after 28th October 1957.[40] This means that normally, both of you will need to meet the conditions of entitlement to income-based JSA, but some couples do not need to make a joint claim – for example, where one of the couple is unable to work because of illness or caring responsibilities or they work for more than 16 hours a week or because they are subject to immigration control. There are exceptions to couples making a joint claim that may apply if you have recently come into the country and contribution-based JSA does not require you to make joint claims.

Income Support

Income Support is a means-tested benefit for people who are not working for 16 hours or more a week.

Eligibility

You can receive Income Support if you satisfy all of the following

- you are aged 16 or over
- you are not in full-time, non-advanced education
- you are not working 16 or more hours a week (there are a few exceptions)
- if you have a partner, they must not be working for 24 or more hours a week

As a newcomer, if you are from abroad you also need to be one of the following:

- not a 'Person Subject to Immigration Control'. But if you are a national of a country which has signed the ECSMA and you are also lawfully present in UK you may qualify[41]

- a Person Subject to Immigration Control who is entitled to Income Support at the lower Urgent Case payment rate because they have been in the UK for less than five years and their sponsor or sponsors, if more than one, have died
- an asylum seeker entitled under transitional protection rules or otherwise self-supporting and funds from abroad have been temporarily disrupted for a limited period
- a worker or family member of one from an EEA state or from an EEA country or a service provider or recipient
- an A8 national who has been registered as a worker for at least 12 months or who has a right to reside
- a British Citizen with the right of abode in the UK[42]

You must also be 'habitually resident' in the Common Travel Area (see page 122).

To qualify for Income Support, you must be in one of a number of particular groups. The most common of these are if you are:[43]

- unable to work because of ill health or a disability.
- caring for a disabled person who has claimed or who receives Disability Living Allowance or Attendance Allowance
- a lone parent responsible for looking after a child aged under 16
- on statutory maternity, paternity or adoption pay

If you have been awarded refugee status and you have been in the UK for less than 12 months and you are also on an English language course lasting at least 15 hours a week, you may also qualify for Income Support.

If you are a Person Subject to Immigration Control you may qualify for a reduced rate of Income Support if your funds from abroad have been temporarily disrupted or you are subject to a sponsorship agreement for less than five years and your sponsor has died.

If you work more than 16 hours a week, you may be eligible for Income Support if you fall into one of the eligible groups listed above, as well as being in one of the following situations:

- you are mentally or physically disabled and your hours or earnings are 75% or less than that of a person without your disability in the same job
- you are living in a care home and working (require personal care because of disablement, past or present dependence on alcohol or drugs, past or present mental disorder or terminal illness)
- you are a volunteer or working for a charity or voluntary organisation and only receive expenses
- you are regularly and substantially caring for another person
- you are a foster parent and paid by a health body, local authority or voluntary organisations to provide respite care in your own home
- you are a childminder working in your own home
- you are on a training course and receiving a training allowance
- you are involved in a trade dispute, but it is more than 7 days since the day you stopped work
- you are working more than 16 but under 24 hours and are still covered by the transitional protection you were awarded in 1991
- you are on statutory maternity, paternity or adoption leave

Note: this is not an exhaustive list.

Earnings

Income Support is a means-tested benefit so your earnings will be taken into account when calculating your eligibility.

Earnings do not include:

- payments in kind
- periodic payments, e.g. because employment has ended through redundancy
- payments made when an employee is on maternity leave
- sick pay

- occupational pensions
- payments of expenses for doing your job for example, specialist clothing, travel expenses, or telephone calls made entirely for work purposes

As well as these, between £5 and £20 of your earnings is ignored; depending on which group you fit into.

Other income

Almost all other income is counted, but some is ignored. For example, these are ignored: Disability Living Allowance, Attendance Allowance, Child Benefit if you also receive Child Tax Credit, Guardian's Allowance, children's earnings, payments in kind, payments made for you to a third party, volunteers expenses, Education Maintenance Allowances, fostering allowances, voluntary and charitable payments (new from April 2006). [44] If in doubt, seek advice.

If you receive Child Tax Credit, this is ignored along with your Child Benefit, but the Income Support calculation will not then take account of any children that you have.

Capital

You must have less than £16,000 in capital or savings unless you live permanently in a residential care home. If you have been between £6000 and £16,000 capital, you will be counted as having £1 weekly income for each £250 (or part thereof) between these limits.

If you have capital assets outside the United Kingdom, it will count as capital for Income Support. If your capital (including property which you or your partner own) is in a country where you are not allowed to transfer the capital to the UK, you will be counted as having capital at its market value in that country. If you can transfer the capital (or proceeds of sale) to the UK, you will be counted as having capital to the value of what it is worth in the UK. In both cases, ten percent is taken off the value to allow for the cost of sale and/or transfer.[45]

If you deliberately get rid of capital to bring your capital down to the level where you can receive extra benefit, you can still be counted as having it and the DWP are allowed to infer an intention from unusually high, one-off expenditure.[46] Seek advice if you are unsure about this or if you are affected by it.

The applicable amount

This is the minimum amount the government sets down that you need to live on. It is normally increased each April. It is made up of a weekly personal allowance for you and your partner and weekly premiums (paid if you are disabled or a carer or bereaved) plus housing cost for things such as interest on mortgages and loans for repairs and improvement and service charges. If you pay rent, this is not included and you should claim Housing Benefit instead. This also means that your applicable amount may vary to take account of some of your circumstances.

If your income is less than your applicable amount, you will normally receive Income Support to bring your income up to the level of your applicable amount.

The Work Focused Interview

When you claim Income Support, you will usually be asked to attend a Work Focused Interview unless an interview would not be appropriate or would not be of assistance. If you do not attend the interview without good cause, your claim will lapse. See page 226 for more information on Work Focused Interviews.

Pension Credit

Pension Credit (also called State Pension Credit), is a means-tested benefit for people aged 60 or over. The amount you qualify for depends on such things as your income, your capital and your personal circumstances. The rules about income and capital are very similar to those used for Income Support.

You can claim Pension Credit for yourself and your partner. You can also receive Pension Credit if you are in hospital.

You can have your Pension Credit claim backdated for up to twelve months if you were entitled and you ask for it to be backdated.

There are two elements to the Pension Credit:

- guaranteed credit
- savings credit

You can receive Pension Credit by qualifying for either one of these or both.

Eligibility

You can get Pension Credit through guarantee credit if you are aged 60 or over (it does not matter if your partner is under 60), and you have a weekly income which is less than amounts fixed by the government (£114.05 for a single person, £174.05 for a couple). Some people have higher amounts – these include people with mortgages, loans or leasehold service charges and people who are recognised by the DWP as carers or as being severely disabled.

You can get the savings credit if you or your partner are aged 65 or over (it does not matter who makes the claim for Pension Credit) and have income between certain levels.

As a newcomer, you also need to be one of the following:[47]

- not a 'Person Subject to Immigration Control'. But if you are a national of a country which has signed the ECSMA and you are also lawfully present in UK you may qualify
- a worker or family member of one from an EEA state or from an EEA country or a service provider or recipient
- an A8 national who has been registered as a worker for at least 12 months
- a British Citizen with the right of abode in the UK

You must also be 'habitually resident' in the United Kingdom or Republic of Ireland.

Income and savings

There are various steps needed to work out if you have low enough income and savings to qualify.

Your income and capital are worked out the same way as for Income Support (see pages 136-137), except that there is no capital limit and you will be treated as having income from capital above £6000 at a rate of £1 a week for each £500 above this level.

The savings credit part of Pension Credit

Working out savings credit is complicated. You can find out more about the calculation at www.thepensionservice.gov.uk/pensioncredit or if in doubt seek advice.

How to claim

To make a valid claim for Pension Credit you must provide (in original documents, unless you don't have these):

- your National Insurance number or evidence to allow the Pension Service to find your number (if you don't have one, you have to apply for one)
- proof of your identity (passport or identity card – you may be asked for more than one piece of evidence)
- evidence of your income (pension payslips, proof of service charges, proof of other money received)

You can make a claim by:

- telephone (0800 99 1234)
- online at www.thepensionservice.gov.uk/pensioncredit or
- filling in form PC1

Pension Credit is usually paid into a bank or building society account. If this is not possible, you can ask for payment to be made in other ways. If you are not able to collect your Pension Credit in person, you may be able to arrange for someone else to do so. Ask the Pension Service about this.

Benefits for ill-health and disability

If you are ill or have an accident, you may need to see a doctor or go to the hospital. Your entitlement to medical care is described below, page 155.

Incapacity Benefit

Incapacity Benefit is the main benefit which is paid to people who are unable to work full-time (i.e.16 hours or more a week) because of an illness or disability.

Eligibility

You can claim Incapacity Benefit if you satisfy both of the following:

- you are aged between 16 and pensionable age (60 for women and 65 for men)
- you are not entitled to receive Statutory Sick Pay from an employer

Incapacity Benefit is not means-tested, so your savings and capital will not affect your eligibility. However, income from occupational pensions may reduce the amount of benefit you are entitled to. If you have a partner, and you receive the long term rate of Incapacity Benefit, you may qualify for an extra mount for an adult dependant. However, their earnings may reduce the amount of this dependant's addition.

To qualify, you must either have paid sufficient National Insurance contributions or be aged under 25 and meet the conditions for receiving this without contributions (this is often called non-contributory Incapacity Benefit or Incapacity Benefit for Youth).[48]

As a newcomer, you can claim Incapacity Benefit if you meet the above requirements and if you are one of the following:

- a Person Subject to Immigration Control (PSIC). But you will need to meet the National Insurance Contribution conditions – which you may have difficulty with if you are not allowed to work. You are also not allowed to receive the non-contributory Incapacity Benefit[49]
- a person with Indefinite Leave to Remain, Exceptional Leave to

Remain, Discretionary Leave or Humanitarian Protection
- a national of a state with a Reciprocal Agreement with the UK
- an EEA worker and family
- an EEA service provider or recipient
- a national of a state with an EU agreement who is lawfully working
- a British Citizen with the right of abode in the UK[50]

Assessment

Claims for Incapacity Benefit must be supported by medical evidence. Usually, for the first 28 weeks of incapacity, you will be judged on your ability to carry out your own job. This is called the Own Occupation Test. You may also be examined by an approved doctor. The Own Occupation Test applies if you have worked for at least 16 hours a week for more than 8 weeks out of the last 21 weeks before you became incapable of work.[51]

You must be assessed using a test called the Personal Capability Assessment after you have been incapable of work for 28 weeks, or from the start of your claim if you had no regular job when you became ill.[52] You may be asked to complete a questionnaire about your illness and asked to obtain a MED4 certificate from your doctor. You may also be examined by an approved doctor.

The decision on whether someone has met the threshold of incapacity is made by a decision maker in Jobcentre Plus. The decision maker is not a doctor, but makes a decision about your ability to work based on all the evidence. This will include the questionnaire, the information provided by your own doctor and the evidence of the approved doctor.

Some people can be exempted from the Personal Capability Assessment – for example, if they have a terminal illness, in which case they receive the highest rate of Disability Living Allowance care component, or if there is medical evidence of certain conditions such as severe mental illness or a severe learning disability or certain serious physical illnesses. It is also possible to be treated as incapable of work even if you are found capable of work if work would cause a substantial risk to your or anyone else's health.[53]

How much is Incapacity Benefit?

Incapacity Benefit is divided into three parts

- the basic amount
- an amount for dependants
- an age addition for some claimants whose incapacity for work started before the age of 45 with a higher age addition for those whose incapacity started before the age of 35

The basic amount increases with the duration for which it is paid. For the first 28 weeks you receive the short-term lower rate. From week 29 to week 52 you will receive the short-term higher rate. If you are entitled to the higher rate care component of Disability Living Allowance or you are terminally ill, you will be paid at the long-term rate after 28 weeks. After 52 weeks the long-term rate becomes payable unless you are over pension age. The additional amounts for dependants or which are age-related are only payable with the long-term rate.

Working while claiming Incapacity Benefit

You cannot usually work while claiming benefits but you may be able to do some work while you are getting Incapacity Benefit. You should tell the office that deals with your benefit before you start any work, and check that the work will not affect your benefit. It is important to contact your local office before you start any type of work.

You may be able to do either voluntary work or permitted work (there are four categories of permitted work). For more information, contact your local Jobcentre Plus office or an advice agency.

Moving into full time work

If you start work or a training course you may be able to protect your entitlement to higher levels of Incapacity Benefit for up to 52 weeks. Contact your local Jobcentre Plus office for further information

How to claim Incapacity Benefit

If you live in an area covered by a Jobcentre Plus office, your first contact with the Jobcentre Plus office will usually be by telephone and you will also have a follow-up interview to complete the claims process.

Statutory Sick Pay

Eligibility

Statutory Sick Pay (SSP) is a social security benefit which is paid through employers to qualifying employees who are absent from work due to sickness, and is paid for up to a maximum of 28 weeks. Self-employed people are not entitled to SSP. The other social security benefits which are also paid by employers in this way, are:

- Statutory Maternity Pay
- Statutory Paternity Pay
- Statutory Adoption Pay

There are no restrictions on people from abroad receiving these statutory payments even if you are not allowed to receive other benefits because of your immigration status (provided you meet the qualifying conditions for payment).

Some employers pay occupational sick pay. This will normally be in addition to SSP. Some employers can reclaim the cost of paying SSP to their staff from HMRC, if they have a high proportion of their workforce sick at any one time.

To receive SSP you must satisfy the following conditions:

- you must be an employee (this means that you work for someone else, even if you don't have a written contract of employment. Your employer can't avoid paying you SSP by dismissing you or writing this into your contract[54])
- you must be incapable of work for four or more days in a row, because of sickness, disability or because you are a carrier of or have been in contact with an infectious disease and a Medical Officer for Environmental Health has certified this or a doctor has advised you not to work as a precaution

- you must be sick on a 'qualifying day' – qualifying days are the days of the week on which you normally work[55]

During the eight weeks before you are sick, your average weekly earnings are at least £84 or more each week before any deductions such as tax and national insurance.

- you are aged over 16
- you have notified your employer that you are unable to come to work because of sickness within seven calendar days of the first day of sickness

You can be entitled to receive SSP for each job that you have – so for example, if you have two part-time jobs (with the same or different employers), you may qualify for two SSP payments if you satisfy all the qualifying conditions for payment.

You cannot receive SSP if:

- you received Incapacity Benefit within the last 57 days (in which case, you should make another claim for Incapacity Benefit)
- there is a strike at your workplace during the time when you first became unable to work
- you have a contract of employment but you have not yet started work
- you are classed as a 'welfare to work beneficiary' and you used to receive Incapacity Benefit or Severe Disablement Allowance in the last 52 weeks. In this case, you should make another claim for one of these benefits
- you are a woman who is on maternity leave
- you are a woman in receipt of Statutory Maternity Pay or Maternity Allowance
- you are in legal custody
- you have already received SSP for 28 weeks

If you are not entitled to SSP, your employer must give you a form known as an SSP1 which you can then use to claim Incapacity Benefit from your local Jobcentre Plus office. They must also send you this form when you

WORKING IN THE UK: NEWCOMER'S HANDBOOK *2ND EDITION*

come to the end of your SSP entitlement.

Even if you are entitled to SSP, you can't receive it for the first three days of sickness unless you have received SSP within the previous eight weeks.

How much is it?

SSP is £70.05 a week for up to 28 weeks. You may have to pay Income Tax on this and you will be credited with class 1 National Insurance Contributions for each week that you receive SSP.

How to claim

Ask your employer how to claim as many employers have their own paperwork and procedures. However, you should tell your employer as soon as you are unable to work and do so in writing within seven days of when you first qualify for SSP. After seven days of being unable to work, you must provide a medical certificate from a doctor confirming that you are unable to work.

Disputes about Statutory Sick Pay

If your employer refuses to pay you SSP, you have the right to ask your employer to explain why. If you disagree with their explanation or if they fail to provide information within a 'reasonable time', you can then ask the local Inland Revenue Office to decide what you are entitled to.[56] You must ask the Inland Revenue to decide matters within six months of when you think you should have received SSP.

If you are dismissed for asking the Inland Revenue to enforce your right to SSP, you will not be able to take action for unfair dismissal unless you have worked for the employer for at least a year. However, if your employer dismisses you in order to avoid paying SSP, they must still pay you SSP until your entitlement ends. This may either be because you have returned to work after a period of sickness, your employment contract ends, you have received the maximum SSP entitlement of 28 weeks, or, if you are pregnant, when the Maternity Pay period begins.

Attendance Allowance (AA)

Attendance Allowance (AA) is a tax-free benefit for people aged 65 or older who are physically or mentally disabled and who:

- need help with personal care or
- need 'supervision' (for example, someone on call in case of danger)

AA is paid on top of other benefits, such as Retirement Pension or Pension Credit and it is not means-tested (indeed, it can increase your entitlement to means-tested benefits).

Eligibility

You must meet the conditions of entitlement for at least six months before your claim and be likely to meet them for at least the next six months after your claim, unless you have a terminal illness which means that your life expectancy can be stated by a doctor as being six months or less.[57]

Try to keep a copy of your claim form (in case you wish to dispute matters or in case the original is lost). You may have a visiting doctor come to your home to examine you after you have sent in a claim and make a report. Inconsistency in your answers may be unhelpful so try to be clear and give full information about your needs.

If you go into a hospital or nursing home funded by the National Health Service (NHS), AA or Disability Living Allowance (DLA) stops after 28 days (84 days if you are aged under 16). Payment starts again when you go home. If you go into a care home and you receive help from public funds with the cost, payment of AA care component DLA stops after 28 days. Payment of the DLA mobility component is not affected unless you are in NHS care.

As a newcomer, you can receive AA or DLA if you meet at least one of the following conditions:

- you are not a Person Subject to Immigration Control unless you are a national of a state which has signed the European Convention on Social and Medical Assistance and you are lawfully present in the UK[58]

- you have Indefinite Leave to Remain, Exceptional Leave to Remain, Discretionary Leave or Humanitarian Protection
- you are a national of a state with a reciprocal agreement with the UK which covers AA and/or DLA
- you are a worker or family member of one from an EEA state or from an EEA country and a service provider or recipient or
- you are a British Citizen with the right of abode in the UK[59]

You must also have been resident in the UK for at least six months – however, you may be able to use time spent in another EU country or a country with a reciprocal agreement to count towards this.

You can claim on-line by going to the DWP website, at http://www.dwp.gov.uk/eservice/

Attendance Allowance Rates

There are two rates of Attendance Allowance – lower and higher.

Lower rate Attendance Allowance is paid if you need attention from another person either during the day or night. This attention might be any of the following:

- you require continual supervision throughout the day
- you require someone awake at night for a prolonged period or at frequent intervals to watch over you
- you need prolonged or repeated attention with your 'bodily functions'.[60]

Higher rate Attendance Allowance is paid when you need attention from another person during both the day and the night. You must have met one of these conditions for at least six months, unless you have a terminal illness.

'Bodily functions' explained

AA provides a contribution towards the extra costs faced by severely disabled people as a result of their disabilities. Broadly, entitlement to

AA depends on the extent to which the person needs help with their bodily functions (i.e. things which the body does) or needs supervision.

Some examples of help from another person with bodily functions which qualify:

- dressing (which can include checking you are tidy)
- prompts and reminders
- washing
- bathing
- guiding
- reading correspondence
- going up or down stairs
- taking medication
- using the toilet
- getting up from a chair

Supervision explained

Continual supervision means it is necessary for somebody to be around on a frequent or regular basis (this does not need to be non-stop), to prevent any accidents to yourself, or to other people.

Examples of need for supervision:

- danger of falls
- needing reassurance
- fits or seizures
- risk of self-harm or suicide attempts
- behaviour which might create a danger for you or others

Disability Living Allowance (DLA)

DLA is designed for people who need help looking after themselves and for people who find it difficult to walk or get around. It is made up of two components:

- care component (paid at one of three rates) and
- mobility component (paid at one of two rates)

Eligibility

You must claim DLA before your 65th birthday but awards already made can continue for as long as you meet the conditions. You can make the claim as soon as you meet the conditions but you must have needed help for three months before payment can begin, unless you have a terminal illness and your death can reasonably be expected within six months.[61] The higher rate of mobility component is payable from age three, and the lower rate from age five. The care component is payable from age three months (or from birth where a child is terminally ill). Attendance Allowance (AA) is available for people claiming from the age of 65. For further eligibility requirements see page 147.

You can claim on-line by going to the DWP website, at http://www.dwp.gov.uk/eservice/

Care and mobility components

Lowest rate care component is paid if:

- you need attention in connection with your bodily functions for a significant portion of the day (i.e. a significant event or an event lasting about 45 minutes) or
- you cannot prepare a cooked main meal for yourself[62]

The cooking test looks at whether you can prepare a main daily meal freshly cooked on a traditional cooker (i.e. not a snack). It is a meal for one person only. Tasks involved in this include:

- planning what to prepare
- using taps
- using a cooker
- peeling and chopping vegetables
- using hot pans
- standing and bending.

Middle rate care component is equivalent to the lower rate of Attendance Allowance and is paid if you need attention from another person either during the day or night. This attention might be:

- frequent attention throughout the day or prolonged or repeated attention at night in connection with your bodily functions or
- continual supervision throughout the day or for prolonged periods or at frequent intervals at night in order to avoid substantial danger to yourself or others[63]

You should put down all the details of help you need from another person on the claim form and why you need someone else to help you (even if you don't actually have anyone helping you).

Highest rate care component[64] is paid when you meet the conditions of entitlement for both the day and night conditions. The definitions of supervision and personal care are explained above (see page 149). Children aged under sixteen must also show that they need substantially more help than a person of their age and gender would normally require.

Lower rate mobility component[65] is paid if you cannot walk out of doors in unfamiliar places because of a physical or mental disability without guidance or supervision from another person most of the time.

This cannot be paid to children under five. Children aged less than sixteen must also show that they need substantially more guidance or supervision than a person their age would normally require.

Higher rate mobility component[66] can be paid to children aged three or over. You can qualify if, because of a physical disability:

- you are unable to walk
- you are virtually unable to walk
- you are unable to walk without pain or severe discomfort (There is no fixed distance and a range of factors must be considered, including how you walk, whether you stop, how fast you walk and how long it takes you to walk somewhere)

- the exertion of walking would endanger your life or lead to a serious deterioration in your health
- you have no legs or feet
- you are both deaf and blind
- you have extremely disruptive and dangerous behaviour and you also receive the highest rate of the care component

Work related illnesses and disabilities

If you have an accident at work or you contract an illness or ill-health condition through work in the UK, you may qualify for a range of benefits commonly called industrial injuries benefits, the most common of which is Disablement Benefit. These benefits are not means-tested but they are taken into account in means-tested benefit calculations.

There are no restrictions on these being awarded to people from abroad or who are subject to immigration control. However if you claim these benefits while you are not allowed to work as part of your conditions of leave to remain in the UK, a claim will reveal that you have been working.[67]

Eligibility[68]

To qualify you must be aged at least 18 and you must have had an accident which arose 'out of and in the course of' your employment. This can include accidents which take place away from your workplace as long as they are 'reasonably incidental'[69] to your work (for example, if travelling in transport provided by your employer or if carrying out your work at home). You must also be an 'employed earner' – in other words an employee or paid 'office holder'.

Alternatively, you should have contracted a 'prescribed industrial disease'. There are over 70 of these and the list of prescribed diseases[70] is amended frequently. The diseases include certain infections caught at work and disabilities caused by exposure to certain substances, as well as certain types of allergy, cancers, respiratory illnesses and repetitive strain injury. An up-to-date list of prescribed industrial diseases can be found in DWP leaflet DB1. For many of the diseases you will need to have been working in a particular type of job when the disease was contracted or started.

You will normally need to have symptoms, whether resulting from an accident or from a prescribed disease, which are present at least 16 weeks after the accident or onset of the prescribed disease, and you will need to be assessed by a doctor working on behalf of the DWP. To qualify for Disablement Benefit, you will normally have to have an assessment that your disability has caused a 'loss of function' of any mental or physical abilities of at least 16%, which means that when compared to someone else of the same gender and age, you have at least 16% less ability to perform normal everyday activities.[71] If your condition changes, you can ask for a re-assessment.

How much is it?

If you are assessed as having a loss of faculty of 95% you may also qualify for additional industrial injuries benefits such as Constant Attendance Allowance and Exceptionally Severe Disablement Allowance. The amount of Disablement Benefit varies according to your percentage loss of faculty. The rates vary between £25.42 and £127.10 a week.

These benefits count as income against means-tested benefits but they may be paid whether or not you are in work and they can also be paid on top of other non-means-tested benefits such as Incapacity Benefit. They are also tax free and are therefore ignored as income when working out any Tax Credits you may be entitled to.

More generous rules apply to people whose work-related accident or illness started before 1st October 1990.

Other help

If your health has been affected by work you have undertaken, you should obtain specialist legal advice – for example from your trade union or (in England and Wales) the Law Society Accident Line on 0500 192939 – because you may be entitled to compensation as well as industrial injuries benefits.

For unwaged people (including those under 18) who are undertaking training on government funded work-based learning, there is the Analogous Industrial Injuries Scheme which pays equivalent benefits. More details are available by phoning 01977 464111 or at www.dfes.gov.uk/aiisnet/idb.shtml.

Carer's Allowance (CA)

Carer's Allowance provides an income if you provide regular and substantial care to a severely disabled person.

There is one basic rate of benefit, increased annually, and child and adult dependency increases may be payable.

If you are a lower income carer who is entitled to CA and get Income Support, income-based Jobseeker's Allowance, Housing Benefit or Council Tax Benefit, you may get an extra amount known as the Carer Premium, or the equivalent amount in Pension Credit.

Carer's Allowance overlaps with other income replacement benefits. If you are entitled both to Carer's Allowance and a contributory benefit, (for example the State Pension) you receive the contributory benefit. If the contributory benefit is less than Carer's Allowance, you get a top-up of Carer's Allowance to ensure that the total is no less than Carer's Allowance.[72]

If you are a disabled person and receive a severe disability premium, you may lose your premium if your carer receives CA. This does not include cases where your carer has claimed CA in order to qualify for the carer premium in their own means tested benefits, but they do not actually receive the Carer's Allowance because they have an overlapping benefit.[73]

Who gets Carer's Allowance?

You must provide care for at least 35 hours per week to a severely disabled person. 'Severely disabled' means receiving the middle or higher rate of Disability Living Allowance care component, Attendance Allowance, or the equivalent rates of Constant Attendance Allowance.

The lower age limit for entitlement to CA is 16 and there is no upper age limit.

You must not be in full-time education (21 hours a week) or receiving more than the current weekly earnings limit (£84), after deduction of allowable expenses, from paid employment.

As a newcomer, you can receive CA if you meet at least one of the following conditions:

- you are a not a Person Subject to Immigration Control unless you are a national of a state which has signed the European Convention on Social and Medical Assistance and you are lawfully present in the UK[74]
- you have Indefinite Leave to Remain, Exceptional Leave to Remain, Discretionary Leave or Humanitarian Protection
- you are a national of a state with a reciprocal agreement with the UK which covers AA and/or DLA
- you are a worker or family member of one from an EEA state or from an EEA country and a service provider or recipient
- you are a British Citizen with the right of abode in the UK[75]

Entitlement to health care

If you become ill or have an accident (in or out of work) you may need to have medical help.

If you need emergency care you can be treated free of charge by the National Health Service (NHS) even if you are subject to immigration control or if you are not a resident in the UK. If you are ordinarily resident you are eligible to receive free NHS treatment at a hospital or from a doctor, called a General Practitioner (GP), in the community.

On arrival in the UK, it is advisable to register with a GP. You can find a list of GPs in any library.

You are not required to show official documentation when registering with a GP, and GP staff have no right to demand to see identity documentation but they will need to see proof of address and other personal details.

If you unable to register with a GP after three attempts, contact your local Primary Care Trust, who will allocate you a GP.

The Primary Care Trust can also provide local information on community dental services and dentists for patients receiving treatment under the NHS.

NHS Direct, on 0845 4647 can also provide information about local GPs and NHS dentists as well as free advice and information about your health or advice if you are unwell.

The Department of Health website has an overview of who is eligible for services. This is available at: http://www.dh.gov.uk/PolicyAndGuidance/International/OverseasVisitors/fs/en

Note: For a full explanation, contact a reputable adviser. This is particularly important if you are an overseas visitor needing primary care as the government has proposed tightening the rules.

Child Benefit

Child Benefit is a tax-free benefit for people who have a dependent child or children. Note that 90% of those who are eligible for Child Benefit are also eligible for Child Tax Credit (see page 170).

Because it is not means-tested, Child Benefit is not based on your assets, income or savings.

Newcomers

Newcomers face additional requirements. You are eligible if you are one of the following:[76]

- a national of state with a Reciprocal Agreement with the UK
- an EEA national working in the UK or a family member of that EEA national
- an EEA service provider or recipient
- a national of a state with an equal treatment agreement with the EU (Turkey, Algeria, Morocco, Tunisia) who is legally working in the UK

- a person who is not a Person Subject to Immigration control, though the immigration status of the child does not matter
- an A8 national who is a registered worker or who has been registered for at least 12 months or who is trading as self-employed
- a British Citizen with the right of abode in the UK

You and the child you claim for (even if you otherwise have no other restrictions on receiving Child Benefit) also need to be 'present' and 'ordinarily resident' in the UK to qualify[77] (the rules are the same as those for Tax Credits). However, some Crown Servants and armed forces personnel can receive Child Benefit when they live abroad. To be 'ordinarily resident' you should be living in the UK as your home at the time you claim.

If you are not ordinarily resident in the UK, you may still be able to receive Child Benefit if you are from a country which has a Reciprocal Agreement which allows it to be paid. In some cases, it is also possible for Child Benefit to be paid for your children living in another EEA country.[78]

Dependent Children

A dependent child is classified as someone who is

- under the age of 16, or
- under the age of 19 and studying up to A-levels/Scottish Highers, GNVQ level 3 or equivalent, and studying for more than 12 hours a week at school or college (not including homework, private study, unsupervised study or meal breaks)

A child stops being dependent on you when they

- get married
- get certain benefits in their own right (e.g. IS, income-based JSA, Incapacity Benefit);
- are an employed trainee
- are in custody

- are in care for more than 8 weeks (unless they come home for at least two nights a week)
- are 16 and over and work for 24 hours or more a week.
- are 16 and over and start a course of advanced education, for example, leading to a degree, a diploma of higher education, a higher national diploma or similar qualifications, or a teaching qualification.

Once any of these happens, you will no longer be entitled to Child Benefit.

The terminal date

If your child reaches 16 and they decide to leave education or unwaged training (which has been funded by the government), your Child Benefit will carry on until the 'terminal date'. This is the first of the following dates after they leave education or training: the last day of August, November, February or May. Some people can also receive this for up to 20 weeks after a child leaves education or training under the Child Benefit Extension period rules (see *Inclusion*'s Young Person's Handbook).

Who should claim Child Benefit?

The person responsible for the child should always make the claim. This person must normally be living with or supporting the child through maintenance.

Help with paying your rent, Council Tax and other housing costs

Housing Benefit

This is a benefit to help people on a low income to pay their rent

Eligibility

You can receive Housing Benefit if:

- you are 'liable' to pay rent or similar payments on a home that you occupy as your main residence[79]
- your income is low enough (you can be either in work or not working)
- your capital/savings are not more than £16,000, (unless you are aged 60 or over and you receive the guarantee credit of Pension Credit which has no capital limit)

As a newcomer, you may qualify if you are also:

- a Person who is Subject to Immigration Control provided you are a national of a state which has signed ECSMA and you are lawfully present in the UK[80]
- an EEA worker or a member of their family or an EEA service provider or recipient. However, if you are a national of an A8 state, you must either meet the conditions on page 124 or if you have been in the UK for less than 12 months, you should be a registered worker in order to qualify for housing benefit[81]
- habitually resident in the Common Travel Area (see page 122)
- a British Citizen[82]

Amount

The amount of Housing Benefit you receive will depend on

- the amount of rent you are liable to pay
- your income and capital
- the number of people you are able to claim for

WORKING IN THE UK: NEWCOMER'S HANDBOOK *2ND EDITION*

However, Housing Benefit is based on 'eligible rent'. This means that you will not receive Housing Benefit towards the cost of some payments which may be included in your rent. These include:[83]

- some service charges
- heating charges
- water charges
- meal charges

This applies whether or not you are in work. The eligible rent is the starting point for all calculations of Housing Benefit.

If you live in privately rented housing, (not including Housing Association tenancies), the maximum amount of Housing Benefit you can receive towards the cost of your rent will be fixed by the Rent Service. In some areas a system of Local Housing Allowance is operating which means that your maximum Housing Benefit in private deregulated rented housing is based on set maximum amounts rather than individual figures from the Rent Service. You can find out the amounts from the local authority for the area.

If you are under 25 and living alone in privately rented housing your eligible rent may be restricted to the average cost of sharing accommodation in the area

If there is a chance that any of these rules apply to you, you should get further information or advice.

Means test

You are only eligible to receive maximum Housing Benefit if:

- you receive Income Support
- you receive income-based Jobseeker's Allowance
- you receive the guarantee credit of Pension Credit
- your income after disregards is less than your applicable amount used for calculating these benefits

If your income is above the applicable amount for these benefits, then your Housing Benefit will be reduced but you may still receive some benefit. You do not have to receive one of these other benefits in order to qualify for Housing Benefit.

Non-dependants

A non-dependant is someone who normally lives with you but is not considered part of your family for benefit purposes, for example a relative, a friend or a child aged 18 or older who is no longer a dependant. Your Housing Benefit and/or Council Tax Benefit will be reduced if you have one or more non-dependants, because it is assumed that they contribute towards your rent and/or Council Tax. Someone who is staying with you temporarily is not a non-dependant.[84].

There will be no non-dependant deduction made from your benefit if you or your partner:

- are registered as blind or ceased to be registered blind within the last 28 weeks
- receive the care component of Disability Living Allowance
- receive Attendance Allowance
- receive Constant Attendance Allowance

Similarly, there will not be a deduction if the non-dependant:

- receives a training allowance as part of work-based training for young people
- is aged under 18
- is aged under 19 and you still claim benefits for them as a dependant
- is aged under 25 and receives Income Support or income-based Jobseeker's Allowance[85]

If you or your partner are aged 60 or older, no non-dependant deduction will be made for the first 26 weeks.

Working and claiming Housing Benefit

If you start working full time then you may be able to get Housing Benefit at the rate paid to you whilst you were claiming Income Support or income-based Jobseeker's Allowance for the first four weeks. This is known as Housing Benefit Run On. See page 183 for further details.

Note: Housing and Council Tax Benefits are awarded without a fixed time limit. This means that it is very important to tell the council that pays your benefit if your circumstances change (for example, if your earnings increase or someone leaves or joins your household). Otherwise you may have an overpayment to repay.

Council Tax Benefit

This is a benefit which helps people on a low income to pay their Council Tax

There are two types of Council Tax Benefit:

- 'Council Tax Benefit' which is the main source of help
- 'Second adult rebate' ('Alternative Maximum Council Tax Benefit')

You can claim either of these benefits if you are in full-time work; part-time work or you are not working. You may be able to get help under the second adult rebate scheme if you have someone aged 18 or older, (your partner does not count), living in your property who is on a low income or is claiming Income Support or income-based Jobseeker's Allowance, even if you have an income which is too high.

Eligibility

Council Tax Benefit is a means-tested benefit and the means-tested rules are the same as for Housing Benefit. If you are liable to pay Council Tax you might be eligible for Council Tax Benefit if you have a low income.

As a newcomer, the same rules for Housing Benefit apply (see page 159).

Council Tax reductions

Council Tax Benefit is based on your council tax liability after you have been awarded any reduction of your council tax (for example, because of a disability or because you live alone).

Even if you receive Council Tax Benefit, it is worth applying for a reduction because it will help if:

- you increase your income or
- at some stage you will no longer qualify for Council Tax Benefit

In Scotland it will also reduce your water charges.

Discretionary Housing Payments

If you receive some Housing or Council Tax Benefit, but not the maximum (because for example, your eligible rents been restricted, because you have non-dependants or because of your income), you can ask the local authority to pay a Discretionary Housing Payment (DHP) if you need additional financial help towards your housing costs.[86] These are discretionary payments with no right of appeal to an independent Tribunal and local authorities are limited in what they can spend. Some local authorities take a very narrow view of entitlement – which you can challenge. You will need to provide information about your circumstances in order to show that you need additional financial help with your housing costs.[87]

DHPs are best used on a short-term basis and they cannot be used either to meet the cost of service charges which are ineligible for Housing Benefit or because your need for help is because you have had a sanction applied to your other benefits.[88]

Help with mortgages and housing loans

The help available with mortgage costs is limited. You can only get help with mortgage interest if:

- you claim the guarantee credit of Pension Credit
- you claim Income Support or income-based Jobseeker's Allowance

In all cases the amount of help is limited to the interest on £100,000 of a mortgage or loan and the interest is calculated using a standard interest rate

You may have to wait until you receive help with your mortgage or loan costs if you and your partner are aged under 60.

An amount towards your mortgage or loan interest is included in the calculation of your entitlement to the above benefits.

The help which is provided is only towards your mortgage interest or the interest on a loan for some repairs and improvements to your home.[89] Help with the cost of endowment policy payments are excluded, as are capital repayments and insurance premiums.

The amount you receive towards your mortgage or loan interest can be reduced in some cases if:

- your home is felt to be too large for you and any family you claim benefit for
- you have non-dependants living with you
- your mortgage or loan was not for acquiring an interest in the property or was not for repairs and improvements which qualify for help

It is also possible to have a 'run-on' of four weeks' help with your housing costs if you start work for at least 16 hours a week for at least 5 weeks after receiving benefit for at least 26 weeks.

It is important to check that you are receiving the correct amount towards any mortgage or loan interest because mistakes are common.

Help with housing services charges for owner-occupiers

Some owner-occupiers have to pay service charges – for example, people who live in a flat or in supported housing. These service charges usually cover things like repairs, maintenance, buildings insurance and cleaning of common areas.

These service charges can be included in the calculation of your entitlement to Income Support, income-based Jobseeker's Allowance and Pension Credit.[90]

Working Tax Credit

Working Tax Credit is paid to people on a low income, who work for at least 16 hours a week. It is administered by Her Majesty's Revenue and Customs (HMRC).

Eligibility

You can receive Working Tax Credit if you satisfy all of the following:

- you are aged 16 or over
- you have a low income
- either you or your partner work for 16 hours or more per week [91]

And if you also fall into one of the following categories:

- you are a lone parent or a member of a couple with a dependent child/young person or children
- you have a physical or mental disability which puts you at a disadvantage in gaining employment and you meet either the 'qualifying benefit' test or the special 'fast-track' rules
- you are aged 50 or over and satisfy the rules for the 50+ element (this is paid for one year only)

If you do not fit into one of the above categories but you are aged 25 or over (even if you are single) and you are working for a minimum of 30 hours a week you can also receive WTC

As a newcomer, you must also be:[92]

- an EEA national working in the UK or a family member of that EEA national
- a 'service provider or recipient' from an EEA country[93] or a national of a state which has an EU agreement and you are working lawfully in the UK

- an A8 state national who is either a registered worker, or who has been registered for at least 12 months or who is self employed and trading
- a person with Indefinite Leave to Remain, Exceptional Leave to Remain, Discretionary Leave or Humanitarian Protection
- a British Citizen with the right of abode in the UK

You must also be present (gaps of up to eight weeks are ignored) and ordinarily resident in the UK. For tax credit purposes, you are 'ordinarily resident' if you normally live in the UK, and your main home is in the UK, or you have decided to settle in the UK for the time being as part of the regular order of your life.

You can't claim if you are:

- a Person Subject to Immigration Control (PSIC) unless you are a national of a state which has signed ECSMA and you are lawfully present in the UK

However, if you are one of a couple where one is disqualified for immigration reasons, you can both claim and you will be assessed as if you are a couple[94] and payment of Tax Credits will not be counted as having recourse to public funds.

Income and capital [95]

When your eligibility for Working Tax Credit is assessed, your income (and that of your partner) from the following sources is taken into account:

- gross annual earnings
- the yearly total of any pensions
- annual profits from self-employment
- social security benefits (but there are some exceptions – see below) – again assessed annually
- annual income received from investments
- annual profits from letting property

- yearly income you receive from abroad such as employment income, trading income, property income, investment income or pensions
- notional income, for example income from stock dividends, which you are treated as having received
- miscellaneous income, that is income which is taxable under income tax rules but does not fall within one of the categories listed above

If you are self-employed, your entitlement is based on your profits in the accounting period which forms the basis of assessment for the year of your tax credit claim. For example, the profit you enter on your 2005-06 self-assessment return is the profit you use for your 2006-07 claim for tax credits.

Some income and capital is ignored. For example:

- there is no capital limit and only actual income of more than £300 a year from taxable income other than earnings, profits, pensions or miscellaneous income is counted
- certain social security benefits are ignored – for example Child Benefit, Guardian's Allowance, Income Support (if you also receive Child Tax Credit), Housing Benefit, Disability Living Allowance, Attendance Allowance, £100 per week of Statutory Maternity Pay, Maternity Allowance and the lower short-term rate of Incapacity Benefit
- all maintenance
- income which is not taxable

You can also offset any pension scheme payments which you make against your income.

How Working Tax Credit is calculated [96]

Working Tax Credit is calculated by adding up any of the following elements that you qualify for:

- basic element (£1665)
- couple element (£1640)

- lone parent element (£1640)
- disability element (£2225)
- 30 hour element (£680)
- severe disability element (£945)
- 50+ element (£1140 if working 16-29 hours, £1705 if working 30+ hours)
- childcare element (towards your 'eligible' childcare costs: 80% up to £175 pw for one child and £300 per week for two or more children)

'Eligible childcare' means formal childcare – for example, a nursery, childminder or after-school club – and to qualify if you are lone parent, you must work at least 16 hours a week, and if you are one of couple either both must work at least 16 hours a week or one must be working and the other be unable to work because of illness or disability or because they are in hospital or prison.[97]

This then gives figures for a maximum possible Working Tax Credit entitlement which is added to any Child Tax Credit that you may be entitled to for your child or children. A further calculation is done which then compares your income to a 'threshold' of £5220 a year. If your income is less than this amount, you will be eligible for the maximum Working Tax Credit and Child Tax Credit. However, if your annual income is above £5220, your maximum possible tax credit award is reduced by 37 pence for every £1 of income over £5220 until you are left with just the family element of Child Tax Credit (£545). This is kept until your income is £50,000 or more when the family element is then reduced by £1 for every £15 of your income above £50,000.

Changes of circumstances

Tax Credits are calculated provisionally at the beginning of the claim with a final decision then being made at the end of each tax year, when your actual income for the year is known. You don't have to tell the Inland Revenue if your income changes in-year, but you risk being underpaid or being asked to pay back any tax credit you have been overpaid if you do not do so. For the tax year 2005-06, if your income increased by up to £2500, your tax credits will not be affected when they are finalised for the end of the tax year. For the tax year 2006-07, any increase in income of up to £25,000 will be ignored when your tax credit award is finalised at the end of this tax year.

However, there are some changes you must not delay telling the Inland Revenue about – a decrease in your childcare cost of more than £10 a week for more than four weeks and a child or adult joining or leaving your family.[98]

Claims for Tax Credits

If you are a couple, then you must both make a joint claim for tax credits[99] and both your hours of work, childcare, income and capital are considered jointly.

A claim for tax credits can be backdated for up to three months if you were entitled during that time.[100] If you believe that you were entitled, you should ask for your claim to be backdated.

How Tax Credits affect other benefits

The amount of Tax Credit you receive counts as income against Housing and Council Tax Benefits, (though arrears and back payments which you receive are ignored).[101] This means that many people receiving Tax Credits will have an income which is too high to receive these benefits unless your rent/Council Tax is higher than average. However, you will still usually be better off receiving Tax Credits even if you lose some or all of your Housing/Council Tax Benefit. If you have been receiving Housing or Council Tax Benefit and you are then awarded Tax Credits, it is important to notify the Housing and Council Tax Benefits service to avoid an overpayment which you may have to repay.

If you are claiming Tax Credits, you are not eligible for child dependant additions within other benefits unless you were receiving these before 6th April 2003.

Overpayments

Overpayments are very likely in a system which uses annual assessments and if you are overpaid Tax Credits you may be asked to repay them. This is done by automatically reducing your current Tax Credits in order to adjust the overpayments or by HMRC sending you a bill. This can cause hardship (for example, if you receive Income Support, it is not increased to make up for the reduced Tax Credit).

In law, HMRC has discretion to waive recovery of any overpayments.[102] In practice HMRC can be reluctant to do so. However, their policy is to consider waiving recovery in cases where the overpayment has been caused by official error and you could not have reasonably known this, and their policy is also to waive in cases of severe hardship.[103] Sometimes HMRC will make 'additional payments' to you to ease the effect of an overpayment, but these will eventually have to be repaid at some time.

If you ask for an overpayment to be waived and your request is refused, you can ask for your case to be considered by HMRC's Adjudicator. You can also complain to your Member of Parliament and a form of legal action known as judicial review may also be possible. You can also ask your MP to refer your complaint to the Parliamentary Ombudsman.[104]

Child Tax Credit

Child Tax Credit is paid to help with the costs of bringing up children.

Eligibility

You can claim Child Tax Credit if you are responsible for a child who normally lives with you, and you are aged 16 or over.

Your eligibility for Child Tax Credit will be assessed at the same time as for Working Tax Credit and the same rules about income and capital are used.

As a newcomer, you can claim Child Tax Credit if you are also:

- an EEA national working in the UK or a family member of that EEA national

- an EEA national who is a service provider or recipient
- a national of a state with an EU agreement who is lawfully working in the UK
- an A8 state national who is either a registered worker, or who has been registered for at least 12 months or who is self employed and trading
- a British Citizen with the right of abode in the UK

You must also be present (gaps of up to eight weeks are ignored) and 'ordinarily resident' in the UK. For Tax Credit purposes, you are 'ordinarily resident' if you normally live in the UK, your main home is in the UK, or you have decided to settle in the UK for the time being as part of the regular order of your life.

You can't claim if you are:

- a Person Subject to Immigration Control (PSIC) unless you are a national of a state which has signed ECSMA and you are lawfully present in the UK

However, if you are one of a couple where one is disqualified for immigration reasons, you can both claim and you will be assessed as if you are a couple[105] and payment of tax credits will not be counted as having recourse to public funds.

How Child Tax Credit is calculated

Child Tax Credit is calculated by adding up the following elements:

- family element (£545)
- family element – extra amount for a baby under a year (£545)
- child element (£1765)
- disabled child element (£2350)
- severely disabled child element (£945)

If you do not meet the work conditions for Working Tax Credit, your maximum Child Tax Credit award is payable in full provided your income does not exceed £14,155 If your income rises above £14,155, your maximum Child Tax Credit award is reduced by 37 pence for every £1 of income over £14,155 until you are left with just the family element of Child Tax Credit (£545). This is kept unless your income is £50,000 or more when the family element is then reduced by £1 for every £15 of income above £50,000. This means that 90% of all families with children qualify for some Child Tax Credit.

Changes of circumstances

Tax Credits are calculated provisionally at the beginning of the claim with a final decision at the end of each tax year, when your award is compared with your actual income. You are not obliged to tell the Inland Revenue if your income changes, but you risk an underpayment or overpayment at the end of the tax year if you do not do so. For the tax year 2005-06, if your income increases by up to £2500, your Tax Credits will not be affected when they are finalised for the end of the tax year. For the tax year 2006-07, any increase in your income of up to £25,000 will be ignored when your Tax Credit award is finalised at the end of the tax year.

However there are some changes you must not delay telling the Inland Revenue about – a decrease in your childcare costs of £10 a week or more for at least four weeks and a child or adult joining or leaving your family.

Claims for Tax Credits

If you are a couple, then you must both make a joint claim for Tax Credits[106] and both your hours of work, childcare, income and capital are considered jointly.

A claim for Tax Credits can be backdated for up to three months if you were entitled during that time.[107] If you believe that you were entitled, you should ask for your claim to be backdated.

How Tax Credits affect other benefits

Any Tax Credits you receive may affect you means-tested benefits. For example, they count as income for Housing and Council Tax Benefit and these benefits will reduce as a result. However, any arrears and back payments which you receive are ignored.[108] If you receive Child Tax Credit, both this and Child Benefit are ignored for Income Support and income based Jobseeker's Allowance.

From some time in 2007, it is planned that Child Tax Credit will eventually completely replace all the existing payments for children in Income Support and income-based, Jobseeker's Allowance. People who receive payments for children in these benefits will be moved onto Child Tax Credit in phases.

If you receive a non-means-tested benefit, Child Tax Credit replaces the child dependant's addition to these benefits, unless you were receiving a child dependant's addition before 6th April 2003.

Some people receiving tax credits can be passported onto other help.[109]

Passported benefit	Tax Credit rate
Free school meals	CTC only and no WTC. Annual income below £14,155
Health benefits (e.g. free prescriptions)	WTC or CTC, or WTC with a disability or severe disability element or CTC with no WTC and income at or below £15,050
Maternity & Funeral grants	CTC higher than baby or family elements or WTC with disability element
Milk and vitamins	CTC and working less than 16 hours pw. Income at or below £14,155

Overpayments

Overpayments are very likely in a system which uses annual assessments, and if you are overpaid Tax Credits you may be asked to repay them. This is done by automatically reducing your current Tax Credits in order to adjust the overpayments or by HMRC sending you a bill. This can cause hardship (for example, if you receive Income Support, it is not increased to make up for the reduced Tax Credit).

In law, HMRC has discretion to waive recovery of any overpayments.[110] In practice HMRC can be reluctant to do so. However, their policy is to consider waiving recovery in cases where the overpayment has been caused by official error and you could not have reasonably known this, and their policy is also to waive in cases of severe hardship.[111] Sometimes HMRC will make 'additional payments' to you to ease the effect of an overpayment, but these will eventually have to be repaid at some time.

If you ask for an overpayment to be waived and your request is refused, you can ask for your case to be considered by HMRC's Adjudicator. You can also complain to your Member of Parliament and a form of legal action known as judicial review may also be possible. You can also ask your MP to refer your complaint to the Parliamentary Ombudsman.[112]

Social Fund

A one-off benefit to pay for a particular need

There are two parts to the Social Fund:

1. The regulated Social Fund – this helps you with expenses which arise for a specified reason: maternity expenses, funeral expenses, cold weather payments, and winter fuel payments

2. The discretionary Social Fund – provides grants and loans to meet a variety of other needs such as for clothing or furniture

As a newcomer, if you are from abroad you also need to be:

- not a 'Person Subject to Immigration Control'. But if you are a national of a country which has signed the ECSMA and you are also lawfully present in UK you may qualify[113]
- a Person Subject to Immigration Control who is entitled to Income Support at the lower Urgent Case payment rate because they have been in the UK for less than five years and their sponsor or sponsors, if more than one, have died
- an asylum seeker entitled under transitional protection rules or otherwise self-supporting and funds from abroad have been temporarily disrupted for a limited period

- a worker or family member of one from an EEA state or from an EEA country or a service provider or recipient
- an A8 national who has been registered as a worker for at least 12 months or who has a right to reside
- a British Citizen with the right of abode in the UK[114]

The regulated Social Fund

Maternity Expenses[115]

You will be eligible to claim the Sure Start Maternity Grant, of up to £500 for each qualifying child, if you have been awarded one of the following:

- Income Support
- Income-based Jobseeker's Allowance
- Pension Credit
- Working Tax Credit with a disability or severe disability element
- Child Tax Credit which is awarded at a rate which is higher than the family element

And also one of the following:

- you or your partner are pregnant and within 11 weeks of giving birth
- you or your partner have given birth in the last three months
- you have adopted a child under the age of one
- you have been granted a parental order for a child born to a surrogate mother

You must also have advice on the health of yourself and your baby from a healthcare professional.

Funeral Payment

You will be eligible to claim a Funeral Payment if:[116]

- you or your partner accept the responsibility for the costs of a funeral which takes place in the United Kingdom. If you are a 'worker' from an EEA country or a family member of a worker, you may receive help

with the cost of a funeral in an EEA country. You must have the 'right to reside' in the UK
- the deceased was ordinarily a resident in the United Kingdom at the time of death
- you or your partner have been awarded Income Support, income-based Jobseeker's Allowance, Pension Credit, Working Tax Credit with a disability or a severe disability element, Child Tax Credit which is paid above the family element, Housing Benefit or Council Tax Benefit
- you claim within three months of the funeral

Cold Weather Payment

You are eligible for the Cold Weather Payment if you or your partner:[117]

- receive Income Support or income-based Jobseeker's Allowance or Pension Credit

and

- are responsible for a child aged under 5 or
- are aged 60 or over, or
- receive a disability premium, including the disabled child premium

These payments are made automatically if the area where you live has had a seven day period of weather with an average temperature of 0°C or less.

Winter Fuel Payment[118]

The Winter Fuel Payment is paid automatically to people aged 60 or over in the week of 18th September 2006. You should be ordinarily resident in Great Britain, but if you live in another EEA country or Switzerland, you may still qualify.

Some people may need to make a claim as their records may not be held by the DWP, so they won't receive a payment automatically (these are usually made by Christmas). If this applies to you, you should make a claim by 31st March by phoning 08459 151515.

The discretionary Social Fund

Community Care Grant

Community Care Grants are for those on Income Support or income-based JSA or Pension Credit to meet costs, which will:[119]

- help them live in the community after being in institutional care
- help prevent them going into institutional care
- ease exceptional pressure on them and their family
- help them set up home as part of a programme of resettlement after an unsettled way of life
- to allow someone to care for a prisoner on temporary release
- to help with certain travel expenses within the UK

Budgeting Loan[120]

Budgeting Loans are interest-free loans to help people who have been on Income Support or income-based Jobseeker's Allowance for 26 weeks or more to buy a specific item. The maximum loan that can be awarded is £2,000. In all cases, the loan should normally be repaid within 78 weeks. However, your local Jobcentre Plus will get it repaid by having your weekly benefit reduced. Because these loans reduce your income, you should always apply for a Community Care Grant instead if you feel you qualify.

Crisis Loan[121]

The Crisis Loan is an interest-free loan for people who are unable to meet a short-term need. You do not have to be receiving any benefits.

To be eligible for a Crisis Loan

- you must be aged 16 or over
- the need you apply for must not be excluded from the Crisis Loan scheme
- the amount awarded must not be more than you can afford to repay
- you must need the loan because of an emergency

- you must not have any other source of income or savings to cover the costs for which you are claiming the Crisis Loan. This includes your wages and the possibility of borrowing from your employer, but does not include Housing Benefit, other Social Fund payments, business assets, or personal possessions

Because these loans reduce your benefits, you should always apply for a Community Care Grant instead if you feel you qualify.

You can apply to have Social Fund loan repayments reduced and the Secretary of State has discretion not to recover.[122] Seek advice if refused.

Benefit decisions and appeals

Decision makers

The Secretary of State for Work and Pensions is legally responsible for assessing each individual claim for benefit. Obviously, she or he cannot do this alone, so the Secretary of State's powers are delegated to decision makers in DWP offices.[123]

Decision makers decide entitlement about claims by reference to the law – Acts of Parliament, Regulations and caselaw. In practice, they refer to guidance (such as the Decision Maker's Guide) which contains guidance on how to apply the law. The interpretation of the law in guidance is often disputable.

Similar arrangements exist for decisions about entitlement to Tax Credits and for these to be made by decision makers acting on behalf of the Board of Commissioners of HM Revenue and Customs.[124]

You are entitled to have a written explanation of the decision provided that you ask for it within one month of being sent the decision, and the decision maker must then send you the explanation within 14 days.[125] You then have a further month after receiving the explanation, to take matters further.

Appeals

You are able to appeal against most of the decisions made by the Decision Maker, such as

- whether you are entitled to benefit
- how your benefit has been worked out
- whether your claim for Jobseeker's Allowance should be suspended or sanctioned and for how long

However, you cannot appeal against decisions such as:

- whether or not the Government have set the right amounts of benefit to live on
- on what day of the week and how a benefit should be paid

An appeal must be in writing within one month of the date on which the decision was made, not the date on which you received the decision.[126] The appeal will then be forwarded to the appeal tribunal. You should normally use form GL24 from the DWP to make your appeal. If you appeal after the one-month date, this time limit may be extended and you may still be able to get your case heard provided that you appeal within 13 months of the decision date, but you will need to show that you have special reasons for appealing late and that it is also in the interests of justice for your case to be heard or that you have a reasonable chance of a successful appeal.[127] It is therefore much better to appeal within a month.

You can also appeal about Tax Credits and Housing and Council Tax Benefits as well as ask for a revision or supersession (see below).

Appeal tribunal

The Appeal tribunal is independent of the Department for Work and Pensions and is able to change the Department's decisions. It is normally made up of one legally qualified member (unless the appeal is about a medically related matter, such as capability for work).

You do not have to attend the tribunal's hearing of your case if you would rather the decision was just made using documents. However, it always is best to be there, as you can then clarify any facts that may not be clear from the documentation and you will have a much better chance of winning your appeal. And remember that you can take along someone to represent or support you if you are not confident to go on your own.[128] Ideally, an adviser who understands social security law should represent you.

If there is more than one member of the tribunal, they will try to reach a unanimous decision. If they cannot, the Chairman (who may be a woman) has the power to make the final decision. Any decision will usually be made on the day of the hearing. You will be told the decision verbally and then sent a short written summary later. You can also ask for a more detailed written decision

Travel costs to and from the appeal hearing will be paid. You may also be able to claim for loss of earnings or childminding costs. You must provide receipts for all expenses that you intend to claim.

Revisions [129]

If you disagree with a decision you can ask for it to be revised within one month of being sent the decision (or within 14 days of being sent a written explanation which you asked for). This is known as the dispute period.

If you would like to have the decision revised after the dispute period, you will normally have to do so within 13 months and if you apply outside the dispute period, you should also show that your application has merit, that it is reasonable to grant your request and that there are special circumstances which prevented you from applying in time.

However, you can ask for a decision to be revised at any time if you feel that it was wrong because the Decision Maker did not use all the evidence that they had or that they applied the law wrongly without having to show additional reasons why the decision should be considered.

The Secretary of State can also revise the decision at any time without a request from you. This may happen if, for example, a decision arose from an official error, if it was based on a mistake about any material fact, or if you were awarded a benefit which meant you became entitled to another benefit or a higher rate of that benefit.[130]

If you appeal, the Decision Maker should look at your case again and consider revising it.[131]

Appeals against revisions

If a decision is not revised in your favour then, in most cases, you can appeal to a tribunal.

Supersessions[132]

You can also ask for a decision to be changed under the 'supersession' rules. These enable a Decision Maker to change a decision if there has been a change of circumstances or if it is thought that there will be a change of circumstances about a benefit you currently receive (this could include a change in your health or disability).

A decision can also be superseded if it was incorrect in law or if evidence was overlooked. This ground is most commonly used by the DWP or HMRC to correct errors they have made or if they feel that you have been receiving benefit you are not entitled to, or if there is new evidence which means you are no longer entitled to benefit.

Normally a supersession only takes place from the date you request it, so if you feel that a decision is wrong, you should either appeal or ask for revision. You can appeal if your benefit is stopped as a result of the DWP using a supersession.

Appeals to Social Security Commissioners

Social Security Commissioners are lawyers who are independent of the Department for Work and Pensions.

If you disagree with an appeal tribunal's decision on a point of law, you may be able to appeal to the Social Security Commissioner. It is very important to get independent advice before doing this.

To follow this course of action, you must apply to the tribunal chairperson in writing. See www.appeals-service.gov.uk for further details and advice.

Complaints

If you do not agree with the way in which a local council made a decision, you can also complain to the Council's Monitoring Officer and to the Local Government Ombudsman.[133] If you wish to complain about something done by the DWP or HMRC, you can write to your MP and you can also make a formal complaint via the DWP's and HMRC's Customer Services staff. If your complaint is not upheld, you can then ask your MP to refer your case to the Parliamentary Ombudsman.[134]

Benefits and Tax Credits if you are in work

Government policy is to make people in work better off compared to people who are out of work. Ways to tackle this include the National Minimum Wage (see page 388) and Tax Credits. There are also universal benefits available to people in and out of work and as well as tax credits, there are a number of other little known benefits to help with the transition into work.

Benefit run ons

Benefit Run Ons are periods where your benefit continues for a short period if you have been receiving benefits and have started paid work for at least 16 hours a week. This helps to ease the transition from welfare to work.

There are three Benefit Run Ons:

- Mortgage Interest Run On
- Extended Payment of Housing Benefit (Housing Benefit Run On)
- Extended Payment of Council Tax Benefit (Council Tax Benefit Run On)

Eligibility

You may receive a Benefit Run On if you satisfy all of the following:

- you have been claiming Income Support or income-based Jobseeker's Allowance, Incapacity Benefit or Severe Disablement Allowance for 26 weeks or more. This does not include any period of Lone Parent Run On (which no longer exists) or Mortgage Interest Run On that you may have received
- you notify your local Jobcentre Plus office that you are working full-time (16 hours or more a week), within 4 weeks of starting or of your hours of work increasing
- you have a job which is expected to last for 5 or more weeks

As a newcomer you must meet the extra requirements placed on those benefits.

Mortgage Interest Run On [135]

This allows you to continue receiving Income Support or income-based Jobseeker's Allowance to cover some of your mortgage or housing loan interest for up to four weeks after you or your partner start full-time work if you have been receiving help from Income Support or income-based Jobseeker's Allowance towards your mortgage, loan or other housing costs.

Extended Payment of Housing Benefit [136]

This allows you to continue receiving Housing Benefit for up to four weeks after you or your partner have started full-time work, at the same rate as when you were on Income Support, income-based Jobseeker's Allowance or Incapacity Benefit or Severe Disablement Allowance.

After the extended period, you may be able to continue to receive some Housing Benefit if you are in full-time work. This will depend on:

- the level of rent you are paying
- your income
- your savings and capital
- your personal or family circumstances

Extended Payment of Council Tax Benefit

The rules for Extended Payment of Council Tax Benefit are the same as for Extended Payment of Housing Benefit.

Job Grant [137]

Job Grant is a tax-free payment for people entering full-time work (16 hours a week or more). It is £100 if you don't have children and £250 if you do have children.

Eligibility

You may receive a Job Grant if

- you are aged 25 or over
- you have received Income Support, Jobseeker's Allowance, Incapacity Benefit, or Severe Disablement Allowance, or a combination of these for at least 26 weeks (if you have been on a New Deal or Employment Zone scheme, it counts towards the 26 weeks providing you were in receipt of Jobseeker's Allowance at the time)
- your full-time work is expected to last 5 weeks or more

If you are working part-time and the hours you are working increase to 16 or more, then you may be able to be paid Job Grant. Similarly, if your full-time work is self-employed, then you may be able to qualify.

This may be paid if you or your partner move into full time work of 16 hours or more a week (24 hours or more a week for your partner).

Newcomers must meet the original requirements for the benefits which make you eligible for the Job Grant.

Adviser Discretion Fund

The Adviser Discretion Fund (ADF) is held by personal advisers at Jobcentre Plus. From this fund, they can buy goods and services (up to a maximum of £100) to help those on New Deal and those who have been receiving certain benefits. The Adviser Discretion Fund is designed to help customers overcome barriers that they may face in looking for or getting work. This may include buying clothes, materials, tools etc. that will help you find work.

The Adviser Discretion Fund is not an entitlement and is at the discretion of your adviser. As a result there is no right of appeal to an independent Tribunal about the Adviser Discretion Fund. However, in most circumstances, advisers will listen to your needs and if you state that you are unable to afford to buy something that you need to look for or start work your adviser may be able to use the Adviser Discretion Fund to help.

In geographic areas where there are Employment Zones or where private-sector New Deal provision exists, there is likely to be similar provision.

Local pilot areas

As part of its welfare to work programme, the government has many local pilot schemes.

These include Pathways to Work for people making new claims for Incapacity Benefit, (except in the West Country where existing claimants are included), which involves a series of work-focused interviews in the early days of the claim (unless you are exempted from the Personal Capability Assessment) and a £40 a week return to work payment if you take a job which pays less than £15,000 a year for up to 52 weeks. If you have been claiming benefit for at least 13 weeks, you may also be paid a £20 week Job Preparation Premium if you agree and adhere to an Action Plan to help you get back to work.

In some areas there are also Pathways to Work for Lone Parents pilot schemes which provide a £20 a week job search premium on top of benefits for lone parents who have been on benefits for at least 52 weeks, followed by a £40 a week payment for up to twelve months if a job is taken.

All the Pathways additional payments are ignored as income for means tested benefits.

Endnotes

1. S 1(1A) & (1B) Social Security Administration Act 1992, & reg 2A Income Support (General) Regulations 1987
2. Reg 2(1) Social Security (Payments on Account, Overpayments and Recovery) Regulations 1988
3. Internal DWP guidance: 'People Requiring Interpreters and Translation Services' available to staff on the DWP intranet under 'Interpreters'
4. Page 10 of DWP Leaflet: Jobcentre Plus. Our service standards. 2006
5. S 179 Social Security Administration Act 1992
6. Levin and Kempf [1986] ECR 1741
7. R v IAT ex parte Antonissen [1991] ECR 1-745
8. EC Regulation 859/2003
9. EC Directive 73/148
10. EC Regulation 1251/70
11. EC Directive 2004/38
12. Article 6: Workers, Article 7: others. EC Directive 2004/38
13. Para 44 DWP Housing Benefit and Council Tax Benefit Circular HB/CTB A9/2006 & The Social Security (Persons from Abroad) Amendment Regulations 2006
14. Article 16
15. British Nationality Act 1981
16. R v Barnet LBC ex p Shah [1983] 1AER 226
17. Nessa v Chief Adjudication Officer [1999] 4 AER 677 & 1WLR 1937
18. Swaddling v. Adjudication Officer, (Case C-90/97) [1999] All ER (EC) 217 & 2 FLR 185
19. Nessa v Chief Adjudication Officer
20. Angela Eagle junior DWP Minister in a Written Answer. Hansard 14th June 1999
21. Secretary of State for Work and Pensions v Bhakta [2006] EWCA Civ 65, February 15 2006
22. Scrivner v Centre d'Aide Sociale de Chastre (C122/84) ECR 1027 ECJ
23. Reg 21 (3) (a) –(d) Income Support (General) Regulations 1987 as amended
24. Swaddling v. Adjudication Officer, (Case C-90/97) [1999] All ER (EC) 217 & 2 FLR 185
25. Nessa v Chief Adjudication Officer [1999] 1WLR 1937)

[26] The Accession (Immigration and Worker Registration) Regulations 2004
[27] Swaddling v. Adjudication Officer,(Case C-90/97) [1999] All ER (EC) 217)
[28] For example, for Income Support see schedule 7 para 16A Income Support (General) regulations 1987
[29] Regulation 3(2) Tax Credits (Immigration) Regulations 2003
[30] Adapted from Migration and Social Security (CPAG, 2002) and reprinted with the kind permission of Child Poverty Action Group
[31] S 1(2) Jobseekers Act 1995
[32] S 115 Immigration and Asylum Act 1999 & Immigration Rules para 6HC 395 as amended
[33] S 115 Immigration and Asylum Act 1999 & Immigration Rules para 6HC 395 as amended
[34] Regs 5, 7 & 8 Jobseeker's Allowance Regulations 1996
[35] Reg 13(2) Jobseeker's Allowance Regulations 1996
[36] Reg 13(3) Jobseeker's Allowance Regulations 1996
[37] Regs 8 & 9 Jobseeker's Allowance Regulations 1996
[38] Reg 55(1) Jobseeker's Allowance Regulations 1996
[39] Sections 19(5)(a) & 20A(2) (a) & (d) – (g) Jobseeker's Act 1995
[40] S 3A Jobseekers Act 1995 & regs 3A - G Jobseekers Allowance Regulations 1995
[41] S 115 (1) & (3) Immigration and Asylum Act 1999, for exceptions see schedule to the Social Security (Immigration and Asylum) Consequential Amendments Regulations 2000
[42] Schedule to the Social Security (Immigration and Asylum) Consequential Amendments Regulations 2000
[43] Schedule 1B Income Support (General) Regulations 1987
[44] Schedule 9 Income Support (General) Regulations 1987
[45] Regulation 50 Income Support (General) Regulations 1987
[46] Regulation 51 Income Support (General) Regulations 1987
[47] S 115 (1) & (3) Immigration and Asylum Act 1999, for exceptions see schedule to the Social Security (Immigration and Asylum) Consequential Amendments Regulations 2000
[48] S 30 Social Security Contributions and Benefits Act 1992
[49] S 115 (1) & (3) Immigration and Asylum Act 1999, for exceptions see schedule to the Social Security (Immigration and Asylum) Consequential Amendments Regulations 2000

50 Schedule to the Social Security (Immigration and Asylum) Consequential Amendments Regulations 2000
51 S 171(B)(3) & (4) Social Security Contributions and Benefits Act 1992
52 Social Security (Incapacity for Work) (General) Regulations 1995
53 Reg 27 Social Security (Incapacity for Work) (General) Regulations 1995
54 S 151(2) Social Security Contributions and Benefits Act 1992
55 S 154 Social Security Contributions and Benefits Act 1992
56 S 14(3) Social Security Administration Act 1992
57 S 66 Social Security Contributions and Benefits Act 1992
58 S115 (1) & (3) Immigration and Asylum Act 1999, for exceptions see schedule to the Social Security (Immigration and Asylum) Consequential Amendments Regulations 2000
59 Schedule to the Social Security (Immigration and Asylum) Consequential Amendments Regulations 2000
60 S 64 (2) & (3) Social Security Contributions and Benefits Act 1992
61 S 72(2) Social Security Contributions and Benefits Act 1992
62 S 71(1) (a) Social Security Contributions and Benefits Act 1992
63 S 71 (1) (b) Social Security Contributions and Benefits Act 1992
64 S 71 (1) (b) Social Security Contributions and Benefits Act 1992
65 S 73 (1) (d) Social Security Contributions and Benefits Act 1992
66 S 73 (1) Social Security Contributions and Benefits Act 1992
67 These benefits are not included in those which are restricted under s115 (1) & (3) Immigration and Asylum Act 1999 or the schedule to the Social Security (Immigration and Asylum) Consequential Amendments Regulations 2000
68 S 94 Social Security Contributions and Benefits Act 1992
69 R v Industrial Injuries Commissioner ex p AEU (No2) 2QB 31
70 Schedule 2 to the Social Security (General Benefit) Regulations 1982 (as amended)
71 S 103 Social Security Contributions and Benefits Act 1992
72 Reg 6 Social Security (Overlapping Benefits) Regulations 1979
73 Para 13 (2) (a) (iii) of schedule 2 to Income Support (General) Regulations 1987 & para 1(a) (iii) schedule 1 to State Pension Credit Regulations 2002
74 S 115 (1) & (3) Immigration and Asylum Act 1999, for exceptions see schedule to the Social Security (Immigration and Asylum) Consequential Amendments Regulations 2000

75. Schedule to the Social Security (Immigration and Asylum) Consequential Amendments Regulations 2000
76. S 115 (1) & (3) Immigration and Asylum Act 1999, for exceptions see schedule to the Social Security (Immigration and Asylum) Consequential Amendments Regulations 2000
77. S 146(2) Social Security Contributions and Benefits Act 1992 & reg 21 Child Benefit (General) Regulations 2003
78. Articles 72 – 76 European Community Regulation 1408/71
79. Regs 7 & 8 Housing Benefit Regulations 2006
80. S115 (1) & (3) Immigration and Asylum Act 1999, for exceptions see schedule to the Social Security (Immigration and Asylum) Consequential Amendments Regulations 2000
81. Para 61 HB/CTB Circular A9/2006
82. Schedule to the Social Security (Immigration and Asylum) Consequential Amendments Regulations 2000
83. Schedule 1 to Housing Benefit Regulations 2006
84. Reg 3 Housing Benefit Regulations 2006
85. Reg 74 Housing Benefit Regulations 2006
86. Reg 2 The Discretionary Financial Assistance Regulations 2001
87. Reg 7 The Discretionary Financial Assistance Regulations 2001
88. Reg 3 The Discretionary Financial Assistance Regulations 2001
89. Paras 15 & 16 of schedule 3 to Income Support (General) Regulations 1987 and parallel regulations for income based Jobseeker's Allowance and Pension Credit
90. Paragraph 17 of schedule 3 to Income Support (General) Regulations 1987 and parallel regulations for income based Jobseeker's Allowance and Pension Credit
91. Reg 4 Working Tax Credit (Entitlement and Maximum Rate) Regulations 2002
92. Reg 3(1) Tax Credits (Immigration) Regulations 2003
93. A 'service provider or recipient' includes a self employed person in the UK. It also includes anyone who receives or provides services in the UK within the meaning of EC law
94. Reg 3(2) Tax Credits (Immigration) Regulations 2003
95. Tax Credits (Definition and Calculation of Income) Regulations 2002
96. Reg 20 Working Tax Credit (Entitlement and Maximum Rate) Regulations 2002
97. Regs 3, 13, 14 & 20 Working Tax Credit (Entitlement and Maximum Rate) Regulations 2002

[98] Sections 6(3) & 32(3) Tax Credits Act 2002

[99] S3 (3)(a) & (8) Tax Credits Act 2002

[100] Reg 7 Tax Credits (Claims and Notifications) Regulations 2002

[101] Regs 45, 46 & para 9 of schedule 6 to Housing Benefit Regulations 2006. Reg 36 & para 9 to schedule 5 Council Tax Benefit Regulations 2006

[102] S28 (1)Tax Credits Act 2002

[103] HMRC Code of Practice No 26

[104] www.ombudsman.gov.uk

[105] Reg 3(2) Tax Credits (Immigration) Regulations 2003

[106] S3 (3)(a) & (8) Tax Credits Act 2002

[107] Reg 7 Tax Credits (Claims and Notifications) Regulations 2002

[108] Regs 45, 46 & para 9 of schedule 6 to Housing Benefit Regulations 2006. Reg 36 & para 9 to schedule 6 Council Tax Benefit Regulations 2006

[109] See HM Revenue and Customs leaflet WTC 6

[110] S28 (1)Tax Credits Act 2002

[111] HMRC Code of Practice No 26

[112] www.ombudsman.gov.uk.

[113] S115 (1) & (3) Immigration and Asylum Act 1999, for exceptions see schedule to the Social Security (Immigration and Asylum) Consequential Amendments Regulations 2000

[114] Schedule to the Social Security (Immigration and Asylum) Consequential Amendments Regulations 2000

[115] Reg 5 Social Fund Maternity and Funeral Expenses (General) Regulations 1987

[116] Reg 7 Social Fund Maternity and Funeral Expenses (General) Regulations 1987

[117] Reg 1A Social Fund Cold Weather Payments (General) Regulations 1988

[118] The Social Fund Winter Fuel Payments Regulations 2000

[119] Direction 4 Social Fund Directions

[120] Social Fund Directions

[121] Direction 3 Social Fund Directions

[122] See use of the words 'repayable' and 'recoverable' in S 139(4) Social Security Contributions and Benefits Act 1992, S 78(1) Social Security Administration Act 1992, & Direction 5 Social Fund Directions

[123] Ss 2(1) & 8 Social Security Act 1998

[124] Ss 2, 3 & 14 Tax Credits Act 2002. Ss 2 & 13 Commissioners for Revenue and Customs Act 2005

[125] Reg 28 Social Security and Child Support (Decisions and Appeals) Regulations 1999

[126] Reg 31 Social Security and Child Support (Decisions and Appeals) Regulations 1999

[127] Reg 32 Social Security and Child Support (Decisions and Appeals) Regulations 1999

[128] Reg 49(8) Social Security and Child Support (Decisions and Appeals) Regulations 1999

[129] Reg 3 Social Security and Child Support (Decisions and Appeals) Regulations 1999

[130] Reg 3 (5) (a) Social Security and Child Support (Decisions and Appeals) Regulations 1999

[131] Reg 3(4A) Social Security and Child Support (Decisions and Appeals) Regulations 1999

[132] Reg 6 Social Security and Child Support (Decisions and Appeals) Regulations 1999

[133] www.lgo.org.uk

[134] www.ombudsman.org.uk

[135] Regs 6 (5) & (8) Income Support (General) Regulations 1987

[136] Reg 71 Housing Benefit Regulations 2006

[137] S2 (2) Employment and Training Act 1973

5 Training and education to help find work

Sean Moley, Centre for Economic & Social Inclusion

Introduction

There is a wide range of help and training available for people newly arrived in the UK. This section covers some of the main types, but the area is huge and this section is far from complete in its scope. For more detailed advice on training you can talk to Connexions, Jobcentre Plus or your local Further Education College or Adult Community Learning service.

For those newly arrived in the UK, the rules around eligibility for training are complex and there are one or two 'grey' areas. Overall though, there is more flexibility in the eligibility rules for training than there is for the employment programmes (see section on employment programmes, page 220). This is especially the case if you are classed as a disadvantaged worker,[1] in which case the course provider will have greater discretion in offering you a place.

Who is a 'disadvantaged worker'?

Disadvantaged workers include migrant workers and minority ethnic workers who require development of their linguistic, vocational training or work experience profile to enhance their prospects of gaining access to stable employment.

The training discussed in this chapter is funded by two distinct organisations:

- Jobcentre Plus – the body responsible for helping people find work
- The Learning and Skills Council (LSC) – the body responsible for training people

Jobcentre Plus offers training to people who are on benefits and are having difficulty finding work. The Learning and Skills Council fund most other forms of training, including training at Further Education Colleges, as well as training in work and in the community. In Scotland some of the functions of the LSC are performed by the Scottish Funding Council, Careers Scotland and by the Scottish Executive committees on Lifelong Learning and Enterprise.[2]

What types of training are covered in this section?

The types of training covered in the sections to follow are:

- Work Based Learning for Adults (WBLA) and Training for Work (TfW)
- Programme Centres
- Learndirect
- Entry to Employment (e2e)
- Apprenticeships
- The Employer Training Pilots (ETPs) and the National Employer Training Programme (NETP)

Who is eligible for this training?

This training provision described in the following chapters is generally available to the following people:

- British and EU citizens
- EEA migrant workers
- refugees, their spouses and children
- people granted Humanitarian Protection (HP) or Discretionary Leave (DL), or Exceptional Leave to Enter or Remain (ELE/R)

It may also be available to asylum seekers (see below) and to non-EEA workers depending on their status.

Asylum seekers

Asylum seekers are eligible for training under certain conditions. As an asylum seeker, when you arrive in the UK you are not allowed to work nor to avail yourself of training delivered in the workplace (often called work-based learning). After 12 months, if you have not received an initial decision from the Home Office, you may be granted permission to work. This will be shown on your Application Registration Card (ARC). See page 72 for information on whether you have the right to work.

From your first day, you can receive training. This might include English for Speakers of Other Languages (ESOL) or Life Skills (courses designed to familiarise you with life in the UK). There are also many opportunities, mainly through Further Education colleges, for asylum seekers receiving NASS support to do a range of vocational courses (beyond basic ESOL and IT) free of charge. For more information on what courses asylum seekers can do, see page 73.

Training providers, colleges, universities and other institutions tend to have slightly different rules on their training for asylum seekers. In general you will find you can attend European Social Fund (ESF) funded as well as UK Government funded courses provided they are non-vocational. If you are aged 16 to 18 you may be eligible for the Learner Support Fund. The best approach is to contact the college or learning institution directly as they are in the best position to advise you.

Note: You may need permission to work to access some types of training due to funding restrictions. It is always best to speak with the training provider directly to ask about eligibility.

If you want to study in Higher Education, then most universities will charge international fees. However, universities are always keen to meet students with the potential to succeed academically, and to demonstrate their commitment to widening participation. It is therefore a good idea to approach them directly to see if there can be any flexibility with fees and possible funding. Each school or department will have an admissions officer, and it is worth approaching them directly. If you gain recognised refugee status you will be treated as a home student and pay the same rate as a British student.

Work Based Learning for Adults (WBLA) and Training for Work (TfW)

If you are aged 25 and over, and are unemployed and on benefits you may be able to get training to improve your prospects of finding a job. In England and Wales, this form of training is called Work Based Learning for Adults (WBLA). In Scotland it is called Training for Work (TfW).

In England Jobcentre Plus is responsible for WBLA, while in Wales, the National Assembly for Wales is responsible. The Enterprise Networks administers TfW in Scotland, through Local Enterprise Companies.

The aim of WBLA and TfW is to:

- give you the skills to improve your employability
- help you build your confidence and develop those skills you lack
- meet the skill needs of local employers

Eligibility

WBLA and TfW are adult training programmes and are usually only available if you are aged 25 or over, have been registered as unemployed for six months or more, and are in receipt of a qualifying benefit, such as Jobseeker's Allowance, NI credits, Incapacity Benefit, Severe Disablement Allowance, Income Support or Maternity Benefit (See pages 130-143 and 466 for details of whether you are eligible for these benefits).

However, you may be eligible for early entry to WBLA or TfW regardless of your length of unemployment if you are a refugee claiming JSA, have a disability, or need help with your spoken English. In addition, a broad range of other eligibility criteria, combined with the fact that you can refer yourself to WBLA, means that as a newcomer you can join even if you have restrictions on your benefit entitlement or you are classed as a 'Person Subject to Immigration Control' (PSIC) (and so normally excluded from receiving benefits).

WBLA provision

WBLA provision is delivered through the following four programmes:

- Basic Employability Training
- Short Job Focused Training
- Longer Occupational Training
- Self-Employment Provision

Basic Employability Training (BET)

BET is particularly focused on helping those who need assistance in overcoming severe basic skills needs and English for Speakers of Other Languages (ESOL) difficulties. The Basic Skills Standards have three Levels: Entry Level, Level 1 and Level 2. BET helps you to improve your basic skills of literacy and numeracy by helping you to reach at least Basic Skills Standard at Level 1, or as a minimum, Entry Level. Prior to BET, you will need to attend an Initial Assessment to identify your level of basic skills need.

Short Job Focused Training (SJFT)

The overall aim is to help you gain soft and occupational skills to enable you to get a job. SJFT also includes Work Placements. SJFT lasts for a maximum of six weeks, and you must complete a minimum of 16 hours of activity each week, over five days. SJFT provision is practical and hands-on, designed to impart straightforward, well-defined skills whilst meeting the needs of the labour market and being tailored to your individual needs.

Longer Occupational Training (LOT)

The overall aim of LOT provision is to help you to acquire new skills or update existing ones through tailored work-focused training to help you to find work. LOT lasts for a minimum of seven weeks and up to a maximum of 52 weeks. You must complete a minimum of 16 hours of activity each week, over five days. LOT seeks to bring together employers and providers to provide work-focused training modules designed to deliver specific soft and occupational skills to prepare you for work. LOT helps you reach local recruitment standards, based on agreements brokered with employers with skill shortages or recruitment shortfalls, or to meet the needs of new employers moving into the district.

Self-Employment Provision (SEP)

This offers you the opportunity to move into unsupported self-employment. SEP also offers support to those participants who decide, during their time on the provision, that they would rather seek employment with an employer than be self-employed.

SEP provides you with access to good quality advice and support and, also, where appropriate, the opportunity to undertake a period of test trading. This allows you to experience the realities of self-employment while continuing to receive help and support from the training provider. SEP has three distinct stages: Stage 1 (advice and information, one day), Stage 2 (development of a business plan, part time over four weeks) and Stage 3 (test trading, maximum period of 26 weeks).

TfW provision (Scotland only)

This is administered by Local Enterprise Companies (LECs) and different programs are available in different areas. The basic structures of TfW are the same as WBLA. For precise information you should contact your LEC directly, or your local Jobcentre Plus should be able to advise you.

You can also obtain information at the Scottish Enterprise website at: http://www.scottish-enterprise.com/sedotcom_home/stp/careersadvice/develop-your-skills-work-based-training-2/trainingforwork.htm

A list of training opportunities is also available at www.scottishtrainingdirectories.co.uk

Getting onto WBLA or TfW

There are several ways of getting onto WBLA or TfW: for example you could:

- be referred by your personal adviser at Jobcentre Plus
- be recruited directly by a local training provider
- apply by yourself because you heard about a particular programme that you believe would meet your needs.

You are also likely to be referred by your Jobcentre Plus Adviser at the six-month restart interview.

Recruited by a training provider

Local training providers can recruit people onto their programmes. For example, you may see adverts in your local paper about programmes and courses designed to help you to improve your employability.

Note: The decision on whether you can take part in WBLA provision does, however, rest with your Jobcentre Plus Adviser. In Scotland, your LEC will make this decision about your participation in TfW.

Refer yourself

You could ask to be put on a WBLA or TfW programme. For example:

- you may know what programme you want to do in order to make yourself more employable
- you may have heard about a relevant programme from a friend or relative
- you may take the initiative to ask about local programmes which you think will help you. See the 'Further Information' section for other ways of finding about activities in your local area (pages 556)

For more information on WBLA and TfW see Chapter 7 of the JCP Provider Guidance http://www.jobcentreplus.gov.uk/jcp/static/Dev_008531.pdf

For more information about Scotland refer to the Scottish Enterprise website at http://www.scottish-enterprise.com

Programme Centres

Programme Centres are run by the public, private and voluntary sectors. They are designed to give jobseekers help and advice on job-search techniques, possible jobs, training, increasing motivation and building confidence in returning to work. Some Programme Centres may also run courses, which are designed to meet the needs of the local labour market. It is the Jobcentre Plus Personal Adviser's responsibility to refer you to whichever Programme Centre module they think will be useful for you.

Modules

The help you receive at the Programme Centre will consist of short courses, one-to-one support and advice. It will be tailored to your needs, teaching you what you need to know to be able to find work.

The Programme Centre will also have a range of free facilities, including photocopying, phones, desks and postage, and a place where you can apply for jobs.

Eligibility

EEA Nationals are able to go to Programme Centres, provided they meet the usual eligibility conditions that apply to UK citizens.

Refugees with Indefinite, Limited or Exceptional Leave to stay in the UK may access Programme Centres provided they satisfy the usual eligibility conditions that apply to citizens of the UK. Asylum seekers who have been given permission by the Home Office to work and train in this country are also eligible, provided they satisfy the usual eligibility conditions that apply to citizens in the UK.

Note: Non-EEA Overseas Nationals who are subject to employment restrictions and/or a time limit on their stay in the UK, are not normally eligible to join Programme Centres.

The eligibility conditions that apply to citizens in the UK are:

- you must be aged 25 or over
- you must have been unemployed for six months or more
- you must be receiving Jobseeker's Allowance, Income Support, or National Insurance Credits

However, there are a number of additional ways in which you may become eligible to access Programme Centres:

- if you are aged 18 to 24 and on the New Deal for Young People you may attend a Programme Centre after your 13 week interview, at the Jobcentre Plus district manager's discretion
- if you are aged 18 to 24 and on the New Deal for Lone Parents, New Deal for Partners, or New Deal for Disabled People
- if you have been away from the labour market for two years because of domestic responsibilities but have not received benefits
- if you are unemployed and have literacy or numeracy difficulties, or your first language is not English
- if you are a victim of a large-scale redundancy

- if you are judged to be at a particular disadvantage in the labour market (this final proviso already covers most asylum seekers and allows them access to Programme Centres)

Note: People participating in an Employment Zone are not eligible to attend a Programme Centre.

Is attendance compulsory?

You cannot be made to attend a Programme Centre, unless you have been referred with a 'Jobseeker's Direction'. If you meet the rules about eligibility, you may be referred to a Programme Centre or you may volunteer to attend.

Referral

Programme Centre providers can recruit you directly, you can be referred by Jobcentre Plus staff after an advisory interview, or you can volunteer to attend.

Your personal adviser should tell you how attending a Programme Centre would help you to find a job. The amount of time for which you attend the Programme Centre will vary according to your needs.

Not completing the programme

If you do not start your programme, your Jobcentre Plus personal adviser will need to know why. You will then be interviewed about other options, such as Work Based Learning for Adults. Your Jobcentre Plus Personal Adviser may refer you again to the Programme Centre to complete a specific course.

If you have been asked to leave the Programme Centre because of disruptive behaviour or because you have been absent too often, you may or may not be re-referred to the same Programme Centre, depending on your situation.

Note: If you are in an 'Employment Zone Programme Centre', your Jobseeker's allowance may be sanctioned and your benefit stopped.

Completing the programme

When you have completed your programme, you should leave the Programme Centre with an Action Plan. Your Programme Centre provider will agree this with Jobcentre Plus, and will send them a copy after which you will have a personal adviser follow-up interview at a Jobcentre Plus office.[3]

Learndirect

Learndirect was designed to help individuals overcome barriers to taking up a course. Home Office research[4] has found that it attracts a large number of refugees and asylum seekers who appreciate the flexibility it offers.

What is Learndirect?

Learndirect is a government-funded initiative that provides computer-based, online courses at more than 2,000 online learning centres in England, Wales and Northern Ireland. The Learndirect centres are based on high streets, in sports and community centres, libraries, churches and even at tourist attractions. They sometimes include facilities like crèches and cafés, and some have weekend and evening opening hours.

How do I find my local Learndirect centre?

To find a centre near you visit http://www.learndirect.co.uk/personal/centres/ or call Learndirect's Learner Services helpline on 0800 101 901.

What courses are available at Learndirect?

The courses provided by Learndirect focus on the skills for employability, and are designed to appeal to those with few or no skills and qualifications, who are unlikely to participate in traditional forms of learning.

Courses available fall into the following categories:

- home and office IT courses (including courses on 'Using Computers', 'The Internet and e-mail', 'Word Processing', 'Spreadsheets' and 'Web Design')
- specialist IT courses (including courses on 'Web Development' and 'Computer Networking')
- business and management courses (including courses on 'Business Start-Up', 'Complying with the Law', 'Project Management' and 'Recruitment')
- languages (including courses in French, German, Spanish, Italian, Japanese, Greek, Welsh and ESOL)
- skills for life (including courses in English, Maths, Lifeskills, and ESOL)

Courses are deliberately flexible, and you can learn as much as you want when you want to learn it, at a pace that suits you. There are no fixed classes, traditional classrooms or teachers, but online or centre-based support is available.

How do I apply?

If you would like to apply for a Learndirect course you should visit your local Learndirect centre to discuss what they have to offer. Skills for Life and ESOL courses are free but Learndirect charges fees for other vocational courses. However, you may be able to get funding to cover this. Talk to your local Learndirect centre or to Jobcentre Plus about this.

Do I have to take the course at the Learndirect centre?

Once you have signed up for a course you can either go along to your local Learndirect centre or you can access the course from home, on your own computer. Unless otherwise stated you will need a computer with a minimum of a 56k modem or an ISDN line for connection to the Internet.

The full computer specifications currently needed to run Learndirect courses are:

- CPU: at least 500MHz
- RAM: 128 Mbytes (256MB recommended)
- Hard Drive with 650 Mbytes of free space
- CD drive: 24x speed
- sound card (16 bit) Speakers or Headphones
- SVGA Graphics card
- 16 bit colour
- keyboard
- mouse
- web connectivity via a 56 kbps modem or a network and web browser software

When you choose to learn at home, at work, or in any Learndirect centre you can access a Learner Services helpline.

Can I get a qualification?

Most Learndirect courses do not lead to qualifications but may help you to work towards a qualification if you so wish. Many Learndirect courses now also include online assessment features to help you practise and prepare for formal assessments.

Formal assessments in Skills for Life and ESOL can be taken online at Learndirect centres. To find out more about the qualifications Learndirect courses are linked to, and to get assessed for these qualifications in the area where you live, please ask at your local Learndirect centre.

Learndirect Scotland

Learndirect Scotland operates approximately 500 Learning Centres throughout Scotland, and have a database listing the courses that are available. Courses are taught in a number of ways including:

- classroom based
- distance learning
- online Learning

Depending on the course, you may be able to study

- in a Learning Centre
- at a college or university
- at home
- in your workplace

Learndirect Scotland also offers advice on choosing a course and on accessing funding.

For more information, visit www.learndirectscotland.com or phone (free) 0808 100 9000.

Entry to Employment (e2e)

Entry to Employment (e2e) is a work-based programme of learning which aims to help young people aged 16 to 19 into Further Education or employment, who are not yet ready or able to directly enter an Apprenticeship.

Eligibility

You are eligible if you are aged 16 to 18 years old, are not participating in any post-16 learning, and you need help to progress into further learning and/or a job.

In Scotland, e2e is not available. Instead, the Get Ready for Work or Skillseekers programmes may be suitable (see below).

Older young people can be admitted at the discretion of the local Learning and Skills Council, provided that the young person is not eligible for New Deal, and their programme of learning can be completed by their 25th birthday.

How can I enrol on to e2e?

Most young people are referred to e2e by Connexions,[5] the careers advice service for young people aged 13 to 19.

Asylum seekers and refugees are entitled to use the Connexions advice service, and you will find branches on high streets up and down the country.

If you visit your local Connexions office for advice they may advise you about e2e opportunities within your local area. Connexions staff will refer you to e2e if this is appropriate – as might other agencies, such as social services, social work or Youth Offending Teams.

Work-based learning providers can also identify young people who may gain from e2e learning programmes. Your Connexions personal adviser is crucial to getting you on to an e2e programme. You can also refer yourself to an e2e programme but you will still be referred to Connexions to confirm that you are eligible and suitable for e2e.

e2e is particularly aimed at young people who:

- are not yet ready to enter a structured learning option
- are currently not engaged in any form of learning and may have had a negative experience of school
- may have one or more barriers to overcome such as alcohol abuse, drug abuse, depression or homelessness

You may be offered e2e as a means of preparing you for entering the UK workforce. An e2e course will allow you to improve your English and your general employability skills. Work placements are available as part of e2e: these provide valuable experience of working life in the UK and will help to build your confidence and skills so as to help you to gain employment.

Initial assessment

There is a period of initial intensive assessment within e2e to identify your individual learning and support needs. This might last between two and eight weeks depending on your individual needs. The aim is to use the initial assessment to help develop personal and social skills.

The arrangements for meeting your own learning and support needs will be set out in a document called the e2e Passport. The passport is made up of the following documents:

- personal adviser Referral Form (Your Connexions personal adviser will use this form when referring you to e2e)
- initial Assessment Summary (Your e2e provider will use this form to provide a summary of your starting point on the programme. It will help set your key objectives that will be used to identify your individual e2e Programme)
- e2e Programme (This will be used to identify the components of your e2e programme and anticipated accredited and non-accredited learning outcomes)
- e2e Activity Plan and Review (this supports the implementation of your e2e programme and provides a record of your progress)

How is the learning programme structured?

All learners undertake learning in the following three areas, which are all linked:

- basic and Key Skills
- vocational development
- personal and social development

Learning takes place in a range of indoor and outdoor settings using different methods. These include classroom type activities, one-to-one coaching, group activities, discussions, projects, presentations from speakers, online e-learning, open learning, work placements and experience, external visits, outward bound activities and volunteering.

Ideally you will, wherever possible, work towards some form of qualification, recognising that acquiring a qualification can be a powerful motivator to continue learning.

How long does e2e take?

The programme is not time limited, but in practice you may find it takes between 22 and 52 weeks to complete. You do not need to have set number of guided learning hours – although you must meet some minimum standards.

You also do not need to get a qualification, but getting one will be encouraged, and there are many options to suit the needs of individual learners.

Education Maintenance Allowance (EMA)

From April 2006 learners on e2e will need to apply for the Education Maintenance Allowance (EMA) to support their learning. EMA[6] is a weekly payment of £10, £20 or £30 a week depending on your household income. The money is intended to help with the day-to-day costs – such as travel, books and equipment for your course.

Importantly, EMA will not affect any other benefits you get. It's paid on top of any other support provided by the government, or any earnings you get from a part-time job.

Am I eligible for EMA?

Around half of all 16 to 19 year-olds studying in England are eligible to get EMA. To qualify:

- you must be between 16 and 19 years old
- your household income must be no more than £30,000 per year
- you must be an UK or EU or EEA citizen, or have Indefinite Leave to Enter or Remain, refugee status or Humanitarian Protection (HP)
- you must have lived in the UK for at least three years and satisfy the Home Student criteria (Check out www.homeoffice.gov.uk for more information)
- your course must require at least 12 hours of guided learning per week

EMA is available to non-British nationals who have been granted Indefinite Leave to Remain, refugee status, or Humanitarian Protection (HP) irrespective of the length of time spent living in the UK. This applies both to former unaccompanied asylum seeking children recognised as refugees or granted HP, and the dependent children of those granted any of these two forms of leave (who will be given the same status as their parents). However, EMA is not available to either accompanied or unaccompanied asylum seeking children or those with Discretionary Leave (DL).

How much will I get if I'm eligible?

The amount you get depends on your household income. For the academic year 2006/2007 the rates are as follows:

If your household income is ...	... you get
up to £20,817 per year	£30 per week
£20,818 to £25,521 per year	£20 a week
£25,522 to £30,810 per year	£10 a week

If you are entitled, you will receive your EMA payment every week of your course, as long as you turn up to your classes and show commitment to your course. The money is paid directly into your bank account so you must have a bank account before you can claim (see page 365). Most young people will be able to get EMA for two to three years depending on how long they need to finish their studies.

You can also get a bonus of £100 in January and July - and again in September if you come back to the course for a second year, but bonuses depend on the progress you make with your course.

The Get Ready For Work Programme (Scotland only)

Get Ready for Work is open to 16 to 18 year olds who are not in school or college, employed, or in training. The emphasis of the program is on building skills and confidence via a personalised training program.

Participants in Get Ready for Work are paid at least £55 per week if they are in full- time training; you may also be able to claim travel expenses.[7]

To find out more contact Careers Scotland on 0845 8502 502.

Skillseekers (Scotland only)

Skillseekers is open to those aged 16 to 18 years old who have left school and are not in education. In certain cases those aged up to 25 may be eligible.

If you have a job, and your employer is willing to train you to NVQ/SVQ Level 2 or above, then you can participate in Skillseekers.

You will either be paid a wage by your employer, or a training allowance; the minimum amount is determined by your Local Enterprise Company (LEC).

If you do not have a job you can still participate in Skillseekers by doing voluntary work.

Participation in Skillseekers may lead to a National Vocational Qualification (NVQ) or Scottish Vocational Qualification (SVQ), usually at Level 2. In some instances it may also lead to entry into a Modern Apprenticeship (see below).

A Skillseekers program would normally take around two years to complete to NVQ/SQV Level 2. During this time you will follow a training plan organised by your employer. You can change to a different job or employer at any time if you decide to do so.[8]

For more information contact Careers Scotland on 0845 8502 502.

Apprenticeships

What is an Apprenticeship?

Apprenticeships[9] are a specific form of work-based training where young workers aged 16 to 24 learn the practical aspects of a specific trade, and are then assessed for their knowledge and proficiency in this trade before receiving certification. Apprenticeships offer young workers a whole package of learning which has been designed to meet the needs of a particular industry or sector of the economy.

Apprenticeships come in two types:

- Apprenticeships
- Advanced Apprenticeships

On an Apprenticeship you'll have a job[10] and a wage. An Apprenticeship takes at least 12 months to complete and leads to an NVQ at Level 2 as well as technical certificates and key skills certificates. The work is mainly practical: you'll develop technical skills and gain valuable work experience. There is also the opportunity to progress to an Advanced Apprenticeship.

On an Advanced Apprenticeship (AA), you'll be in full-time employment with an appropriate wage. You should be aiming for a technical, supervisory or junior management role. The training, which usually lasts at least 24 months, leads to an NVQ at Level 3, technical certificates and key skills certificates. For many people, an AA is a stepping-stone to university to do a Foundation Degree.

How do I become an Apprentice?

You can become an apprentice in three ways:

- your employer offers to train you as an apprentice
- you apply for and get a job with apprenticeship training included
- you secure an apprenticeship with an unpaid work placement

To be an Apprentice you must be entitled to work and study on vocational courses, so asylum seekers must first obtain permission to work before applying for Apprenticeships. You can apply for permission to work if you have been waiting a year for a decision of your application for asylum.

How difficult is it to get an Apprenticeship?

You will find a lot of competition for places on Apprenticeship programmes, with the result that employers can ask for certain qualifications (for example GCSE passes) before considering your application. If you have non-UK qualifications you should obtain a 'letter of comparability' explaining how your qualifications compare to those in the UK. See page 326 for more details.

The kind of skills and attributes employers are looking for in a potential apprentice are:

- motivation to succeed in the industry or trade of your choice
- willingness to learn and apply that learning in the workplace
- ability to demonstrate that you have the potential to complete the qualifications which are part of the programme
- willingness to communicate with a range of people
- willingness to undergo a criminal record check (you need to do this to enter employment in areas such as childcare)

Apprenticeships are designed to raise standards so that people who have been on these programmes can be successful in the workplace.

Contact your local Connexions service for advice on becoming an Apprentice. They will know which local employers provide

Apprenticeships. You can also apply for an Apprenticeship online at www.realworkrealpay.info

In Scotland contact 0845 8502 502 to find out your local Careers Scotland Centre which will provide you with advice and information on becoming an apprentice.

Information on apprenticeships is also available at: http://www.scottish-enterprise.com/modernapprenticeships

What is there to learn?

Because Apprenticeships are based on learning you:

- develop your personal and social skills
- develop the knowledge and skills you need to do the job
- develop other skills that help people to be successful in the workplace such as communication skills, numeracy, information technology, working with others, and problem solving
- learn how to apply what you have learned in the workplace

As you progress through the Apprenticeship programme you become qualified in a number of areas and you will collect certificates to demonstrate this. As you develop you will collect:

- technical certificates
- key skills certificates

Technical Certificates are qualifications that show that you have learned the occupational knowledge required to do a job. In order to be awarded a Technical Certificate you will need to do an external assessment where you could be required to:

- complete a case study, project or assignment
- take a multiple choice question paper or written examination
- attend a 'viva' where you could be asked to make a presentation and answer interview questions

Key skills are a range of essential skills that you will need in your working and personal life. You will be able to apply these skills as you continue to learn, work and run your personal life. The key skills qualifications of 'Communication' and 'Application of Number' are now an integral component of all Apprenticeship frameworks. Opportunities will be available for those who wish to take key skills at a higher level.

Once you have proved that you can apply the knowledge and skills required for the job you will be assessed on your ability to do the job for real, in the workplace. When you pass you will be awarded with the appropriate NVQ certificate. NVQs assess occupational competence, which is the ability to apply all your knowledge and skills in the workplace to get jobs done on time and in the right way. The idea of an NVQ is to see if you can cope with the unplanned and unexpected, and respond to the additional demands, requests, pressures and problems that arise in jobs every day. Once you have proved that you have met the occupational standards contained in the NVQ specification you will be awarded an NVQ certificate, which is recognised across the UK.

Once you have obtained all your Technical, Key Skills and NVQ certificates you can claim your Modern Apprenticeship certificate. This is like a final diploma, which confirms that you have completed all the requirements. You may also get a reference from your employer at this stage.

Pay and holidays

As an Apprentice you will receive a training allowance of at least £40 a week if you are on an unpaid work placement or a basic wage of £70 to £80 per week if you are employed – you could get more than this depending on your employer. You'll also get at least 1.5 days' paid holiday for each month of your training. On top of that you'll get paid for Bank Holidays.

Leaving

If you want to leave, your job gets made redundant, or your relationship with your employer breaks down, the normal rules contained in your employer's terms and conditions of employment will apply. See page 370 for the section on employment rights. Your learning provider will try to help you find an alternative Apprenticeship program.

The Employer Training Pilots (ETPs) and the National Employer Training Programme (NETP)[11]

What are ETP and NETP?

The Employer Training Pilots (ETPs)[12] are designed to engage employers in training their employees to gain their first NVQ level 2 and/or a basic skills qualification Level 1 or 2. The pilots offer free training and make a funding contribution to the costs of releasing staff during working hours. A maximum of 70 hours of training is provided free, though the size of contribution to the employer's release costs is dependent on the size of the employer.

Six pilots were originally set up in September 2002 in six local LSC areas: Birmingham & Solihull, Derbyshire, Essex, Greater Manchester, Tyne & Wear and Wiltshire & Swindon. Six more were added in September 2003 in Berkshire, Kent & Medway, Leicestershire, London East, Shropshire and South Yorkshire. In April 2004 the Chancellor of the Exchequer announced in the budget that a third phase of pilots would be set up in Lancashire, West Yorkshire, the Black Country, Cambridgeshire, Devon & Cornwall and in the rest of the North East region (Durham, Northumberland and Tees Valley).

From April 2006 the National Employer Training Programme (NETP)[13], known as 'Train to Gain' will replace ETP, and by August 2006 the programme will be applied to the whole of England. While NETP will build on the lessons learned from the ETP pilots, it is seen more as a business support and skill development service than ETP was.

Who is eligible for ETP and NETP?

ETP and NETP are employer-led and so organisations and companies rather than individuals must approach their local Learning and Skills Council (LSC). However, if you are an employee there is nothing to stop you asking your employer about ETP and NETP and if you are an employer yourself your status has no effect on eligibility.

Non-governmental organisations and companies can participate in

ETP and NETP. Until August 2006 it will remain limited to those within the pilot areas but after that date non-governmental organisations and companies from across England can take part. Those employing less than 50 people are a particular target for the programme.

Who is eligible?

Employees are eligible if they:

- have no qualifications, or qualifications below NVQ Level 2
- are employed within the local LSC area
- are over 19
- are not already registered on an LSC-funded course

Employers are eligible if they:

- employ learners within the local LSC area
- are not a central Government Department
- agree to pay employees while they train

In order for the training to be eligible it must:

- be relevant to the learner's job
- be recognised on the DfES website Section 97[14] as a National Qualification at Level 2

or

- lead to a nationally recognised qualification in basic skills Level 1 or 2

How does it work?

Each local LSC is responsible for implementing the ETP and NETP in their area. Procedures may differ slightly from one LSC to another, but in general the steps involved are:[15]

1. The employer registers their interest online or by phone
2. ETP / NETP allocate a dedicated programme adviser
3. The programme adviser outlines the project and makes an assessment of the employer's and employees' eligibility

4. *The programme adviser and employer work together to:*
   - identify basic and vocational skills gaps which affect the employer's productivity
   - identify which type of vocational or basic skills training is required to improve business performance
5. The employer selects a preferred training provider (the programme advisers may make recommendations at this stage if asked)
6. The programme adviser creates a training profile to meet employer needs
7. The training profile is formalised in a training contract for the training provider to sign
8. The training provider visits the employer to:
   - meet with learners
   - assess learners' needs in detail
   - gather information on the employees' jobs (so as to produce job-relevant training)
9. The training provider delivers a maximum of 70 hours of training on site. This should be job relevant, tailored to the learners' needs and should lead to the award of a nationally recognised qualification

Qualifications

An essential first step for many people who are planning to study or work in the UK is to have their qualifications recognised. This will help both you and the UK organisations you deal with understand how your qualifications relate to those in the UK.

Employers will want to know this, as they will want to know if you are sufficiently qualified for the jobs they offer you, and universities, colleges and other training providers will want to know this before accepting you onto one of their courses.

Please see the section on qualification recognition, pages 326-335 for more information.

Endnotes

[1] Commission Regulation (EC) No 68/2001 of 12 January 2001 on the application of Articles 87 and 88 of the EC Treaty to training aid Official Journal L 010, 13/01/2001 P. 0020 – 0029 see http://europa.eu.int/smartapi/cgi/sga_doc?smartapi!celexplus!prod!CELEXnumdoc&numdoc=32001R0068&lg=en

[2] http://www.fssc.org.uk/cgi-bin/wms.pl/UK_representation/52

[3] For more information on Programme Centres see Chapter 8 of the Jobcentre Plus Provider Guidance http://www.jobcentreplus.gov.uk/JCP/static/Dev_008532.pdf

[4] Integration Matters: A National Strategy for Refugee Integration, IND Corporate Communications, (2005) http://www.ind.homeoffice.gov.uk/ind/en/home/laws__policy/refugee_integration0.Maincontent.0002.file.tmp/267218_RefugeeFinal_240205.pdf

[5] Working Together: Connexions supporting young asylum seekers and refugees (Series Title: Making a difference Emerging Practice) http://www.connexions.gov.uk/partnerships/publications/uploads/cp/Asylum%20Seekers%20(For%20Web).pdf

[6] Get in the know! A students' guide to EMA http://www.dfes.gov.uk/financialhelp/ema/uploads/docs/ema_leaflet_final_a-w.pdf

[7] http://www.scottish-enterprise.com/sedotcom_home/stp/education-and-skills/adult-education/get-ready-for-work.htm?siblingtoggle=1

[8] http://www.scottish-enterprise.com/sedotcom_home/stp/education-and-skills/adult-education/skillseekersinformation.htm?siblingtoggle=1

[9] Your Guide 2... Apprenticeships: Policy and strategy (August 2005) see http://senet.lsc.gov.uk/guide2/apprenticeships_policy/G2ApprenticepolicyG042Sep05.pdf

[10] If you cannot find a job with apprenticeship training you may be able to go on a work placement. Discuss this option with your local Connexions service.

[11] As with the LSC, these do not apply in Scotland

[12] Employer Training Pilots: First Year Evaluation Report http://www.dfes.gov.uk/research/data/uploadfiles/ETP1.pdf

[13] National Employer Training Programme - Design Framework 2006-07 (2005) http://readingroom.lsc.gov.uk/LSC/2005/internaladmin/procurement/netp-design-framework-2006-07.pdf

[14] See http://www.dfes.gov.uk/section97/

[15] This particular example is based on the process used in Wiltshire & Swindon ETP see http://www.free2learn.org/providers.php

Training and education to help find work

6 Employment programmes

Bee Brooke and Alex Doyle,
Centre for Economic & Social Inclusion

National Employment Programmes

There are a number of national employment programmes, usually provided if you have spent a period of time on benefit. They are generally known as the 'New Deal'. Some of New Deal provision is mandatory (i.e. you have to do it) and other provision is voluntary. It very much depends on your circumstances.

This section covers:
- Work Focused Interviews
- New Deal for Young People
- New Deal for Musicians
- New Deal for 25 Plus
- New Deal 50 Plus
- New Deal for Lone Parents and New Deal for Partners
- New Deal for Disabled People

For each of these programmes you have to meet the 'eligibility criteria'. Many of these eligibility criteria are based on a social security benefit. For a full and in-depth examination of benefits, see the relevant section on pages 108-191. However, for ease of reference, here are some of the key benefits and your eligibility for them:

	Jobseeker's Allowance (JSA) – You are eligible if:	
Eligibility	<ul><li>You are aged 18 to pension age</li><li>You are out of work or working less than 16 hours a week</li><li>You are available for work for at least 40 hours a week</li><li>You are capable of work</li><li>You are not in full time education</li></ul>	
Immigration status	<ul><li>You have Indefinite Leave to Remain</li><li>You have Exceptional Leave to Remain</li><li>You have Discretionary Leave or Humanitarian Protection</li><li>You are a national of a state with a Reciprocal Agreement with the UK which includes JSA</li><li>You are an EEA worker or dependant</li><li>You are an EEA service provider or recipient</li><li>You are a British Citizen with the right of abode in the UK</li><li>You are a national of a state with an EU agreement who is working lawfully</li></ul>	
	But not if:	<ul><li>You are a Person Subject to Immigration Control unless you are a national of a state which has signed ECSMA and you are lawfully present in the UK</li><li>You are not habitually resident in the Common Travel Area</li><li>You are a national of an A8 country and have been registered as a worker in the UK for less than a year</li></ul>

Income Support – You are eligible if:

Eligibility
- You are aged 16 or over
- You are out of work or working less than 16 hours a week and do not have a partner working more than 24 hours a week
- You are not in full time, non-advanced education
- You are unable to work because ill-health or disability, or caring for a disabled person who has claimed DLA or AA or a lone parent responsible for a child under 16 or have maternity, adoption or paternity leave
- You are working more than 16 hours a week and you fulfil certain other criteria, such as you are mentally or physically disabled, or you are a childminder working in your own home (see page 135 for the full list of criteria)

Immigration status
- You are not a Person Subject to Immigration Control unless you are a national of a state which has signed ECSMA and you are lawfully present in the UK
- You are a Person Subject to Immigration Control who has been in the UK for less than 5 years and whose sponsor, or sponsors, have died, or who is an asylum seeker entitled under transitional protection rules, or who is otherwise self-supporting and whose funds from abroad have been temporarily disrupted
- You are an EEA worker or dependant
- You are an EEA service provider or recipient
- You are a national of an A8 country and have been registered as a worker in the UK for more than a year
- You are a British Citizen with the right of abode in the UK

But not if:	• You are not habitually resident in the Common Travel Area

Pension Credit – You are eligible if:

Eligibility
- You are aged 60 or over
- Your income is under £114.05 for a single person or £174.05 for a couple (although if you are a carer or if you have a mortgage, loans or leasehold service charges you may be eligible even if you have a higher income)

Immigration status
- You are not a Person Subject to Immigration Control unless you are a national of a state which has signed ECSMA and you are lawfully present in the UK
- You are an EEA worker or dependant
- You are an EEA service provider or recipient
- You are a national of an A8 country and have been registered as a worker in the UK for more than a year
- You are a British Citizen with the right of abode in the UK

But not if:	• You are not habitually resident in the Common Travel Area

Council Tax Benefit – You are eligible if:

Eligibility
- You are 'liable' to pay council tax
- Your income is low enough (either working or not working)
- Your capital savings are not more than £16,000
- You are not a full-time student (some exceptions apply)

Immigration status
- You are not a Person Subject to Immigration Control unless you are a national of a state which has signed ECSMA and you are lawfully present in the UK
- You are an EEA worker or dependant
- You are an EEA service provider or recipient
- You are a national of an A8 country and have been registered as a worker in the UK for more than a year
- You are a British Citizen with the right of abode in the UK

But not if:	• You are not habitually resident in the Common Travel Area

Housing Benefit – You are eligible if:

Eligibility
- You are 'liable' to pay rent or similar payments on a home that you occupy as your main residence
- Your income is low enough (either working or not working)
- Your capital savings are not more than £16,000

Immigration status
- You are not a Person Subject to Immigration Control unless you are a national of a state which has signed ECSMA and you are lawfully present in the UK
- You are an EEA worker or dependant
- You are an EEA service provider or recipient
- You are a national of an A8 country and have been registered as a worker in the UK for more than a year
- You are a British Citizen with the right of abode in the UK

But not if:	• You are not habitually resident in the Common Travel Area

Carer's Allowance – You are eligible if:

Eligibility
- You are aged 16 or over
- You provide 35 hours or more a week to a severely disabled person (who receives middle to higher rate DLA care component or Attendance Allowance)
- You are not earning more than the current weekly earnings limit (after deduction of allowable expenses)
- You are not in full time education (21 hours a week or more)

Immigration status
- You have Indefinite Leave to Remain
- You have Exceptional Leave to Remain
- You have Discretionary Leave or Humanitarian Protection
- You are a national of a state with a Reciprocal Agreement with the UK which includes DLA and/or AA
- You are an EEA worker or dependant
- You are an EEA service provider or recipient
- You are a British Citizen with the right of abode in the UK

But not if:	• You are a Person Subject to Immigration Control unless you are a national of a state which has signed ECSMA and you are lawfully present in the UK

	Disability Living Allowance – You are eligible if:
Eligibility	• You are younger than 65 when you make your first claim • You have needed help for at least three months unless you have a terminal illness and your death can reasonably be expected within six months • You need significant attention in connection with your bodily functions for a significant portion of the day or cannot prepare a cooked meal for yourself • You cannot walk outdoors in unfamiliar places without guidance or supervision from another person most of the time For further information on the different care and mobility components and the different rates please see page 150
Immigration status	• You have Indefinite Leave to Remain • You have Exceptional Leave to Remain • You have Discretionary Leave or Humanitarian Protection • You are a national of a state with a Reciprocal Agreement with the UK which includes Incapacity Benefit • You are an EEA worker or dependant • You are an EEA service provider or recipient • You are a British Citizen with the right of abode in the UK • You are a national of a state with an EU agreement who is working lawfully
But not if:	• You are a Person Subject to Immigration Control unless you have made the necessary National Insurance contributions which may be difficult if you are not lawfully allowed to work

Work Focused Interviews

What is a Work Focused Interview?

Work Focused Interviews (WFI) are designed to help people out of work to overcome their barriers to employment.[1] They require people making a new or repeat claim for certain benefits to attend an interview with a personal adviser to talk through work options.

Note: If you don't attend when required, your benefit may be affected. If you attend an interview you do not have to accept work.

Work Focused Interviews (WFIs) aim to:

- encourage you to see work as a realistic option, where this is appropriate
- help you build upon your skills and potential
- help you tackle any obstacles to work
- offer you ongoing support through further interviews, or referral to other provision, for example New Deals

Eligibility

To find out if you have to attend a WFI, answer the following questions:[2]

	YES	NO
Question 1 - Age Are you of working age (from 16 to 59)?	YES	NO
Question 2 - Work Are you not working, or working less than 16 hours a week on average?	YES	NO
Question 3 - Benefits Are you making a new or repeat claim for:[3] Income Support / Incapacity Benefit / Severe Disablement Allowance?	YES	NO
Question 4 - Where you live Do you live in a WFI area? (contact Jobcentre Plus to find out)	YES	NO
If you answered **YES** to every question, then you probably do have to attend a WFI. If you answered **NO** to any of the questions, then you do not have to attend a WFI		

Work Focused Interviews for Partners

You may also have to attend a WFI if you are the partner of someone claiming for certain benefits. To find out if you have to attend a Work Focused Interview for Partners answer the following questions:[4]

Question 1 - Benefits Has your partner been receiving one of the benefits listed below and an increase for you, for at least 26 weeks: Income Support Income-Based Jobseeker's Allowance (other than joint claim JSA) Incapacity Benefit Severe Disablement Allowance Carer's Allowance. (To find out if you are eligible for these benefits see pages 110-116)	YES	NO
Question 2 – Where you live Do you live in a Jobcentre Plus area?	YES	NO
Question 3 - Age Are you and your partner both aged under 60?	YES	NO
Question 4 - Work Are you working under 24 hours a week?	YES	NO
If you answered **YES** to every question, then you probably do have to attend an interview If you answered **NO** to any of the questions, then you will not have to go to the interview unless your circumstances change		

Who can choose to attend a WFI?

If you are claiming Maternity Allowance or Industrial Injury Disablement Benefit, or you are aged between 60 and 65, you can choose to have a WFI.

Arranging the WFI

You will have a WFI before your first claim is processed (this only applies to new claims after 22nd October 2001).

If you are claiming Incapacity Benefit your initial meeting will take place eight weeks after the start of your claim.[5] The interview is mandatory (i.e. you must attend).

Note: If you fail to attend your benefit may be affected.

If you are eligible for a WFI because of the benefits your partner is claiming, Jobcentre Plus will contact you to arrange a WFI when your partner has been making the claim for around 26 weeks. The interview is mandatory (i.e. you must attend).

Note: If you fail to attend your partner's benefits may be affected.

If you are in a Jobcentre Plus area you should speak to someone at the Jobcentre Plus Contact Centre to arrange your interview. The Contact Centre will take your details and ask you what you want to claim. They will also send you claim forms to fill in and take to the WFI.

You should be given or sent a letter telling you the date, time and place of your WFI, along with the name of the Adviser you will be seeing. You should also receive a leaflet telling you about WFIs.

Special arrangements

In exceptional circumstances, for example due to health problems or difficulties in arranging childcare, it may be possible for interviews to take place at home or away from the Jobcentre Plus office.

Translation

If you need someone to provide translation, this should be arranged for you. See page 113 for details of the Jobcentre Plus translation policy. You can choose to bring a friend or a relative if you wish.

Arrangements should also be made if you are deaf or have a hearing impairment.

Assistance with costs

You may be eligible for assistance with travel and / or childcare costs if you:

- have a health condition or disability
- are a lone parent
- are a widow or widower
- are a carer

Overview of a Work Focused Interview

When you first attend you will have a meeting with a financial assessor that will take about twenty minutes. The financial assessor will first do an identity check and will then go over the details of your benefit claim. The Personal Adviser will then take over the meeting.

The interview with the personal adviser will last about 40 minutes. You will not be required to look for work, but the initial interview will tell you about the help you can get from Jobcentre Plus. The Adviser should try to take account of your individual situation when considering what advice to give you.

Participating

Participation means attending the WFI and answering certain questions about:[6]

- your educational qualifications
- your past employment history
- other work skills you have acquired or vocational training you have done
- whether you are currently doing any unpaid or paid work
- any medical conditions
- whether you have caring or childcare responsibilities

These questions are designed to establish basic information about you that will help the personal adviser to provide the right support for you.

Note: If you do not answer the questions your benefit may be affected.

If you are a lone parent or are claiming Incapacity Benefit you will be required to help your Adviser to complete an Action Plan but you will not be required to comply with the content of the Action Plan.[7]

Trigger point interviews

Trigger point interviews are similar to the initial interview but will not include a discussion with a financial assessor.

Work Focused Interviews for Partners: if you are eligible, you will only have to attend a single WFI.

All other WFI interviews: if you are eligible, you will be invited for further interviews at certain trigger points. These interviews are mandatory.

Type of customer	2nd interview	3rd interview	4th interview	5th interview
Lone parent with youngest child aged 14 or over[8]	3 months after first interview	3 months later	3 months later	3 months later
Other lone parents	6 months after first interview	6 months later	12 months later	12 months later
Other customer	3 years from date of last WFI or other face to face meeting with personal adviser	3 years later	3 years later	3 years later

Other trigger points

You can arrange further interviews at any point during your claim by contacting your personal adviser. However, there are other trigger points:

- starting or ending part-time work
- staying on Incapacity Benefit or Income Support following a Personal Capability Assessment
- reaching the age of 18
- finishing or reducing caring responsibilities
- starting or ending a training course arranged by Jobcentre Plus

Deferring or waiving interviews

In some circumstances the interview might be deferred (postponed) to a later date or you might not have to attend at all. You will be offered a deferral if it would be unreasonable for you to attend a WFI at this point, for example if you have just had a baby. Every situation will be considered on its own merits. If your interview is deferred you can still proceed with your benefit claim and start getting benefits so long as you agree to attend a WFI at a specified time in the future.

The WFI will be waived when it is unlikely to be of any assistance to you in the foreseeable future, for example if you are very severely disabled. If your interview is waived you can proceed straight away with your benefit claim.

If you are 16 or 17

If you are 16 or 17 and making a claim for a WFI benefit, you will have to attend a Learning Focused Interview (LFI). This will be held at a Careers Service or at Connexions. The interview will cover education, training and future work options. This is unlike the WFI in that you are not required to answer any particular questions. You may be entitled to help with travel costs.

Your first claim will be processed once you have attended the interview. However, you will not be required to attend any further interviews.

What happens if I do not attend?

If you fail to attend mandatory interviews, your benefit (or your partner's benefit[9]) may be reduced.[10] You will be given three chances to attend a

WFI before any action is taken that could affect your benefit claim.

If you are late for an interview or make contact after the time of the interview has passed, you may be treated as having failed to attend. It is important to contact an Adviser as soon as you know you are unable to attend an appointment.

New Deal for Young People

Aim

The primary aim of the New Deal for Young People (NDYP)[11] is to move you into sustainable work. It provides a wide variety of support, including training, advice, jobsearch support and work experience.

NDYP consists of three stages:

- Gateway
- four NDYP options
- Follow-through

Eligibility

Compulsory or mandatory participation

If you are aged between 18 and 24, and have been claiming Jobseeker's Allowance (see page 130 to find out if you are eligible for JSA) for six months, entry to NDYP is compulsory.[12]

Voluntary participation (early entry)

In some circumstances individuals are allowed early entry to NDYP. personal advisers use their discretion to determine which customers get early entry[13] but you may be eligible if you fall into one of the special groups below.[14] As a newcomer you should check if you are eligible.

Special groups:

- refugees
- ex-offenders
- homeless people (including rough sleepers)
- people affected by drug addiction (including alcoholism)
- people who have been in residential care
- ex-regular members of the armed forces
- benefit recipients with language, literacy or numeracy problems (if they do not enter Work Based Learning for Adults)
- lone parents, people with disabilities and carers on JSA (instead of other benefits)

The Gateway

The Gateway period is the first stage of NDYP. It can last up to four months and may involve several different organisations. During this time you will remain on Jobseeker's Allowance and are subject to the normal Jobseeker's Allowance requirements of taking steps to look for work and being available to start work. The Gateway aims to prepare you for work by addressing any barriers, and to help you to find work.

Content

The activity you undertake during the Gateway activity will depend on your particular needs. Certain elements from the list below may be available to everyone, while other elements are only available to those with particular needs.

The Gateway can include:

- an initial phase of intensive help to find unsubsidised jobs, including help with searching for jobs
- independent careers advice, including motivation and confidence building, the identification of learning and training needs
- access to a mentor who will provide advice, guidance and encouragement on a non-official basis

- specialist assistance if you are disabled, from an ethnic minority, have problems relating to homelessness, debt, drug or alcohol abuse
- short refresher courses to help with basic and key skills, confidence and motivation
- referral onto Short Intensive Basic Skills provision (an 8 week course)
- a Gateway to Work course to improve your chances of moving into work
- help preparing you to join a New Deal Option, including discussion with providers and taster options
- help if you are interested in self employment including short awareness seminars, advice and information
- initial help with moving into self-employment which may include a basic awareness and information session, one-to-one counselling and a short four week part-time course at which you will develop a Business Plan

The initial New Deal interview

The Gateway starts with an initial New Deal interview that is always undertaken by a Jobcentre Plus New Deal personal adviser. The interview will:

- tell you about New Deal, how it operates locally and the involvement of partner organisations
- begin the process of drawing up a New Deal Action Plan, that will record any action you plan to undertake and do undertake to move closer to work
- screen for basic skills needs
- where appropriate, refer you to partner organisations that deliver relevant activity

Subsequent interviews

Following the Initial New Deal Interview, you will attend interviews with your New Deal personal adviser on at least a weekly basis. These interviews will last around 30 minutes. Where you have significant barriers to employment due to health or disability that need addressing you should be referred to the disability employment adviser, who will take on the role of New Deal personal adviser.

Gateway to Work courses

If you have not found work after four weeks on the Gateway you must attend a Gateway to Work course. The course will help you to improve:

- your communication skills
- how you present yourself
- your punctuality, time-keeping and time-management
- your team working and problem solving skills
- your ability to search for jobs, your CV, and your performance in interviews

The course is mandatory and if you do not go your benefits may be affected. If no course is running then you must attend the next available one. The courses last two weeks, and you are required to attend for a minimum of 30 hours each week.

End of the Gateway

At the end of the Gateway period, if you have not found work, your New Deal personal adviser will work with you to find a suitable placement on one of the four options. You will also be referred to a mentoring provider, although you will be able to opt out of this.

New Deal Young People Options

Once you enter the flexible Options period you will be able to choose between four possible Options. Your adviser will help you decide which is most appropriate for you. As well as your chosen Option, an equivalent of one day per week will be spent job searching.

1. Full Time Education or Training (FTET)

The FTET Option is designed to help jobseekers reach S/NVQ level 2 or equivalent, or offer support to those who have basic skills needs. The Option aims to equip those without a relevant S/NVQ level 2 or equivalent with the employability and occupational skills for work. Basic skills training is also available on this Option.

There are two types of programme:

- A short, job focused course that last eight weeks with a certificate awarded on completion
- A course of up to 52 weeks with an education and training provider which will lead to an S/NVQ level 2, involving work experience

2. Employment Option (EO)

You can participate in the Employment Option at any time during NDYP, including during the Gateway and Follow-Through. The aim of the Employment Option is to help improve the participant's chances of finding permanent employment by offering a period of work with an element of training to an approved level. The length of this option is up to 26 weeks.

Employers will be expected to pay you the going rate for the job. They will be offered a subsidy towards the cost of employing you. If they take on a full-time employee (30 hours or more a week), they will receive up to £60 per week, and if they take on a part-time employee (24-29 hours a week) they will receive up to £40 per week.[15] They may also receive up to £750 towards the cost of certified vocational training.

The employer will sign an agreement stating that they will:

- keep you on as long as you show the aptitude and commitment needed
- provide or arrange training as appropriate
- monitor and record your progress and identify areas of action, in the same way as they would for any other employee to help them settle in and progress

The Employment Option includes a Self-Employment Option that aims to prepare you to set up and run a successful business and to equip you with the transferable skills to help you into work with another employer if appropriate. It involves a basic awareness and information session, one-to-one support and a short part-time course that will include the development of a business plan. These elements of the Self-Employment provision are also available during the Gateway and Follow-Through. During the Option period, the provision can also include test trading for up to 26 weeks and must also include some training.

3. Voluntary Sector Option (VSO)

This involves a work placement or employment in the voluntary sector to benefit your local community. It will also involve support and education or training towards an approved level.

4. Environment Task Force Option (ETFO)

This involves a work placement or employment in work designed to improve the environment, and will also include support and education or training towards an approved level.

If you participate in either the VSO or the ETFO, your participation will be reviewed at 10 weeks and can then be extended to 13 weeks.

Finance and your choice of Options

If you are on:

- the Employer Option: you will be paid a wage by the employer and will be eligible for tax credits and other in-work benefits (see page 165), but you will not be eligible for passported benefits such as free prescriptions or free dental care
- the Full-Time Education and Training Option: you will receive a training allowance equivalent to your Jobseeker's Allowance plus a training allowance of £15.38, and travel expenses will be paid
- either the Environment Task Force or the Voluntary Sector Options: some providers will pay a wage, while others pay an allowance equivalent to your Jobseeker's Allowance plus £15.38, plus travel expenses

Support while on a New Deal Option

While you are on a New Deal Option, you will still have access to your New Deal personal adviser and you should contact them if you have any problems. The adviser is supposed to keep in touch with you, and to monitor your progress throughout your time on your Option.

Note: You are not required to attend weekly or fortnightly meetings.

The Referral Process

If you find it difficult to choose an Option, you can do a taster that gives you the opportunity to try out one of the options for a short time. You can stay on JSA while doing a taster.

Once you have agreed to start an option you will have a pre-entry interview with your New Deal personal adviser. You will be asked to agree a personal development plan that will form part of the New Deal Action Plan.

Although you will have a choice about which Option you join, once a decision is reached participation on the Option is mandatory. If you repeatedly fail to start you may be sanctioned.

Transferring between Options

If one Option is not working for you, you may be able to move onto a different Option.[16] If you approach your personal adviser, they can agree to a transfer between providers and options.

Note: If you simply leave and then try to claim Jobseeker's Allowance at a Jobcentre Plus office you will be referred for possible sanctions for leaving your Option.

Where you are permitted to transfer from Full Time Education and Training Option, you can spend no more than 39 weeks on Options, i.e. 26 weeks on Full Time Education and Training Option, followed by 13 weeks on either Voluntary Sector or Environment Task Force Options, or a combination of both.

However, you can participate in the full 26 week Employment Option at any point during the Option period, even after a full 13 week Voluntary Sector or Environment Task Force Option, after 52 weeks of Full Time Education and Training, or during Follow-through (see below).

If you transfer within the same Option, you can only have a total of 26 weeks on the Employment Option (including the Self Employment route), 13 weeks, with extensions allowed in exceptional circumstances, on Voluntary Sector or Environment Task Force Options, and 52 weeks maximum on the Full Time Education and Training Option.

Follow-through

If you have completed your option and remain without a job, you will have to re-claim Jobseeker's Allowance. At this point, you will be referred back to your New Deal personal adviser, who will start a Follow-through period.

You will receive intensive help to find jobs, as well as advice and guidance to identify further action to improve the prospects of finding work. You may be offered:

- jobsearch help including help with job applications, CVs and job interviews
- enhanced vacancy filling services for employers
- work trial placements with employers
- access to specialist programmes and measures where there are complex barriers to work because of disability

Leaving the programme

If you are seriously considering giving up your Option placement, you should discuss this with your personal adviser, who may be able to resolve the issue that is causing problems with your Option, or may be able to refer you to an alternative placement.

You may leave New Deal to receive another benefit, for example, Income Support, Incapacity Benefit or Invalid Care Allowance, if you fulfil the conditions for receipt of that benefit (to find out if you are eligible see page 110-116). Similarly, you can leave New Deal if you join a full-time education course or take up a job.

Note: New Deal for Young People is only available to Jobseeker's Allowance claimants, and if you cease to claim, other than because you have gone on an Option or left to a job, then you automatically leave New Deal.

If you still require assistance to find employment, a further range of help is available through more intensive employment and training measures. The follow-through period can last for up to four months, during which time you will have interviews with your New Deal personal adviser. There is no set frequency for these meetings, and your adviser will agree a course of action that best suits you.

Note: You can be sanctioned for repeatedly failing to start an Option, for leaving an Option without agreeing this with your personal adviser, or for being dismissed due to misconduct.[17] Jobcentre Plus is the only organisation that can sanction you.

New Deal for Musicians

Aim

New Deal for Musicians (NDfM)[18] is delivered to participants as part of New Deal for Young People and New Deal 25 Plus. It aims to help aspiring unemployed musicians into a sustainable career in the music industry either as artists under contract or as self-employed artists.

It does not directly provide musical tuition, but rather advice and guidance on the business aspects of work in the music industry. It caters for all genres of music including, rock/pop, dance, jazz, blues, country and folk, and classical. The provision is designed for musicians in a range of roles, including vocalists, composers, and performing DJs.

It does not extend to those interested in careers allied to the music industry, such as management, technicians, and road crew.

NDfM can have three elements:

- access to advisory support from Specialist Music Industry Consultants (MIC)
- full Time Education and Training Open Learning Pack from a Music Open Learning Provider (MOLP)
- subsidised or Self-Employment

Eligibility

NDfM is available to jobseekers who are eligible for either New Deal for Young People (NDYP) or New Deal 25 Plus (ND25 Plus)[19] (to find out if you are eligible for these programmes see page 232 and page 244). It is a voluntary route within these programmes.

However, you will not automatically be allowed to participate in NDfM just because you are eligible for either of these New Deals and express an interest to do so. It will be left to the discretion of your personal adviser and an MIC to decide whether NDfM is suited to you. This will depend partly on whether you:

- are an active musician or have previously been working as an active musician
- have instrumental or other music related qualifications
- have a work history within the music industry
- live where there is little or no local provision or would experience difficulty travelling to provision
- have a preferred learning style of independent study with access to support and would find regular time-tabled attendance difficult because of your chosen career path

Programme elements

Music Industry Consultant (MIC)

You can request to be referred to an MIC at any time during New Deal. MICs have extensive experience in the music industry and are able to provide impartial support and guidance, including advice about the business environment. They are not expected to assess your talent or abilities. The interviews with a MIC are in addition to the required hours on an Option or IAP. The use of an MIC is voluntary and is not a pre-condition for accessing support from a Music Open Learning Provider.

In association with your personal adviser, the MIC will help you draw up an Action Plan to monitor progress and record activities.

Your relationship with your MIC is confidential. MICs are not required to disclose any information to your personal adviser without your consent. However, they are expected to provide information to enable your personal adviser to decide on the best way forward for you.

Meetings with MICs can take place outside working hours and away from the Jobcentre Plus office or provider environment. Meetings with MICs should be arranged between yourselves.

Your access to MICs is intended to be flexible – you may see an MIC for your entire time on New Deal or just during the Gateway. MICs will reimburse you with the travel costs of getting to interviews.

Music Open Learning Provider (MOLP)

MOLPs will support you and monitor your progress, and will help you to select appropriate open learning modules. Your MOLP will help you to keep a log to record activity and time spent on learning. This can be used towards a recognised qualification or a module within a qualification.

The available open learning modules are:

- Business Skills
- Technology

- Management and Enterprise
- Performance Skills
- Composition and Song Writing
- Music Business Affairs

NDYP participants

If you participate in NDfM within NDYP, you can receive support from a MOLP through the Full Time Education and Training open learning route. The maximum time spent on this route will be 26 weeks. You will be required to complete an average of 30 hours' activity a week. You should meet your MOLP at least every month, and should be in contact on a weekly basis. Your travel expenses will be reimbursed by your MOLP. The MOLP is responsible for ensuring that you continue to undertake jobsearch activities. You may request a Leaver Certificate on leaving to start work.

ND25 Plus participants

If you participate in NDfM within ND25 Plus, MOLPs can provide up to 60 hours of music related support during the Gateway and IAP, in addition to the 30 hours of required ND25 Plus activity per week. In exceptional circumstances it may be arranged for you to undertake more MOLP-supported activity, but this must still be in addition to your 30 hours of required activity.

Moving into Employment or Self-employment

You can opt to move into subsidised employment at any time through NDYP and after the fourth week of the Gateway through ND25 Plus.

Alternatively, you could try a Self-Employment route. You can access initial help during the Gateway. You will also have the opportunity to 'test trade'. This would normally happen during the Option / IAP period. Examples of test trading include providing instrumental tuition, and performing at concerts or gigs. You could be part of a group or band of other musicians where one or more of the other members are employed. In these circumstances any earnings by the group will be apportioned and those relating to you will be held in a special dual signature account with the self-employment provider until test-trading is completed.

If you access NDfM through NDYP you can continue to receive support from your MOLP, and can use the open learning materials as part of the training element of Self-Employment.

For more information on Self Employment Provision available through ND25 Plus please see page 249. For more information on Self Employment Provision available through NDYP please see page 237.

Follow-through

Follow-through support and advice is available if you do not find work immediately at the end of your NDfM help.

New Deal for 25 Plus

Aim

New Deal for 25 Plus (ND25 Plus)[20] aims to help unemployed adults into sustained work. It provides a wide variety of individually tailored support, including training, advice, guidance and work experience.

ND25 Plus has three stages:

- Gateway
- Intensive Activity Period (IAP)
- Follow-Through

Eligibility

Compulsory participation

You are required to participate in the ND25 Plus if you:[21]

- are aged 25 or over
- have been claiming Jobseeker's Allowance for 18 out of the previous 21 months (even if you have just been receiving National Insurance Credits)

- you do not live in an Employment Zone (EZ) area where there is alternative provision which you must participate in instead (to find out if you live in an EZ area see page 270)

Claimants for these purposes include both members of a Joint Claim couple if the claim satisfies the eligibility conditions.

If you are a Joint Claim couple the following matters are also taken into consideration:

- when a Joint Claim is considered to start
- when an existing Jobseeker's Allowance claimant claims for a new partner
- whether the claimant has any children who are no longer in full-time education or children who are over 18 years old

Voluntary participation (Early entry)

If you are claiming Pension Credit, you can voluntarily enter ND25 Plus.[22]

In some circumstances individuals are allowed early entry to ND25 Plus. personal advisers use their discretion to determine which customers enter early[23] but you may be eligible if you fall into one of the groups below:[24]

- ex-offenders
- refugees
- homeless people (including rough sleepers)
- people affected by drug addiction (including alcoholism)
- people who have been in residential care
- ex-regular members of armed forces
- benefit recipients with language, literacy or numeracy problems (if they do not enter Work Based Learning for Adults)
- lone parents, people with disabilities and carers on JSA (instead of other benefits)

The Gateway

The Gateway is the first stage in the ND25 Plus and lasts for up to four months. During this you will have weekly meetings with and receive help from a New Deal personal adviser. You will remain on Jobseeker's Allowance and will be subject to the normal Jobseeker's Allowance requirements of taking steps to look for work and being available to start work. The Gateway aims to help prepare you for work by addressing any barriers, and by helping you to find unsubsidised employment.

Gateway content

The activity you undertake during the Gateway activity will depend on your particular needs. It can include:

- careers advice and guidance
- training needs analysis
- Basic Skills assessment and short Basic Skills courses
- short job focused training courses covering key skills (see page 197)
- help with motivation and confidence building
- mentoring
- short work tasters
- short Intensive Activity Period (IAP) tasters
- initial help with moving into self-employment which may include a basic awareness and information session, and one-to-one support and a short four week part-time course at which you will develop a Business Plan
- support from a Music Industry Consultant (MIC)
- specialist assistance to help improve job prospects and specialist help with other problems, such as homelessness, debt, alcohol, drug and substance misuse
- help for participants with a disability or health problem, jobseekers from ethnic minorities, or those in rural areas
- Gateway to Work courses which include training to improve communication skills, presentation, punctuality, time-keeping and time-management, and problem-solving and team-working

At your initial interview you will begin the process of drawing up a New Deal Action Plan, which will record any action you plan to undertake and do undertake to move closer to work.

Intensive Activity Period (IAP)

If you have not found work by the end of the Gateway, you will move into the Intensive Activity Period (IAP). This consists of flexible packages of support that can be tailored to suit your individual needs. Providers will record any action taken in your individual Action Plan.

The IAP is designed to:

- address 'deep-seated' barriers to work
- provide valuable experience of the world of work
- act as an added incentive to people to move into work

If you are between 25 and 49 years old, participation in the IAP is mandatory.[25]

Note: If you do not take part, you risk losing your benefit.

If you are aged over 50 and are not claiming Pension Credit, you will be required to participate in the Gateway, but entry to the IAP will be voluntary.

For most people the IAP lasts for 13 weeks, however for those who need additional assistance it can last for up to 26 weeks. About 11 weeks into the IAP there will be a review where the eventual length of the IAP will be finalised. In almost all cases you will be required to do a minimum of 30 hours of IAP activities, over five days.

During IAP you will receive a training allowance that is equivalent to your Jobseeker's Allowance plus a top up, currently £15.38, unless you are on some form of waged provision.[26]

IAP Routeway

In most cases the IAP is provided by a single organisation. This is called the IAP Routeway.

The IAP Routeway will:

- provide you with occupational skills such as motivation, timekeeping, communication
- support you in finding work which builds on those skills
- provide you with experience of a real work environment and a work reference
- encourage you to continue learning once in work

IAP content

Your IAP will consist of at least one of the following activities:

- help with basic skills problems
- work placements with employers (see also page 343)
- work experience placements
- training with strong labour market links – short job focused training or longer occupational training
- motivation, soft skills and job search skills provision
- any other support which will help you to overcome barriers to work
- help with moving into self-employment

Subsidised employment

You can move into subsidised employment during the IAP and Follow-through. The job should be expected to last at least 26 weeks and wherever possible, be permanent. The subsidised employment element of the ND25 Plus differs from the New Deal for Young People in that there is no formal training commitment or payment for training accompanying the subsidy. However, employers will be expected to provide the participant with the same training as that undertaken by any of their other employees.

You will receive a wage, and employers will be expected to pay you the going rate for the job. They will be offered a subsidy towards the cost of employing you. Employers can receive £75 per week for six months if the post is full-time (30 hours or more), and £50 per week if the job is part-time (16 to 29 hours).[27]

Employers will sign an agreement stating that they will:

- keep you on as long as you show the aptitude and commitment they need
- give you the same preparation and training as anyone else doing the job
- monitor and record your progress and identify areas for action, as they would with any other employee to help them settle in and make progress

It may also be possible to do subsidised employment in conjunction with other Jobcentre Plus programmes such as Work Trials (see page 344).

Self-Employment provision

The Self-Employment Option aims to prepare you to set up and run a successful business and to equip you with the transferable skills to help you into work with another employer if appropriate. It involves a basic awareness and information session, one-to-one support and a short part-time course which will include the development of a business plan. These elements of the Self-Employment provision are also available during the Gateway and Follow-through. During the IAP period, the provision can also include test-trading for up to 26 weeks.

Unlike what happens under the New Deal for Young People, training is not a compulsory element of the ND25 Plus Self-Employment provision. However it is available to you if you need some specific training in order for you to succeed during your test-trading but this does not necessarily have to be towards an approved qualification.

Work-based learning for adults (WBLA)

Work-based learning for adults is available to ND25 Plus participants as part of the IAP. This might include, for example, Basic Employability Training (BET) or Longer Occupational Training (LOT). For more information about what this might involve see page 195.

Education and Training Opportunities

Education and Training Opportunities (ETO) are designed for those participants who face barriers to employment through their lack of educational qualifications following on from basic skills screening, assessment and subsequent training.

ETO provision can consist purely of Basic Skills provision (where it is for a relatively short period, for example an eight to ten week course) or can include Basic Skills provision as a minor element of a longer course.

ETO provision can last for up to 52 weeks. While on ETO you will work towards a recognised qualification, which can be up to NVQ level 3, or equivalent. ETO could include other elements, including help with IT skills, counselling to address personal problems, and financial advice.

ETO activities can be part-time with other IAP activities, such as work experience or work placements, making up full-time attendance.

Work experience

The aim of work experience is to help you move into work, and where this is not possible, to improve your employability.

Work experience placements provide you with the opportunity to:

- develop or refresh soft skills and attributes
- update your CV
- gain a recent work reference
- undertake jobsearch which may include attending Jobcentre interviews

Work experience placements take place in a work environment but offer a higher level of support and supervision than you might expect at work. A work experience placement may be followed by a work placement, either within an overall period of work experience, or after a period of work experience. See also 'volunteering' on pages 336-342.

Follow-through

If you reach the end of ND25 Plus and have been unsuccessful in gaining employment, you will return to JSA and move into Follow-through. Follow-through usually lasts six weeks but if you need additional help it may be extended to 13 weeks.

The support available will be tailored to your particular needs. It will include jobsearch support, guidance, training and specialist support, in addition to the help you received during the Gateway and IAP stages of ND25 Plus.

Leaving the programme

If you leave the New Deal programme without securing employment, you may be able to claim another benefit such as Incapacity Benefit, or you will have to re-claim Jobseeker's Allowance.

Note: If you leave ND25 Plus without previously agreeing this with your New Deal personal adviser, of if you fail to turn up to appointments, you will be referred for possible sanctioning.[28]

New Deal for 50 Plus

Aim

New Deal for 50 Plus (ND50 Plus)[29] offers a route back into paid employment from long term unemployment for older workers.

Note: The programme is entirely voluntary, which means that you will not lose any benefits if you decide not to take part.[30] You can take a job if you want to regardless of whether or not you will be better or worse off.

Eligibility

You are eligible[31] for ND50 Plus if you are aged 50 or over and have received one of the following benefits (to find out if you are eligible for these benefits see page 130) for at least 26 weeks:

- Income Support
- Jobseeker's Allowance
- Incapacity Benefit
- Severe Disablement Allowance
- Pension Credit

You may also be eligible if you have been receiving National Insurance Credits or Invalid Care Allowance or Bereavement Allowance.

You are also eligible if your partner has been receiving one of the following benefits with an increase for you, for at least 26 weeks:

- Income Support
- Jobseeker's Allowance
- Severe Disablement Allowance

Programme elements

There are three elements to ND50 Plus:

- Help to find paid employment through a New Deal personal adviser or to move into self-employment
- The opportunity to claim the 50 Plus element of the Working Tax Credit once you have secured paid employment
- Access to a training grant once you have secured paid employment

You do not have to take part in all three elements of the programme, for example:

- you can find work or become self-employed without using the services of the Jobcentre Plus or the help of a personal adviser, and still claim your Working Tax Credit and Training Grant

- you can get help from a personal adviser to find work, but do not have to apply for the Training Grant

Finding paid employment (caseloading)

Caseloading is a series of about six thirty-minute interviews with your personal adviser over a period of between three and six months. The amount of time will depend on your needs. Each interview will last 30 minutes. If you are disabled you may have interviews with a Disability Employment Adviser instead.

Note: During this caseloading period, your benefits will not be affected.

If you want to find paid employment with an employer, your personal adviser will help you by offering advice and assistance with writing CVs, writing application letters, and preparing for interviews, and will provide you with information about programmes and services that could help you. You will also receive money to cover the costs of travelling to interviews, including overnight stays.

Moving into self-employment

You could use ND50 Plus to start your own business and become self-employed.

You can participate in basic awareness and information sessions, one-to-one counselling and a short part-time course that will include the development of a business plan. You may also have the opportunity to do test-trading for up to 26 weeks, but this is not available to IB claimants.[32]

Additional elements

While on ND50 Plus, you may also have access to:

- Work Based Learning for Adults (see page 195)
- Work Trials (see page 344)
- Travel to Interview scheme (see page 348)
- Programme Centres (see page 199)

Your New Deal personal adviser may also discuss with you the benefits of doing voluntary work, which you could do to develop and maintain new and existing skills, provide an up to date reference, open up job opportunities or provide you with a talking point at interviews.

The end of caseloading

Caseloading will end when:

- you move into a job or enter a training programme
- you no longer wish to participate (as the programme is voluntary)
- your personal adviser thinks this element is no longer appropriate
- you move into another New Deal or Employment Zone

Working Tax Credits

ND50 Plus will give you access to Working Tax Credit payments:

- if you have found paid employment with an employer
- during your start-up year if you are self employed.

A Working Tax Credit is a payment from the Government designed to top up your wages that is paid through the Tax Credits system (see page 165).

Training Grant

Once you have taken up work with the help of ND50 Plus and have successfully claimed the 50 Plus element of the Working Tax Credit, you can make a claim for a Training Grant up to the value of £1,500 where:

- £1,200 can be awarded at any time during the two year eligibility period for training that is relevant to your current job
- £300 can be awarded at any time during the two year eligibility period for lifelong learning

The grant will be paid on production of a detailed receipt or invoice. It cannot be used to pay:

- for equipment (except workbooks or open learning)

- for job induction programmes
- for foreign language training unless this is a requirement of the job

If you are self-employed, you could use the Training Grant to go on general courses such as business administration or marketing, which you would use to run and develop your business.

To start the process of claiming the Training Grant, you must complete an Individual Learning Plan, which you can get from Jobcentre Plus. Once the Individual Training Plan has been approved your personal adviser will help you complete the Training Grant Application Form.

Note: It is up to you to take advantage of the Training Grant. You have two years in which to claim it.

Leaving the programme

The programme is voluntary so you can leave at any time without your benefits being affected.

New Deal for Lone Parents and the New Deal for Partners

Aim

The New Deal for Lone Parents (NDLP)[33] and the New Deal for Partners (NDP)[34] are designed to help lone parents and partners to improve their job readiness and increase their employment opportunities.

Eligibility

NDLP and NDP are voluntary programmes.[35]

Note: If you are eligible but choose not to take part your benefits or your partner's benefits or allowances will not be affected.

New Deal for Lone Parents

You are eligible to participate in NDLP if you:[36]

- are aged 16 or over
- have a dependent child under 16
- are not working or are working less than 16 hours a week
- are not an asylum seeker[37]

New Deal for Partners

You are eligible[38] if you are not working, or are working less than 24 hours a week, and your partner is claiming one of the appropriate benefits listed below:

- Jobseeker's Allowance
- Income Support
- Incapacity Benefit
- Severe Disablement Allowance
- Carer's Allowance
- Pension Credit

You are also eligible if you are not working, or working less than 16 hours a week, and you or your partner are receiving Working Tax Credit.

You are counted as a partner if you are married or living together as if you were married, and your partner is claiming benefit for you[39] (to find out about eligibility for these benefits see page 130).

Note: If your partner is on New Deal, Work Based Learning for Adults, Training for Work, or an Employment Zone, and you fulfil the other criteria, you are still eligible for NDP.

Note: You are not eligible if you have a Jobseeker's Allowance claim in your own right, or if you are making a Joint Claim for Jobseeker's Allowance.

Programme elements

The programme elements are made up of a series of interviews between you and the New Deal personal adviser. The number and length of interviews will depend on you. Your adviser will give you help and advice about moving into work or training, as well as in work support to 'smooth' the transition into work.

Role of the New Deal personal adviser

Your personal adviser will offer a package of advice and support including:

- advice about job vacancies, jobsearch, writing applications and CVs, and interview technique
- drawing up an Action Plan to monitor progress and record action
- advice about what benefits and incentives are available to help you when you start work, such as Childcare Subsidy and the Adviser Discretion Fund
- advice on childcare available locally (your adviser should have links to the local Sure Start for possible jobs, childcare help and so on)
- arrangement of training to update skills and payment of the Training Premium, if you are eligible
- an in-work support service

Help with Costs

When you attend an interview with a personal adviser or an employer you are eligible for help with the costs you incur. These include childcare and travel. You may also qualify for travel costs if you are attending approved training and other activities.

Training Premium

The Training Premium is a sum of £15, which is paid weekly in arrears, and is available to NDLP and NDP participants who undertake approved training for at least two hours a week.

Note: If you receive a Training Premium it is your responsibility to tell the Inland Revenue that you are in receipt of NDLP or NDP funding and the Training Premium.

In most cases it would be anticipated that participants on NDLP and NDP would attend at least 16 hours of training per week. These hours can be split between training and jobsearch according to your needs.

While on NDLP or NDP you will have access to a range of training provision. This includes:[40]

- training provision available via Work Based Learning for Adults (WBLA) and Training for Work (TfW) (except employed status WBLA and TfW) (see page 195)
- Work Trials and work experience (as part of an approved training course) (see page 344)
- NDYP Full Time Education and Training, Environmental Task Force, Voluntary Sector Options
- ND25 Plus IAP Education and Training
- ND25 Plus Self-Employment Provision, including advice, training, the development of a business plan, and 26 week test-trading
- ND Music Industry Consultant and Music Open Learning Provider
- ND Basic Skills Training (non-Short Intensive Basic Skills)
- ND jobsearch training, Key Skills training, IT training, Motivational training, vocational training

Childcare

You can also receive funding for childcare provision while you attend approved activities or interviews, so long as the childcare is either:

- provided by carers registered with Ofsted (payment cannot be authorised for childcare provision by friends or family members unless they are registered childminders)
- run on school premises or by the Local Authority

Childcare costs can be paid up to the first Tuesday in the September following your child's 15th birthday. The maximum amount of childcare costs payable depends on the amount of time you are spending attending approved activity or training, and on how many children you have.

Childcare Subsidy

The Childcare Subsidy is available to NDLP or NDP participants who move into part-time work of up to 16 hours. Help is available towards the cost of childcare while you are working, up to a maximum of £67.50 per week for one child and £100 per week for two or more children.[41] You are entitled to the Childcare Subsidy for a one off period of 42 weeks. There is no help towards travel costs when undertaking part-time work.

The Childcare Assist scheme entitles all lone parents moving into work through the NDLP to funding to cover the costs of childcare for the first week of work.[42]

Additional support

If you are a healthcare professional, you could go on the NHS-funded return to practice course. This is specifically aimed at encouraging former healthcare professionals to return to the NHS. These courses are often funded by the NHS.[43]

If you live in certain areas, further support may be available:

- Lone Parent Work Search Premium (LPWSP), available in eight Districts, giving lone parents an extra £20 per week for jobsearch[44]
- a Work Search Premium, available in eight Districts, giving those in a family in receipt of the Working Tax Credit who agree to join NDP, an extra £20 per week for jobsearch for up to 26 weeks[45]
- Lone Parent In Work Credit (LPIWC), giving an extra £40 a week in work credit for up to 52 weeks, to all parents claiming certain benefits (London Districts), or lone parents claiming certain benefits (outside London).[46] The In Work Credit is piloting in a total of 22 areas (extended to London in April 2005 and the South East in October 2005)

Leaving the programmes

Since the programmes are voluntary you can leave at any time without your benefits being affected.

New Deal for Disabled People

Aim

The New Deal for Disabled People (NDDP)[47] is a voluntary programme designed to help people in receipt of a disability or health related benefit to prepare for, find, and sustain paid work. NDDP Job Brokers will provide help with looking for a job and any support or training that is needed.

Eligibility

NDDP is a voluntary programme, so your benefits will not be affected if you choose not to participate.

There is no qualifying length of incapacity. To participate in NDDP you need to be between the age of 18 and pension age (60/65) and must be in direct receipt of one or more of the following[48] (to find out if you are eligible for these benefits see pages 110-116):

- Incapacity Benefit
- a benefit equivalent to Incapacity Benefit that has been imported into the UK under the European Community Regulations on the co-ordination of social security and the terms of the European Economic Area Agreement
- National Insurance credits on the grounds of incapacity (which may be awarded on their own or in addition to payments of income related benefits – Income Support, Housing Benefit, Council Tax Benefit, or War Pension)
- Income Support with a disability premium
- Income Support pending the result of an appeal against disallowance from Incapacity Benefit
- Severe Disablement Allowance
- Disability Living Allowance provided you are not in receipt of Jobseeker's Allowance, and you are not in paid work of 16 hours or more per week
- Housing Benefit with a disability premium, provided you are not in receipt of Jobseeker's Allowance, and you are not in paid work of 16

hours or more per week
- Council Tax Benefit with a disability premium, provided you are not in receipt of Jobseeker's Allowance, and you are not in paid work of 16 hours or more per week
- Industrial Injuries Disablement Benefit with an Unemployability Supplement

Note: If you are between 16 and 20 and registered with Connexions or the Careers Service you are eligible for NDDP. In some other circumstances you may be entitled to participate if you are 16 or 17, or beyond state retirement age.

NDDP Job Brokers

Jobcentre Plus contracts a range of organisations on a Local Authority basis to be Job Brokers. You need to register with a Job Broker to receive their services. It is up to you to choose a Job Broker. You can only register with one Broker at a time, and their services vary, so it is advisable to find out about all the different Brokers in your area and what services they offer before choosing one.

Jobcentre plus advisers can inform you about all the Job Brokers in your local area and the services they offer. This should happen at your initial Work Focused Interview (see page 226) if you are making a claim for a disability or health related benefit. There is no formal referral to a Job Broker, but after the interview, you may be contacted to check whether you have registered with a Job Broker. If you have decided not to, the adviser may offer you the opportunity for further interviews or referral to a disability employment adviser.

You can find out which Job Brokers are in your area either by ringing the NDDP Helpline on 0800 137 177 (or textphone 0800 435 550), or by visiting www.jobbrokersearch.gov.uk

Note: If, once you have registered with a Job Broker, you feel you are not progressing, or you are unhappy with the service they are offering, you may de-register and then re-register with a different Job Broker.

Programme elements

Once you have registered with a Job Broker you will have regular and direct contact with them regarding your search for work. The services they offer may include:

- offering careers advice
- assessing how taking a job would affect you financially, including information about in-work benefits
- offering basic training, for example on interview techniques
- matching you to employers, by looking at your skills, interests and experience
- helping and advising on adaptations such as special chairs or computer equipment, and how to fund them
- an in-work support service for you and your employer to make sure the first few months in the job go smoothly

Job Brokers have access to other Jobcentre Plus services and may refer you to another programme if you meet the eligibility criteria.

Leaving NDDP

There is no time limit for your participation on NDDP – you can continue to access support for as long as you want.

As NDDP is a voluntary programme you may choose to leave it at any time without it affecting your benefits. You are however encouraged to discuss any concerns with your Job Broker before you de-register.

Geographic Employment Programmes

The employment programmes above – such as the New Deals – are national programmes. There are also a number of programmes that are 'geographic' in the sense that they only operate in certain areas. The following looks at:

- Action Teams
- Employment Zones

- Pathways to Work
- Jobseeker Mandatory Activity
- Progress2Work
- Progress2Work – LinkUP
- Building on New Deal.

The eligibility criteria are similarly very dependent on claiming particular social security benefits. For a quick guide see the introduction to this chapter. For more detail see the section on benefits, pages 108-191.

Action Teams for Jobs

Aims

Action Teams for Jobs (ATs)[49] work in disadvantaged areas with high unemployment, and high numbers of people from ethnic minority backgrounds, to increase the numbers of people in work. They aim to secure sustainable employment for the most inactive clients in the local labour market. ATs are not a programme and as such there is no single description of what they offer. Action Teams currently operate in 65 areas. Direct funding for Action Teams will end in December 2006. Where there is still considered to be a local need for Action Teams local Jobcentre Plus managers will be expected to spend Deprived Areas Funding (DAF), a new localised funding stream, to continue Action Team activities.

Eligibility

ATs target all people out of work within the area in which they operate. There is a clear focus on those 'furthest away' from the labour market and those who experience 'significant barriers' to employment.

Note: No one is excluded from the help of an AT so long as they live within the area in which an AT operates. For this reason, clients are usually asked for their postcode when they first come into contact with an AT.

Features

One of the main characteristics of ATs is their flexibility in response to local problems. Each AT will identify what the local problems and key priority groups are for their services locally. They can provide flexible and tailored support to help to you overcome whatever problems you face in getting a job.

Through an AT you will be offered the support of an adviser. They will talk through your work options, and any barriers you face, and will offer practical advice, for example about writing CVs, interview technique, and financial assistance. They are all fully trained and work closely with local organisations and employers, to match you up to suitable vacancies. Your adviser will also continue to support you once you move into work.

There is no time limit to the support you can receive from your adviser. The support is entirely voluntary, so you can stop seeing your adviser whenever you want.

The main approach adopted by ATs falls under three headings:

Outreach

ATs aim to be proactive and reach people where they are. They operate from outreach sites on local housing estates. There are also 28 mobile units that take the work of the ATs out to people in the community.

Providing what people need

ATs offer individually tailored help from an adviser to help you secure and retain employment by for example, helping with financial assistance, help with debt management and budgeting, and individual employment related training packages.

Working with employers

ATs develop links with employers locally and help to tackle recruitment problems.

Note: From 2007 new DAF funding will continue to support the localised approach that Action Teams have pursued, even where it is not used to continue Action Teams.

Operational areas[50]

Action Teams currently operate in 65 areas, these are:

- Barnsley and Rotherham
- Barrow-in-Furness
- Birmingham North
- Birmingham South
- Blackburn with Darwen
- Blaenau Gwent
- Brent
- Brighton and Hove
- Caerphilly
- Chester-le-Street
- Cornwall
- Doncaster
- Dundee, City
- Easington
- East Ayrshire
- Glasgow Central and East
- Glasgow North
- Glasgow South
- Glasgow West
- Greenwich
- Hackney
- Halton
- Haringey
- Hartlepool
- Highlands and Islands
- Islington
- Kingston Upon Hull, City
- Knowsley
- Lambeth
- Lewisham
- Liverpool Central
- Liverpool North
- Liverpool South
- Manchester Central
- Manchester North
- Manchester South
- Merthyr Tydfil
- Middlesborough
- Neath and Port Talbot
- Newcastle Upon Tyne
- Newham
- North Lanarkshire
- North West Wales
- Nottingham
- Pembrokeshire
- Plymouth
- Redcar and Cleveland
- Rhondda Cynon Taff
- Salford
- Sefton
- Sheffield
- South Tyneside
- Southwark
- St Helens
- Stockton-on-Tees
- Sunderland
- Thanet
- Tower Hamlets
- West Wales and the Valleys
- Waltham Forest
- Wansbeck
- Wear Valley
- West Dunbartonshire
- Wirral
- Wolverhampton

Employment Zones

Aim

Employment Zones (EZ)[51] aim to help long term unemployed people to move into sustainable employment. The thirteen Zones operate in fifteen areas of the country which have high levels of long-term unemployment. Each Zone is designed slightly differently, depending on the contractor involved, but all operate within the same broad structure.

The Department of Work and Pensions contracts service providers to run EZs. There are two types of contract – single provider Employment Zones where one contractor providers the service, and multiple provider Employment Zones where more than one contractor provides the service.

Eligibility[52]

Compulsory participation

If you are aged between 25 and 60, you must take part in Employment Zones if:

- you live in an Employment Zone area
- you have been claiming Jobseeker's Allowance for 18 out of the last 21 months

If you are aged between 18 and 24, you must take part in Employment Zones if:

- you live in an Employment Zone area
- you have previously participated in New Deal for Young People
- you have been claiming Jobseeker's Allowance for at least six months without breaks totalling more than 28 days

Note: You are not eligible if you have an outstanding referral to another programme, or are currently being sanctioned, disallowed or awaiting a decision outcome.

Note: Once you have started on the Zone you can't leave to join another Jobcentre Plus programme.

Early entry

In some circumstances individuals are allowed early entry to EZ's. Personal advisers use their discretion to determine which customers enter early [53] but you may be eligible if you fall into one of the groups below:[54]

Early entrant groups include:

- people with a physical or mental disability
- people who need help with reading, writing or numbers
- people whose first language is not English, Welsh or Gaelic
- anyone who is a lone parent who does not live with a partner and is responsible for at least one child living in their household
- people who have served in the regular armed forces
- people who were looked after as a child by a local authority
- people with a criminal record
- people with a drug problem
- people who have participated in Progress2Work
- people who have been told by the Home Office that they are officially a refugee
- people who have been given Exceptional Leave to enter the United Kingdom by an immigration office

If you are an early entrant in a multiple provider EZ you will not be able to choose which contractor you go to. The contractor will be randomly selected for you. Once you start the EZ you must remain on the programme.

Lone parents

If you are a lone parent living in an EZ area you can volunteer for EZ help as long as:

- You are not working more than 16 hours a week
- You are not receiving Jobseeker's Allowance
- You are not an asylum seeker

WORKING IN THE UK: NEWCOMER'S HANDBOOK *2ND EDITION*

Note: You can choose to leave at any time and your benefits will not be affected.

In London, EZ provision has replaced the New Deal for Lone Parents. These Zones are delivered by multiple providers and you can choose which one you work with.

In EZ areas outside London, you can choose between New Deal for Lone Parents and any of the EZ providers in a multiple provider area, or New Deal for Lone Parents and the EZ provider in a single provider area.

Note: If you choose to participate in the EZ you can no longer participate in the New Deal for Lone Parents. If you are a lone parent and fulfil the criteria for compulsory participation as written above, you must take part in the EZ.

Note: If you live in an Employment Zone area, and you are claiming Pension Credit[55] you may volunteer for Employment Zone help.

People claiming Pension Credit

If you are claiming Pension Credit and are not working more than 16 hours a week you can volunteer for EZ help.

Note: You can choose to leave at any time and your benefits will not be affected.

In the Multiple Provider EZs, people claiming Pension Credit can choose which of the contractors they wish to work with.

Key elements

There are three stages within the Employment Zone. Each contractor has flexibility to design their own programme, while meeting the essential requirements outlined below.

Stage One

Jobcentre Plus is responsible for identifying, referring and re-referring eligible jobseekers to the Employment Zone.

Stage One lasts up to 4 weeks. You are appointed a personal adviser by the EZ contractor. They will help you draw up an individually tailored Action Plan. An Action Plan is an agreement between you and the EZ contractor. The Action Plan is an agreed plan of structured activities that will help you move closer to work. When this is agreed the EZ Contractor notifies Jobcentre Plus and you move to Stage Two, where the agreed activities are carried out.

Stage Two

This stage can last up to 26 weeks. The contractor will enable you to carry out whatever activity was outlined in your individual Action Plan. You may receive financial assistance with travel and clothes for interviews. You may also receive training or assistance with moving into self-employment. You will also carry out an intensive jobsearch.

During this stage you will be paid your benefits by the provider and will no longer need to attend Jobcentre Plus.

Stage Three

Stage Three lasts 13 weeks and begins once you have started work. The contractor will provide in-work support to help you sustain work.

The EZ contractor receives a payment when you start work and a further payment if you are still in employment after thirteen weeks. As a result the contractor has a strong incentive to find you a job that lasts.

Follow On

If you are a compulsory participant in an EZ and you have not found a job by the end of Stage 2 you will return to the Jobcentre Plus office to claim benefit.

Note: You can volunteer to get help from the EZ for another 22 weeks.

Benefits and entitlements

If you are a voluntary participant your benefits will not be affected. If you are a compulsory participant, you will continue to receive your benefits or entitlements from Jobcentre Plus during Stage One, and during Stage Two you will receive from the contractor payments that are equivalent to benefit payments.

Leaving early

If you leave the EZ during Stage One and sign on within thirteen weeks, you will be referred back to the EZ immediately. If you leave during Stage One and don't sign on within thirteen weeks, you must re-qualify for the EZ.

If you leave during Stage Two or Three and your time on the EZ combined with your time in employment comes to less than 22 weeks, you will immediately be re-referred to the EZ contractor. If you leave during Stage Two or Three and your time on the EZ combined with your time in employment comes to more than 22 weeks, you must re-qualify for the EZ.

Note: If you are a compulsory participant, your benefits may be affected if you fail to do what is expected of you whilst on the EZ. Reasons for benefits sanctions might include:

- failing to turn up to appointments
- failing to comply with your Action Plan
- dismissal from an employment programme
- leaving early

Pilot areas[56]

The single provider Employment Zones are:

- Brighton and Hove
- Doncaster and Bassetlaw
- Heads of the Valleys, Caerphilly and Torfaen
- Middlesborough, Redcar and Cleveland
- North West Wales
- Nottingham
- Plymouth

The multiple provider Employment Zones are:

- Glasgow
- Liverpool and Sefton
- Birmingham
- Tower Hamlets and Newham
- Brent and Haringey
- Southwark.

Pathways to Work

Aim

The Pathways to Work Pilots[57] aim to help disabled people and people with health conditions claiming incapacity benefits to return to work.

Eligibility[58]

If you are making a new or repeat claim for Incapacity Benefit in one of the pilot areas you will automatically be screened for eligibility to participate in Pathways to Work. If you are already receiving Incapacity Benefit or Income Support on health grounds you may be contacted to take part.

Note: If you are living in a pilot area and are receiving incapacity benefits you can volunteer to take part by contacting Jobcentre Plus. Pathways to Work is currently being rolled out nationally, and will be available in every Jobcentre Plus district by April 2008.

Programme elements

Mandatory work-focused interviews

If you started an IB claim (excluding Personal Capability Assessment exempt cases) in the two years before the respective pilots went live, you will have to take part in six mandatory Work Focused Interviews. These are likely to be with the same adviser at monthly intervals. During the interviews the adviser will help you to identify future life and work goals and any barriers to achieving them, and will support you in overcoming these barriers. You will agree an Action Plan with your adviser that outlines the activities that you will undertake. This will be reviewed at each meeting.

Note: From October 2006 in some areas IB claimants whose claims started over 2 years ago will also be mandated to take part.

Other elements

If you are a new or existing customer in a pilot area, you may be entitled to the following support:

- a job preparation premium of £20 per week for a maximum of 26 weeks if you agree an Action Plan and participate in activity that supports a return to work
- a Return to Work Credit of £40 per week if you move into work of 16 hours or more per week and earn less than £15,000 per year. This lasts for 52 weeks
- access to existing training, employment programmes, and financial help, including the Adviser Discretion Fund (ADF) (see page 184)
- Condition Management Programmes – short courses run by local NHS providers that aim to help you to understand and manage your health condition

Pilot areas[59]

The current pilot areas are:	From April 2006:
Argyll	Barnsley Rotherham and Doncaster
Bridgend	County Durham
Bute	Lanarkshire and East Dunbarton
Cumbria	Liverpool and the Wirral
Cynon	Manchester and Salford
Derbyshire	Sunderland
Essex	Swansea and West Wales

East Lancashire	
Gateshead	**From October 2006:**
Glasgow	Eastern Valleys
Inverclyde	Greater Mersey
Lancashire West	Staffordshire
Refrewshire	
Rhondda	
South Tyneside	
Somerset	
Taff	
Tees Valley	

Pathways to Work is set to be rolled out across the rest of the country during 2007. It is likely that it will be delivered by private and voluntary sector providers. In most areas it will continue to focus on new claimants, although existing claimants can voluntarily join the programme, and in some areas will be mandated to join.

Jobseeker Mandatory Activity

Aim

The Jobseeker Mandatory Activity (JMA) Pilot[60] aims to help customers who are aged 25 or over to become better prepared for work, and to find work.

Eligibility

If you live in a pilot area, are aged 25 or over, and have been claiming Jobseeker's Allowance or National Insurance Credits for six months, you will be required to participate.

Note: If you do not participate, your benefits may be affected.

Programme Elements

The programme consists of:

- a three-day motivational course, that will be delivered by external providers, and will help you improve your job-search skills, explore your job goals, and draw up a personal Action Plan
- three mandatory follow-up interviews with a personal adviser who will help you to pursue your Action Plan and actively search for a job

Leaving early

The programme is mandatory for those who fulfil the eligibility criteria, so if you leave early or fail to participate, your benefits are likely to be affected.

Pilot areas[61]

In April 2006, the JMA pilot will be launched in:
Bedfordshire and Hertfordshire
Berkshire, Buckinghamshire and Oxfordshire
Cheshire and Warrington
Cumbria
Lanarkshire and East Dunbartonshire
South East Wales
South London
Staffordshire
Surrey and Sussex
West Yorkshire

Progress2Work

Aim

Progress2Work[62] is a national programme aiming to support people with a history of drug misuse to take up and remain engaged in mainstream provision, such as New Deal and Work Based Learning for Adults, and to secure and sustain employment.

The programme has three key strands:

- contracted specialist providers of support, guidance and advice
- awareness training for Jobcentre Plus staff so they are better able to identify and refer appropriate customers
- a co-ordinator in every Jobcentre Plus District who links up key local partners and ensures that drug treatment and employment services are joined up effectively

Eligibility

You are eligible[63] for the programme if you are disadvantaged in the labour market because of drug misuse, but have made sufficient progress in your recovery to be drug free or stabilised. This includes people who have completed a drug treatment programme, who are undergoing a drug treatment programme, or who are identified by Jobcentre Plus as recovering drug misusers.

In addition, you must be claiming one of the following benefits:

- Jobseeker's Allowance (see page 130)
- Income Support (see page 134)
- Incapacity Benefit (see page 141)
- Severe Disablement Allowance (see page 151)
- Disability Living Allowance (see page 149)
- Pension Credit (see page 138)[64]

In exceptional cases you may be able to participate even if you are not claiming any benefits.

Note: Participation in Progress2Work will not affect your benefits.

Programme Elements

Specialist Employment Worker

If you participate in Progress2Work you will be allocated an employment support worker. They will work in consultation with other agencies with whom you are involved. They will:

- assess your employment and drug related history and any other factors that might impact on your chances of moving into and sustaining work
- work with you to draw up an individual action plan which will be updated to include planned and undertaken activities
- help you to prepare you for work, for example through providing confidence building training and life skills
- help you to access specialist agencies to address any other issues that are acting as barriers to work, such as debt, housing, health and residual criminal justice issues

Once you are ready to access the agreed employment measures, the employment worker will negotiate with the mainstream provider to make sure that the content and pace are suitable. The employment worker will continue to support you to complete the provision, and where the original plan is not working out, negotiate a revised programme.

Support will continue for up to 13 weeks after you have moved into work.

Leaving the Programme

There is no fixed time for participation in the programme. Providers are expected to assess progress and take appropriate decisions about continuation. Progress2Work is a voluntary programme so you can drop out at any time without your benefits being affected.

Progress2Work-LinkUP

Jobcentre Plus has also introduced Progress2Work-LinkUP. Progress2Work-LinkUP provides employment-related support services for people facing significant labour market disadvantage due to an offending background, homelessness or alcohol misuse. It operates in a similar way to the Progress2Work model.

It currently operates in the following areas:
London South
Liverpool
Tayside
Fife
Bridgend Rhondda Cynon Taff
Rotherham / Barnsley
Bristol
Bradford
Manchester
Lancashire West
Berkshire
Birmingham and Solihull
Sheffield
Greater Nottingham
Gateshead and South Tyneside
Eastern Valleys
Glasgow
Wakefield
Lancashire East
Knowsley and Sefton
Leicester
Sussex

Building on New Deal

Aim

Through Building on New Deal (BoND)[65] the Government aims to develop the New Deal model. One of the main objectives is to increase local discretion and flexibility so that provision meets the needs of the local labour market.

Programme elements

Although many current programmes will be replaced, there will still be core entitlements and requirements – for example, participation in provision will still be mandatory after a given period of claiming Jobseeker's Allowance.

Note: There is currently no fixed timetable for the roll out of BoND

Current provision will be replaced with a 'flexible menu' of modular provision (individual blocks of learning). The modular format means that advisers will be able to build a programme combining different elements that are tailored to your requirements and capabilities. Some examples of modules are:

- job search
- careers guidance
- mentoring
- Gateway to Work (see page 235)
- work experience
- literacy and numeracy
- self-employment provision
- specialist support for those with particular barriers to work, for example, those with histories of drug and alcohol misuse

Where appropriate provision is not available, district managers will be able to work with providers and partners to develop innovative schemes that meet the needs of individual customers and the local labour market.

Pilot areas

At the time of writing, the pilot was planned to start in the following areas:
Ayrshire, Dumfries, Galloway and Inverclyde
Buckinghamshire and Oxfordshire
Cardiff and Vale
Cheshire and Warrington
Cornwall
Northamptonshire
North East London

Endnotes

[1] Jobcentre Plus Decision Makers' Guide, vol 1, ch 5

[2] Reg 3, Social Security (Jobcentre Plus Interviews) Regulations 2002

[3] DWP, 'Changes to Work Focused Interviews' [December 2005] Touchbase 41, 23

[4] Reg 2(1,2), Social Security (Jobcentre Plus Interviews for Partners) Regulations 2003

[5] DWP, 'Changes to Work Focused Interviews' [December 2005] Touchbase 41, 23

[6] Reg 11(2), Social Security (Jobcentre Plus Interviews) Regulations 2002

[7] DWP, 'Changes to Work Focused Interviews' [December 2005] Touchbase 41, 23

[8] DWP, 'Changes to Work Focused Interviews' [December 2005] Touchbase 41, 23

[9] Reg 3(1), Social Security (Jobcentre Plus Interviews for Partners) Regulations 2003

[10] Reg 4(2), Social Security (Jobcentre Plus Interviews) Regulations 2002

[11] Jobcentre Plus Provider Guidance ch 11, and Jobcentre Plus Decision Makers' Guide, vol 3, ch 14

[12] Jobcentre Plus Provider Guidance, ch 11, para 2

[13] DWP 'New Deal streamlining changes' [June 2004] Touchbase 35, 20

[14] DWP. New Deal for Young People and Long-Term Unemployed People Aged 25+: Background Information. In DWP Resource Centre. Retrieved 28 February, 2006, from http://www.dwp.gov.uk/asd/ndyp.asp

[15] DWP. New Deal for employers. In Jobcentre Plus New Deal. Retrieved 28 February, 2006, from http://www.jobcentreplus.gov.uk/JCP/Employers/Ourservices/Programmes/New%5FDeal/

[16] DWP 'New Deal streamlining changes' [June 2004] Touchbase 35, 20

[17] Jobcentre Plus Provider Guidance, ch 11, para 75 and 77, and Jobcentre Plus Decision Makers' Guide, vol 3, ch 14, 14225

[18] Jobcentre Plus Provider Guidance, ch 6, 134-190

[19] Jobcentre Plus Provider Guidance, ch 6, 134

[20] See Jobcentre Plus Provider Guidance, and Jobcentre Plus Decision Makers' Guide for more information

[21] Jobcentre Plus Decision Makers' Guide, vol 3, ch14, 14335

[22] DWP 'Extra help for older people' [September 2004] Touchbase 36, 6

[23] DWP 'New Deal streamlining changes' [June 2004] Touchbase 35, 20

[24] DWP. New Deal for Young People and Long-Term Unemployed People Aged 25+: Background Information. In DWP Resource Centre. Retrieved 28 February, 2006, from http://www.dwp.gov.uk/asd/ndyp.asp

[25] Jobcentre Plus Provider Guidance, ch 9, para 8

[26] DWP. New Deal 25 Plus. In Jobcentre Plus New Deal. Retrieved 28 February, 2006, from http://www.jobcentreplus.gov.uk/jcp/Customers/New_Deal/New_Deal_for_25_plus/Dev_011413.xml.html

[27] DWP. New Deal for employers. In Jobcentre Plus New Deal. Retrieved 28 February, 2006, from http://www.jobcentreplus.gov.uk/JCP/Employers/Ourservices/Programmes/New%5FDeal/

[28] Reg 75(1)(a)(iv) Jobseekers Allowance Regulations

[29] DWP. New Deal for 50 Plus. In Jobcentre Plus New Deals. Retrieved 28 February 2005, from http://www.jobcentreplus.gov.uk/jcp/Customers/New_Deal/New_Deal_for_50_plus/index.html and Jobcentre Plus Provider Guidance, ch 1, para 20

[30] Jobcentre Plus Provider Guidance, ch 1, para 20

[31] DWP. New Deal for 50 Plus. In Jobcentre Plus New Deals. Retrieved 28 February 2005, from http://www.jobcentreplus.gov.uk/jcp/Customers/New_Deal/New_Deal_for_50_plus/index.html

[32] Prime. Roadblock on the Route from Incapacity Benefit to Test-Trading'. In Prime What's New?, retrieved 28 February, 2005.

[33] Jobcentre Plus Provider Guidance, ch 13, and Decision Makers' Guide, vol 3, ch 14

[34] Jobcentre Plus Provider Guidance, ch 14, and Decision Makers' Guide, vol 3, ch 14

[35] Jobcentre Plus Decision Maker's Guide, vol 3, ch 14, 14402

36. DWP. New Deal for Lone Parents. In DWP Resource Centre. Retrieved 28 February, 2005, from http://www.dwp.gov.uk/asd/asd1/ndlp/NDLP_Background_Information.pdf

37. Refugee Council. Government Training Scheme. In Refugee Council Info Centre. Retrieved 28 February, 2005, from http://www.refugeecouncil.org.uk/infocentre/entit/sentit006.htm

38. DWP, 'New Deal for Partners – new eligibility rules' [September 2004] Touchbase 36, 9

39. Reg 2(1) Social Security (Jobcentre Plus Interviews for Partners) Regulation 2003

40. Jobcentre Plus Provider Guidance, ch 13, para 1 and 14, and Jobcentre Plus Provider Guidance, ch 14, para 2 and 19

41. BBC. Paying for childcare. In BBC Parenting. Retrieved 28 February, from http://www.bbc.co.uk/parenting/childcare/paying_loneparents.shtml

42. HM Treasury, Child Poverty Review (Spending Review 2004), ch 3

43. NHS. Frequently Asked Questions, in NHS Careers. Retrieved 28 February, 2005, from http://www.nhscareers.nhs.uk/nhs/cb_faqs.html

44. DWP 'Disregard of Lone Parent Work Search Premium and Lone Parent In Work Credit' [2004] Housing Benefit and Council Tax Benefit Circular, HB/CTB A9

45. HM Treasury, Budget 2004, ch 4,

46. DWP 'Disregard of In Work Credit [2005] Housing Benefit and Council Tax Benefit Circular, HB/CTB G3

47. DWP. 'New Deal for Disabled People'. In Jobcentre Plus New Deals. Retrieved 2 March 2005, from http://www.jobcentreplus.gov.uk/jcp/Customers/New_Deal/New_Deal_for_Disabled_People/index.html

48. Directgov. 'New Deal for Disabled People'. In Directgov Disabled People. Retrieved 2 March 2005, from http://www.direct.gov.uk/DisabledPeople/Employment/WorkSchemesAndProgrammes/WorkSchemesArticles/fs/en?CONTENT_ID=4001963&chk=cV3TWD

49. DWP, 'Action Team for Jobs'. In Jobcentre Plus Action Team for Jobs. Retrieved, 3 March 2006, from http://www.jobcentreplus.gov.uk/jcp/Customers/Programmesandservices/Actionteams/index.html

50. DWP, 'Action Team for Jobs'. In Jobcentre Plus Action Team for Jobs. Retrieved, 3 March 2006, from http://www.jobcentreplus.gov.uk/jcp/Customers/Programmesandservices/Actionteams/index.html

51. DWP, 'Employment Zones: background information'. In DWP Resources. Retrieved, 3 March 2006, http://www.dwp.gov.uk/asd/emp_zones/EZ_Background_Information.pdf and DWP, 'Employment Zones'. Retrieved, 3 March 2006, from http://www.employmentzones.gov.uk/

[52] DWP, 'Employment Zones – changes to the programme' [June 2004] Touchbase 35, 18

[53] DWP. 'Employment Zones: background information'. In DWP Resources. Retrieved, 3 March 2006, http://www.dwp.gov.uk/asd/emp_zones/EZ_Background_Information.pdf

[54] DWP, New Deal for Young People and Long-Term Unemployed People Aged 25+: Background Information. In DWP Resource Centre. Retrieved 28 February, 2006, from http://www.dwp.gov.uk/asd/ndyp.asp

[55] DWP, 'Extra help for older people' [September 2004] Touchbase 36, 6

[56] DWP, 'Employment Zones'. Retrieved, 3 March 2006, from http://www.employmentzones.gov.uk/

[57] DWP, 'Pathways to Work'. In Jobcentre Plus Pathways to Work. Retrieved, 6 March 2006, from http://www.jobcentreplus.gov.uk/jcp/customers/programmesandservices/pathways_to_work/index.html

[58] DWP, 'Pathways to work' [September 2004] Touchbase 36, 17 and DWP, 'Pathways to Work' [June 2005] Touchbase 39, 10

[59] DWP, 'Pathways to Work'. In Jobcentre Plus Pathways to Work. Retrieved, 6 March 2006, from http://www.jobcentreplus.gov.uk/jcp/customers/programmesandservices/pathways_to_work/index.html and HM Treasury, Budget 2005, chapter 4

[60] DWP, 'Jobseeker Mandatory Activity' [March 2006] Touchbase 42, 7 and HM Treasury, Budget 2005, chapter 4

[61] DWP, 'Jobseeker Mandatory Activity' [March 2006] Touchbase 42, 7

[62] DWP. 'Progress2Work'. In Jobcentre Plus Progress2Work. Retrieved 2 March 2006, from http://www.jobcentreplus.gov.uk/jcp/Partners/progress2work/index.html

[63] DWP. 'Progress2Work'. In Jobcentre Plus Progress2Work. Retrieved 2 March 2006, from http://www.jobcentreplus.gov.uk/jcp/Partners/progress2work/index.html

[64] DWP, 'Extra help for older people' [September 2004] Touchbase 36, 6

[65] DWP, 'Building on New Deal' [September 2004] Touchbase 36, 12

Employment programmes

7 How can I improve my English?

Helen Sunderland, LLU+

What is ESOL and where can I find ESOL courses?

ESOL stands for English for Speakers of Other Languages. There are lots of places that run ESOL courses. You can find ESOL courses:

- in Further Education (FE) colleges
- in Learndirect centres (see page 202)
- in adult and community learning centres
- in organisations that provide training for work (training providers)
- through your local Jobcentre Plus office
- in some universities which provide ESOL at higher levels. Many now provide language support (see below)
- in the workplace – some employers now provide ESOL

If you want to find a course, under 'How do I get on to a course?' on page 286.

ESOL courses are aimed at people who intend to live and/or work in England. Some organisations also provide English as a Foreign Language (EFL) courses, aimed at short term visitors and students. In schools, English for speakers of other languages is called EAL (English as an Additional Language).

In England, Wales and Northern Ireland, ESOL courses follow a national curriculum at different levels. The first five levels are currently funded under the Skills for Life initiative along with literacy and numeracy courses. These levels are named Entry 1, Entry 2, Entry 3, Level 1 and Level 2. Entry 1 is the lowest level and Level 2 is the highest of these five. Higher level courses do exist, but at the moment are not publicly funded.

Benefits of ESOL

There are many benefits to learning another language. In the UK, research has demonstrated that fluency in English is associated with a rise in the chances of getting a job and in progressing to higher paid jobs, as well as helping you settle more quickly in the UK.

Can I learn ESOL?

Anyone can learn ESOL provided they can find a course. However, to qualify for free ESOL courses, there are a number of requirements (see below for details).

While officially everyone who lives and works in the UK is entitled to ESOL, in practice there are more opportunities in some areas than others. In rural areas, courses are often for a few hours a week only. In the big cities, courses are often full.

Do I have to pay for ESOL?

At the time of writing, ESOL courses in FE and ACL up to and including level 2 are free for:

- asylum seekers (but see asylum seekers section below)
- refugees
- people who have been ordinarily resident (see page 122) in the UK or the EU for three years
- spouses of UK residents who have been in the country for one year

It is probably best to check that this is still the case, as changes are currently being discussed.

Some ESOL courses above level 2 are publicly funded. If this is not the case with the course you want to do then you will have to pay for it.

For ESOL courses in the adult training sector see page 195.

Asylum seekers

For asylum seekers, the courses are usually free but charges are sometimes made for higher level courses (Level 3 and above). Some organisations also offer to reimburse travel costs and provide childcare facilities.

There is no limit to the number of hours you can study English and continue to receive support from NASS. Proof of immigration status in the form of an Application Registration Card (ARC) card is usually needed.

ESOL courses can be for general English, but may also be combined with a particular skill or vocational area: for example, ESOL with IT or ESOL for health and social care. Many of these will be available although you may have to pay for some specialist courses. It is best to discuss what ESOL course is appropriate with a student or training adviser where the course is being run. For more information see 'How can I get language help?' on page 74 in the chapter for refugees and asylum seekers.

Note: The Home Office has recently clarified that asylum seekers are allowed to engage in unpaid or voluntary work whilst awaiting their asylum decision (see page 73).

How do I get on to a course?

There is no central source of information about ESOL courses. Local careers advice centres or Learning and Skills Councils can help you find your nearest learning centre or college, or you can try your local further education college. If you are also looking for work, ask the Jobcentre Plus office to refer you to a training provider that runs ESOL or training for work with language support (see below).

If you are working, your union learning rep (Representative) may be able to give you information about courses. If you are in work you may also be in an Employer Training Pilot (ETP) area which would mean you may be able to get support to improve your English at work (see page 215). Equally, you may access ESOL courses in your local college even if you are in work through ETP area funding.

The Learndirect helpline 0800 101 901 or the Learndirect website http://catalogue.learndirect.co.uk/browse/sfl/category25/ can tell you about Learndirect ESOL courses in England, Wales and Northern Ireland. For more information about Scotland, see the later section in this chapter.

If none of these can help, try the local library for more information.

Interviews and waiting lists

When you apply for a course, most places offering courses will arrange for you to have an interview and will then either place you straight on a course or put you on a waiting list.

If you are in an area with long waiting lists, it may be best to have your name on more than one list.

Teacher, trainer or tutor?

The language of education and training can be confusing. Further education usually talks about education, teaching and teachers. A course tutor is usually the person in charge of the course and the person you should go to if you have any queries. The course tutor may or may not also be your teacher.

In Training for Work in Scotland, the person who teaches you is usually called a trainer and the course is called a training programme.

If you are studying in Further Education (FE) you are known as a learner, in a training scheme you are a trainee, and in a university you are a student.

Can I get qualifications in ESOL?

ESOL students are encouraged to take Skills for Life qualifications at the appropriate level for them. The college or training provider which runs the courses will organise the exam entry.

If you want to take higher level qualifications, for instance IELTS for university entry, or professional qualifications, you may need to pay for them. Since January 2006 some of these have been government funded, you will need to check this when you apply for a course.

What is language support?

If you are studying on a vocational or academic course at college or with a training provider, it may be possible to get additional support for your English. This is often called language support.

Language support comes in different formats; it may be a workshop, as one-to-one teaching, or having an English teacher working alongside the subject teacher for some of the time. Some universities also provide language support for students on their courses.

How do I get language support?

Not everyone provides language support, so it is a good idea to ask about it before you sign up for a course. If you have not done so, but find you are having difficulties with English when you are on the course, ask your course tutor. Most FE colleges will screen learners to find out whether they need some help with their language, literacy and numeracy needs before they take them on a full-time course.

Do I have to pay for language support?

At the time of writing, language support on publicly funded courses is free. You should check with the organisation providing your course that this is still the case and that you do not have to pay extra for language support.

What will I study in ESOL or language support?

In most ESOL courses you should have a chance to study speaking, listening, reading and writing. Some courses specialise and this should be made clear to you at your interview. For instance, there are ESOL courses which specialise in learning, reading and writing, in learning

English for job-search, or English and study skills. Many organisations now run ESOL with citizenship courses (see the section on UK citizenship, page 550). Some organisations provide courses where English is taught at the same time as other skills, such as computing.

In language support, the English you learn is likely to be closely associated with the English you need for your vocational or academic course.

You may find the teaching methods in England different from those you are used to.

How long will it take me to learn English?

The answer to this is 'it depends'. It has been estimated that it will take an average learner around 300 notional hours of study per ESOL level.

The following are likely to help:

- learning English for 10 or more hours per week
- using English in your everyday life
- doing homework
- having learnt languages before
- being able to read and write the script that English uses
- being highly motivated to learn

Translation assistance for people whose first language is not English

It is best to use a trained interpreter if your first language is not English. Children, relatives and friends should not be used as interpreters.

There are some telephone based interpretation services (for example, Language Line). These can be useful for emergency interpreting or for very brief contact.

Public Services

Public services should arrange and pay for any interpreting which is required. Public services should not expect you to provide your own interpreter. If they don't you should make a complaint as this will be less favourable service and therefore discriminatory. It is also likely to be against their policies.

A number of websites offer leaflets and information about various public services and legal rights in languages other than English. For example, www.multikulti.org.uk and www.refugeecouncil.org.uk

Benefit claim forms are not available in languages other than English but can be completed with the help of an interpreter. The Department for Work and Pensions and local authorities should help you complete these if you have any difficulties with English – you can complain if they don't when you have asked. Please see page 113 under 'interpreters' for further information.

ESOL in Scotland, Rob Whelton and Philomena De Lima, Policy Web

At present, there is no overall policy on ESOL provision in Scotland. The provision that exists is fragmented and lacks overall coordination. However, there are a number of different organisations which may offer courses in your area:

- Adult Basic Education Department of your Local Authority
- Further or Higher Education Institutions
- Trade Unions
- a number of voluntary sector providers

A wide range of classes may be available. These may include:

- English language courses at levels ranging from very basic to advanced, which may in some cases lead to recognised qualifications.
- classes specialising in English language for academic or employment purposes

- college provision for English as a Foreign Language (EFL) with the option of obtaining relevant qualifications

Tuition may be available in a workplace, college, or community-based environment.

In 2006 the Scottish Executive plans to implement an 'Adult ESOL Strategy for Scotland'. This will aim to coordinate ESOL providers within a common framework. It will also seek to ensure 'that all Scottish residents for whom English is not a first language have the opportunity to access high quality English language provision'.[1]

Provision is likely to be free to those who meet the Executive's criteria: 'A person who has little or no literacy in his/her own mother-tongue and who has little or no literacy in English and whose spoken English may range from basic to fluent'.[2]

If you are an asylum seeker and want to attend a college to access ESOL provision, you are eligible for an automatic fee waiver for any ESOL course that you are attending.

If you are not an asylum seeker and are not primarily in the EU for education purposes, you will be means-tested for a fee waiver for a part-time ESOL course at a college.

The Further Education Hardship Fund can provide assistance for ESOL students:

- when emergency financial support is needed for the student to get to college and take part in the course
- by providing a childcare place while the student is attending an ESOL course, if no other source of childcare is available

Given the present nature of ESOL provision in Scotland, there are a number of means of contacting providers mostly operating in local communities. Some suggested points of contact are:

- Edinburgh: Stevenson College (0131 5354700)
- Glasgow: Anniesland College (0141 3576063)

- Aberdeen: Aberdeen College (01224 612 000)
- Inverness: Spectrum Centre (01463 221842)

At the time of writing, the Open University is preparing a 'Diversity Pack' which is likely to provide guidance on ESOL in Scotland. Contact the OU on 0131 226 3851 for more information.

Further information

DfES (2001) Adult ESOL Core Curriculum, available from DfES Publications 0845 60 222 60

LSC website www.lsc.gov.uk for the latest information on funded courses.

Endnotes

[1] Adult ESOL Strategy for Scotland, Consultation Paper Enterprise, Transport and Lifelong Learning Department, Scottish Executive, July 2005

[2] ibid

How can I improve my English?

7

8 Finding and starting work

Beryl Randall, Employability Forum

Finding work

There are many different ways to find out where the vacancies are in the UK. This includes looking in national, local and trade press, making use of contacts through friends, family and community groups, using recruitment agencies (both on the street and on the internet) and in Jobcentre Plus offices. Jobs are also advertised in shop windows, in newsagents, community centres and libraries.

Libraries and college careers services will stock copies of newspapers, both national and local, and some will also have trade/professional magazines. Most national press and recruitment agencies are also available free of charge over the internet and have search tools you can use to find vacancies. Most libraries have free internet access.

For many people finding work is not so much of a problem as finding appropriate work that meets their skills and experience from their home country. This is particularly true for refugees and there are specialist voluntary organisations that can help to point you in the right direction, though these are mainly based in London.

Often there will also be a contact within the relevant professional body, for example the British Medical Association or the Royal College of

Nursing, or you may need to go through a national organisation such as the Refugee Council to find projects in your area.

For a list of useful organisations, see the further information chapter, page 556.

Applying for work

The labour market in the UK is competitive and unless you already have work arranged before you come to the UK it is likely that you will have to apply for several posts before you find a job.

The main methods for applying for a job are by CV (Curriculum Vitae – see below) or application form. Both the CV and application form will give approximately the same information to an employer, but an application form gives you space to describe your experience, showing how it fits with the criteria the employer is looking for. It is important to show how the criteria in the job and person specifications match your skills and experience. Unless the application form gives this as an option, you should not send a copy of your CV either as extra information or as a substitute for answering questions. As with CVs, it is usual to list education and employment with the most recent first, and a brief description of what the role involved. When you are describing achievements and responsibilities you should bear in mind what the employer is looking for and highlight those that are most appropriate. Some forms have an open section for you to complete. Usually there is some guidance to show what the employer is looking for, but if not and depending on what has already been asked in the form you could outline:

- skills and experience that are directly relevant to the post you are applying for (not necessarily all from work experience, but also from leisure interests or community work)
- achievements to date
- extenuating circumstances

Some application forms are completed online, others are paper-based. In all cases it is helpful to make copies of the forms to practise on and later, to get your answers checked by an adviser or a friend if you can.

An application form does not usually need to be sent with a covering letter, but if there is no opportunity to say why you want to work for that particular company, or if you have particular circumstances that you feel need more explanation, it might be useful to send one (unless the guidance specifically says not to).

A CV is usually sent with a covering letter which outlines in more detail why you think you should be interviewed for the job you are applying for. The job advertisement will usually say whether you should apply by CV and letter, or whether there is an application pack you should complete. More information on CVs and cover letters is described below.

Equal opportunities monitoring

In the UK there is legislation to protect you from discrimination on the grounds of gender, marital status, sexual orientation, disability, race, nationality, religion or belief, or age (age legislation comes into effect from 1 October 2006). Some employers advertise their commitment to encourage diversity in their workforce by stating in vacancy adverts that they are 'Equal Opportunities employers'.

Employers are often keen to know whether their company is attractive to all members of the labour market and will include monitoring forms with their application packs so that they can check to see if they are reaching all potential jobseekers. These forms are removed when the application is returned to the organisation and are not used as part of the application process. You do not have to complete these forms if you do not want to.

CV writing in the UK

A CV is an advertisement about you, your skills and experience. It is a way of promoting yourself to an employer, and what you write and how you write it are important as a demonstration that you are the right person for the job.

Most CVs are two pages long. The average employer spends between 30 seconds and a minute scanning CVs, so you need to think carefully about how to make a positive impact. Using headings, setting out your experience using bullet points or short paragraphs, making sure that there are no spelling mistakes and printing the CV on good quality paper will all help.

There are two main styles of CV: chronological or skills-based. The former outlines your work experience and education, with the most recent first. The second is more complicated and groups experience in themes, for example team-working or training. It is becoming more standard in the UK to include a personal/skills profile, which is a couple of sentences or bullet points outlining your key skills and qualities. It is also common practice to tailor the CV to each job applied for, and you should keep copies of the letters and CVs sent to apply for each job. When you are writing about your experience, remember that all experience counts, whether it is paid or unpaid, including voluntary work.

You can get free help with CV writing from careers advisers in college or university or at the Citizens Advice Bureau, from Jobcentre Plus or from voluntary sector agencies providing help to refugees and/or migrants. There is also free help on the internet.

Covering letters

A covering letter usually accompanies an application by CV rather than an application form. It is an opportunity for you personalise your approach to an organisation, to highlight key points from your CV (without repeating the text), to give a little more detail on aspects that may not be fully covered in the CV, and to show how your particular skills and experience match those required for the job.

You can also use it to explain 'problem' areas in your CV, for example gaps in your work history.

Each covering letter should be tailored to the company you are applying to. It is usually one page long and follows a business letter format. The aim of the letter is to get you an interview, not to outline your experience in a lot of detail. The content should include:

- a paragraph outlining which job you are applying for, where you saw the job advertised (for example a newspaper and date) and a little detail about who you are

- one or two paragraphs about why you want the job and what interests you about it
- one or two paragraphs illustrating how your particular skills and experience match those that the employer is looking for
- a couple of sentences outlining that you would welcome the opportunity to discuss this in more detail at an interview and also stating any dates that you are not available

Before sending the letter, check that it is addressed to the correct person, that there are no spelling mistakes and that what you have written is clear and concise and avoids jargon – it may help to get a friend or adviser to read it through for you.

Your letter will be competing with those from other people applying for the same position. On average the employer will spend 20-30 seconds skim-reading each letter, so what you have written needs to be easily understood in that time. Some tips on formatting are:

- sans serif fonts such as Arial or Tahoma are more modern, but take longer to read than serif fonts such as Times or Garamond
- use a font size of between 10 and 12 points
- do not use more than two fonts or font sizes on your letter, as this makes it look untidy
- left-justified text is easier to read than fully-justified, which creates uneven word spaces
- use short sentences (approximately 15 words) where possible
- black type on a white/cream background is easier to read than black type on colour
- if you are sending it in the post, make sure that it is printed on good quality paper

Application forms

Completing an application form for a job is becoming more and more popular. The form allows organisations to ask specific questions about experience and skills they feel are important for the job they are advertising.

Application forms are often sent with guidance on how to fill them in, either separately or included on the form. This includes whether it should be completed in block capitals or not, handwritten or typed, in blue or black ink. Many can be completed online.

Note: Not completing the form as you have been asked to will probably mean that your application will not make it past the first stage.

Most application forms do not need to be sent with a covering letter – in fact many state that you should not send a letter with the form. However if you feel you need to explain particular circumstances, for example gaps in your history, and there is no space for this on the form, a letter may help.

In addition to sections on your education and employment history, there may be questions where you are asked to provide evidence of skills, for example describing your experience of working in a team. Here it would be useful pick one example of team working; to outline the size of the team, your role within it, how you worked with others, how you overcame any difficulties within the team or with its project. Do not copy sections from your CV for these questions – the employer is looking to see how you tailor your experience to their requirements. Make sure that your language is concise and not informal or full of jargon.

There may also be an open question (often called a supporting statement) where you are asked to give any other information relevant to the job you are applying for. This is an opportunity to draw on skills and experience you have not mentioned so far, including voluntary or community work and things you do in your free time. Use the information in the job description and person specification to structure your answer.

It is important to give evidence of your experience, rather than giving a general response – for example, rather than 'I am a good communicator' you could go into more detail about how your experience meets what the employer is looking for. This could include dealing with customer complaints, working with the public, teaching children or adults, giving presentations. Highlight your achievements – what happened as a result of your communication?

Application form tips

- unless the guidance states that this is acceptable, do not send a copy of your CV instead of filling in the application form
- save a copy of the form or photocopy the form a number of times, so that you are able to practice completing the questions within the space allowed
- complete the education and work experience sections with the most recent first (reverse chronological order)
- if your education or experience cannot be fitted into the spaces allowed, most forms will allow you to continue on an additional sheet.
- when you are completing the work experience/employment section, emphasise the responsibilities and skills the employer is looking for in the job you are applying for
- focus on key words that demonstrate your skills, for example, formulated; designed; implemented; managed
- if a section is not relevant, write 'not applicable' or N/A in the section rather than leaving it blank
- if you have been asked to send evidence of your training or qualifications, send photocopies rather than the originals
- make sure that your form has no spelling mistakes – ask a friend or adviser to check it
- if you are submitting extra pages, make sure that they have your name, the vacancy title and any reference number and the section that the page is linked to
- check the envelope or email before sending to ensure that all the information is there – letter, application form, equal opportunities monitoring form etc
- if you are posting the form, use a large envelope so you do not need to fold it
- make sure that the form is sent in the correct format and in good time so it arrives before the closing date – if you are posting the form you may want to send it by registered post so that you have proof of postage
- keep a copy of everything you have sent so that you can prepare if you are called for interview

WORKING IN THE UK: NEWCOMER'S HANDBOOK 2ND EDITION

You can get more help from advisers in careers centres, Citizens Advice Bureaux, refugee agencies or from a number of sources on the internet.

Speculative applications

In addition to advertised vacancies, you can make a speculative application. A speculative application is sent to an organisation you would like to work for, but which has not advertised any current vacancies. Speculative letters do not have a high success rate, but you can increase your chances of success by:

- finding out who is the right person to write to in the company
- tailoring your CV to the company and type of vacancy that you are looking for
- including a covering letter that outlines why you are contacting the company, the skills and experience you can offer, and that asks the company to consider you for suitable vacancies as they arise
- making sure that the letter and CV are free from grammatical or spelling mistakes. It might help to get a friend or an adviser to check it
- enclosing a stamped, addressed envelope to encourage the employer to respond. If you do not hear anything, follow up your letter with a phone call
- keeping a record of whom you wrote to and when

How can I work out how much I need to earn?

An important consideration in looking for a job is how much money you actually need, how much you would like to earn and what compromises you might make between the two in order to get into work.

The following is a brief checklist to help you work out what income you should aim for, given your spending. It is intended as a guide, and should not be taken as exhaustive:

- rent and deposit (usually one month's rent as a deposit, and rent is payable one month in advance)
- Council Tax

- bills – gas, electricity, water, mobile phone and/or landline, TV licence, TV/video rental
- insurance (home contents, car)
- food
- clothing
- furniture
- travel (public transport, petrol)
- childcare
- socialising
- saving
- prescriptions
- other

The Citizens Advice Bureau can help you work out your average monthly costs. Your local Jobcentre Plus can give advice on any in-work benefits you may be entitled to in addition to your earnings.

Some benefits information is available on the Department of Work and Pensions website. (http://www.dwp.gov.uk/lifeevent/benefits) This will give you a general idea of whether you are able to claim additional benefits if you are on a low income, but for a definitive answer you should talk to an adviser at Jobcentre Plus.

Salary guide

The table below outlines how much money you would be paid per month on annual salaries of between £10,000 and £30,000 after tax and National Insurance deductions had been made by your employer. The allowance for a single person in the tax year 2006-07 has been used to calculate the tax contributions.

Annual Salary	Pre-tax (gross)	Tax contribution	National Insurance	Net pay (month)
£10,000	£833.33	£69.95	£45.47	£767.91
£11,000	£916.67	£88.21	£54.63	£773.83
£12,000	£1,000.00	£106.69	£63.89	£829.42
£13,000	£1,083.33	£124.95	£73.04	£885.34
£14,000	£1,166.67	£143.21	£82.13	£941.33
£15,000	£1,250.00	£161.69	£91.30	£997.01
£16,000	£1,333.33	£179.95	£100.47	£1,052.91
£17,000	£1,416.67	£198.21	£109.63	£1,108.83
£18,000	£1,500.00	£216.69	£118.10	£1,165.21
£19,000	£1,583.33	£234.95	£127.97	£1,220.41
£20,000	£1,666.67	£253.21	£137.13	£1,276.33
£21,000	£1,750.00	£271.69	£146.30	£1,332.01
£22,000	£1,833.33	£289.95	£155.47	£1,387.91
£23,000	£1,916.67	£308.21	£164.63	£1,443.83
£24,000	£2,000.00	£326.69	£173.80	£1,499.51
£25,000	£2,083.33	£344.95	£182.97	£1,555.41
£26,000	£2,166.67	£363.21	£192.13	£1,611.33
£27,000	£2,250.00	£381.69	£201.30	£1,667.01
£28,000	£2,333.33	£399.95	£210.47	£1,722.91
£29,000	£2,416.67	£418.21	£219.63	£1,778.83
£30,000	£2,500.00	£436.69	£228.00	£1,835.31

The recruitment process

Employers take differing approaches to recruitment, depending on the type of work they want to offer and what skills they are hoping to attract. The recruitment process can last from a few weeks to six months but in general will include the following steps:

1. the employer or recruiting organisation produces a job description and a specification of the skills and experience their ideal candidate will have
2. the vacancy is advertised

3. a shortlist of candidates to interview is drawn up, based on the information given in their applications. Some organisations use telephone interviews as a way of shortlisting people who have applied
4. first interview. Many employers use one interview as the only method to decide who will get the job, and you may be told on the day whether or not you have been successful
5. references can be requested before or after your interview. If your CV states 'references are available on request', you will be asked for your referees' contact details
6. second interview. Larger employers or organisations looking for specific skills or experience may use a second interview
7. conditional job offer or unconditional job offer (see below)
8. employment starts

References

You will probably be asked to provide contact details for one or, more likely, two 'referees' when you are applying for work. These are people who know you and who can confirm the information you have given about yourself in a work and a personal context. You must ask their permission before giving their names as referees.

A personal referee is usually someone who has a position of responsibility in the community and who has known you for some time – it could be a teacher, a social worker, a manager in a voluntary organisation, a member of a refugee community organisation or a person who has helped you during your asylum application. Family members are not usually accepted as referees.

You may not have a recent work reference from a UK employer. If you have work references from your previous job in your home country, these should be translated where necessary and include full contact details.

Getting into work without a work reference or UK experience can be very difficult. Many employers are unwilling to take on someone without UK work experience and references. Voluntary work can help you, in that you may be able to get a reference from the organisation you volunteered with for use as a work reference. Alternatively you or your adviser might be able to negotiate starting work for a probationary period (see below).

The interview process

If an employer thinks that you may fit what they are looking for, they will ask to meet or speak with you for an interview. Depending on what kind of job you are applying for, you will have one or more interviews before you find out whether you have been successful.

There are lots of internet sites offering free advice on interviews and common tips on how to do well. In addition you may be able to get some help on interview skills and identifying your skills and experience from advisers in Jobcentre Plus, college careers services or organisations working with refugees and/or migrants. You should not be charged for this advice.

Some basic tips to remember are:

- confirm that you will be attending
- make sure that you know where you are going and how long it will take you to get there. It is important to be on time, or a little early if you can, so that you have a few minutes to relax
- plan what you are going to wear and make sure that it is smart and presentable – if you look good you will feel more confident
- take copies of your CV or application with you, as well as the letter inviting you to interview and any certificates or records of achievement that you will need
- interviewers know that you will probably be nervous and will make allowances for this
- if you don't understand the question, ask the interviewer to repeat it again, or to explain what they mean
- body language is important

A standard interview will begin with an introductory conversation outlining the structure for the interview and moving to specific questions on your skills and experience as set out in your application. From there, more information about the company and the role may be discussed, before finishing with an opportunity for you to ask some questions of your own. On average an interview will last between 30 minutes and an hour.

For all interviews it is important to prepare answers to common questions. These might include:

- why do you want the job?
- tell me about your previous experience
- what experience do you have of working in a team?
- give me an example of a time you had to work to a deadline and tell me what you did to meet it
- what are your strengths and weaknesses?
- describe a time that you had too much to do and had to prioritise your tasks. How did you decide which was most important?
- what can you bring to this company?
- what do you know about our company/this sector?
- what do you do in your spare time?

An interviewer is interested in personality and presentation as well as someone who meets what the company needs in terms of skills and experience, and these skills and experience don't have to be from your previous work experience, but can also come from hobbies, or family life.

They are also usually looking for someone who has taken the time to find out about their company – its products, its competitors, its sector, how long it has been established and where it operates – so it is important to do a bit of research beforehand.

It is good to have questions to ask too, but avoid asking about money, holidays or other benefits at the first interview. In the UK this is usually left until the end of the second interview or until you have a job offer. Your questions are an opportunity to find out more about the job and the company.

There are several different types of interview. The following covers:

- panel interviews
- one to one interviews
- telephone interviews
- competency-based interviews

Panel Interviews

Panel interviews are being used more often in recruitment because they can be more consistent in approach than one to one interviews – based on more than one person's opinion they can give a more balanced decision. They are also more efficient: staff meet you together and can compare notes on the same day. They are used either as part of an interview process or as the only interview. If you know you are going to be interviewed by a panel, find out in advance who will be on it and what roles they have in the company.

A panel varies from two to about five individuals, though the average is two or three. Sometimes there is a person there who is just at the interview to take notes. It is important to make contact with all the members of the panel, from the first handshake when you are introduced. Don't rush the introductions as the first few seconds are a key opportunity to making a good impression. Even though only one person might be asking the questions, or more questions than the others, you are being interviewed by the entire panel. When you are asked a question by one member, you should respond to that person, but include the other members of the panel by making eye contact with them.

Questions in the panel interview are likely to be the same as those used in a one to one interview, but the panel may have decided, as a tactic, that one person will ask all the difficult questions to see how you react. Remember that you are considered as a candidate for the job, or you would not have been invited. Remaining calm and answering each question thoroughly is the best approach you can take.

Remember to clarify what the next steps are in the process, and when you may hear from the company. Thank each person individually as you leave, and follow this up with thank you letters.

One to one interviews

A one to one interview is still the most common format. Depending on the size and type of the organisation and the type of job you are applying for, this might be the start of an interview process or the only interview you will have. In general they will follow the format described at the beginning of this chapter. Some interviewers will be trained recruitment interviewers and some may be the line manager for the job in question. As with the panel interviews you need to maintain a comfortable level of eye contact, and answer questions clearly and thoroughly. If it's appropriate, smiling when you speak will also help to relax you. Remember again to clarify at the end of the interview what happens next, and to thank the interviewer for the opportunity, followed by a letter.

Telephone interviews

Telephone interviews are becoming more common for lower-skill and bulk recruitment. They can be used to assess how interested you are in the job, identify an interview shortlist from a large pool of candidates or to go through an in-depth interview.

Talking on the phone is not as easy as people think, particularly if English is not your first language. It helps to practise with a friend or an adviser using typical questions, and also to record your practice. When you play back the recording you will be able to hear how you sound, whether your tone varies, or whether there are certain words that you say a lot, for example 'okay' or 'um', and you can then practise your conversation.

One of the advantages of a telephone interview is that you can have your information in front of you – your CV, any application letters or forms that you may have sent, information on the company and any questions that you want to ask about the job or company. You could write down important points about your experience or the company you want to work for, and use them in the interview, but be careful that you don't write too much – it is easy for someone listening to you to tell that you are reading out loud, and they will want to know that you can answer spontaneously.

The telephone interviewer may call unexpectedly. If this happens you need to decide if it is a good time to talk for you, and if not (you may be in the middle of something else or somewhere noisy) you should arrange a time that is more convenient.

Tips for telephone interviews:

- keep a drink to hand in case you get a dry mouth
- speak slowly and make sure that you are talking clearly
- smile when you are talking – this changes your tone of voice
- don't interrupt the interviewer
- if you do not understand a question, ask the interviewer to repeat it
- give short answers to the questions, don't ramble
- don't feel you have to answer immediately. It is perfectly acceptable for you to take a few seconds to gather your thoughts
- take notes about what you were asked and what you said – either during the interview or afterwards
- address the interviewer by their title and surname. Only use their first name if they ask you to
- ask when you will hear whether you have an interview or a job offer
- remember to thank the interviewer at the end of the call

Competency-based interviews
(Amar Dhudwar, Working Lives Research Institute)

Many organisations now use competency-based interviews in place of more traditional methods of recruitment, such as CVs or one to one interviews. These interviews are designed to enable the interviewer(s) to gather information about your knowledge, abilities and motivation, and compare these with those required for the job.

The questions will concentrate on the most important parts of the job and will be broken down into specific competencies, such as communication skills, team working or organisational skills. You will be expected to provide examples of where you have used such skills and may possibly be asked about any difficulties you came up against and how you dealt with them.

When giving examples you should be demonstrating your ability to perform successfully in the job, by matching your skills and knowledge with those required for the position. These examples could come from your previous employment, but also from voluntary work, study at school or university, travel or personal experiences.

If some of the examples you have prepared involved a group situation, the focus should still be on you, as interviewers will want to know what your specific role was in achieving the outcome. You should try and structure your answers around four key themes:

- describe the situation/task you were involved with
- what was your objective? What were you trying to achieve?
- what action did you take?
- what was the outcome of your action?

You will be able to identify which competencies the employer is likely to explore by checking out the job advert or job description. Some employers may already have asked you competency type questions on their application form. You need to be ready to talk about these and other examples at the interview.

The questions you are likely to be asked will be directly linked to the job description and will generally being asked in the following ways:

- 'tell me about a time when ....'
- 'describe an occasion when ....'
- 'when has it been important to ....'
- 'please give me an example when.......'

So if an employer had listed the ability to work co-operatively as part of a team on the job description, an interviewer might ask:

- tell me about a time when you worked with others on a piece of work/project?
- what role do you tend to take in a team situation?

WORKING IN THE UK: NEWCOMER'S HANDBOOK 2ND EDITION

You will need one or two examples from different aspects of your life and preferably taken from the last three years, to demonstrate each skill or competency.

Feedback

You can learn a lot from attending an interview, whether or not you are actually offered the job. Asking for feedback can help you prepare for future interviews. If they are a good employer they should give you at least a few minutes to point out where they think you performed well and where you could have improved.

You can then use the feedback in a mock interview with a friend to help you prepare for your next job interview.

Starting work

Offer Letters

Although you may initially hear over the telephone that you have been successful in your employment interview, your future employer should send you a formal offer letter.

This is often a conditional offer and will set out:

- the job title
- to whom the job is offered
- where the job will be based
- what conditions you are expected to meet. For example, you may have to:
    - provide evidence that you have permission to work in the UK
    - provide satisfactory references
    - undergo a criminal records check
    - show that you have a satisfactory health record
- if there is any probationary period
- the terms of the job (e.g. the pay, hours, holiday entitlements)
- what the employer expects you to do now and when you have to do it by

You may be asked to sign and return the offer letter. This is to ensure that both you and your employer have a record of what has been agreed.

Once your prospective employer knows you meet the conditions, they should send you an unconditional offer letter. When you have accepted an unconditional offer an employment contract exists between you and your employer.

Your potential employer (or actual employer if you have started work) can withdraw the offer if they find that you do not meet the conditions.

It is a good idea to wait for an unconditional offer letter before giving notice to your current employer if you can.

Probationary periods

When you get your job offer, you might be told that this is subject to successfully completing a probationary period. This is typically three to six months and is used by an employer to assess whether you are able and willing to do the job.

At the start of the probationary period you should have an initial meeting with your manager to explain:

- what the period is
- what standards are expected of you
- how and when these standards will be reviewed
- what training will be available to you
- what will happen at the end of the probationary period

You should establish whether there are any contractual differences during the probationary period. For example is the rate of pay lower in that period or is absence from sickness dealt with differently?

In terms of holiday, you will start to accumulate leave from the beginning of your contract. You have a right to four weeks paid holiday per year (see 'What are my rights in work?' on page 376).

Note: your employer can require you to accumulate the holiday entitlement before you take it, and is able to refuse holiday requests when these conflict with business needs.

During your probationary period the contractual notice period to terminate employment on either side is usually shorter, for example one week rather than a month. Sometimes the notice period differs for employer and employee. For example you may be asked to give a week's notice while the employer will give you 24 hours' notice.

At the end of the probationary period you will usually have a meeting with your manager to review your employment so far. In the majority of cases your employer will confirm that you have been successful and that you have completed the probationary period. Sometimes an employee's performance might have fallen below the expected standards and the employer will want to extend the probationary period a little longer.

However if your performance has not met the standards set out at the beginning of the probationary period and the employer feels that you are unsuitable for the position, they may wish to end your employment at this point. If this is the case, under the Employment Act 2002 (Dispute Resolution) Regulations 2004, your employer must follow a minimum required procedure. If you are told that you will not be continuing after the end of the probationary period and you are not asked to a meeting to discuss this, you must request a meeting in writing. For more information on dismissal please see the section on what happens when something goes wrong, page 399.

Induction

The induction process is intended to help a new employee to integrate into their new working environment. It is a mixture of explaining the culture of the organisation (or how things are done in the company), a detailed discussion with you about your new position and where it fits into the company, introductions to other staff members, organisation procedures (including how and when you will be paid), and explaining company policy about health and safety.

An employer has a legal responsibility to ensure your health, welfare and safety while you are working for them. An employer with more than five employees must have a written health and safety policy which should be explained to you. Health and safety legislation also includes rules about making sure that you are able to take rest breaks and your holiday entitlement. You also have responsibility for your own health and safety and you can refuse to do something that is unsafe without disciplinary action from your employer.

An induction can include a tour of the workplace, meetings with your line manager, reading assignments, visits to partner organisations, suppliers or customers, attending internal meetings or shadowing other members of staff. Depending on the job and how big the organisation is, an induction can vary between a day or two to a structured two week programme.

In larger organisations with a regular flow of new employees, there may be a formal induction course to attend. In smaller organisations there may be more one to one training, but both should feature a large element of contact with other staff for the new person. Relationships and contacts are the routes for the organisation to function. Meeting and getting to know other people are essential aspects of the induction process.

A fact sheet with more information on induction can be found at: http://www.cipd.co.uk/subjects/recruitmen/induction

or on the ACAS website: http://www.acas.org.uk

More information on health and safety can be found on the DirectGov website http://www.direct.gov.uk or the ACAS website http://www.acas.org.uk, or you could ask for help at your local Citizens Advice Bureau.

Self-employment and setting up a business

Setting up a business or becoming self-employed is often an attractive option for newcomers to the UK. Many have previous experience of working for themselves and others may see it as an alternative to requalifying for their previous profession.

However, setting up a business or becoming self-employed may affect your immigration status (for example if you are in the UK on a work visa) and you should consult an experienced adviser before you start.

Starting up a business is complicated, and there are specific barriers that newcomers can face in terms of establishing what the legal regulations are, putting together a business plan and accessing finance or financial planning advice, but there are several organisations that can help you to navigate the process.

Business Link is part of the Government's campaign to encourage enterprise in the UK. It is a national business advice service in the UK, comprising independent Business Link organisations for each geographical area of the country. http://www.businesslink.gov.uk

It has an online resource to take you through the process of starting up a business and tools you can use to find out what licences you might need to apply for and what regulations you will need to comply with. The online service is linked to local offices which can also provide information on funding you can access in your area or sector.

National organisations such as the Citizens Advice Bureaux provide information on self employment and their website has a useful section on where to find more help and support (http://www.adviceguide.org.uk/index/life/employment/self-employment_checklist.htm#Who_can_give_further_advice).

The National Federation of Enterprise Agencies (NFEA) runs the Small Business Advice Service, an online resource that you will need to register for, but registration is free. The NFEA website or enquiry line can help you to find an Enterprise Agency in your area who will be able to provide more information and guidance. They also provide information on funding available in the area. You can find more information on their website:
http://www.smallbusinessadvice.org.uk

In scotland you may find information from the scottish enterprise: http://www.scottish-enterprise.com/

In addition to national and regional organisations, some local councils offer help, in particular to people from ethnic minority backgrounds. You can also find information through banks and local Chambers of Commerce. If you are a refugee there are specialist agencies such as the Refugee Council, The Prince's Trust and the Refugee Education and Training Advisory Service (RETAS) which provide training and support to start a business. If you are in Scotland or Wales you should contact the Welsh or Scottish Refugee Council.

Finding and starting work

8

9 Documentation
Will Somerville

Introduction

In order to get a job in the UK, you will need to demonstrate your entitlement to work. This means that your employer will ask you for proof that you can work when you start a new job.

If you work for an employment or recruitment agency, you will have to provide the agency with proof that you can work in the UK.

Your employer or your employment agency will photocopy your documents and return them to you. It is best to do this while you are with the employer so that your documents are not lost.

There are no rules on when an employer will ask you for proof of your entitlement to work. However, it is normal practice to ask for documentation when you are short-listed for an interview or, more often, when you are offered the job but before you start work. If you are applying to work for an employment or recruitment agency, they will often not let you register with them until you have produced documentation proving that you are entitled to work in the UK.

Note: New rules (see below) mean that some newcomers may be required to prove their entitlement to work on a regular basis.

Background

The law requiring employers to check documentation is often referred to as 'Section 8' after the relevant section of the 1996 Asylum and Immigration Act. The law was amended in the 2002 Nationality, Immigration, and Asylum Act (which came into force May 1 2004) and the new legislation requires stricter documentation checks from one of two lists. This is the current law and the one described below.

Forthcoming changes

The recently passed Immigration, Asylum and Nationality Act 2006 provides for more checks on your entitlement to work and penalties for employers who employ irregular migrants. If you are a newcomer with limited leave to remain, you will be checked more than once during the period of your employment.[1] This is likely to be on an annual basis.

Note: If an employer refuses to employ you despite the fact that you have valid residence, it may be racial discrimination (see page 433). The Home Office has produced a code of practice on the new checks so that employers do not discriminate when employing newcomers. This also details the documentation that you can produce to prove your entitlement to work.

Exceptional Leave to Remain and varying leave

If you are coming to the end of your period of Exceptional Leave to Remain (ELR) and you have applied in-time for a further period of residence (i.e. you applied for an extension before your leave expired) you are legally allowed to work.

The application for a further period of residence is called a variation of leave (usually people apply for Indefinite Leave to Remain). However, even though you are legally allowed to work, some employers can be concerned that they are breaking the law. There are a several ways you can reassure an employer:

In your application for varying leave, the standard response letter should contain the following paragraph:

> You were granted leave to remain in the United Kingdom on an exceptional basis until [date]. In your particular circumstances your conditions have been extended, and you may take up employment whilst the application is outstanding.

You can show the employer this paragraph which should be enough proof.

If they still need to be convinced, direct them to Question 32 of the Q&A in the short guidance on Illegal Working (available on the Home Office website or from the employer's helpline on 0845 010 6677) or suggest they follow the new verification system.

The verification system

The new verification system has been in operation since April 2006. It allows employers to check if those with an outstanding application for varying leave can work. If you are in this situation, you could ask your employer to use the verification system.

Employers can ring the employer's helpline on 0845 010 6677 and request a pro-forma. You and the employer then fill in the pro-forma and fax it to a designated number. The employer should then receive a response from IND within five working days as to your eligibility to work.

Glossary of documentation terms

The following is a glossary of some of the key documents you may have and will assist you in proving your right to work.

Certificates of entitlement

People who have the right of abode in the UK but who are not travelling on British passports need to get this right confirmed by the British Embassy or High Commission before travelling. You will be given a certificate of entitlement to the right of abode, which is embossed into your passport.

EEA residence permits and documents

EEA nationals and their family members have rights of free movement derived from EU law and these rights are not dependent on whether or not they possess any particular documentation. You are entitled to possess documents known as 'residence permits' and 'residence documents'. Residence permits are available to EEA nationals exercising free-movement rights.

Residence documents are also issued to non-EEA national family members of EEA nationals who have the right to reside under EU law.

Application Registration Card (ARC)

An Application Registration Card is a credit card sized form of identity issued to applicants for asylum and their dependants during the asylum screening process.

Immigration Status Documents

Immigration Status documents (ISD's) are issued to those granted refugee status, and to those given Humanitarian Protection or Discretionary Leave where it is not appropriate or possible to place a UK Residence Permit (UKRP) vignette in the holder's national passport.

Refugees

Refugees' national passports are not stamped, because they cannot use them without forfeiting their refugee status. If you are a refugee, you will be issued with an Immigration Status Document (ISD) containing a UK Residence Permit (UKRP) which will grant leave for a period of five years. You will also be given a letter from the Home Office which explains your position as a refugee and some of your rights as such in the UK.

Humanitarian Protection and Discretionary Leave

When Humanitarian Protection (HP) and Discretionary Leave (DL) are granted you will be issued with a 'status' letter and may be issued with an ISD. For those given HP, the ISD or national passport will contain a

UKRP vignette granting leave for a period of five years. For DL, the ISD or national passport will contain a UKRP vignette granting leave for a maximum period of three years initially, though it may be less.

Note: The period of leave for DL will be raised to five years.

UN travel documents

As a refugee, you may be given refugee travel documents, issued by the Home Office under the 1951 Convention relating to the Status of Refugees, and leave will be endorsed in them on a UKRP vignette. The travel documents are valid for all countries except your country of origin.

Certificates of Identity

If you are granted HP, DL or Exceptional Leave to Remain (ELR) you may have leave to enter or remain stamped in your national passports where possible and appropriate. Otherwise you will be issued with an ISD containing a UKRP vignette. However, if you wish to obtain a travel document and you do not have a passport, you may apply for a Home Office travel document called a 'Certificate of Identity'.

UK Passport

A passport showing that the holder is a British citizen, or has the right of abode in the United Kingdom.

Letter from Home Office

A letter issued by the Home Office which indicates that the person named in it has been granted Indefinite Leave in the UK or which indicates that the person has current leave to be in the UK, and which allows them to take jobs applied for.

Proof of the right to work

The current law states that you have to produce a document(s) from one of two 'lists'.

If you have one document in the following table (table 1) that is all the proof you require.

TABLE 1
Any one of the documents in this table will be acceptable proof of your right to work in the UK. An employer does not require any further proof.
A passport showing that the holder is a British citizen, or has a right of abode in the United Kingdom
A document showing that the holder is a national of a European Economic Area country or Switzerland. This must be a national passport or national identity card. See the introduction to this handbook for a list of EEA countries
A residence permit issued by the Home Office to a national from a European Economic Area country or Switzerland
A passport or other document issued by the Home Office which has an endorsement stating that the holder has a current right of residence in the United Kingdom as the family member of a national from a European Economic Area country or Switzerland who is resident in the United Kingdom
A passport or other travel document endorsed to show that the holder can stay indefinitely in the United Kingdom, or has no time limit on their stay
A passport or other travel document endorsed to show that the holder can stay in the United Kingdom; and that this endorsement allows the holder to do the type of work the employer is offering even if they do not have a work permit
An Application Registration Card issued by the Home Office to an asylum seeker stating that the holder is permitted to take employment

If you do not have a document listed in the Table above, you will need to produce two documents. The documents are listed below. You must produce two documents from either Table 2 or from Table 3 (not both).

If you have a different name on the two documents, for example you have been married, you will need to produce a third document.

Note: If you have the necessary documentation from Table 1 or Table 2 or Table 3 you do not need to provide anything else.

TABLE 2
Provide two documents, one from each column.

ONE document from this column	**PLUS**	**ONE** document from this column
A document with a permanent National Insurance Number (NINO) and name. For example a letter from a Government agency		Full birth certificate issued in the United Kingdom, which includes the names of the holder's parents
National Insurance card		Birth certificate issued in the Channel Islands, the Isle of Man or Ireland
P45		Certificate of registration or naturalisation stating that the holder is a British citizen
P60		Letter issued by the Home Office to the holder which indicates that the person named in it can stay indefinitely in the United Kingdom, or has no time limit on their stay
		Immigration Status Document issued by the Home Office to the holder with an endorsement indicating that the person named in it can stay indefinitely in the United Kingdom, or has no time limit on their stay
		Letter issued by the Home Office to the holder which indicates that the person named in it can stay in the United Kingdom, and this allows them to do the type of work being offered
		Immigration Status Document issued by the Home Office to the holder with an endorsement indicating that the person named in it can stay in the United Kingdom, and this allows them to do the type of work being offered

TABLE 3
Provide two documents, one from each column.

ONE document from this column	PLUS	ONE document from this column
Work permit or other approval to take employment that has been issued by Work Permits UK		Passport or other travel document endorsed to show that the holder is able to stay in the United Kingdom and can take the work permit employment in question
		Letter issued by the Home Office to the holder confirming that the person named in it is able to stay in the United Kingdom and can take the work permit employment in question.

Note: Some documents are not accepted. They include a Home Office Standard Acknowledgement Letter or Immigration Service Letter (IS96W) which states that an asylum seeker can work in the United Kingdom or letters issued by the Home Office stating that the holder is a British citizen.

Endnotes

[1] Immigration, Asylum and Nationality Act 2006, s 15 7 (e)

10 Recognition of qualifications
Will Somerville

Introduction

Many new migrants and refugees have higher level qualifications in the fields of medicine, engineering, research, teaching, accountancy and in other major professions.

However, qualifications (and particularly higher level academic and professional qualifications) are often undervalued in the UK, especially if they are from certain countries. For example, qualifications from countries such as Iran, Iraq, Sri Lanka and Cameroon are usually poorly understood in the UK.

As a new migrant or refugee, it is crucial that you clearly communicate the academic value and learning outcomes of your studies to employers and learning institutions (learning outcomes are what you know or are able to do as a result of your studies). You should also highlight the practical value of work experience, particularly if you have gained experience overseas.

In terms of getting jobs, it is typically up to the employer whether or not your qualifications are recognised. However, there are other ways of proving you can do a particular job and of improving you knowledge of UK work culture. See, for example, the section on volunteering, pages 336-342.

This chapter covers:

- Formal recognition from NARIC
- Professional body exemptions and membership and projects specialising in qualification recognition
- Portfolios, APEL and recognition of trade experience
- Key tips for how to present qualifications on your CV

NARIC

NARIC stands for the National Academic Recognition Information Centre which exists to offer advice and information about academic recognition and the comparability of international and national qualifications. NARIC is a national agency, under contract to the Department for Education and Skills (DfES). Their website is a good source of information: see www.naric.org.uk

NARIC has an on-line database that organisations such as careers services and universities can access on payment of a registration fee.

The database gives NARIC's opinion of the UK equivalence of many overseas academic and vocational qualifications. This can be very useful. For example you can put the equivalence on your CV or application form. However, NARIC can only compare 'like with like' in terms of course content, and many qualifications are not seen as equivalent to UK qualifications.

A NARIC certificate holds no legal value and is therefore not necessary. It is much more important to clearly describe the qualification than to show a NARIC certificate.

Vocational qualifications

Vocational qualifications is dealt with by the UK National Reference Point for Vocational Qualifications (UK NRP).

UK NRP is independent but part of NARIC and is a resource for UK skilled worker, trade and technician level qualifications. If you wish to work in a specific trade or occupation, send certificates that are relevant to that trade such as technical certificates, Apprenticeship certificates, or trade or registration cards. Always send photocopies as NARIC does not return certificates.

NARIC and NRP Guidelines

NARIC and NRP assess overseas awards which constitute national standards in the country of origin. They only:

- evaluate courses of at least 200 hours duration
- assess certificates of awards – they are not able to assess certificates of attendance

Translation and waiver scheme

You can obtain an official translation of your certificate through a translation agency. As NARIC does not return documents, make sure you send a photocopy of your official translation.

You cannot make a translation yourself.

UK NARIC operates a translation waiver scheme for holders of Bulgarian, Catalan, Chinese, Danish, French, German, Norwegian, Russian, Spanish and Swedish qualifications.

If you have a certificate in one of the languages above, you do not need to have it translated.

Cost

A written individual assessment of your own academic qualifications, which results in a letter of comparability (this advises how your qualification compares against UK qualification levels) costs £42.30 (including VAT) for people in the UK and EU.

There is a premium service for individuals or companies who need a statement in a maximum of 48 hours. The cost of the service is £235 for a 24 hour turnaround and £176.25 for a 48 hour service.

All payments must be made payable to ECCTIS Ltd and you can pay by cheque, card, or postal order. Include your name and address on the back of the cheque if you do send a cheque. You can also make an on-line application.

NARIC will not proceed with an enquiry until they receive your payment – i.e. you have to pay in advance. However, if you are receiving help from Jobcentre Plus you might wish to ask your personal adviser to pay for the cost of NARIC through the Adviser Discretion Fund (see page 184). If you are a refugee you may receive this for free.

Note: If you are a refugee or have Exceptional Leave to Remain (ELR), Humanitarian Protection (HP) or Discretionary Leave (DL), you need not pay any fees to NARIC because a registered NARIC service such as a careers service can provide the information required at zero cost.

National Awards Information Service from NARIC

You may request an additional 'National Awards Information Service', which is an additional document that can be included with your letter and qualification certificates to employers. The total cost for this is £76.38 (including VAT) and you must apply by post.

Note: There is no evaluation evidence of whether this helps you to get a job or not.

What do you need to send?

For a written assessment statement, you need:

- a letter detailing the service you require (giving your full contact details)
- a photocopy of the final qualification certificate / diploma
- photocopies of the course record / transcript / mark-sheet
- a copy of an official translation into English

NARIC and NRP only provide assessment statements for fully completed qualifications. However, if you are unable to get a copy of your certificate, or it has not yet been issued, it may still be possible to get a statement (for example if you have a transcript). Contact a NARIC information officer for more details.

The address for NARIC or NRP is:

UK NRP/ UK NARIC
ECCTIS Ltd
Oriel House
Oriel Road
Cheltenham,
Gloucestershire
GL50 1XP

+44 (0) 870 990 4088
info@naric.org.uk
www.naric.org.uk

Appeals against NARIC decisions

You can appeal against a NARIC decision. There is no charge for appealing if made on the grounds listed below.

You can appeal against a NARIC decision on the following grounds:

- Disputing the comparable level of an award
- Disputing the information provided in the assessment
- Disputing the level of service and conduct towards an individual during the assessment process

Once an appeal has been received, NARIC undertakes to re-examine the information originally provided, which will always be carried out by a senior member of staff as appeals officer.

The appeals officer will undertake a re-evaluation of the assessment using all available evidence and will seek further clarification from appropriate authorities where necessary. In addition the assessment will be peer reviewed by the divisional manager.

Professional body exemptions and membership

This is an area commonly overlooked by newcomers to the UK. If you are a doctor, lawyer, engineer, or teacher (or a member of any profession) you should contact the professional body. They will tell you how your qualification compares with those in the UK.

Some overseas qualifications, such as accountancy qualifications, can be accredited by professional bodies in the UK. For example, ACCA (Association of Certified Chartered Accountants), have comprehensive lists of exemptions on their website for specific university/college courses around the world.

You should also explore the criteria for joining the relevant UK professional body of your job area, usually as an associate or student member (especially if you are continuing your studies in the UK).

It is important that you explore this so that employers and educational institutions, many of whom operate globally, are fully aware of the international aspect of some qualifications.

Note: If you work in some professions, it is a legal requirement to have a qualification approved by the profession's society, association, board or council, or by a government department.

Projects specialising in qualification recognition

There are a number of projects and services that specialise in qualification, advice and recognition services. These include:

RAGU

The Refugee Advice and Guidance Unit (RAGU) offers a range of services for refugees with higher level educational or professional qualifications, through specialist training organisations and work placement schemes.

They are also responsible for this very useful website www.info-for-asylumseekers.org.uk

which provides information on various aspects of qualification recognition.

RETAS

RETAS, part of Education Action International, offers a service for Doctors. This involves Education Action's employment team which provides initial advice on medical re-qualification and employment opportunities in the NHS. This is followed by a mentoring stage where a UK doctor coaches a refugee doctor. It is evident that employment support is a necessary adjunct to recognition of qualifications.

Engineers

Education Action International has produced 'The Employment Handbook for Refugee Engineers' (J Rogic and P Feldman, 2004). The handbook also contains sections on the UK education system and engineering qualifications, including details of engineering qualifications, entry requirements for engineering courses, recognition of overseas qualifications and general detail on the engineering profession in the UK.

The Migrant Qualifications project

This is a pan-London project, involving the five London LSCs and the LDA. This project aims to identify the transferable skills and qualifications of migrant workers (including refugees) with a right to work in the UK and supports them to fulfil their potential in the employment market. The project is targeted towards skills shortage sectors, such as construction, engineering and teaching. The first stage is concerned with 'identification' of eligible clients (often through Information Advice and Guidance partnerships), onward referral to UK NARIC and support to complete a Migrant Skills Questionnaire. In the second 'qualification comparability' stage, NARIC completes qualification comparability documentation and informs the client accordingly. The third stage is 'skills analysis', in which each client receives from NARIC a document that 'maps' the additional training/learning needed to be qualified and competent to UK industry standards. The fourth stage embraces 'local guidance, support and active brokerage', involving one-to-one counselling and guidance, production of a personal development plan, brokerage of additional skills (basic ESOL, vocational, academic, etc) and arranging work experience.

Breckland New Communities (BNC) – Keystone Development Trust

Breckland New Communities (BNC) is a project managed by Keystone Development Trust in Thetford, Norfolk with funding from the European Social Fund, Home Office and Breckland Council. The project assists migrant workers to access jobs and services, through tackling barriers such as language, lack of information and difficulties in demonstrating UK equivalence of overseas qualifications.

The BNC Project bought in the worldwide general qualifications and interskills (European Region) databases from NARIC to assist clients/beneficiaries to demonstrate the value of their overseas qualifications to local employers.

The majority of users in the first year were Portuguese nationals who used the system for secondary school leavers' certificates or degree level comparisons. Project staff and volunteers are able to issue a comparability statement printed from the NARIC database. This service is free to clients. Almost 80% of clients who used this service and were questioned in a recent evaluation said they found it useful in seeking work. The project is also able to link clients to training and employment opportunities in the area through its network of contacts in the public and private sectors.

Portfolios, APEL and recognition of trade experience

Portfolio

A portfolio is an organised folder of documents and other evidence that shows what you have done. It tells someone else who you are and what you can do. A portfolio should be constantly updated.

Your portfolio will show evidence of a range of your skills and experiences. If you want to use your portfolio for a specific occasion, such as for a job interview or when applying to university, you may decide to take some of the information out. Your portfolio should be relevant for each time you use it.

It might include:

- CV (Curriculum Vitae)
- references from employers (paid or voluntary)
- learning outcomes (including a description of skills)
- transcripts of units / modules covered at college or university
- certificates of achievement you may have
- short summaries or abstracts of theses, dissertations or research projects
- photographs of creative work (for artists, designers, architects)
- action plans you have made with an adviser
- any other evidence of academic or work achievement

It is advisable to present a portfolio as well as you can (such as in a file) and to keep the originals safe (presenting only photocopies).

Assessment of Prior Experiential Learning (APEL)

After you have created a portfolio, you can apply to a college or university and they may accept your portfolio rather than insist on your meeting their stated entry requirements. This process is often called Assessment of Prior Experiential Learning or APEL.

Note: This does not apply to doctors, lawyers, and teachers although it does apply to the majority of courses at learning institutions.

Recognition of trade experience

In addition to formal recognition through UK NRP (see above under NARIC) you can get recognition of trade experience by taking a National Vocational Qualification (NVQ) in your trade area. An NVQ is a vocational qualification. You may be able to take an NVQ while working, as many employers want their staff to have NVQs. You may also be able to get an NVQ through On-

Site Assessment and Training (OSAT). Also see page 215 for details of the Employer Training Pilot (ETP) and the section on training on page 192.

An NVQ is a qualification that shows an employer that you can work at a certain standard within your trade. This type of qualification is very flexible and can be taken at college or as part of your normal job. Your abilities will be assessed and you will start at the appropriate level, so you do not have to start from the bottom if you have experience.

OSAT (On-Site Assessment and Training) can be arranged through your employer. An assessor will visit your workplace to identify the skills that you have and any gaps in these skills. You do not go to college but learn at work and collect evidence of your skills. You will be visited at work by the assessor four or five times over a six month period. If you are successful you will be given an NVQ (or SVQ in Scotland).

Key tips for presenting qualifications

The following are three key tips in how to lay out overseas qualifications on your CV or on an application form. For further advice on interviews and the recruitment process, see pages 302-310.

- translate the name of the qualification into English and put the NARIC equivalence in brackets after the translation (if the NARIC view is positive – otherwise leave it out)
- include three or four bullet points of selected key study areas/ learning outcomes, relating this very closely to what the employer/ educational institution is looking for wherever possible
- use your portfolio (if you have one) as a basis for selecting the key study areas and to assist you if you have to write a covering letter
- include UK professional body exemptions/membership in the qualifications section

11 Volunteering, work experience, placements and mentoring

Beryl Randall, Employability Forum

Volunteering

In Britain an estimated 22 million people volunteer within their local community every year. Whether for a few hours or for a few days each week, volunteering is recognised as a key method for newcomers to gain relevant work experience in the UK, and has been found to be particularly valuable for refugee jobseekers.

What is volunteering?

Volunteering is about giving your time to an organisation, a project or a cause without being paid for it, other than receiving expenses such as travel.

What is the difference between volunteering and unpaid work?

There is a difference between volunteering and employment.

An example of unpaid employment would be an arrangement in which a person makes an arrangement to help out in a business, perhaps on behalf of a relative, in return for some non-monetary benefit.

But where the work is unpaid and is carried out on behalf of a charity, voluntary organisation or body that raise funds for either, then it will be accepted for immigration law purposes as volunteering.[1]

Eligibility

If you are an asylum seeker in the UK you are allowed to volunteer, but you cannot undertake unpaid work.

Newcomers with refugee status, Humanitarian Protection or Discretionary Leave, or exceptional or Indefinite Leave to Remain, are able to volunteer as well as to take paid employment. EU or EEA nationals have no restrictions on their ability to volunteer.

If you come from outside the EEA you will not be able to volunteer unless you have a work permit or unless you have applied for a volunteering permit before entering the UK. If you are coming to the UK as a student your college may impose some restrictions on volunteering, for example you might be restricted to volunteering for less than 20 hours per week during term-time in order not to affect your studies. Your college should be able to give you more information.

Benefits and volunteering

You are allowed to do voluntary work without it affecting your benefits. To count as voluntary work you must not receive any payments except for reasonable expenses for the work that you do, but you are allowed to work for unlimited hours for a charitable or voluntary body.

Note: You cannot volunteer for a member of your close family.

If you receive Jobseeker's Allowance you should inform your Jobcentre

Plus office that you are doing voluntary work. You will then be allowed to give a week's notice before starting work, but you must be available for any job interviews within 48 hours. You can include voluntary work as one of your steps to find work as it improves your chances of getting paid work and it improves your skills.

Seek advice if you have difficulty with benefits because of any voluntary work.

How long can I volunteer for?

It is possible to volunteer for as little as one hour per month. Volunteering does not necessarily have to take place during office hours – there are opportunities for evening positions through befriending and mentoring schemes or through organisations such as the Samaritans.

You do not necessarily have to give a long-term commitment to a voluntary position, though you will probably find the experience more useful if you can stay there for a few months. Some organisations require a minimum commitment – for example three to six months. Short term volunteering, where you volunteer for a certain project or for a specific period of time, is becoming more common and may be more appropriate if you are not sure that you will be living in the same town for a long period (for example if you are an asylum seeker).

Why volunteer?

Apart from providing relevant work experience and helping you keep your skills up to date, volunteering has many other benefits. It can give you an opportunity to meet new people, learn new skills, improve language skills and to contribute to a cause you feel is worthwhile or which interests you.

An important benefit is that you might be able to gain a reference from the organisation you volunteer for, which you can then use when applying for work.

Some potential issues

English language skills can be an issue for newcomers and you should explore what options are available if language is a barrier. In some cases the organisation will have volunteers or staff who speak your language and it may be possible to volunteer alongside these individuals to help your language improve in an informal setting.

You may need to have your expenses paid on the day that you volunteer in order to avoid hardship. This needs to be explained sensitively to any organisation from the outset.

Cultural issues should be identified and flexibility may be required to accommodate needs such as family or religious commitments. Most organisations will do everything that they can in order to work around an individual's needs as long as they are clearly explained.

Some newcomers, for example asylum seekers, will not know how long they will be staying in a given location and will feel uncertain about their future. This may translate into anxiety or a reluctance to take on new commitments.

Note: If you are a provider of services, or you are a newcomer interested in setting up a volunteering scheme, see the annex at the end of this section.

Will I be interviewed?

Most organisations will want to talk to you before you start with them, but this may not be a formal interview. An interview does not guarantee that you will be offered a position, but it is an opportunity for you to meet with them and ask any questions that you may have as well as answering their questions. They will probably want to discuss why you want to volunteer, what skills you have and what you would like to do or learn, and, crucially, how much time you are able to give and how often.

You may want to ask them about what flexibility there is to take account of your needs (e.g. prayer facilities and timings) whether your expenses will be paid, how regularly you can volunteer and at what times this might be, and whether there will be any training for the position and what supervision you will have – either initially or routinely.

Will my expenses be paid?

Many organisations will repay your travel expenses and may give you an allowance towards subsistence (lunch and/or refreshments). Some may be able to either provide or reimburse you for childcare.

If you are an asylum seeker you cannot accept a flat-rate contribution towards expenses, but rather must be reimbursed for actual expenditure. However expenses are not guaranteed and you should ask about this before starting any volunteering position.

Note: Recent guidance from the DWP states that if you are receiving an income-related benefit you must declare any expenses payments you receive. The full guide can be viewed at http://www.dwp.gov.uk/publications/dwp/2006/volunteering/vg1.pdf
The DWP have however recently clarified that lunch expenses paid to volunteers are exempt from declaration, and that such payments can be disregarded for benefits purposes.

What information will I need to give?

It is important that an organisation checks that you are the person you say that you are, and you will be asked to provide proof of identity. This may include information that can be used for security checks.

In the UK an organisation will need to check whether you have a criminal record if you will be working with certain groups of vulnerable people, for example, children or those dependent on others for their nursing or personal care. In England and Wales this check is carried out through the Criminal Records Bureau (CRB) (www.crb.gov.uk) and involves checking police records for any criminal record for the individual.

A drawback of the system is that the police checks cover five years, and a newcomer may not have been in the UK for this length of time. Where there are reciprocal agreements with the UK it is sometimes possible to check records in the person's country of origin. The police checks take time, and while the CRB aims to provide a response within a certain period, at some times in the year (for example before the new school year) the service is very busy and there are likely to be some delays.

In Scotland, criminal record checks are conducted by Disclosure Scotland. Disclosure may be to Basic, Standard, or Enhanced level, and should normally take two weeks or less to process. For more information, contact Disclosure Scotland on 0870 609 6006 or visit www.disclosurescotland.co.uk, remembering that it is the organisation you want to volunteer for that will carry out the check. There is a charge of £20, although this is waived for (non-paid) positions in voluntary organisations. This is also the case in England.

References

Most organisations will ask for at least one referee before offering a volunteering post. This is someone who knows you but is not a relative and who can confirm the information you have given about yourself. You should ask this person's permission before you give their name and contact details for reference purposes.

If you are a refugee, it is unlikely that you will be able to provide a reference from a previous employer if your last employment was outside the UK. Sources of references could be an employee in your local refugee agency, such as the Refugee Council, an English tutor from the college or your solicitor or landlord. If you cannot find a referee, the organisation may offer you a slightly different and supervised position for a few months.

Other newcomers may face similar issues and can volunteer and receive references in the same way.

What happens when I start?

You should be given an induction to the organisation, the workplace and to your position. This will include information on your working hours and duties, health and safety policies and practices, such as first aid, fire precautions, general and personal security in the workplace, and safety.

All organisations have an obligation to make sure that they are not exposing their volunteers to risks to health and safety (see page 401). Depending on where you are working, you may also be made aware of other risks, such as infectious diseases, or policies such as the use of panic buttons.

The organisation should make clear whom you can go to for support when you are volunteering and/or who will be supervising you and what that will involve.

What happens if I don't like it?

You are under no obligation to stay with the organisation, but it is often helpful to talk about any problems with your supervisor or with any of the organisation's management as soon as they arise, as they may be able to do something to resolve them. If you do decide to leave it is good practice to give the organisation some notice, so that they can replace you before you leave.

Where can I find out more?

Volunteering opportunities are often advertised in local libraries, charity shops, Jobcentre Plus offices, community centres, Citizens Advice Bureaux offices or in the Volunteer Bureaux or Councils for Voluntary Service, which can be found in most areas. These opportunities will cover a range of organisations and professions.

The Volunteer Bureaux in particular play a role in collating the various opportunities available locally and matching them with potential volunteers. For example it may be possible for a trained accountant to gain a volunteering placement working for a charity in their accounts section. If you do not know where you might find volunteering opportunities in your area, you can register your details with an organisation such as TimeBank, who will forward you to the relevant organisation in your area and ask you to contact them directly for what is available, or alternatively search for opportunities on www.do-it.org.uk

Mentoring

Mentoring is 'a one-to-one non-judgemental relationship in which an individual mentor voluntarily gives time to support and encourage a mentee. The relationship is typically developed at a time of transition in the mentee's life and lasts for a significant and sustained period'.[2]

Mentoring is a very useful tool for a newcomer to find out more about aspects of life in the UK, and is a more formal relationship than befriending. It is often arranged by an organisation and sometimes is used by organisations as support for their new employees. Mentors are members of the general public and are usually used to work on specific areas, such as employment or education. They provide guidance, support and encouragement for the individual in an informal setting. Mentors can be drawn from specific groups. For example refugees who have been in the UK for some years may be encouraged to mentor new refugees.

There are several mentoring projects in the UK which target refugees. These include the Time Together scheme run through TimeBank, the Refugee Council, Refugees into Jobs, RETAS, RAGU and SOVA. For all contact details please see the Further Information section on page 556.

Work placements

What is a work placement?

Work placements provide an ideal opportunity to gain some experience of a UK workplace, to gain a recent reference, to update existing skills, improve language skills and to demonstrate to employers that you are capable of undertaking paid employment in a particular position.

In the main, work placements will fit into normal working hours, and although they are unpaid, you should be able to claim expenses, either from the employer or from Jobcentre Plus if you are claiming benefits.

How long will they last?

Work placements should last a minimum of four weeks to provide useful experience, although three to six months is better. To be of most use to the individual and the employer, the placement can be structured around a particular project or job role, with regular reviews of progress and achievement.

Who is eligible?

Most newcomers are eligible for work placements in the UK. If you are an asylum seeker, see page 72. Refugees and those with Indefinite, Exceptional and Discretionary Leave to remain or with Humanitarian Protection are able and often encouraged to take work placements in the UK to gain recent and relevant work experience. If you are claiming benefits, you or the employing organisation might be eligible for extra allowances for attending a work placement and you should check this with your Jobcentre Plus personal adviser.

You might also want to ask your Jobcentre Plus personal adviser about programmes to help you get into work and when it would be possible to start these (see page 220).

Expenses

As part of the work placement your expenses should be paid by the employing organisation and they may give you an allowance towards subsistence (lunch and/or refreshments). Some may be able to either provide or reimburse you for childcare.

If you are claiming benefits you may be eligible for extra money for participating in a work placement, though if this is not organised through your Jobcentre Plus office you need to discuss the placement with your personal adviser. If you will have difficulties in paying for a season ticket the employer may, in some cases, be willing to buy this for you.

References

It is quite likely that you will not have a reference (from a 'referee' – usually your previous employer). This might be because your previous employer is unavailable or a reference cannot be easily provided. In this situation a work placement is particularly useful as an employer should be able to provide one.

References from people who have known you for a short time or only in a personal capacity are also useful. These include solicitors, landlords or your adviser.

Work Trials, Bee Brooke, Centre for Economic & Social Inclusion

Work Trials are a specific scheme organised by Jobcentre Plus. You can organise a Work Trial through Jobcentre Plus or you can suggest one to an employer.

They last up to 15 working days (i.e. 3 weeks) and give employers the chance to try out someone for a particular job before deciding whether or not to employ them, which gives you the opportunity to prove that you can do the job. Work Trials are designed for people who have the motivation to work but are often sifted out before the employer interviews, or people who tend not to perform well in interviews.

A Jobcentre Plus personal adviser can arrange a Work Trial, or you can suggest a Work Trial to a potential employer.

Benefits of Work Trials

The key benefits of Work Trials are:

- you can decide whether the job is suitable without losing your benefit. You will also be paid meals and travel expenses
- if you leave a Work Trial or decide you do not want the job, your benefit is not affected
- it gives you the opportunity to prove you can do the job
- it is a good way to persuade an employer to try you out
- it is an opportunity to find out what problems you may have in a working environment and get support to overcome them

Eligibility

If you are aged 18-24 then you can be offered a Work Trial only if you are on the New Deal and the Jobcentre Plus district manager has decided to make Work Trials available to this group. For other age groups, you must meet the following eligibility requirements:

- you must be aged 18 or over
- you must have been unemployed for six months or more

- you must be receiving Jobseeker's Allowance, Income Support, or National Insurance Credits

Note: To check if you are eligible for these benefits, see page 130.

The following groups can participate in a Work Trial regardless of how long they have been unemployed:

- people who require basic training in English
- people with literacy or numeracy difficulties
- people leaving Work Based Learning for Adults
- participants on the New Deal for Lone Parents
- people with disabilities who are unemployed
- victims of large-scale redundancies, at the discretion of the Regional Director
- returners to the labour market who have been out of the labour market for two years or more due to domestic reasons

Work Trial vacancies

It is important that Work Trials are only used where there is a genuine vacancy for a permanent and full-time job.

Part-time jobs

If the advertised job is part-time, then a Work Trial is only justified if it could result in enough earnings to enable you to sign off benefits. If a job is part-time, Jobcentre Plus suggest that a Work Trial of less than five working days should be enough.

Temporary jobs

If the job is temporary, a Work Trial should only be used if it enables someone who has been out of work for a particularly long time to start work. If a job is temporary, Jobcentre Plus suggest that a Work Trial of less than five working days should be enough.

Jobcentre Plus staff are given guidance to ensure the vacancy is genuine. If the Work Trial is not in your best interests, staff are advised to cancel the Trial.

Is it compulsory to participate in a Work Trial?

A Work Trial is completely voluntary. You can terminate the Work Trial at any time and you retain the right to refuse employment. This will not affect your benefit entitlements.

Contract with employer

Before you begin your Work Trial, the employer must agree:

- to provide you with the opportunity to do tasks which will give you suitable work preparation and experience
- to interview you as a potential permanent employee for the vacancy which has been advertised, or another which they think you may be suitable for
- not to fill the vacancy you are on trial for until you have completed the Work Trial and have been interviewed

What should be explained to you before you start

Your Jobcentre Plus personal adviser should explain to you:

- why you are doing the Work Trial
- what the job will involve
- how it will work, the hours you will work and how long it will last
- that the Work Trial is voluntary
- that you will continue to receive benefit
- that you must still be available for work whilst you are on the Work Trial
- that you should attend an interview for another job whilst you are on the Work Trial
- the arrangements for travel and meal expenses
- that the employer is not allowed to make any further payments
- the terms and conditions of the Work Trial
- that you will be visited during the Work Trial

- whom to contact if you have any problems

Arrangements when you start

On the first day of the Work Trial, the employer should:

- make sure you understand what the organisation does
- introduce you to the people who will be responsible for you during the Work Trial
- explain any arrangements the employer has with trade unions at the location of the Work Trial

Unauthorised absences and termination of the Work Trial

If you stop attending the Work Trial for more than four consecutive days, it will be assumed that you have withdrawn from the placement. Similarly, if you are sick, and are likely to remain so for more than a few days, the Work Trial may be terminated.

The employer has the right to terminate your Work Trial at any time for reasons relating to changes in the operating needs of the organisation, or your behaviour or welfare.

Expenses

When you are participating in a Work Trial, you continue to receive your full benefit entitlement. You can also claim expenses from Jobcentre Plus of up to £10 a day for travel and £3 a day for meals. These expenses do not affect your benefits.

The end of the Work Trial

If you are offered the job after the Work Trial and you accept it, then the Work Trial has been successful. If you are offered the job and decide not to take it, your benefit entitlement will not be affected. In this situation, your Jobcentre Plus personal adviser will agree a further course of action with you. If you are not offered the job, your Jobcentre Plus personal adviser should liaise with the employer to find out why.

Travel to Interview Scheme, Kelsey Froehlich, Centre for Economic & Social Inclusion

The Travel to Interview Scheme is designed to help unemployed people attend job interviews they would otherwise be unable to attend. Travel costs and any unavoidable overnight expenses, up to a maximum of two nights, are paid by Jobcentre Plus.

Eligibility

To be eligible for the Travel to Interview Scheme you must be either directly or indirectly claiming one of the following benefits:

- Jobseeker's Allowance
- Incapacity or Disability Benefits
- Maternity Benefits
- Carer's Allowance
- National Insurance credits
- Income Support as a lone parent or a person in receipt of Invalid Care Allowance
- Jobcentre Plus/New Deal Allowance (for participants on Work Based Learning for Adults (WBLA), Work Based Learning for Young People, Work Based Learning in Wales, Training for Work in Scotland, and New Deal)

As a newcomer you will face the additional qualifying criteria explained under the benefit section (see page 113).

16-18 year old jobseekers must also be registered with Connexions/Careers Office, in receipt of Bridging Allowance, or on a Work Based Training for Young People Scheme.

If you are aged 18 to 24, you face additional eligibility requirements. If you have been unemployed for fewer than 26 weeks, you may apply for the Travel to Interview Scheme. If you have been unemployed for longer than 26 weeks, you can only apply if you are a New Deal participant and the District Manager has agreed to fund this out of the New Deal budget.

You will normally be required to demonstrate that you have lived in your home area for more than four weeks, but if you cannot show this, the personal adviser has discretion to allow you to apply for the scheme.

An interview is eligible for payment under the Scheme if it meets the following requirements:

- the job is 30 hours or more per week
- if it is for a short-term contract, it has the potential to become permanent
- the job may be a self-employed position, provided it is for a specific employer (this includes commission-only jobs)
- voluntary work is eligible, if it would require you signing off as unemployed
- employment agency positions are eligible only if for a specific vacancy.
- if an employer requires a proficiency test to demonstrate your job skills, it can be covered under the Scheme

An interview is not eligible if it is for one of the following:

- a seasonal, temporary or short-term fixed contract lasting less than 12 months
- a government employment or training programme, or other type of education or training course
- a discussion about the possibility of setting up in business
- a general assessment at an employment agency
- a speculative interview where the employer does not have a current vacancy

Each application is considered individually, but Jobcentre Plus staff must generally take the following guidelines into account:

- the location of the interview (but not necessarily the location of the place of work) must be beyond your normal daily travelling distance
- if local people commonly travel to the place where the interview is, then it is probably within normal daily travelling distance

- if the interview is more than 25 miles from your home (40 miles if it is in central London) it is likely to be beyond normal daily travelling distance
- if the journey takes more than one hour (1 hour 20 minutes for journeys including the London area) it is likely to be beyond normal daily travelling distance

Confirmation

It is usual practice to produce a letter inviting you to interview with your application. The letter should include a statement that no help will be given with your travel costs, and Jobcentre Plus will confirm this with the employer or employment agency.

Note: For this reason, you may not want to use the Travel to Interview Scheme, as the employer is informed that you are currently claiming benefit. If you are on New Deal, your personal adviser may be able to assist you with travel costs using the Adviser Discretion Fund instead (see page 184).

Approval

Once your application has been accepted, you will be issued with a travel warrant, which you can exchange for the ticket that is the cheapest and most direct route to your interview. In most cases it will be recommended that you travel by coach or bus. However, if you give suitable reasons for travelling by rail, you should be allowed to do so.

It is possible to request an overnight sleeper if you would otherwise have to claim for daytime travel plus one or two overnight stays. You will be allowed to travel by air if the cost of the journey is less than by other modes of public transport plus one or two overnight stays.

Non-attendance and overpayments

Jobcentre Plus will always check whether you have attended the interview. If you have not, it is likely you will be referred to a personal adviser who will consider further action. You will also be asked to pay back any help you have received from the Scheme.

Advice for refugee and migrant community organisations

If you are an adviser or a newcomer who wants to set up a volunteering scheme or a work placement, there are a range of issues to consider. This section covers some of the key issues.

Setting up a volunteering scheme

Establishing a volunteering scheme is complex and it is important to take time to consider all the implications. Issues that you should consider are set out in the following table:

Issues to consider if setting up a volunteering scheme
Is there a local organisation already providing this service? Why will it be needed?
Why do you need volunteers?
What will the volunteers do?
Will they be working with vulnerable groups and need screening by the CRB?
What will the volunteers receive from volunteering (training, references, experience etc)?
How many volunteers do you need and where will you get them from?
How long will they be needed for?
How will you ensure that you have enough volunteers at the right time and what happens if you do not have enough?
What information will you need from volunteers about themselves and how will you ensure that you comply with data protection legislation?
What training will they need?
Do you need to take references for the volunteers or send their information for a police check?
Who will supervise them?
Will their managers be paid and what training will they need?
What additional support might they need?

What risks might they be exposed to and how can these be minimised or eradicated?
Are you sufficiently insured and will the volunteers be covered under that policy?
What space and equipment will the volunteers need?
Can you pay for travel expenses/childcare?
Can you provide childcare?
Do you have a clear handbook for the volunteers that outlines the policies and procedures in the organisation and includes a clear volunteer agreement?
How will the scheme be evaluated?
Do you have sufficient funding for the above and how long will it last?

The above list is by no means definitive and you should seek advice before setting up any scheme. A list of contacts and further information is included at the end of this chapter, and you may find it helpful to talk to other organisations running volunteering schemes in your area to find out what issues they face and whether these might apply to you.

If you are providing services to newcomers suffering from low self-esteem, who are concerned that their skills are not relevant in the UK or who may have little knowledge of work practices in the UK, it might be useful to explain how the application process will work (for example if someone needs to fill in a form, be interviewed or offer references).

In addition, some newcomers may struggle to understand the concept of formal volunteering as it may not exist in their country of origin. Similarly, some newcomers may therefore also not understand the benefits of volunteering or why they are not being paid. If you are providing services, you should take this into account.

Setting up a work placement

Working with employers

The most successful work placements have been found to be those where a voluntary or specifically refugee agency works closely with the employer. It is important for advisers in agencies to take the time to establish what the employer's expectations are of the work placement and what support might be needed throughout the selection process as well as when the person is in post.

A lot of this work can be done before the work placement is advertised, and will ensure that there is a thorough foundation in place. Equally it is essential for advisers to explain clearly what the placement will involve and what it might or might not lead to, so that those undertaking the placement do not, for example, expect that it will lead to a permanent position when this has never been envisaged.

The employing organisation should be aware that newcomers are likely to need significant supervision and/or support, in the same way that any new employee would need help when moving to a new role. The employer is likely to need regular and ongoing support from the organisation referring newcomers to them in order to ensure that any unexpected issues are dealt with efficiently and promptly.

The adviser should also encourage the employer to brief their staff on issues that may arise from taking newcomers for work placements, for example language issues, lack of knowledge of current systems or routine tasks. Flexibility, helpfulness and patience are of key importance when settling into a new post.

Issues for advisers

If you are an adviser, there are several things to think about when designing a placement:

- visits (see below)
- applications and interviews (see below)
- selection and feedback (see below)
- references (see below)
- induction (see below)
- health and safety (see below)
- in-placement support (see below)
- supervisions and review of progress (see below)
- leaving (see below)
- language issues (see page 284)

- documentation (see page 318)
- retention
- costs for the employer (time and money)
- preparing the existing workforce

Visits

Newcomers, and refugees in particular, may lack confidence in their abilities or previous experience and be intimidated by the process of applying for any employment, whether paid or unpaid. Encouraging employers to visit the agency is an important step in increasing their confidence in taking on newcomers. These visits do not necessarily have to concentrate on recruiting for specific work placements or employment. Other activities that advisers/agencies might suggest that employers become involved in are:

- explaining the general context of the UK work culture
- discussing work placements and their benefits
- exploring recruitment processes in the UK
- advising on CV structure or completing application forms
- conducting mock interviews
- mentoring individuals or groups of individuals
- cultural or community activities arranged by your organisation to raise awareness of the issues faced by your clients when first coming to the UK
- arranging office tours for candidates

Application and Interviews

Newcomers may find being in an interview situation intimidating and may have been subject to discrimination in the past. You and the prospective employer may find it helpful to talk through the general purpose of interviews with the person in advance, and even give them a copy of the questions that will or might be asked.

Employers should be made aware that the culture of interviews in the UK may be very different from the culture of applying for work in other countries of origin.

It can be difficult to transfer previous experience and skills into a UK context, for example working on a community project or within the family business doesn't necessarily equate to employers' ideas of customer relations and budgeting skills.

Employers should be clear that newcomers may find filling in application forms difficult and that they may be unlikely to apply for jobs where there are lengthy forms to fill in. One to one advice on how to fill in these forms is very useful and advisers should talk to the employer about alternative methods of applying, such as through a CV.

It is essential that newcomers understand why they are being interviewed, what will happen to the information that they give, and that they do not feel pressurised to give information that they are not comfortable with sharing. It is also important that they are interviewed in an appropriate space, i.e. a private room.

It may increase their confidence to be interviewed in familiar surroundings, for example within your agency, and you might discuss the possibility of holding interviews there rather than on the employer's premises.

If there is an expectation that the placement will lead to a permanent job this should be made clear from the outset and the employer should interview the newcomer as a potential employee.

Selection and feedback

It is extremely important that the selection process for work placements is clear and based on criteria that are fair and easily understood. It is helpful if these criteria are circulated so newcomers can appreciate if they have done well and where there is room for improvement.

If a candidate is unsuccessful, advisers should work closely with the employer to give the newcomer detailed and constructive feedback on why someone was not selected, what aspects could be improved for future applications and how this might be achieved – for example by expanding skills through volunteering.

References

Newcomers are unlikely to be able to provide a reference from a previous employer if their last employment was outside the UK. This is especially true for refugees or people with Humanitarian Protection or Discretionary Leave.

Sources of references could be an employee in the local refugee agency, such as the Refugee Council, an English tutor from a college or a solicitor or landlord.

If no referee can be found, employers are still able to offer the post or instead offer a slightly different and supervised position for a few months.

Induction

Induction is a process through which newcomers are provided with information to find their feet in a new organisation and position. It includes briefings on health and safety at work, the rules and regulations of the organisation, the people in the organisation (usually introduced on a tour of the workplace), the duties and responsibilities newcomers will carry out, as well as details of whom they will report to and whom to go to if they have any questions, problems or worries. Some organisations use 'buddies', in the form of senior members of staff, who will help newcomers to settle in. This system is very helpful, as often newcomers may have queries about how things are done, or what systems are normally used in the office.

It is important for your adviser to work with the employer on the amount of information newcomers are given, in what form and over what period of time. If newcomers have language needs, they may not be able to understand all the information in an employee handbook for example. Advisors may play a role in explaining to newcomers before they start in the placement, or in advising the employer to spend more time with them to ensure that it is clearly understood.

Advisers should work with the employer and highlight areas that the employer may not have not thought of, such as explaining the UK work culture in more detail, extending the period of induction to allow newcomers to take all the information in, or building in a feedback session for newcomers to ask questions on induction. More information on induction can be found on the ACAS website www.acas.org.uk and on pages 314-315 of this book.

Health and safety

It is good practice for the adviser to visit the site where newcomers will be employed and look for any health and safety issues that might arise – for example will newcomers be able to understand the information on health and safety measures in the workplace, and if not could this be translated or related through diagrams? The adviser should also check that newcomers will be adequately covered by the organisation's employer's liability insurance. More information on health and safety can be found on the government website www.hse.gov.uk

In-placement support

During the placement advisers and their advice organisation should be in close and regular contact with the employer, if only to check that all is going well. In some cases newcomers may feel more able to talk to the adviser who arranged the work placement about issues that they are facing, than to the employer.

Supervision and reviews of progress

During the placement, and in particular when the placement is part of a specific project, progress and achievements should be regularly reviewed. Advisers should encourage newcomers to participate fully in these sessions and they should be written up to provide a record of progress.

Advisers can encourage the employer to involve the advice agency in this process at the planning stage or additionally as part of a steering group during the placement. The agency may also want to offer newcomers a confidential service where they can discuss any issues that are arising from the placement that they do not feel comfortable discussing with the employer.

Leaving

If a work placement does not result in a permanent position with the employer – and many do not – advisers should work with the employer on support structures and help for newcomers once the placement has finished. Advisers should ensure that newcomers are able to use the employer as a reference in future job applications and the organisation may want to help newcomers further. If this is to include an extension of the work placement advisers should make sure that both sides are clear on what this will entail in terms of expectations, benefits to the client and implications for any benefits that newcomers may be claiming.

All future post-placement support should be clearly agreed, if possible in writing and in particular where further support has been offered. Advisers should also agree the time period for support with newcomers and the employer, so that expectations are clear on both sides of what service can and cannot be expected.

Checklist for work placements

An adviser may want to consider the following when thinking of establishing a work placement scheme:

- what are the individual's needs?
- what positions are they aiming for and in which professions?
- are they ready for work?
- what will happen to any benefits that they are claiming?
- does this affect how many hours they could work for?
- can they apply for extra allowances for expenses whilst on a work placement, in particular if it has not been organised through Jobcentre Plus?
- are there organisations in the area who can offer suitable placements?
- are they open to taking newcomers for work placements?
- are newcomers covered by the employer's insurance?
- are there any health and safety risks? What assessment has been made?

- what supervision and/or training will be offered as part of the placement?
- what support will be available after the placement finishes?
- what is the induction process?
- what support networks will be available through the employer during the placement?
- how will the referring agency be updated on progress and/or problems?

Endnotes

[1] http://www.ind.homeoffice.gov.uk/news.asp?NewsId=365&SectionId=3
[2] Home Office Active Communities Unit

11
Volunteering, work experience placements and mentoring

12 UK work culture

Beryl Randall,
Employability Forum

Introduction

There are a number of aspects of UK work culture that may be alien to newcomers. This section looks at some of the practicalities and includes:

- National Insurance
- Finding a tax code
- Bank accounts
- Pay slips
- Driving licences
- Car insurance

National Insurance

National Insurance is a form of social insurance that helps to fund state benefits and the National Health Service (NHS). Each unique National Insurance number or NINO (a combination of letters and numbers such as AB 12 34 56 C) is linked to a record of your contributions and is a reference number for the social security system.

A NINO is not a proof of identity or of permission to work and you do not need to have a NINO to start paid employment.

To apply for a NINO you will probably need to have an 'evidence of identity interview' at your local Jobcentre Plus. It can take some time to make an appointment for this interview and for the number to come through.

Some groups of people (including asylum seekers with a positive decision) are eligible for a fast-track process which does not include the interview. You will need to bring original documents to prove your identity with you to the interview. For more information on documents see pages 390 and 332.

You can find out more information about National Insurance numbers on: The Department for Work and Pensions website: http://www.dwp.gov.uk/lifeevent/benefits/ni_number.asp

Directgov: http://www.direct.gov.uk/MoneyTaxAndBenefits/Taxes/BeginnersGuideToTax/BeginnersGuideToTaxArticles/fs/en?CONTENT_ID=4015904&chk=izW7Qe

HM Revenue and Customs: http://www.hmrc.gov.uk/nic/

Information on fast-track National Insurance numbers (including refugee NINOs) can be found at: http://www.hmrc.gov.uk/manuals/nimmanual/NIM39610.htm

Contact details for your local Jobcentre Plus can be found in your phone book or via: http://www.jobcentreplus.gov.uk/JCP/Aboutus/Ouroffices/LocalOfficeSearch.aspx

Finding my tax code

Every working person in the UK is given a tax code, which is a combination of numbers and letters. The amount of tax you pay varies by factors including age and income (see page 302). If you are employed by an organisation, your employer will arrange for tax to be deducted from your wages. If you work for more than one employer you will get a special tax code.

If you do not have a tax code your employer will ask you to fill in a P46 form which they will send to the Inland Revenue to process and to check that the code your employer has given you is correct. You may be charged emergency tax until you have the correct code.

A P45 is a form sent to you from the Inland Revenue via your employer when you leave your job. It is a statement of the money you have earned, the tax you have paid and the amount you are expected to pay in the tax year. When you start a new job, your employer will ask for parts 2 and 3 of the P45. If you lose your P45 you should contact your Tax Office with your National Insurance number and, if you have it, a tax reference. If you leave your job before you have a correct tax code, or if you think that you might be able to claim back some of your tax, you should contact your local tax office.

Contact details of all tax offices can be found at: http://www.hmrc.gov.uk/local/individuals/index.htm

If you are self-employed you must register with HM Revenue and Customs within 3 months of starting to work by either calling the HMRC Newly Self-Employed Helpline on 0845 915 4515 from 8.00am to 6.00pm, Monday to Friday, English Language Service only, or completing the form Becoming self-employed and registering for National Insurance contributions and/or tax (CWF1).

You can download the form at www.hmrc.gov.uk/forms/cwf1.pdf or collect it from any HM Revenue & Customs Enquiry Centre.

If you are a student you will still pay tax on your earnings unless you are:

- in full time education in the UK, working only in the holidays
- you are going back to full-time education after a holiday
- your total income is lower than your personal allowance

You will need to ask your employer for form P38S to make sure that tax is not deducted from your earnings.

It is illegal for anyone to work 'cash in hand' without their employer making deductions for National Insurance and tax, even if you are working on a part-time, casual or temporary basis. If you are found out you risk losing your right to work and some of your rights to benefits.

If you are self-employed you can accept cash for work that you do, but it is illegal not to declare this on your Self-Assessment Tax Return and illegal not to pay tax and National Insurance on these amounts if they are due.

Bank accounts

You will need to have some form of bank account in the UK for salary or benefits payments and to manage your money. Some employers have a special agreement with a bank and will be able to open an account for you when you start employment. If you are coming to the UK as a student, your student union, welfare officer or student services department may be able to help you.

If you have a bank account in your home country you should check to see if they have any links or special relationships with a UK bank that could help you open an account here. If you have a cash card from your bank you may be able to use it in the UK while you are waiting for a new account to be set up, but you may be charged more money for this service.

On average it can take from two to three weeks to open a bank account. If you do not have the documents the bank requires to set up an account it will probably take longer than this. Different banks have different policies on the documents they ask to see, but they are all required to check your identity (that you are who you say you are and that you live where you say you live) before an account is opened.

In general you will be asked to show the originals of at least one current proof of identity and at least one current proof of address. If you are not a UK national, the proof of identity will most likely be a passport or national identity card. Banks recognise that if you are new to this country, you may not have a UK bill with your address on. To prove where you live a bank may also accept a letter from your employer in the UK or a tenancy agreement from your landlord. If you do not have the documents the bank asks to see, you should ask a member of staff in the bank to send your application to someone who is responsible for exceptional cases.

The Immigration Status Document issued by the Home Office has recently been accepted by the British Bankers Association as an acceptable form of establishing identity, and this has been included in the guidance sent to banks. This should be introduced across all banks by September 2006.

There are several different types of account and you should talk to the bank to find out which one is best for you. You may be offered a basic bank account at first. This account allows you to access your money with a cash card and to set up direct debits, transfers and standing orders, but you do not have access to credit.

With all accounts you should check the bank's restrictions on taking out your money – some have maximum withdrawals per day, and you may only be able to use your cash card to take out money for free at certain locations. If you use your cash card to take out money from a cash machine run by another bank or company you may be charged. If you are offered a basic bank account you may be able to change to a different account after a certain period of time.

You may also wish to investigate whether there is a credit union in your local area. Credit Unions enjoy slightly different identification requirements for opening accounts. For example, they are permitted to accept a letter from a responsible person in the absence of traditional identification. To locate a credit union, see the credit union search facility on the Association of British Credit Unions Limited website, www.abcul.coop or call their helpline on 0161 832 3694.

You may also want to send some of your money back home. For information on this please see the remittances section on page 534. To find out if credit unions operate remittances contact the Association of British Credit Unions Limited (details above).

Problems or poor service

You may experience problems or receive a poor service when setting up a bank account. If so, you could:

Stage 1

Contact the bank and ask for their complaints procedure (the major UK banks are covered by the Banking Code, which has a set of standards that you can check against the service you received)

Stage 2

If you not satisfied with the bank's response, contact the Financial Ombudsman Service at:

The Financial Ombudsman Service
South Quay Plaza
183 Marsh Wall
London E14 9SR

0845 0801800
enquiries@financial-ombudsman.org.uk
www.financial-ombudsman.org.uk

Bank account information

More information about basic bank accounts see this information from The Financial Services Authority:
http://www.fsa.gov.uk/consumer/pdfs/bank_account.pdf

The Islamic Bank of Britain is the UK's first stand-alone Sharia'a compliant retail bank for Muslims and non-Muslims and offers current and savings accounts, amongst others:
http://www.islamic-bank.com

For more information about money matters and bank accounts you can contact your local Citizens Advice Bureau. Contact details will be in the phone book or can be found online at http://www.adviceguide.org.uk/ or http://www.citizensadvice.org.uk/

For issues in Scotland, refer to http://www.cas.org.uk

Pay slips

At the end of each month (or in some cases at the end of each week) you should receive a pay slip. This typically (but not always) comes in the form of an A5 sized-paper record with its own envelope.

You should always keep your pay slip for your own records.

Receiving a pay slip is a legal entitlement in the UK. If you are not receiving one, you can take action against your employer. See page 386 for more information.

Driving licences

If you are going to drive in the UK you must hold a current recognised driving licence. If you hold a full licence from your home country this may be valid for driving in the UK for a certain period of time. After this time it may no longer be valid and you will have to get a full UK driving licence if you want to drive. You should check with the Driver and Vehicle Licensing Agency (DVLA) to see if it is valid. If you do not have your driving licence with you, or if it is not valid in the UK, you will need to apply for a provisional driving licence and pass a theory and practical test to get a full UK driving licence.

There are two types of licence in the UK, provisional or full. The provisional driving licence has restrictions on what and how you may drive. You must display 'L' plates (Learner), you cannot drive on a motorway and you must be accompanied by someone who is over 21 and who has had a full licence for more than 3 years.

To apply for a driving licence you need to complete an application form (available online or at your local post office) and send it with your fee (£38.00) for the licence, your passport or birth certificate and a recent colour passport photograph to the address on the form. If you do not have a UK, EU or EEA passport, the photograph must be verified by a doctor, lawyer, teacher, police officer, MP or minister of religion who has known you for at least 2 years. You should not be charged for this. If you have been in the UK for less than 2 years you should take the photo, application and documents to the local DVLA office who will be able to authorise it for you.

If the Home Office has your passport and you need it back to apply for a driving licence you should contact the Immigration and Nationality Directorate on 0870 606 7766.

If you do not have a passport or birth certificate the DVLA will accept a Home Office issued travel document in support of the application. The DVLA has been working with the Home Office on documentation issues and has added the Immigration Status Document to its List A documents for proving identity. If none of these documents is available, DVLA will consider whatever alternative evidence of identity an individual can submit, which may include bank statements and utility bills.[1]

For more information on Driving Licences, costs and requirements, please visit http://www.dvla.gov.uk

Car insurance

Driving without insurance is illegal in the UK. All vehicles must be taxed, registered and insured. The law requires every driver to have insurance to cover them, or any driver they allow to drive the vehicle. If the car does not belong to you, even if it is insured, you may not be insured to drive it.

There are 3 types of insurance policy:

- Comprehensive – the fullest and usually most expensive cover
- Third Party, Fire and Theft
- Third Party only (the minimum required cover)

The cost of insurance varies depending on factors such as your age, how long you have been driving, the age and type of car you are driving, and whether you have any penalties on your licence.

The cost can also vary from company to company and you should get several quotes before buying insurance. Insurance companies can be found in the phone book or online. If you are driving in Northern Ireland you should make sure that the cover includes Northern Ireland – this is likely to be more expensive than driving in the rest of the UK.

Endnotes

[1] Hansard answer to Question 158461 dated 24 April 2001 http://www.publications.parliament.uk/pa/cm200001/cmhansrd/vo010424/text/10424w04.htm

13 Employment rights

Alison Balchin, TUC

Introduction

This chapter aims to help you to understand your employment rights as a migrant worker in Britain. The rights that are available to newcomers who are working in the UK are affected by issues such as nationality, whether your employment status is legal, and if so, whether that status is as employee or worker, and whether you are residing under the provisions of European law and policy or domestic UK rules and regulations.

In this chapter we will look at the different groups of migrant workers and any restrictions on their rights to work in Britain. We will then look at the range of employment rights that exist in Britain and who is entitled to these, and finally we will consider employment issues that are particularly likely to affect and be of concern to groups of migrant workers.

Who can work in Britain?

Information on who can lawfully work in Britain is set out in the section on immigration status, pages 24-69. The following pages show a summary of who can lawfully work in Britain.

At a glance guide to working in Britain

You can work if

- you are a citizen of a country in the European Economic Area (EEA)
- you are a citizen of Poland, Lithuania, Estonia, Latvia, Slovenia, Slovakia, Hungary or the Czech Republic and have been required to apply to register with the Home Office under the 'Worker Registration Scheme'
- you are a refugee or have humanitarian protection/discretionary leave, formerly known as Exceptional Leave to Remain in the UK
- you are an international student studying in the UK and working for 20 hours per week or less during term-time. There is no limit on the amount of work that can be done during academic holidays. Graduates in some subjects may be able to work for one year after finishing their studies without restriction
- you are a Commonwealth citizen aged 18 to 30, working under the Working Holidaymakers Scheme
- you are a Non-EEA national for whom your employer has obtained a work permit or on the Highly Skilled Migrant Programme (HSMP)
- you are a worker admitted under the Seasonal Agricultural Workers Scheme or Sector Based Scheme
- you are an au pair

Note: There are different restrictions on the length of time that you are allowed to remain in the UK and work, depending on which of the above categories you fall into.

Working rights at a glance

Category of Worker	Criteria	Documents	Maximum length of stay	Renewable / extendable?	Any restrictions on work?	Can change employers?	Access to employment rights
EEA Nationals	National of an EEA state or family member of EEA national	Passport or National ID card/ Worker registration card and certificate for A8 nationals in first 12 months	Indefinite	N/A	No – possible exception being higher level public sector / civil servant jobs	Yes	Yes
A8 workers on registration scheme	National of an A8 country (see page 26)	Passport	Initial grant of 12 months then indefinite	Indefinite after first 12 months	No	Yes	Yes
Work Permit Holders	Non EEA nationals who are offered work by UK-based employer	Work Permit Passport	Five years	Yes – can apply for indefinite leave to remain after four years	Yes – limited to employer that recruited them and applied for permit	Restricted – only if another employer applies for work permit for worker	Yes

Working rights at a glance (continued)

Category of Worker	Criteria	Documents	Maximum length of stay	Renewable / extendable?	Any restrictions on work?	Can change employers?	Access to employment rights
Workers under the Fresh Talent Scheme	Outside EEA who studied in Scotland for HND, Degree, Masters, PhD and who lived in Scotland while studying	FLR form Valid degree certificate	Two years	Yes – can apply for a work permit, HSMP, Business person or innovator	Can only work in Scotland	Yes	Yes
Overseas students	Proof of acceptance on approved course of study	Visa Passport	Duration of course	Can in some cases transfer to work permit employment following course	Yes – no more than 20 hours per week during term-time. Must not interfere with study	Yes	Yes
Working holiday makers	Commonwealth citizens aged 17-30, with no dependent children over 5 years old	Visa Entrance clearance certificate	Two years	Two years maximum – but can apply for extension as work permit holder if meet requirements	Allowed to do any work, but must also take a holiday of 12 months out of a stay of 24 months	Yes	Yes

WORKING IN THE UK: NEWCOMER'S HANDBOOK *2ND EDITION*

Working rights at a glance (continued)

Category of Worker	Criteria	Documents	Maximum length of stay	Renewable / extendable?	Any restrictions on work?	Can change employers?	Access to employment rights
Seasonal Workers in Agriculture (SAW)	Students in full-time education	Home Office Work Card	From 5 weeks to six months maximum	Can apply again after three months	Agricultural work	Not without agreement of scheme operator	Yes – but limited access due to short length of stay
Domestic Workers in private households		Stamp in passport indicates length of stay	Six months if employer is here as visitor 12 months if employer is staying longer	Yes – further 12 months. Once worker has worked continuously for employer for four years can apply for Leave to Remain	Yes – if time limited employment No restrictions if granted Indefinite Leave to Remain	Yes – but only to similar post as domestic worker in private household (unless granted ILR)	Yes – with some exemptions from some elements of discrimination law and working time regulations
Asylum seekers	Applied for protection in UK under international conventions	Application Registration Card (ARC)	N/A	N/A	Not allowed to work if applied for asylum after July 2002	Yes	Yes

WORKING IN THE UK: NEWCOMER'S HANDBOOK *2ND EDITION*

Working rights at a glance (continued)

Category of Worker	Criteria	Documents	Maximum length of stay	Renewable / extendable?	Any restrictions on work?	Can change employers?	Access to employment rights
Refugees	Protection given under 1951 Convention Relating to Status of Refugees or under Human Rights Act 1998	Immigration Status Document (ISD)	Granted either Indefinite Leave to Remain or ELR, HP or DL	N/A	No restrictions	Yes	Yes
Illegal workers	Overstayed visa, in breach of visa, failed asylum claim or entered clandestinely	N/A	N/A	N/A	Not allowed to work	N/A	Case law is unclear on whether there is protection

What are my rights at work?

Starting work – having the right documents

Under immigration law, employers are required to ask all new employees to give them proof of their right to work in Britain.[1] Section 8 of the Asylum and Immigration Act 1996 threatens employers with a fine if they employ people who are subsequently found not to be entitled to work by virtue of their immigration status. As a result, employers may be reluctant to offer jobs to prospective employees if they feel that their immigration status might be problematic.

In some cases, even when the worker is clearly entitled to work in the UK, employers have been more inclined to withhold the offers of jobs on the grounds that they do not want to risk the possibility of being prosecuted or fined.[2]

Key documents

There is a range of documentation that you can use to prove your entitlement to work. Work Permits, the Worker's Registration Certificate and National Insurance Numbers are detailed below. See pages 318-325 for a complete overview of all documentation.

Work Permits

If you have obtained work through a Work Permit, then this will be sufficient to give proof of your right to work.

National Insurance Numbers

For all other employees the most commonly accepted proof is the National Insurance (NI) Number. However, recent changes to the law mean that employers can no longer rely solely on the NI card, but must have a second document – usually one including a photograph. A NI number is a unique number that identifies every individual liable to pay National Insurance Contributions. NI numbers are issued by the Inland Revenue's National Insurance Contributions Office. They are in the form of two letters followed by six numbers and a letter (for example AB 12 34 56 C).

If you are a migrant worker from another EEA state you may be able to use your identity card to obtain an NI number. You will need to make an appointment at a local Jobcentre Plus for what is called an 'evidence of identity' interview. You must attend this interview in person and should bring along your EU card and any other documentation such as a passport or birth certificate. Work permit holders from outside the EEA can obtain a NI number by similarly presenting evidence of identity. If you claim any benefits you will have to provide your NI number, or if you don't have one you will have to apply for one.

There can be long delays in issuing NI numbers but some employers are able to fast-track NI applications for some employees in the business and commercial sectors or under the Highly Skilled Migrants Programme. If you are not in work, you can ask for an interim payment of benefits while you are waiting – seek advice if this is refused or if you are refused a NI number.

It is best to produce original copies of documents about your date of birth, identity and marriage. However, some people will not have these, in which case, you may need to contact the place in the country where these are and/or try to provide other evidence – such as letters from advisers, relatives and friends who have known you for a long time or provide evidence about traditional record-keeping systems. You will need to be interviewed by the Inland Revenue contributions staff if they don't feel that they have sufficient evidence of your identity.

Worker's Registration Certificate

Workers from eight out of the ten new member states that joined the EU from 1 May 2004 have to register with the Home Office under the new Worker Registration Scheme within 30 days of starting work. On registering, a Worker's Registration Certificate will be issued for 12 months initially. Employers will have to check that any new worker from the A8 member states has registered and it will be unlawful for them to employ a national from the new member states if they are not registered for the job they are doing. The exceptions to this will be nationals from Malta and Cyprus and those who are self-employed who will have full free movement rights and will not be required to obtain a Worker's Registration Certificate.

Under arrangements agreed with the Home Office, workers registering will also receive a TUC leaflet outlining their basic employment rights and the benefits of trade union membership.

Registered workers can change jobs within the year, as long as there is no more than one month in the year during which they are not employed. Each time they change jobs they will have to renew the certificate, although there will be no charge for this. During the year, they have restricted rights to benefits (see page 119). Following a year of work, workers will be provided with evidence that they have achieved free movement rights.

Discrimination

Employers who impose too high a burden of proof of entitlement to work or who unreasonably reject an applicant because they fear asylum and immigration complications may be guilty of discrimination under the Race Relations Act 1976. The Home Office has issued guidelines which advise employers to treat all applicants in the same way at each stage of the application process in order to avoid discriminating against some groups of workers. For example, if an employer only sought proof of entitlement to work from migrant workers who are Black, this could be challenged under the Race Relations Act 1976. See the section on racial discrimination on page 424.

Legal rights

If you have legal employment status, that is, you are legally entitled to work in Britain and have registered for National Insurance purposes and been given an NI number, then you will be entitled to certain minimum rights at work. If you do not have legal employment status, and you are not 'on the books', then you will probably have no legal employment rights. This is particularly the case if the employer was not aware of any illegality. Employment tribunals may agree to hear cases even where there is some question of the legality of the employment relationship, if they believe that this would be in the public interest (See also page 364 regarding working without paying tax and National Insurance).

In Britain, everyone who is legally entitled to work has two kinds of employment right. The first kind are the rights given to you by the law, by legal Acts passed by Parliament, and by Regulations made under these Acts. These are called statutory rights and they set out the minimum entitlements that employers must offer, for example, to ensure that a worker is paid the minimum wage. The second kind are the rights provided by your contract. These will be different for every job. They may offer better terms than your statutory rights or cover areas where there are no statutory rights. They should not offer less generous terms than your statutory rights however, as this is unlawful.

Employment status: worker or employee?

In Britain, the employment rights that you are entitled to depend on your employment status, that is whether by law you are considered to be a 'worker' or an 'employee'. The working relationship that you have with your employer will determine whether you are classed as a 'worker' or an 'employee'. This is more than just a different title or label: it has real consequences in terms of whether you can claim important legal rights at work. For guidance on 'worker' or 'employee', please see the section on tribunals, page 488.

Some workers are not classed as employees of the company that is providing them with work; instead they are classed as 'workers' under a contract for services. However, many workers are employees and will be entitled to additional rights only available to employees.

Please note that the law in this area is complex and it is not possible to provide a definitive guide to who is an employee and who is a worker in this handbook. Please see the further information section for advice on whom to contact, pages 556-630.

The guidance below will give you a general idea of the factors that the courts and tribunals take into account when deciding whether someone is an employee or a worker:

- is your employer obliged to provide you with work and to pay you for being available to work?

- does your employer control what you do and lay down how and when you do it?
- do you have to carry out the work personally, (ie. you cannot provide for another worker to carry it out on your behalf?)
- does your employer supply the tools or other equipment for the job?
- do they pay tax and National Insurance on your behalf (although this alone does not prove that you are an employee)?

If you answered 'Yes' to most or all of the above, you are more likely to be classed as an employee.

Or:

- has the employer stated that they will only offer work as and when you are required?
- do you decide when you will work, and can you turn down work when offered?
- can you provide another worker to carry out the work in your place if you want?
- do you pay your own tax and National Insurance?

If you answered 'yes' to most or all of the above, you are more likely to be classed as a worker.

However, as this area is so complicated, you should always check your contract and if in doubt about your employment status, you should seek further advice from your union or from an advice agency such as a Citizens Advice Bureau or Law Centre.

Key rights

All workers are entitled to some basic rights at work, and as a worker you will generally be entitled to the following rights from the day you start work:

- the right to be paid the National Minimum Wage (NMW)[3]
- the right not to work more than 48 hours a week (unless you sign an agreement saying that you are willing to work longer hours)[4]

- the right to a rest break of 20 minutes where your working day is longer than six hours.[5] If you are aged less than 18, you are entitled to a 30 minute break after working four and a half hours
- the right to four weeks' paid annual leave[6]
- the right to health and safety protection[7]
- protection from discrimination. You have the right not to be treated less favourably by the employer on the grounds of sex, pregnancy, race, disability, sexual orientation and religion or belief. From 2006 onwards, it will also be unlawful for employers to discriminate against workers and job seekers on grounds of age. See page 400 for more information
- the right to join a union of your choice[8]

There are some exceptions to the above and it is not a definitive statement of the law. If you are in doubt about any of your legal employment rights, you should seek further advice as soon as possible.

Additional rights for employees

Some important employment rights are only available to those who are classed as 'employees'. These include:

- the right to claim unfair dismissal before an employment tribunal, where you are sacked without notice or good cause[9]
- the right to redundancy pay[10]
- the right to take maternity, paternity and parental leave and to request flexible working[11]
- the right to paid time off for ante-natal care[12]
- the right to a written statement of your main terms and conditions of employment[13]

Many employee rights are however, subject to additional qualifying conditions beyond passing the 'employee' test. In many cases you have to work for the same employer for a set length of time in order to qualify for protection. These time limits are set in the following sections.

Rights timetable

Not all employment rights start from your first day at work. Some rights are only granted when you have worked for the same employer for a certain period of time of time. This applies to both statutory and contractual rights. For example, under your contract of employment, you may get more paid holidays and sick leave after you have spent a number of years with the company. The same applies to some important statutory rights.

The timetable below shows how long you must work for your employer in order to gain important legal rights at work.

When you apply for a job

You should not be discriminated against in a job selection process because of your sex, race, disability, sexual orientation, religion or belief or because you are a trade union member. From October 2006 it will also be unlawful to discriminate on grounds of age in the recruitment and selection process (Employment Equality (Age) Regulations 2006). See page 501 for more details.

From your first day at work

You have the right to:

- the national minimum wage if you are aged 16 or over
- not have deductions made from your pay unless you have agreed to them or they are required by law
- 26 weeks' maternity leave, even if you were pregnant when you started the job (employees only)
- time off for antenatal care (employees only)
- unpaid leave for family emergencies (employees only)
- health and safety protection – you are entitled to work in a place which is safe and which does not cause you to injure yourself or become ill
- protection from dismissal on some limited grounds such as pregnancy, sex, race or disability discrimination, trade union membership

- equal pay with a member of the opposite sex who is doing the same job as you or a comparable one
- take a trade union representative or fellow worker into a disciplinary or grievance hearing
- claim Statutory Sick Pay (SSP) after you have been off sick for four days in a row (if you are paying National Insurance contributions)

After one month

You have the right to receive one week's notice of dismissal.

You are also required to give one week's notice if you wish to leave the job. These are the legal minimum requirements; your contract may provide for longer notice periods and if it does, these will apply.

After two months

Employees are entitled to a written statement of their main terms and conditions of employment. This must include pay, hours, where you are expected to work, holiday entitlement and any other benefits such as pension entitlement. The written statement is not a contract of employment in itself, but it is very important that you have one, as it can be used as evidence in court or tribunal hearings if problems arise.

After six months

You have the right to an additional 26 weeks' maternity leave (in addition to the 26 weeks that you are entitled to from the start of your employment) (employees only).

You have the right to request flexible working arrangements (if responsible for bringing up a child aged less than six). This can be extended to age 18 where the child has a disability (employees only).

After one year

Employees are entitled to written reasons for dismissal.

Employees are entitled to claim unfair dismissal if they are dismissed without a good reason. Your employer cannot make you sign away your right to claim unfair dismissal even if you are on a short-term or fixed-term contract.

You have the right to request parental leave (for a child under the age of 5).

After two years

You can claim a redundancy payment if your job has ended because the company has closed down completely or closed the particular place where you work or has reduced the number of staff employed in your type of job (employees only).

When you start work

You should make a written note of any arrangements discussed and terms agreed at your interview or when you are offered work with the company. Ideally, the terms should be agreed in writing and you should ask for written confirmation as this avoids later misunderstandings about what has been agreed. See Starting Work, page 312, for more details.

If you are taken on as an employee of the company, you are entitled by law to have a written statement of your main terms and conditions within eight weeks of starting work.[14]

Before accepting a job offer, try to find out the following details and keep a note of them:

- the type of work that you will be doing
- how long the work will last
- how much you will be paid
- who will be responsible for paying your tax and National Insurance. If the employer says that this is your responsibility, then ask them why and write down what they say. You should also seek further advice from an advice agency in this situation
- when and how you will be paid
- how to do the work and what training you will receive, particularly if work has to be done in a certain way or to a specified standard of quality
- whether you will be provided with all the necessary materials,

components, tools and equipment
- whether you are entitled to holiday pay, sick pay and paid maternity leave.
- whether there is a pension scheme that you can join
- are there any health risks associated with the job? If so, what advice does the company offer on working safely?

Written statement of main terms and conditions for employees

If you are taken on as an employee of the company that is providing you with work, then you are entitled to receive a written statement of your main terms and conditions within eight weeks of starting week. This is a legal right.[15]

The written statement must include the following information:

- your name and that of your employer
- the date your employment started
- your rate of pay (this must be at least the rate of the National Minimum Wage)
- your hours of work and your holiday entitlement (these must comply with your minimum entitlements under the Working Time Regulations)
- the title or description of your job and your place of work
- your notice period – both the notice that your employer is required to give to you in order to terminate the employment and the notice that you must give to the employer if you wish to leave
- details of the employer's grievance and disciplinary procedures
- details of any pension entitlement
- where employment is not intended to be permanent, the period for which it is expected to continue, or if it is for a fixed term, the date on which it is to end
- any collective agreement directly affecting terms and conditions of employment

Pay

By law all workers are entitled to be paid for work that they have carried out.[16] If you are not paid wages due to you for work done, this is called an 'unlawful deduction' or 'non-payment of wages' and you can bring a claim before an employment tribunal for the money that you are owed.[17] If you are in this situation, you should seek legal advice immediately, as there are strict time limits on taking a claim to an employment tribunal (usually three months from the date of the offence).

Pay slips

Every time you are paid, you should receive a pay slip. This should show:

- the total amount of your pay before deductions
- a breakdown of any deductions made (such as tax and National Insurance)
- your pay after these deductions, which is referred to as your net pay

This is a legal entitlement, which you can enforce at a tribunal if your employer is refusing to give you pay slips.[18]

Deductions from pay

Your employer should not make any deductions from your pay[19] unless:

- the deduction is required by law (income tax and National Insurance fall into this category)
- your contract contains an express clause which allows for the deduction
- you have signed a written agreement authorising the deduction

Employer deductions from workers' pay for transport to work

Your employer may make a deduction from your pay to cover the cost of any transport that they provide to work. However, they should not do so unless this is set out in your contract of employment or you have agreed to this deduction in writing. Any deductions from your pay for transport costs must be made before calculating the minimum wage. In other words, you must be paid at least the NMW after any deductions for benefits such as transport provision.

Employer deductions from workers' pay for accommodation

If your employer provides you with accommodation, they can deduct an amount from your pay or can charge you for the accommodation. As with other deductions, this should be agreed in advance and should be included in your contract or in a separate written agreement.
There is also a limit to the amount of the deduction or charge that the employer can count towards Minimum Wage pay. This is called the 'accommodation offset', and it is set out as a maximum daily or weekly amount. Since October 2005 the maximum daily offset has been £3.90 and the maximum weekly offset is £27.30. The accommodation offset is the maximum amount that employers can count towards Minimum Wage pay. In other words, if your employer deducts £45 per week from your pay for rent for accommodation provided, only the excess rent above the accommodation offset of £27.30 per week (£45 minus £27.30 = £17.70) will be counted when determining if you are receiving the NMW. So to be able to charge £45 per week rent, the employer would have to pay at least £17.70 per week above the normal Minimum Wage rate.

No other benefit in kind counts towards Minimum Wage pay so if, for example, your employer provides meals (e.g. canteen service) they cannot say that free or subsidised meals are part of a package that makes up your minimum wage pay.

Employer deductions from workers' pay for tools, equipment, and clothing

If your employer deducts an amount from your pay to cover the cost of providing clothing, a uniform, tools or other equipment necessary for the job, then the amount deducted will reduce your pay for the purposes of Minimum Wage calculation. Your employer must pay you at least the Minimum Wage, after any such deductions are made.

Employer deductions from workers' pay for breakages

Such deductions will be lawful if they are allowed by a term in your contract or if you have agreed to them in writing. You should still be paid the NMW after any such deduction has been made.

Overpayments

If your employer has overpaid you, they may be able to recover the money, but should not deduct any money from your wages without first explaining the overpayment to you and consulting you on the repayment. Seek advice if you have been overpaid and your employer wishes to recover the money from you.

Shop workers

Shop workers have additional legal protection to limit the level of deductions from their pay to cover till shortages or stock deficiencies. No more than 10% of pay can be deducted from any one pay packet to cover till shortages or stock deficiencies.[20] The exception to this is the final payment of wages, where more can be deducted if necessary.

If you have not been paid wages due to you or if your employer has imposed a pay cut or made a deduction from your pay that is not allowed under your contract, you can bring a claim for 'unlawful deductions from wages' before an employment tribunal.[21] The complaint must be made within three months of the non-payment or underpayment (see page 522).

Your union or an advice centre may be able to help you, either by negotiating with your employer or helping you to apply to a tribunal or to the small claims court to recover wages that you are owed. You should contact them for further advice on this.

The National Minimum Wage (NMW)

Under the National Minimum Wage regulations, all workers are entitled to be paid at least the National Minimum Wage rate for each hour that they work.[22] If your employer says that you are not entitled to the NMW because you are 'self-employed', it is up to them to prove why you are not an employee or a worker. Even if you are classified as self-employed for tax and National Insurance purposes, you may still be entitled to the NMW. If in doubt, seek advice.

There are three NMW rates:

- one for workers aged 22 and over
- a lower rate for workers aged between 18 and 21
- a third rate for workers aged 16 and 17. This was introduced in October 2004. Before then, 16 and 17 year olds did not have the right to be paid the NMW

The current rates are:

Population	Rate per hour
'Adult' rate (aged 22 or over)	£5.05 an hour
Workers aged 18 to 21	£4.25 an hour
Young workers aged 16 to 17	£3.00 an hour

Workers aged over 22 may be paid the lower rate of £4.25 per hour but only where they are receiving accredited training during the first six months of a job. After this they must be paid the full adult rate even if the training is continuing.

The rates are usually uprated in October of each year. From October 2006, the rates will be:

Population	Rate per hour
Adult rate (aged 22 and over)	£5.35 an hour
Workers aged 18 to 21	£4.45 an hour
Young workers aged 16 to 17	£3.30 an hour

Hourly pay for the NMW is worked out as an average over your 'pay period'.[23] If you are paid weekly, your pay period is a week. If you are paid daily, then the pay period is a day and if monthly paid, then the pay period is a month. For many workers, working out their hourly pay is simply a matter of dividing total pay before tax and other deductions (known as gross pay) by the number of hours worked. But for some workers the situation is more complicated, as they have no fixed hours but are paid by what they produce (their output) or paid on completion of a specific job.

There are some special provisions for output workers because employers often have no way of checking how many hours such workers have actually worked.

On 1 October 2004, the 'rated output work' system providing for 'fair' piece rates was introduced. It was an attempt to provide for a fairer way of paying output workers than the previous system of 'fair estimate agreements' that had been widely abused by employers. The rated output work system requires employers to either pay the worker the Minimum Wage for every hour worked or to pay at least a 'fair' piece rate for each piece produced or task performed. This is determined by reference to the rate of performance of (the time taken by) an average worker of the same employer doing the same job.

If you think that you are not being paid the NMW you can make a complaint directly to the NMW Helpline on 0845 6000 678 (England, Scotland or Wales) or 0845 6500 207 (Northern Ireland). The helpline is open 24 hours a day, 7 days a week and callers can be assisted in 30 different languages. You can also seek further advice from your union if you are a member, or an advice agency.

Tax and National Insurance

You will have to pay tax and National Insurance if you are earning above a certain limit, called a 'threshold', which is set each year. If your earnings fall below the threshold you will not have to pay tax or National Insurance. These levels usually change in April at the start of each new tax year.

The tax and National Insurance contributions that you pay depend on whether you are classified as an employee or self-employed. Most workers are employees or workers, rather than genuinely self-employed, although employers may argue otherwise. As always, if in doubt, seek advice.

Tax code

Your tax code is usually made up of a combination of numbers and letters. It should be displayed on your pay slip. All workers are legally entitled to receive a pay slip, each time they are paid. The pay slip must contain certain information, including itemised deductions and the tax code and National Insurance number.

The number in your tax code is used to work out the tax due on your income from your employment. It is usually followed by a letter, which is used to show how the tax you pay should be adjusted, according to any tax allowances that you are entitled to. 'L' is the tax code for the basic personal allowance for a working person aged less than 65. The personal allowance is the amount that you are allowed to earn tax-free. You will be required to pay tax on all earnings above this amount. See page 363 for help with finding your tax code.

National Insurance Contributions (NICs)

You will have to pay class 1 National Insurance Contributions if:

- you work as an employee in the UK
- you are aged 16 or over but under state retirement age (currently 60 years for women and 65 for men)
- your earnings are more than a set minimum level, called the Earnings Threshold (ET)

You do not currently pay NICs on earnings of less than £84 per week before tax (from April 2006).

If you are an employee

The advantage for you is that your employer or supplier of work is responsible for tax and National Insurance contributions. If you earn enough to pay these, they should be deducted from your pay and shown as itemised amounts on your pay slips. If you are earning enough to pay tax and NI, your contributions will be contributing towards entitlement to benefits such as Jobseekers' Allowance, Incapacity Benefit, Statutory Maternity Pay (SMP), and the state pension. If you do not earn above the threshold, you should not have to pay tax and NI. The downside to this is that you will not be building up your contributions record, which is used to determine entitlement to these benefits.

There are good reasons to ensure that you are properly registered for tax and National Insurance:

- it is a legal requirement, and failing to do so leaves you vulnerable to exploitation by unscrupulous employers
- National Insurance contributions count towards several benefits such as Jobseeker's Allowance and Retirement Pension
- National Insurance contributions can count towards your benefit and pension entitlements in other EU member states
- if you are not registered for National Insurance, then not only are you not building up a contributions record, but your employer is also getting out of paying their share of contributions to the state scheme. The employer has to make NI contributions for you too and this should be viewed as part of your total pay

If you are not registered for tax and NI and you later run into problems at work, you may be disqualified from taking action at an employment tribunal. If the tribunal considers that you knowingly acted with your employer to avoid paying tax and NI, they may rule that you have been working under an illegal contract and you cannot enforce any employment rights under that contract. However, the legal position is more complicated than this and you may have some rights in this situation. It is vital that you seek further advice on this from an advice agency or your union.

Having more than one job

Migrant workers are more likely than settled workers to be doing more than one job. If you are working very few hours for a number of different employers in low paid jobs, you could find that you are earning less than the National Insurance threshold in each of these jobs. The threshold is currently £84 a week.

The result of this is that you will not be building up NI contributions to entitle you to benefits such as Statutory Sick Pay, Maternity Pay and State Pension.

Statutory Sick Pay (SSP)

To be entitled to Statutory Sick Pay, you must meet certain conditions, in particular:

- you must be in work
- you must be aged between 16 and 65 when your sickness began
- you must be earning enough to pay National Insurance contributions (£84 per week from April 2006). If your pay varies, your entitlement depends on your average pay over the last eight weeks
- you must be absent from work due to illness for at least four consecutive days

You will not qualify if you are self-employed or have not started work yet. Temporary workers are entitled to SSP on the same basis as permanent workers.

For more information on SSP see page 144.

You may be entitled to more generous sick pay under your employer's own scheme and should check your contractual information to see if this is the case.

Rights for working parents

Maternity leave

If you are classed as an employee, you will be entitled to 26 weeks' maternity leave from the day you start your job. However you cannot usually begin maternity leave any earlier than the 11th week before your baby is due. Whether you receive maternity pay during this period of leave depends on whether you meet the qualifying conditions for Statutory Maternity Pay (SMP) or whether your contract gives you a right to more generous maternity pay. The conditions for receiving Statutory Maternity Pay are set out in the following sections.

Some women are entitled to a further 26 weeks' maternity leave after the first 26 week period, giving them an entitlement to a year's leave in total. In order to qualify for this additional six months' leave, you must have worked for your employer for at least six months by the 14th week before your baby is due. Unless your contract provides for this additional maternity leave to be paid, it will be taken as unpaid leave, as there is no entitlement to SMP beyond the first 26 weeks' entitlement. Also see pages 467-471 for more information.

Proposed changes

The Work and Families Bill is draft legislation that is currently before Parliament. It proposes improvements to the current statutory maternity and 'family friendly' entitlements. Specifically, it proposes an extension to paid statutory maternity leave from six to nine months initially and later to a year's paid leave (date to be determined). It is proposed that six months of the mother's paid maternity leave will be transferable on request to the father. It is also proposed to extend the right to request flexible working to carers of adults. If enacted, these new entitlements will come into force from April 2007 onwards.

See also Maternity Benefits, page 467.

Statutory Maternity Pay (SMP)

You will be entitled to SMP from your employer if they deduct tax and National Insurance from your pay through PAYE, and you qualify under the following rules:

- you have worked for the same employer for at least 26 continuous weeks by the 15th week before the week in which your baby is due (this is known as the 'qualifying week') and you are still working for this employer in the qualifying week (you do not have to work a full week for the week to count)

and:

- you earn at least the earnings threshold for NI contributions, that is, you have average earnings of at least £84.00 a week (from April 2006) before tax in the eight weeks (if weekly paid) or two months (if monthly paid) before the end of the qualifying week

and:

- you stop work because of your pregnancy on or after the 11th week before the week in which your baby is due

If you qualify for SMP you will receive maternity pay for 26 weeks and this will be paid at 90% of your average pay for the first six weeks and then at a flat rate for the remaining 20 weeks. The flat rate SMP is currently £108.85 per week (from April 2006).

If you do not qualify for SMP, you may be able to claim another benefit called Maternity Allowance from your local Jobcentre Plus office. The TUC maternity leave and pay leaflet has further details. This can be obtained from the TUC 'know your rights' line on 0870 600 4882. Also see pages 467 471.

Paternity leave and pay

Paid paternity leave was introduced in April 2003 by the Paternity and Adoption Leave Regulations 2002. You can now claim two weeks' paternity leave if you meet the following conditions:

- you are an employee working under a contract of employment
- you are the baby's father or the partner of a woman on maternity leave
- you have worked for your employer for at least 26 weeks by the 15th week before the baby is due (in practice this means you must have worked for the employer for about 10 months by the time you apply to take the paternity leave)
- you have written to your employer to request the time off to care for the baby or to support the mother of the baby
- you must take the leave within the first eight weeks after the baby's birth

If you meet these conditions and you are earning at least £84 per week (from April 2006) and are liable to pay National Insurance contributions, you will be entitled to Statutory Paternity Pay (SPP) for the two weeks' leave.[24] SPP is paid at a flat rate of £108.85 a week, the same as the basic rate of Statutory Maternity Pay (from April 2006).

The TUC 'paternity leave and pay' leaflet has further details. This can be obtained from the TUC *'know your rights'* line on 0870 600 4882.

Parental leave

You will be entitled to take up to 13 weeks off work to spend with your children if:

- you are an employee
- you have worked for your employer for one year
- your child or children are aged under five
- you have given your employer at least 21 days' notice that you want to take time off

Both parents have the right to take 13 weeks' leave and the 13 weeks' entitlement is for each child.[25] The leave is to be taken over the first five years of the child's life (or until the child's 18th birthday if s/he has a disability and is receiving Disability Living Allowance) with four weeks usually being the maximum amount of time that can be taken in any one year. The right is to take leave, but it is not an entitlement to paid leave – this is at the discretion of your employer and you will need to check your contract, employee handbook or other information to see if you will be paid for any parental leave. The right is transferable so that if you change employers and have only taken seven weeks of your entitlement with your former employer, the remainder of your 13-week entitlement carries forward to the new employer.

Time off for dependants

Employees also have a legal right to take a reasonable amount of time off work to deal with domestic emergencies relating to their family.[26] This right applies from the day that you start the job.[27] Time off for dependants rights are designed to help you deal with unexpected accidents and illnesses affecting either a parent, partner, a child or other relative or person dependent on you. It covers short-term, emergency situations only and does not apply to long-term or ongoing illnesses. Again the right is to take time off, but it is up to your employer whether this is paid time off. Your contract, employee handbook or other employee information may give further details.

The TUC 'time off for families' leaflet has further details of both parental leave and time off for dependents entitlements. This can be obtained from the TUC 'know your rights' line on 0870 600 4882.

Working time rights

These rights are set out in the Working Time Regulations and cover rest breaks, holidays and holiday pay, night work and how long you can work each week. Working time rights are complicated and not all rights apply to everyone at work. There are a lot of exemptions (for example some transport workers are not covered by the Regulations) and in some cases, workers can 'opt-out' of the right or can agree to vary arrangements with their employer. If you are in any doubt as to whether a particular right applies to you, you should seek advice from your union or from an advice agency before taking any action.

- rest breaks: the right to a rest break of 20 minutes where your working day is longer than six hours. If you are under 18 however, you are entitled to a 30-minute break after working four and a half hours
- holidays: you should receive four weeks' paid annual leave. Holiday entitlement is explained in more detail in the section below
- night work: Regular night workers should not work more than eight hours in each 24-hour period. The Working Time Regulations allow for night work to be averaged over a 17-week period in the same way as weekly hours of work. Night workers are also entitled to a free health assessment
- working week: You have the right not to work more than 48 hours a week on average. This limit is averaged over a 17-week period. This means that it is legal to work more than 48 hours in some weeks, so long as this is balanced out by weeks in which fewer hours are worked, making an average of not more than 48 hours over the whole 17 weeks. You can sign away this right, but cannot be pressured to opt out, and can opt back in again at any time, though you can have to wait for up to three months to gain protection

If you are employed as a domestic worker in a private household, you are excluded from the key limit on working time under the Working Time Regulations, the 48-hour maximum working week. You are also excluded from the restrictions on the length of night work. However, you are entitled to the daily and weekly rest periods, rest breaks and annual leave entitlements under the Regulations.

Holiday entitlement

Under the Working Time Regulations, everyone at work is entitled to a minimum of four weeks' paid holiday a year. These are the minimum holiday entitlements that you are entitled to by law. You should always check your contract or employment handbook as well to see if your employer offers more generous holiday entitlements.

The number of days you will actually receive as holiday depends on how many days a week you work. If you work full-time five days a week, you should therefore get 4 x 5 = 20 days' paid leave per year. If you work regular part-time hours, for example, three full days per week, you should get 4 x 3 = 12 days' paid leave per year.

The position is more complicated for workers who do not have any set hours, or have hours that vary considerably over time. Under the Working Time rules, where hours vary from week to week or where a worker is employed and paid on 'piece-work', weekly holiday pay should be the average weekly pay that you earned over the last 12 weeks. Any week during the last 12 in which no pay is received is replaced by the week before, until you have a total of 12 weeks on which to work out your average weekly pay.

Public or 'bank' holidays

In England and Wales, there are eight national or public holidays which are known as bank holidays. In Scotland, there are 9 bank holidays (though these are mostly not general public holidays) and also local public holidays. There is no automatic right to a day's leave with pay on bank holidays however, that is entirely up to your individual employer and whether your contract says that you are entitled to time off with pay on these days.

Unfortunately, the Working Time Regulations do not require the four weeks' paid leave to be in addition to paid bank holidays. Therefore, if your employer does pay you for some or all of the bank holidays, they can quite lawfully count these towards your four weeks' paid leave entitlement. The current government have said that they are going to review the existing legal position with a view to making bank holiday entitlement additional to the entitlement to four weeks paid leave under the Working Time Regulations, but it remains to be seen if and when this will actually happen.

Some employers try to avoid paying holiday pay by saying that your hourly pay rate already includes holiday pay and that they therefore do not have to give extra pay if you take a break. If in doubt about your entitlement, seek further assistance from your union, or from an advice agency such as the CAB, as there are clear legal rules on what employers can and can't do when it comes to calculating your holiday pay. At the very least, your contract must clearly state that your pay includes a sum for holiday pay and must say exactly what amount of pay is actually holiday pay.

What happens when something goes wrong?

This section looks at problems that can arise at work, from accidents at work to being dismissed from your job. In all such cases, it is helpful to have access to legal advice and assistance and this is where membership of a trade union can be extremely useful. The first section below looks at the benefits of union membership and provides further contact details if you wish to find out more about joining a union.

Trade union membership

Everyone in the UK has the right to join a trade union. Joining a union is a private matter and you do not have to tell your employer that you have joined. On the other hand you do not have to join a trade union. You have legal protection if you are discriminated against either for joining or refusing to join a trade union.

You are free to join any union that you wish to. The TUC website can provide more information on the variety of unions that exist and guidance on finding the right union for you and your job. To find out more about joining a union, call the TUC 'know your rights' line on 0870 6004882, or go to www.tuc.org.uk and click on 'Britain's Unions' for more information.

If your employer recognises a union already, then it makes sense to join that one, as it will be in a strong position to look after you at work. Even if your employer does not recognise a union however, it can still be very worthwhile to join one as the union can offer invaluable legal advice and assistance if you run into problems at work. Union representatives also have a legal right to accompany their members to formal grievance and disciplinary meetings and to support them at such meetings.

Finally unions provide a range of other benefits for their members ranging from financial benefits such as insurance to education and training courses and opportunities and legal advice on issues unrelated to employment. Obviously the range of benefits offered will vary from union to union and you can find out what is offered by contacting the union and requesting information on joining and on benefits of membership.

Discrimination

UK employment law gives you the right not to be discriminated against at work on the grounds of your sex, pregnancy, race, disability, sexual orientation or religion or belief. Your employer should not treat you less favourably on any of the above criteria.

For EU citizens, discrimination on grounds of nationality is also prohibited (except in a few cases such as employment in the civil service).

From October 2006, the Employment Equality (Age) Regulations will also make it unlawful to discriminate against someone on grounds of their age. The protection applies to workers, not just to the narrow category of employees and also applies to job seekers, not just to those already in work.

If you feel that you have been treated less favourably than a colleague or have suffered abuse or harassment from your employer on any of the above grounds, then you should seek further advice as soon as possible. Further information on race and sex discrimination can be found in sections 14 and 15 (see pages 424 and 466).

Health and safety

If you are worried that your work may be affecting your health, or that of your family, contact your union or an advice centre, as they may be able to help and advise you further. As a worker, you have certain rights under Health and Safety laws.

The main law governing health and safety at work in the UK is the Health and Safety at Work Act 1974 (HSWA). Under the HSWA, employers have a legal duty to protect the health, safety and welfare of their workers. Employers have a duty to protect the mental as well as the physical health of their employees and they must:

- maintain plant and work systems so that they are safe and do not present health risks
- have in place arrangements to ensure the safe use, handling, storage and transportation of items and substances
- provide a safe working environment including the provision of health and safety information, training and supervision, maintaining entrances and exits to the work place so that they are safe
- ensure that their premises and processes are safe and do not pose health threats to other workers, sub-contractors, visitors to their premises and the public in general (employers' duties extend beyond their own employees)
- must keep an up to date written health and safety policy in situations where more than five people are employed, and must ensure that employees are aware of this and have access to it. They should also ensure that where workers have limited understanding of English, that the health and safety policy is explained to the workers and in particular that any specific guidelines for example, on operating machinery or dealing with hazardous substances are clearly understood by the worker

The need for health and safety guidance to be clearly accessible and understandable is particularly important where the employer engages workers with either literacy difficulties or where English is not the worker's first language and his or her understanding is limited. In this case, the employer will need to ensure that safety information is displayed in such a way that it is easily recognised and understood. For example, the 1994 Construction (Design and Management) Regulations require effective communication between the main contractor and workers on site where necessary for reasons of health and safety. The guidance that accompanies the 1999 Management of Health & Safety at Work Regulations 1999, states that:

'Information [on health and safety risks] can be provided in whatever form is most suitable in the circumstances as long as it can be understood by everyone. For employees with little or no understanding of English, or who cannot read English, employers may need to make special arrangements. These could include providing translation, using interpreters, or replacing written notices with clearly understood symbols or diagrams.'

Section 2 of the HSWA requires employers to consult safety representatives of recognised trade unions when developing health and safety arrangements. Where two or more health and safety representatives request that the employer sets up a safety committee, the employer must comply with this request.

Enforcement

The HSWA established the Health and Safety Commission (HSC) to oversee the development of occupational health and safety policy in Britain, and also the Health and Safety Executive (HSE) which is responsible for enforcing the legal requirements of the Act. In practice, the enforcement of health and safety at work is split between the HSE Inspectorate and local council environmental health departments. Environmental health officers are employed by local authorities and are responsible for health and safety in offices, shops, warehouses and leisure centres whilst HSE Inspectors deal with factories, agriculture, mines, railway and offshore installation safety.

Under the HSWA, there are three main enforcement measures: improvement notices, prohibition notices, and prosecution.

Improvement notices can be issued where an inspector visits a workplace and has health and safety concerns. If they do so, the employer is obliged to take the recommended action to put things right within a given time period. If they fail to do so, a prohibition notice may be served, requiring the employer to cease the activity that is causing concern for health and safety immediately. Prohibition notices may also be issued where there is an immediate danger to health and safety. If an employer wishes to appeal against the issue of one of these notices, they must make a complaint to an employment tribunal.

If an employer fails to comply with an improvement or prohibition notice, they may face a fine or imprisonment. If the case is heard at a higher court (i.e. not a magistrates court) the fine may be unlimited and imprisonment may be for up to two years.

Risk assessment

The management of Health and Safety at Work Regulations 1999, require the employer to carry out a risk assessment of the work activities carried out by the worker. This assessment will include identifying any hazards in the workplace and who is at risk of harm from these, assessing the risks and taking appropriate action to remove them or to reduce them as far as possible.

The results of the risk assessment should be recorded in writing and follow-up checks should be carried out from time to time and further action taken if necessary.

The Health and Safety Executive has made it clear that they regard all workers as being entitled to this protection, even if they are not working legally.

Further information can be found on the HSE website www.hse.gov.uk or by calling the HSE infoline on: 0845 345 0055 or their publications line on: 01787 881165.

Accidents at work

Employers of 10 or more people must record all accidents at work, however minor. This is a requirement under the Social Security (Claims and Payments) Regulations 1987. Accidents will normally be recorded in an accident book (BI 510) which should be kept in an accessible place and be available for inspection. Trade union safety representatives have a legal entitlement to information on accidents at work. Employers should keep accident books for three years after the date of the last entry.

Under the Health and Safety (First Aid) Regulations 1981, employers are obliged to provide adequate and appropriate first aid provision. This includes maintaining first aid equipment and providing a suitable number of trained and qualified first-aiders. It is for employers to determine their own first aid needs taking account of factors such as the number of workers, the nature of the business, and proximity of emergency medical services. A Code of Practice (CoP) to the Regulations provides that every workplace should have at least one first aid box and that this should be readily accessible to employees. The CoP suggests a minimum supply of first aid items for the box but this is guidance only and not a requirement.

Employers should provide information to their workers about first aid facilities, personnel and their location. This information should take account of the needs of workers with disabilities, and with language or with literacy needs.

Bullying and harassment

Bullying and harassment is conduct that is unwelcome, offensive and which has a detrimental affect on the worker who is subjected to such behaviour. They are health and safety issues and although there is no specific legislation dealing with bullying and harassment at work, employers have general duties under the HSWA to ensure both the physical and mental health and safety of their workers.

In some cases, the bullying or harassment may be based on a worker's sex, race, disability, sexual orientation or religious belief and in such cases, the laws which prohibit discrimination and victimisation on these grounds will apply. Further details on the application of discrimination legislation in tribunals can be found on page 501. If the harassment or bullying is racial, please see page 424.

According to the Advisory Conciliation and Arbitration Service (ACAS) which has produced guidance for employers on bullying and harassment, 'bullying may be characterised as offensive, intimidating, malicious or insulting behaviour, an abuse or misuse of power through means intended to undermine, humiliate, denigrate or injure the recipient.'[28]

They define harassment as 'unwanted conduct affecting the dignity of men and women in the workplace. It may be related to age, sex, race, disability, religion, nationality or any personal characteristic of the individual and may be persistent or an isolated incident. The key is that the actions or comments are viewed as demeaning and unacceptable to the recipient.'

Key features of acts of bullying and harassment are that they are unwelcome to the recipient and that s/he considers them to be offensive, irrespective of whether the intention was to cause offence.

Examples of bullying behaviour include:

- verbal abuse – shouting or swearing at the individual, name-calling
- unjustified criticism of the individual's work
- exclusion from work or social events
- withholding information necessary for the worker to carry out their job
- work overload or setting impossible deadlines
- constant supervision

Examples of harassment include:

- unwanted and offensive comments, e.g. of a sexual or racial nature
- sexist, racist or homophobic jokes
- unwanted physical contact
- sending offensive material to the worker (by e-mail, computer, post) or displaying material in the workplace that is likely to cause offence and which creates a hostile or intimidating working environment

What can I do if I am being bullied or harassed at work?

It is important to get support if you feel that you are being bullied or harassed at work:

- is there anyone that you can speak to at work about this – for example a sympathetic colleague or a trade union representative?
- do you feel able to approach the bully / harasser and ask them to stop their behaviour as you find it offensive?

It is important to make it clear that the behaviour is unacceptable and that you find it offensive. However, you may need support in approaching the harasser or may simply find it too intimidating to do this alone.

Formal complaints

Your employer may already have an anti-bullying policy and this should give details of how to raise your concerns. Your workplace must also have a grievance procedure and you can use this to raise your concerns. Again it is advisable to seek advice and support, ideally from a trade union representative or colleague in the workplace or alternatively from an external advice agency before making a formal complaint. They will be able to advise you on the best way of raising your concerns.

You should keep a written record of bullying or harassing incidents together with evidence (offensive e-mails for example).

Legal action

Hopefully you will be able to put a stop to the bullying or harassment either informally or formally through using your employers internal anti-bullying or grievance procedures. If the unacceptable conduct continues, however, you may need to consider legal action. As always, you should seek further advice before initiating any such action.

Health and safety law

Under the common law (law made by judges through their legal decisions in individual cases) your employer may be liable for any psychiatric or psychological damage caused by bullying or harassment. Your employer may also have breached her or his duties under the HSWA.

Unfair dismissal law

Persistent bullying and harassment which has been brought to your employer's attention, but which is not addressed, could amount to a breach of the 'duty of mutual trust and confidence' which is implied in every contract of employment.

Such a fundamental breach of your contract could entitle you to resign from your employment and claim that you have been 'constructively dismissed'. In other words your employer's conduct has left you with no alternative but to resign from your job.

Constructive dismissal cases can be extremely hard to prove and as they require you to actually leave your job, they are a high-risk option. Any worker contemplating this form of action is strongly advised to seek legal advice first and to do so promptly.

Discrimination law

There is legislation to protect workers from discrimination and specifically from harassment on grounds of their sex, race, disability, sexual orientation or religious belief and if you have suffered discrimination on any of these grounds, you should seek further advice on how to take action.

Protection from Harassment Act 1997

This Act was introduced to tackle other forms of harassment such as stalking and was not designed specifically to tackle abuse in the workplace. However, in 2005 the Court of Appeal ruled that the Act could potentially be used to pursue a claim that an employer was vicariously liable for harassment carried out by his or her employees.[29]

This decision has opened up another potentially very useful route for workers to seek compensation for abuse at work, one that does not require some element of prescribed discrimination or for the employee to actually resign from their job. However, it is a very recent legal development and there is little case law as yet. It remains to be seen how this will develop in the longer term.

Redundancy and dismissal

Dismissal

A dismissal takes place where your contract with your employer comes to an end and this is not through your choice or free will. It covers the following situations:

- your employer terminates your contract – either with or without notice
- you are on a fixed term contract which ends but is not renewed
- you leave but claim that the employer's behaviour towards you left you with no choice but to leave (this is called a 'constructive dismissal')
- you are made redundant. You are made redundant if your company either closes down completely, or closes the particular places where you work, or where your company needs to employ less people in the job that you are employed to do. In these circumstances you may be offered an alternative job with the company. If you are, you should seek advice on this because if you unreasonably turn down an alternative job, you may lose your right to a redundancy payment

Is your dismissal fair or unfair?

You have been dismissed by your employer. This may be fair if it is for one of these reasons:

- your conduct – for example, you stole from the company or were fighting with a colleague at work
- your capability – your skills, qualifications or ability to do the job. For example, if you lied about your qualifications on your application form. Capability dismissals also include dismissal for long-term sick leave or a series of sickness absences
- you are made redundant

- to comply with the law – for example if you lose your driving licence and driving is an essential part of the job
- for 'some other substantial reason' relating to the interests of the business

Dismissal for any other reason will be unfair. Even if your employer says that your dismissal is for one of the above reasons, you may be able to take action against them if you believe this was not the real reason for your dismissal or the way in which you were dismissed was unfair. If you have been dismissed you must seek advice as soon as possible as there are strict time limits on bringing a claim of unfair dismissal before an employment tribunal. See page 522 for more information.

New statutory disciplinary and dismissal procedures

Since 1 October 2004, all employers have been legally required to have disciplinary and dismissal procedures in place for all employees. If an employer dismisses an employee and has failed to comply with the new procedures, the dismissal will be deemed to be automatically unfair and the amount of compensation awarded will be increased.[30]

Where an employer is considering formal disciplinary action and potentially dismissing an employee, they will usually be required to follow a standard three-stage procedure. This involves:

- a written statement – the employer writes to the employee setting out the conduct or other circumstances that may lead to dismissal or other disciplinary action
- a disciplinary meeting – the employee must be invited to a meeting to discuss the circumstances and must be given a reasonable opportunity to consider his or her response before the meeting takes place and to state their case and be accompanied at the meeting. The employer must inform the employee of the decision in writing and offer the right of appeal
- an appeal – where possible this should be heard by a more senior manager not involved in the initial decision. After the appeal hearing the employee should be notified of the final decision and have this confirmed in writing

There is provision for a shorter two-stage (written statement, appeal) modified dismissal procedure to be used in cases of gross misconduct where the employer feels that it is necessary to dismiss the employee without notice because of their conduct. However, in most circumstances the standard three-stage procedure should apply.

Employers are required to provide details of their disciplinary and grievance procedures to all employees. Details must be provided in writing and can be provided as part of the written statement of main terms and conditions, as part of the contract of employment, or in the letter of appointment.

Grievance procedures

The Employment Act 2002 (Dispute Resolution) Regulations 2004 also introduced new requirements for employees to have initiated grievance proceedings before bringing certain claims before an employment tribunal. The new requirements apply to a wide range of grievances including those concerning:

- equal pay
- discrimination
- unauthorised deductions from pay
- breach of contract (on termination of employment)
- working time

Where the new requirements apply, the employee will not be able to bring a claim to an employment tribunal unless they have:

- written to their employer setting out the grounds for the grievance
- waited 28 days after presenting the grievance to the employer

The standard three-stage grievance procedure involves:

- writing to the employer setting out the grounds for the grievance
- attending a grievance meeting to discuss the issue after which the employer informs the employee of their decision and of the right of appeal

- an appeal hearing – where possible to be conducted by a more senior manager not involved in the first stage hearing. This will include a notification of the final decision

Again there is a modified two-stage procedure that can be used where the employee has left employment and has not initiated the standard procedure before leaving and the parties agree in writing to use the modified procedure. In this case the two-stage process involves:

- the employee's written statement of grounds for grievance
- the employer's written response

The new statutory disciplinary, dismissal and grievance procedures apply to employees only and not to the wider group of workers.

The procedures have significant implications for the way in which employment tribunals deal with cases, and for the time limits for submitting claims. You should therefore seek further advice if you are considering a claim to a tribunal. Pages 488-530 have more information about employment tribunals and making a claim.

Unfair dismissal and redundancy – claims to employment tribunal

A complaint of unfair dismissal will be heard before an employment tribunal and there are strict time limits on bringing a case. The tribunal office must receive your application within three months of the date of your dismissal. It is very rare for this time limit to be extended and if you do not get your claim in on time, it is very likely to be rejected. There is detailed information on taking a claim to an employment tribunal on pages 522-530.

Your rights to redundancy pay, and to claiming unfair dismissal if your employer dismisses you without good reason, depend on showing that you are an employee. Put simply, if you are not an employee, you have no legal entitlement to claim redundancy pay or unfair dismissal. Even if you clear this first 'hurdle', you face another: both redundancy pay and unfair dismissal claims require you to have worked for your employer without breaks for a minimum amount of time.

Redundancy pay

In order to claim statutory redundancy pay you must have worked for the same employer for a continuous period of two years.[31] Workers such as agency workers often find it particularly difficult to meet this requirement.

However, if you have worked for one employer for two years or more and the work stops or the company closes down, you may be entitled to some redundancy pay. If you are in this situation you should seek legal advice.

Unfair dismissal

In order to claim that you have been unfairly dismissed before an employment tribunal, you are usually required to have worked for the same employer for a continuous period of one year.

If you have worked for your employer for one year, then you are entitled to have the reason for your dismissal given to you in writing, and can make a complaint to an employment tribunal if you ask for written reasons and your employer refuses this.[32]

Exceptions to the one year of employment rule

Where an employer has dismissed an employee because of their sex, race, disability, pregnancy, trade union membership, or because the employee was claiming an entitlement that they have under UK employment law, this is considered to be 'automatically unfair'.

In these circumstances you do not need to have a year's continuous service with the employer in order to bring a claim and you are protected from the day on which you start working for the employer.

Rights of specific groups of workers

Agency Workers

The employment status of agency workers is often problematic: the agency worker has a 'triangular' relationship with both the agency that provides placements to them and the end user company that they are placed with. Unfortunately, when things go wrong, it is often the case that both the agency and the end user company deny that the agency worker is their employee. As a result, agency workers are often denied access to important employment rights.

In practice, the employment status of an agency worker will depend on the specific circumstances of each case. A key criterion in determining employment status is whether there is any 'mutuality of obligation' between either the agency and the agency worker or between the agency worker and the company that the agency worker is placed with. In other words is there an obligation on either the agency or the end user company to provide work to the agency worker and in turn is s/he obliged to accept the work and to carry it out personally? Many cases fail on this criterion, as employment tribunals have often ruled that this mutuality of obligation is absent. This is not always the case however, and in the case of Brook Street Bureau v Dacas (2004) the Court of Appeal held that there were circumstances where it might be possible for an agency worker to demonstrate that they were an employee of the company they were placed with, rather than of the agency that had placed them there.[33]

The second criterion is the extent to which the agency or the end user company exercise control over the agency worker's work (timing, conduct, appearance, location etc). The greater the degree of control, the more likely it is that the worker is an employee, although this will often be insufficient by itself and it will be the total picture which will be taken to determine employment status. As this area is so complicated, it is always worth seeking legal advice before launching a claim against an employment agency and/or a company that you have been placed with.

The Gangmasters Licensing Authority (GLA)

The Gangmasters (Licensing) Act 2004 was passed to protect workers in the fresh produce supply chain from exploitation. The need for such protection was graphically illustrated by the tragic deaths of the cockle pickers in Morecambe Bay in early 2004.

The Gangmasters Licensing Authority (GLA) was established on 1 April 2005 to curb the exploitation of workers in the agriculture, horticulture, shellfish gathering and associated processing and packaging industries.

In general terms, a person is acting as a Gangmaster if they:

- supply a worker to do work to which the Act applies
- use a worker to do work to which the Act applies in connection with services provided to them by another person, e.g. subcontracting
- use a worker to do certain types of work (in particular gathering shellfish)

The new licensing scheme will ensure labour providers and labour users meet the minimum standards required by law.

The sectors that are being licensed have been defined as:

- agricultural activities
- horticulture
- gathering shellfish
- processing and packaging
    - any produce derived from agricultural work
    - shellfish, fish or products derived from shellfish or fish

Applications for licenses can be made online or by telephone from 6 April 2006. See the GLA website for further information: www.gla.gov.uk

From 1 May 2006 a public register listing the licensed labour providers will be available online at the GLA website (www.gla.gov.uk). You will be able to check this to see if your current employer is licensed to provide labour.

From Autumn 2006 it will be an offence to:

- operate as a Gangmaster without a licence
- use an unlicensed Gangmaster

The maximum penalty for operating without a licence is a prison sentence of 10 years and a fine.

The maximum penalty for using workers or services by an unlicensed Gangmaster is a prison sentence of 51 weeks and a fine.

A labour provider would also commit an offence if they hold:

- a relevant document that is known or believed to be false
- a relevant document obtained by deception and known or believed to have been so obtained
- a relevant document that relates to someone else with the intention of causing a third party to believe that the person in possession of the documentation or that another person is a licensed Gangmaster.

It will also be an offence to obstruct a GLA officer in the course of their duties.

Compliance

The GLA will conduct inspections to ensure compliance with the Licence Standards (the standards are still to be published at the time of writing).

Inspections will either be at the application stage (with an application inspection) or once the licence has been issued (with a compliance inspection).

The GLA will use risk-based techniques to determine whether an application inspection or compliance inspection is necessary.

The GLA says that for both application inspections and compliance inspections, evidence of compliance is likely to be gathered from a range of sources:

- face to face interviews with workers

- data collected from the labour provider
- interviews with the labour provider
- evidence collected by the GLA's own officers
- data provided from other government sources
- data collected from the application process
- other intelligence sources

The GLA will work closely with a range of government departments and the police to ensure that all legal requirements are met and enforced in the licensable sectors.

The GLA website states that following the commencement of licensing, they will be keen to hear from anyone who believes a labour provider is:

- operating in breach of licence conditions
- operating without a licence

or that a Labour User is:

- using an unlicensed labour provider.

A reporting line is available on 0845 602 5026 between 9am-5pm Monday -Friday. You can also call Crimestoppers anonymously on 0800 555 111 at any time. Further details on this and on the licensing process are available from the Gangmasters Licensing Authority (GLA) website at the following address: www.gla.gov.uk

Homeworkers

Homeworkers' employment rights depend on whether they are classed as an employee or a worker under UK employment law. See the section above on employment status for further information on this important distinction.

Most homeworkers are not classed as employees of the company that gives them work and so do not have a contract of employment. Instead the agreement that they have with the company is called a contract for services and they are classed as workers.

There is no easy test to determine whether you are an employee or a worker. Ultimately only a court or tribunal can decide and they will do this by looking at the reality of your employment situation, including whether the company is obliged to offer you work and if they do, whether you are obliged to accept it. They will also consider other factors such as how closely the company supervises your work, when and how it is done and who provides any special materials or equipment in order to carry out the work. Even if your employer says that you are not an employee, an employment tribunal may disagree, if you are unsure of your status, you should seek further advice.

Searching for work

Be careful about replying to adverts for homework that ask you to send money in advance, for example, as a 'deposit' or 'registration fee'. Often these are swindles and you are unlikely to see your money again or to receive any work.

If you have been cheated by a company offering bogus homework, you should tell your local council's trading standards department, and they can investigate if the company is acting fraudulently. See the Further Information section on page 556 for more details.

Keeping records

Only employees are legally entitled to receive a written statement of their main terms and conditions of employment. You are therefore advised to keep your own records of what was agreed at the time of interview or when you were offered the job. It is also important to keep a record of any work carried out for the employer, how long this has taken to complete and the agreed rate for the job. Keeping records in this way will help if you ever have a dispute with your employer or supplier of work.

All workers are entitled to some basic rights at work and as a homeworker you will generally be entitled to the following rights from the day you start work:

- to be paid at least the National Minimum Wage
- to refuse to work more than 48 hours per week (unless you sign an

agreement waiving this right)
- to have a rest break of 20 minutes where your working day is longer than six hours. If you are under 18, you are entitled to a 30 minute break after working four and a half hours
- to have four weeks' paid annual leave (for homeworkers who are paid on 'piece-work' or whose hours vary considerably, weekly holiday pay should be worked out as the average weekly pay earned over the last 12 weeks, omitting any weeks during which you did not have any earnings)
- to have health and safety protection
- to have protection from discrimination on grounds of your sex, pregnancy, race, disability, sexual orientation, religion or belief, and from 2006 onwards, on grounds of your age
- to join a trade union of your choice

Other rights are only available to employees, for example, the right to claim unfair dismissal. Further details on these rights are set out on pages 381-385.

Working in private households

Employment rights can be affected by where you work and in Britain one of the most notable examples of this is working in a private household.

When you apply to come to Britain as a domestic worker, you will normally be given permission to stay for up to six months if your employer is coming to Britain as a visitor, or for up to 12 months if your employer plans to live here for a longer period. The date your permission to stay ends will be marked on your passport. You can apply to extend your stay and if granted, this will usually be for a further 12 months. After four years' continuous employment as a domestic worker, you can apply to stay in the UK indefinitely.

You can change jobs while you are in Britain, but if your permission to stay has a time limit, you can only change to another job as a domestic worker in a private household.

This restriction does not apply if you have permission to stay in Britain indefinitely. If you have permission to stay indefinitely, you can take any job.

Under section 4(3) of the Race Relations Act 1976, employment in private households is specifically excluded from discrimination law which means that employers are able to discriminate in their choice of whom to employ. This does not extend to any advertisement for the job so an employer cannot discriminate in advertisements.

Seafarers

The vast majority of the world's seafarers are essentially migrant workers, being employed under the ship registers of foreign ships. Seafaring is one of the world's most dangerous jobs and many seafarers are employed under appalling terms and conditions. Ship owners are able to exploit seafarers because they can sail under a 'Flag of Convenience' or FOC. This means that they register the ship in a country which has very low employment standards and then issue contracts which reflect these standards.

As a seafarer, you will only be able to claim protection under UK employment laws if you are employed on a vessel registered in Britain. You must also be 'ordinarily resident' in Britain. If you do not meet these conditions, you will not have any employment protection under UK law.

Seafarers not ordinarily resident in the UK are not protected by UK discrimination law as this does not generally cover seafarers recruited abroad (see page 439). The Posted Workers' Directive does not ordinarily cover foreign seafarers as they are technically hired in another country.

Work permit holders

The purpose of the work permit scheme is to enable non-EEA nationals to come to the UK to work. The scheme operates by giving permission to UK-based employers to employ a named person from a non-EEA state. The scheme requires that the worker remains in the employment of that specific employer and in the same category of work. The permit can run for up to five years. In fact a worker on the work permit scheme can change employer, but only if offered employment by another employer who has applied for a work permit to take them on.

Workers recruited under work permits are supposed to get market rates of pay, and conditions comparable to those of resident workers doing the same type of job. The rate of pay should be shown on the work permit, a copy of which the worker should receive. Work Permits UK can revoke a work permit if they think this condition is not being met.

Work Permits UK have no powers at present to force the employer to pay these rates. Failure to pay the promised rate of pay, would however be a breach of contract, and would probably constitute an illegal deduction from wages.

A worker employed on a work permit for less than four years may apply for an extension and at the end of four years' employment on a work permit, the worker may apply for indefinite leave to remain in the UK. In order for this to be granted, the employer is required to support the application by confirming that the employment has been satisfactory and that they would be willing to continue employing the worker.

Those working in the UK on a work permit have access to the same employment rights as all other UK workers, provided that they meet the relevant qualifying criteria such as employment status and length of service with the employer.

Sector based schemes (SBS)

These apply to workers recruited by employers in the hospitality industry and parts of the food-processing industry (meat and fish processing and mushroom growing). Only workers aged 18 to 30 may take part, and permits are for a maximum of one year, after which workers must leave the country for at least two months, before returning on a new permit. Workers must be directly employed (i.e. not by an agency) and receive the same rate of pay as other workers at the same workplace. If there is a collective agreement, agreed pay and conditions must apply to SBS workers as well.

Undocumented workers

'Undocumented' workers are those who do not currently have the right to work. Whilst some may be illegal migrants, many may have entered the country legally, but their permission to stay has since expired. Undocumented workers are particularly vulnerable to exploitation by unscrupulous employers as they will be reluctant to complain about their treatment for fear of deportation.

If you are in this position you should seek advice from an agency such as Joint Council for the Welfare of Immigrants (JCWI) who may be able to assist you with bringing your documentation up to date or seeking fresh permission to work. Their contact details can be found at the end of this handbook.

Police raids

Raids can be carried out where the police suspect that workers are being employed illegally. Prejudices and assumptions make it more likely that raids will take place in workplaces with visibly migrant workers, like workers from the Far East or Africa. If you are concerned about your legal position in the UK, you can seek advice from one of the agencies listed at the end of this handbook. If you are a union member, your union should be able to arrange advice for you on this.

Employers are under a legal obligation to ensure that you have permission to work in the UK. If they are new to employing newcomers they may be concerned about the tests.

If you are a refugee, your potential employers may not have seen the Home Office documentation issued to refugees before, and there are several documents about which they will need to be aware. Grant of status letters and the new immigration status documents are currently part of list two of documents to provide an employer with a statutory defence under section 8 of the Asylum and Immigration Act 1996. This means that you will need to provide additional documentation, for example proof of a National Insurance number. Further and more detailed guidance from the Home Office can be found on their website www.ind.homeoffice.gov.uk. There is also an employers' helpline: 0845 101 6677.

If you are working informally in the construction industry there is a special scheme that allows you to enter the formal economy – the CIS card. However, the CIS card is for those working informally and is not to do with breaches in immigration law.

If you are an irregular resident who has been living in the UK for 14 years and who has not been actively evading enforcement measures and is otherwise of good character, you can normally expect to be granted settlement according to the Immigration Rules. See page 62 for further details.

Endnotes

1. Asylum and Immigration Act s 8
2. See for example, case studies contained in 'Migrant Workers a TUC Guide.' 2002
3. National Minimum Wage Act 1998 s 1 (1)
4. The Working Time Regulations 1998 4 (1)
5. The Working Time Regulations 1998 12 (1) (3) (4)
6. The Working Time Regulations 1998 13 (1)
7. Health and Safety at Work Act 1974
8. Trade Union and Labour Relations (Consolidation) Act 1992 Part III Rights in Relation to Union Membership and Activities
9. Employment Rights Act 1996 s 94
10. Employment Rights Act 1996 s 135
11. Employment Rights Act 1996 Part VIII
12. Employment Rights Act 1996 ss 55-56
13. Employment Rights Act 1996 s 1
14. Employment Rights Act 1996 s1
15. Employment Rights Act 1996 s1
16. Employment Rights Act 1996 s 13
17. Employment Rights Act 1996 s 23
18. Employment Rights Act 1996 s 8
19. Employment Rights Act 1996 ss13-14
20. Employment Rights Act 1996 ss 17-22
21. Employment Rights Act 1996 s 23
22. National Minimum Wage Act 1998 s 1
23. National Minimum Wage Act s 1(4)
24. The Paternity and Adoption Leave Regulations 2002 s 4 (1)

[25] The Maternity and Parental Leave Regulations 1999 ss 13-14
[26] Employment Rights Act 1996 s 57A
[27] Employment Rights Act 1996 s 57A
[28] 'Bullying and Harassment at work: a guide for managers and employers' and 'Bullying and Harassment at work: guidance for employees'
[29] Majrowski v Guys & St Thomas's NHS Trust (2005) IRLR 340
[30] Employment Rights Act 1996 s 98 A
[31] Employment Rights Act 1996 s 135
[32] Employment Rights Act 1996 s 92
[33] Brook Street Bureau v Dacas (2004) IRLR 358

14 Racial discrimination

Ranjit Singh Rana with Graham O'Neil, Commission for Racial Equality

Introduction

This section of the handbook is about racial discrimination. It provides an overview of your rights and explains race relations law, and how to make a complaint of racial discrimination. It also covers a number of the key issues facing newcomers in the UK.

All workers have the right to work free from unlawful racial discrimination and harassment. You therefore have the right not to be treated less favourably than another worker on racial grounds:

- in access to job opportunities
- in the terms and conditions under which you are employed
- in the opportunities you have for promotion, transfer or training or in the access to benefits, facilities or services
- in matters of dismissal or redundancy

You also have other rights, including:

- not to be subjected to unwanted behaviour that violates your dignity or creates an intimidating, hostile, degrading, humiliating or offensive environment
- not to be victimised for claiming unlawful racial discrimination or harassment, or for supporting someone else's complaint under the

Race Relations Act 1976 (RRA)
- not to be instructed or pressured to discriminate unlawfully against, or harass, someone, on racial grounds
- to have your complaint considered by your employer, who must adhere to the statutory grievance and disciplinary procedures
- to take your complaint to an employment tribunal, if you are not satisfied with the way your employer has dealt with it

If you believe your employer or a colleague is harassing or discriminating unlawfully against you, on racial grounds, you have several options. You can:

- consult your trade union (if there is one where you work and you are a member) or workplace representative
- report the matter to your manager (unless this person is the alleged discriminator) and/or to someone in the personnel department (if there is one)
- use informal procedures, such as mediation, and, if unsuccessful, the employer's grievance procedure, which must be followed if you are considering taking the matter to an employment tribunal
- seek legal advice about pursuing your claim in an employment tribunal, if you are not satisfied with the result of the grievance procedure

Who is covered?

The Race Relations Act 1976 (RRA) gives protection from racial discrimination and harassment in employment.

Migrant workers or newcomers

If you feel that you have been discriminated against as a migrant worker or newcomer based on your Immigration status, it does not mean you can automatically pursue a complaint under race relations law.

It is not possible to make a complaint of racial discrimination solely and expressly on the grounds of being an asylum seeker, refugee or migrant worker. Asylum seekers, refugees and migrant workers are not racial groups as defined by the RRA.

However, depending strictly on the facts of your complaint, it may be possible to link discriminatory treatment that you think was motivated by your status as an asylum seeker or migrant worker, with the racial grounds outlined below.[1]

Therefore, in practice, as a migrant worker or newcomer, you are likely to be covered based upon your racial group(s). For example, you may suffer discrimination not only because of being a migrant worker but also because you are of Afghani nationality.

Racial grounds and racial and ethnic groups

The RRA offers protection from discrimination on racial grounds, that is, race, colour, nationality (including citizenship) or ethnic or national origins.[2]

Racial groups are groups defined by racial grounds. All racial groups are protected from unlawful racial discrimination under the RRA. Romany Gypsies,[3] Irish Travellers,[4] Jews[5] and Sikhs[6] have been explicitly recognised by the courts as constituting racial groups for the purposes of the RRA. A person may fall into more than one racial group; for example, a 'Nigerian' may be defined by 'race', 'colour', 'ethnic or national origins' and 'nationality'. However, other groups, such as Muslims[7] and Rastafarians[8] have not been so recognised, as case law has established that such groups cannot be considered to be a distinct racial group by virtue of certain characteristics.

Religious or faith groups

If you feel you have been discriminated against owing to your religion, faith or belief you may be able to make a complaint under the Employment Equality (Religion or Belief) Regulations 2003 (the Religion or Belief Regulations).

These Regulations offer greater protection against discrimination (direct and indirect), victimisation and harassment on the grounds of religion or belief, which covers any religion, religious belief or similar philosophical belief.

For information and advice on Religion or Belief Regulations, and your rights under them, see page 509.

You may also be able to make a claim of racial discrimination if the act of discrimination amounts to unlawful indirect discrimination against a 'racial group' (for example, discrimination against Muslims and Hindus could in certain circumstances amount to unlawful discrimination against Pakistanis or Indians).[9]

What is racial discrimination?

There are five main types of discrimination: direct, indirect, victimisation, harassment, and segregation.

Direct discrimination[10]

Direct discrimination occurs when a person is treated less favourably, on racial grounds, than another person is, or would be, treated in the same or similar circumstances.

There can be no justification for direct discrimination. Apart from limited exceptions to the general prohibition of discrimination under the RRA (see page 220), direct discrimination is unlawful, whatever the reason for it.

The following are examples of direct discrimination:

- you are not appointed to a job because of your racial group, even though you have more experience and better qualifications than the successful candidate
- more background checks are carried out on members of your racial group compared to others in the recruitment process
- you are required to work longer hours or for less pay compared to other racial groups

Segregation[11]

Segregating a person from others, on racial grounds, automatically means treating her or him less favourably, and constitutes unlawful direct discrimination.[12]

The segregation of workers, by racial group, will be unlawful even if they have the same access to promotion, training or pay and conditions as other workers.

Examples of segregation could include:

- separating racial groups through shift patterns
- isolating certain racial groups into certain departments or occupations
- having separate facilities for different racial groups in the workplace

Indirect discrimination[13]

There are two definitions of indirect discrimination in the RRA. One covers indirect discrimination on the grounds of race, ethnic or national origins. This definition is relatively new, and originates from the EC Racial Equality Directive (2000). The other definition relates to indirect discrimination on the racial grounds of colour and nationality.

Indirect discrimination, definition 1: Race, ethnic or national origins

There are four elements to the definition:

- when an apparently race-neutral provision, criterion or practice is applied to everyone
- when this provision, criterion, or practice would put persons of specific race, ethnic or national origins at a particular disadvantage
- that it actually does place persons within this group at a particular disadvantage
- that it is not proportionate to achieving a legitimate aim

Indirect discrimination: definition 2: colour or nationality

Again there are four elements:

- when an apparently non-discriminatory requirement or condition is applied to all
- that those able to meet this requirement or condition are considerably smaller among persons of a certain colour or nationality than is the case with other groups
- which is to the detriment of those persons because they can't comply with the requirement or condition
- that the requirement or condition cannot be justified on non-racial grounds

Indirect discrimination may occur as a result of other requirements, such as qualifications or experience, dress, language, area of residence, or recruitment techniques.

For example, a rule saying that workers must not wear headgear could exclude Sikh men who wear a turban, Jewish men who wear a yarmulka or Pakistani women who wear a hijab.

Victimisation[14]

It is unlawful to treat a person less favourably on racial grounds because he or she has:

- brought proceedings under the RRA
- given evidence or information in connection with any proceedings under the RRA
- alleged that an act of unlawful discrimination has been committed
- done anything under the RRA in relation to someone, or intends to do so, or is suspected of having done or intending to do so

Victimisation could emerge as a result of a worker or workers:

- complaining of discrimination against themselves
- encouraging a colleague to pursue their complaint

- providing information to support another member of staff in their complaint
- highlighting issues around poor race equality practice within the workplace

Harassment[15]

The definition of harassment introduced by the 2003 Race Regulations applies when the conduct in question is for reasons of race or ethnic or national origins, but not colour or nationality.

A person harasses another on grounds of race or ethnic or national origins when she or he engages in unwanted conduct that has the purpose or effect of:

- violating the other person's dignity
- creating an intimidating, hostile, degrading, humiliating or offensive environment for that person

Harassment on grounds of colour or nationality involves less favourable treatment and may constitute unlawful direct discrimination.

The following examples could amount to harassment:

- racist name calling or taunting
- racist attacks
- sending racist emails or notes

Key issues for newcomers

The following provides an overview of specific employment areas most relevant to newcomers and migrant workers.

Checks before starting work

Before you start work you will be required to prove to your employer that you are legally allowed to work in the UK. Prospective employers will ask you to provide documentation, such as a passport or Immigration Status Document (ISD) to prove your right to work. For further details, see page 318.

If other groups of workers are not asked for such documentation this requirement may constitute unlawful racial discrimination.

Language

A language requirement for a job may be indirectly discriminatory and unlawful unless it is necessary for the satisfactory performance of the job.

This does not only apply to getting a job (i.e. the recruitment phase), it also applies to promotion opportunities within employment. Therefore if you are denied advancement because of your language and language is not related to the satisfactory performance of the job, then this requirement may be indirectly discriminatory.

Where the workforce includes people who are not proficient in the language of the workplace, the CRE's statutory code of practice in employment indicates that employers should consider taking reasonable steps to improve communication.[16] These might include providing:

- interpreting and translation facilities
- multilingual safety signs and notices, particularly for health and safety requirements
- training in language and communication skills
- training for managers and supervisors on the various populations and cultures that make up Britain today

Qualifications

If your employer does not recognise your qualifications, you can refer them to the relevant professional body (for example the Qualifications and Curriculum Authority). You may also be able to have your qualifications recognised by NARIC. For details on qualification recognition, see page 326.

Otherwise you might have to undergo further training for your qualification to be relevant in the UK.

If you have had your training accredited or your qualification recognised (e.g. through NARIC) and an employer does not accept the qualification, this requirement may be indirectly discriminatory.

Dismissal or transfer on racial grounds

It is unlawful for employers to discriminate against, or harass, workers on racial grounds, by dismissing them or subjecting them to any other detriment. Any other detriment potentially includes transfer.

Dismissal includes termination of a contract by the employer (with or without notice), and non-renewal or expiry of a fixed-term contract.

Volunteering

If you are a volunteer and you experience racial discrimination or harassment then you may have a level of protection under the RRA.[17] While at present there is no direct protection under the RRA for volunteers as a class of persons, you may still be able to use the RRA. This may depend on any contractual arrangements, which will be evident from your duties and responsibilities and pay.

Asylum seekers

If you are an asylum seeker, then you can use the RRA if you suffer unlawful racial discrimination while in employment (and you have permission to work) like any other individual.

In practice, it is very likely that you will be able to identify yourself with one or more of the racial groups outlined on page 426.

Irregular, undocumented and illegal migrants, or asylum seekers without permission to work

If you are an asylum seeker or migrant worker and you become aware that you are working illegally, the situation is more complex in terms of how the RRA applies to your circumstances.

Case law[18] indicates that if you bring a claim, several factors would need to be taken into account. At the time of writing, and based on present case law, whether you are covered under the RRA depends very much on the facts of the case and in particular on:

- the relationship between the discrimination alleged and the illegality of your contract of employment
- whether you or your employer were conscious that your work relationship was illegal

While employment tribunals are unwilling to condone illegal activity it should be stressed that, depending on the relationship between the discrimination and the illegal contract, they may hear your case and perhaps also award remedies if you are successful.

This is due to the fact that discrimination is a statutory tort, and is not dependent on your having a legal contract of employment. Importantly, EC Directives relating to equal treatment on racial and ethnic origins unambiguously require member states, including the United Kingdom, to provide for effective remedies in domestic law when such discrimination is proven.[19] This means that even if your contract is illegal you may still be able to pursue a discrimination claim through the employment tribunal, and receive remedies to compensate for the unfair treatment suffered. For example the remedies may be for injury to feelings, as opposed to wage compensation. As noted above this will depend strictly on the facts of your case.

Note: If you pursue a racial discrimination claim and you are working illegally then the employment tribunal and/or county or sheriff courts may use this information to make the relevant referrals to the authorities, who then may make their own separate enquiries.

Unlawful racial discrimination

Employment[20]

The Race Relations Act 1976 (RRA) gives employers a legal duty not to discriminate against or harass applicants for employment, workers, and former workers, on racial grounds.

Employers must not discriminate on racial grounds or subject a person to harassment:

- in the arrangements they make to decide who should be offered employment
- in the terms on which they offer to employ a person
- by refusing or deliberately failing to offer employment

It is also unlawful for employers to discriminate on racial grounds against a worker, or to subject him or her to harassment:

- in the terms of employment provided
- in the way they make opportunities for training, promotion or transfer, or access to any other benefits, facilities or services, available
- by refusing access to such opportunities or benefits, facilities or services
- by dismissing the worker or subjecting him or her to some other detriment

It is unlawful to discriminate against a former worker on racial grounds, or to subject him or her to harassment, after the employment relationship has come to an end, if the discrimination or harassment has arisen from, or is closely connected with, the employment.[21]

Legal responsibility for discrimination[22]

Legal responsibility for unlawful racial discrimination rests with employers.

Discriminatory acts or conduct by workers or agents (for example, contractors) 'in the course of their employment' are treated as having been done by their employer, unless the employer can show that he or she has taken all reasonably practicable steps to prevent such acts.

Employers can be held liable whether or not those acts were done with their knowledge or approval. An employer's liability for racial discrimination may extend to a worker's behaviour when 'off duty', but in a work-related situation, such as at a social event for staff, for example a Christmas party.

A worker who discriminates against, or harasses, someone, on racial grounds, in the course of her or his employment may be personally liable for his or her actions. Under the RRA, the employer will also be liable, unless she or he can show that all reasonably practicable steps were taken to prevent unlawful racial discrimination or harassment. In this case, the worker may be solely liable for the unlawful act.

Aiding unlawful acts[23]

A person who knowingly helps another person to discriminate against, or harass, someone unlawfully on racial grounds, will be treated as having discriminated similarly themselves. Their only defence would be that they had been told the act would not be unlawful, and that it was reasonable for them to believe that statement – it is an offence to make a reckless statement on such matters.

In an employment situation, anything a worker does in the course of his or her employment is treated as having been done by her or his employer as well, whether or not the employer knew about it or approved of it. A person who knowingly takes part in an act of unlawful discrimination or harassment will therefore be deemed to have helped his or her employer in acting unlawfully.

Trade unions, employers' associations, and professional and trade associations[24]

For the purposes of the Race Relations Act 1976 (RRA), trade unions, employers' associations and professional and trade associations (referred to as trade unions and other membership organisations) are both employers and providers of services specifically covered by the RRA.

In their role as employers, these organisations have all the responsibilities outlined above. They are also responsible for making sure their representatives do not discriminate unlawfully on racial grounds.

As providers of services for their members, trade unions and other membership organisations must make sure services are provided without unlawful racial discrimination or harassment.

It is unlawful for trade unions and other membership organisations to discriminate against a person, on racial grounds:

- in the terms on which they offer membership, or by refusing membership
- in the way they make benefits, facilities or services available or by refusing or deliberately failing to make them available[25]
- by depriving the person of membership, or varying the terms on which he or she is a member
- by subjecting the person to some other detriment

Trade unions and other membership organisations must not harass members or potential members on racial grounds.

Pressure or instructions to discriminate

It is unlawful for members of trade unions and other membership organisations, or their representatives, to put pressure on workers or instruct them to discriminate against, or harass, someone, on racial grounds, in the decisions they make:

- when recruiting, promoting, transferring, training or dismissing staff
- in the terms of employment, benefits, facilities or services, for example, by restricting the numbers of workers from a particular racial group in a section, grade or department
- by resisting changes to practices that are designed to remove indirect discrimination, such as mobility between departments, or rights of seniority

It is unlawful to discriminate against, or harass, a person because he or she has complained of unlawful racial discrimination or brought legal proceedings under the RRA, or provided information or evidence in connection with such proceedings, or has otherwise done (or intended to do) anything else under the RRA.

Employment Agencies[26]

The RRA covers employment agencies. In their role as employers, employment and recruitment agencies, including online recruitment agencies, have the same responsibilities as employers. They also have responsibilities as suppliers of job applicants and workers to other employers.

It is unlawful for employment and recruitment agencies to:

- discriminate against, or harass, a person, on racial grounds, in the way they provide any of their services
- job advertisements that suggest or could be taken to suggest that applications from certain racial groups will not be considered, or will be treated more favourably or less favourably than others
- act on instructions or pressure from employers, to reject, prefer or restrict the numbers of applicants from certain racial groups, unless a statutory exception applies, see page 438 for more information.
- act on indirectly discriminatory instructions from employers, so that applicants have to meet requirements or conditions that could unreasonably exclude or significantly reduce the number of applicants from a particular racial group (or groups)
- knowingly aid an employer in an act of unlawful racial discrimination or harassment

Pressure or instructions to discriminate

Employment and recruitment agencies, or their representatives, should not put pressure on workers or clients or employers, or induce or instruct them, to discriminate unlawfully against, or harass, someone, on racial grounds.

It is unlawful for employment and recruitment agencies, or their representatives, to discriminate against, or harass, a person because she or he has complained of unlawful racial discrimination or brought legal proceedings under the RRA, or provided information or evidence in connection with such proceedings, or has otherwise done (or intended to do) anything else under the RRA.

Commission for Racial Equality (CRE)

There are several acts of discrimination where only the CRE can take legal action. These include:

- discriminatory advertisements
- pressure to discriminate and
- instruction to discriminate

Complaints concerning these acts should be referred to directly to the CRE. For further information please see the CRE section, page 460.

Exceptions to unlawful racial discrimination

Private households[27]

When employment is in a private household, you can't use the RRA when the direct or indirect discrimination or harassment that you suffer is based on the racial grounds of colour and/or nationality.

However if the unfair treatment takes the form of victimisation and it is based upon your colour and/or nationality then you can use the RRA.

Positive action[28]

The term 'positive action', which is distinct from unlawful positive discrimination, refers to the measures that employers may lawfully take to provide access to facilities that meet special needs in relation to education and training or welfare, or to train or encourage people from a particular racial group that is under-represented in that particular area of work.[29]

National security[30]

An act of discrimination in employment, on racial grounds, may be permitted if it is done to safeguard national security, and if it can be justified.

Employment for training in skills to be used outside Great Britain[31]

Employers may discriminate on grounds of colour or nationality, but not race or ethnic or national origins, in employing a person who does not normally live in Britain for work at an establishment in Britain, in order to train him or her in skills that will only be used outside Britain.

Genuine Occupational Requirement and Genuine Occupational Qualification[32]

It is lawful for an employer to discriminate on racial grounds in recruiting people for jobs where being of a particular race or ethnic or national origin is a 'Genuine Occupational Requirement' (GOR), or being of a particular colour or nationality is a 'Genuine Occupational Qualification' (GOQ).[33]

Seamen recruited overseas[34]

Employers may discriminate (i.e. it is lawful to discriminate) in recruiting a person for a job on a ship with regards to pay, where the person was recruited overseas, and where it amounts to discrimination on the racial ground of nationality.[35]

Making a complaint of racial discrimination

If you feel that you have been discriminated against on racial grounds, you have the right to make a complaint of racial discrimination.

Pursuing a complaint can be very stressful and time-consuming. It is not a decision that should be taken lightly. However, this should not deter you if you feel strongly about the complaint.

If you choose to pursue your complaint of racial discrimination, there are several options available to you:

- raising the complaint with your employer (see below for dispute resolution procedures)
- using mediation to resolve the complaint
- progressing the complaint with the employment tribunal

It is important to seek advice from a qualified adviser in racial discrimination casework about your complaint as soon as possible. You may want to approach one of the organisations highlighted below and in the Further Information chapter (see page 556). The adviser should:

- establish how your complaint constitutes racial discrimination
- explore the different options available to you
- ensure any relevant requirements (such as strict time limits of employment tribunal procedures) are met

Raising the complaint with your employer

Since the introduction of the Employment Act 2002 (Dispute Resolution) Regulations 2004, which came into force on 1 October 2004, there are new compulsory procedures that all employers and employees must use in attempting to resolve issues of grievances (such as a claim of racial discrimination), disciplinary action and dismissal (see page 410).

The purpose of their introduction was to encourage employment disputes to be resolved internally without the need for costly and time-consuming employment tribunal claims.

Before using the statutory grievance procedures you and your employer should attempt to resolve any dispute informally where possible (see pages 443-446). If you do pursue a grievance and a complaint is formalised, the Dispute Resolution Regulations must be followed by all employers and employees. These are only a minimum standard and some employers may already have grievance procedures which go further.

Note: These procedures do not apply to other workers such as contractors or freelance workers as the 2004 Regulations apply only to employees and not 'workers'. Therefore if you are a contract or freelance worker, you should pursue your complaint directly with the employment tribunal (see page 490).

To assist you with your complaint, you may want to send your employer a race relations questionnaire (RR65 form)[36]. A RR65 questionnaire can be used to inform the grievance procedure, although you should note that the questionnaire does not count as a grievance statement. In practice, this means that you can use the answers on the questionnaire to to build your case. This especially effective if used early on in the process. For further details on the RR65 form, see page 453.

You should follow one of the two procedures below depending on whether you are still in the job or whether you have left. You must follow these procedures otherwise you may not be able to make a claim, or your compensation may be reduced by up to 50 per cent.

Procedure if you are in the job

Stage 1: written statement of grievance and first meeting

If you have a grievance you are required to send a written statement explaining your grievance to your employer. Your employer must then arrange a meeting to discuss your grievance. You have a right to be accompanied to this meeting by someone who works with you or a trade union official. The meeting must be held at a time and place which are reasonable for you and anyone accompanying you. Please note that you must take all reasonable steps to attend this meeting.

After the meeting the employer must tell you what she or he has decided, and inform you of your right of appeal. If you do not agree with his or her decision, then you should consider using this right.

Stage 2: the appeal

If you feel your grievance has not been satisfactorily dealt with, you should tell your employer you are going to appeal. She or he must arrange another meeting to discuss this and the same rules apply to this as to the original meeting, although you should note that the employer should be represented by a more senior representative than was the case at the first meeting.

After the appeal meeting the employer must tell you what he or she has decided and that this decision is final.

Stage 3: employment tribunal

If you are still not satisfied with the way you have been treated you can begin a claim in the employment tribunal. Please be aware that the employment tribunal will expect you to have complied with the Dispute Resolution Regulations, and that the RRA's statutory time limit for lodging your application to the employment tribunal remains within three months of the last act of racial discrimination.[37] However this time limit will be extended by an extra three months when you have either

- lodged your grievance, in accordance with the above regulations, and within a period of three months since the last act of racial discrimination

or

- submitted your application direct to the employment tribunal within the statutory timescales but have not yet engaged the above regulations

Procedure if you have left the job

If you leave a job but still have an outstanding grievance, you can still pursue your claim using a shorter procedure (known as the modified procedure).

This procedure applies only if:

- you and your employer agree in writing to use the modified procedure and
- the employer did not know about the grievance procedure or the procedures were either not started or started but not completed before you left the employment

Stage 1: written statement

You must send a written statement of grievance to your former employer.

Stage 2: employer's reply

Your former employer must write back to you, answering the points you have raised.

Stage 3: employment tribunal

If the issue has not been resolved to your satisfaction, you can pursue the complaint through the employment tribunal as long as it is commenced within the required time limits.

Please note that the modified grievance procedure will not apply if it is also decided by an employment tribunal that in circumstances where the employment relationship has ended, no grievance has been commenced, or it is not reasonably practicable to require you to follow this procedure.

In general, and in order to protect your rights under the RRA, you should ensure that you adhere to both the statutory timescales under the RRA and you follow the Dispute Resolution Regulations as well.

Mediation

What is mediation?

Mediation is a process of resolving disagreements or disputes, on a voluntary basis, without having to go to an employment tribunal. A person, who has no relationship with you or the employer, works with you and the employer to reach an agreement that resolves the identified problems in the worker-employer relationship.

This approach has the following benefits:

- you may be able to assess the strengths and weaknesses of the case
- you could minimise the time, expenses, risks and stress of pursuing the claim through an employment tribunal

- the agreed settlement would be on terms agreed by you and the employer, rather than another person

Your workplace may already have internal mediators whom you can ask to help. If not, there are now many companies that specialise in this area of work.

Alternatively, the Advisory, Conciliation and Arbitration Service (ACAS) (see page 593 for details) should be able to help. Their aim is to promote good employment relations. As part of their remit, they have a legal duty to offer conciliation in most cases when someone has a complaint about their employment rights.

Participation in mediation

Both you and your employer have to agree to participate, regardless of who requested the assistance. If you are not happy to participate in mediation, you do not have to.

Confidentiality and mediation

Mediators should maintain the confidentiality of both parties and only disclose information to third parties when they have the relevant consent. You should ensure that mediators do this when dealing with your case.

Cost of mediation

Other than where ACAS is involved, there may be a charge for mediation. In some cases the employer may be in a position to cover the cost of mediation.

Time limits for mediation

There are no formal time limits in which mediation can be used. However, where this is seen as a genuine option, this should take place prior to the final hearing at the employment tribunal if a complaint has been lodged. Note that there are time limits for tribunal cases (see page 522).

ACAS can get involved as soon as you have a complaint about your employment rights, even if the complaint has not been formally registered with the employment tribunal.

If you register a complaint with the employment tribunal, copies are automatically provided to your local ACAS office. ACAS has a duty to consider whether they can help you or your employer to reach a settlement without the need for an employment tribunal hearing. Under the Employment Tribunals Regulations, there is no fixed period for ACAS to attempt to resolve the dispute by conciliation in relation to claims of racial discrimination.

Impact of mediation

With reference to the mediation process and employment tribunal procedures, if a complaint has been lodged, each will operate completely separately. It is therefore important to continue complying with any instructions you receive from the employment tribunal.

Tribunal procedures will only stop if the complaint has been heard or withdrawn for some reason or if you have settled the complaint with the assistance of ACAS.

Settlement through mediation

When aiming to settle your complaint, you should ensure the settlement meets your needs, requirements and expectations. It may be helpful to seek legal advice prior to reaching this stage.

If you settle the complaint with your employer, the agreement will be legally binding. The agreement does not necessarily have to be in writing for it to be legally binding. ACAS Officers will record the agreement on an ACAS form for proof of the agreement. ACAS will also require you and the employer to sign it.

Where a complaint has been made to the Employment Tribunal, ACAS will notify the employment tribunal office that settlement has been agreed and they will close the case.

Terms of settlement through ACAS

In general, it is best to try to settle your case before it gets to a full hearing (if you can agree terms that an employment tribunal would consider reasonable in the circumstances).

In practice, a significant proportion of all cases are settled on agreed terms. You may for example, agree to settle your complaint by accepting a sum of money or an apology instead of going to an employment tribunal.

Other areas of settlement could, depending on the circumstances of the complaint, include:

- other outstanding monies (such as worked overtime)
- other acts of discrimination or employment rights
- agreed references
- future acts of victimisation

Appointed representatives

If there is an appointed representative, you can direct her or him to conciliate on your behalf. However, it is important that they are clear about your needs, requirements and expectations as any agreements reached are legally binding where ACAS is involved.

Unsuccessful mediation

If you and the employer are unable to reach a settlement, and neither you nor the employer have withdrawn a logged complaint, the complaint will progress to a full employment tribunal hearing.

Employment tribunal

What is an employment tribunal?

Cases involving unlawful racial discrimination in the employment field are heard in employment tribunals.[38] For further details see the section on employment tribunals, page 488.

If you think you have been discriminated against at work and you can't resolve your complaint with your employer through the statutory grievance procedures you can start a claim in an employment tribunal.

Lodging a complaint

To register your complaint, you need to complete an ET1 form, which asks you to provide details about your complaint. Copies are available from your nearest employment tribunal office.

Time limits to lodge a complaint

Generally, you must make the complaint to the employment tribunal within three months, less one day, from the date of the incident that you are complaining about.[39] Late applications are considered at the discretion of the employment tribunal.[40] However, where the statutory grievance procedures apply, the time limit must be extended by a further three months to allow you and the employer to try to resolve the dispute.

Costs when lodging a complaint

You do not have to pay a fee to make a complaint to the employment tribunal. See page 520 for more information.

Employment tribunal procedures

There are different types of hearing that form part of the process to resolve a complaint. The type of hearing applied will depend significantly on the nature of your complaint.

Employment tribunal decisions and appeal

The employment tribunal will decide if your employer has discriminated against you. If your case is successful it will also decide whether compensation should be awarded, and if so how much.

After the employment tribunal, you will be sent a written copy of its decision.

In some circumstances, if you lose your case you may be able to ask for a review of the decision, or appeal to the employment appeal tribunal.

If you win your case but the employment tribunal does not make a decision on what compensation you should receive, then a 'remedies hearing' will be held.

For further details on all the above, see the section on employment tribunals, pages 488-533.

Remedies

Where an employment tribunal decides in your favour, it may award one or more of the following remedies:

- an order declaring the rights of the parties
- an order requiring the employer to pay you compensation
- a recommendation that the employer take action to remove or reduce the effects of the discrimination on you (such as a written apology or removing discriminatory documents from your personnel file)[41]

A remedies hearing may involve more detailed evidence. You will need to provide details of any loss of earnings or benefits and any other evidence that will help the employment tribunal decide what compensation you should receive. This may include evidence from doctors or psychiatrists indicating any physical or mental effect the racial discrimination has had on you.

Withdrawing the complaint

You can withdraw your complaint at any time. However, this should be done on the advice of a racial discrimination expert. Please see 'Information, Advice and Assistance' (page 458) for more information.

Legal representation

You are strongly advised to seek legal representation. Please see suggestions in this section and the Further Information chapter on page 556.

Evidence in a case of racial discrimination

The standard applied by employment tribunals to determine whether racial discrimination has taken place is based on the balance of probabilities. This means, what is the likelihood of racial discrimination taking place, compared to it not taking place?

If your case involves other claims under employment law (including other forms of discrimination), please see the section on employment tribunals, page 488.

Employment tribunals assess the chances of racial discrimination taking place by identifying the key facts and then making reasonable inferences to determine whether racial discrimination took place.

The Race Relations Act 1976 (RRA) prohibits unlawful racial discrimination, but not prejudice, which means prejudging people. The law is concerned with people's actions and the effects of their actions, not with their opinions or attitudes. It is not necessary to show that someone intended to discriminate against you, just that the effect of their actions was that you were treated less favourably.

Burden of proof

As a result of the EC Race Directive, the burden of proof used by employment tribunals will vary according to the grounds of discrimination. For further details, see the section on tribunals, page 488.

On grounds of race or ethnic or national origins[42]

If you can establish facts from which an employment tribunal can conclude that an act of racial discrimination or harassment on grounds of race or ethnic or national origins has occurred, the employer will have to prove that any difference in treatment was not due in any way to discrimination or harassment. If the explanation is inadequate or unsatisfactory, the tribunal must find that unlawful discrimination or harassment has occurred.[43]

On grounds of colour or nationality[44]

In cases where the discrimination is on grounds of colour or nationality, if you establish facts from which an employment tribunal could conclude that you have suffered racial discrimination, the tribunal will ask the employer for an explanation. If the explanation is unsatisfactory, the tribunal may find that discrimination has occurred.

Direct discrimination (including segregation)

If you pursue a claim of direct discrimination, it is necessary to demonstrate that you were treated differently (or would have been) compared to another person and that the difference in treatment is at least partially attributable to your perceived membership of one or more racial groups.

Discrimination based on someone else's racial group

The RRA does not specify that discrimination has to be based on your racial group. Therefore, there is scope to be discriminated against because of another person's racial group.[45] This could include:

- being reprimanded or dismissed for not excluding certain racial groups at the direction of your employer
- being excluded by your colleagues because of a friendship or relationship with someone of another racial group

Indirect discrimination

The test of indirect discrimination is the same under both definitions. It involves drawing an objective balance between the discriminatory effects of the provision, criterion, practice, requirement or condition and the employer's reasonable need to apply it.

When assessing the justification for policies and practices that could have a disproportionate effect on some racial groups, it would be useful to consider the following questions:

- does the provision, criterion, practice, requirement or condition correspond to a real need?

- does the employer's need pursue a legitimate aim, for example health and safety?
- are the means used to achieve the aim appropriate and necessary?
- is there any other way of achieving the aim in question?
- is there a way of reducing any potentially unlawful discriminatory effect?

Justification, legitimate aim and proportionate means

If an employment tribunal considers that a race-neutral provision or practice places persons of specific racial groups at a particular disadvantage, then, to justify this, the respondent will have to show that:

- the aim of the provision was legitimate
- the means used to achieve that aim were proportionate

'Proportionate means' may be defined as means that are appropriate and necessary to achieve a legitimate aim, for example an aim of maintaining a safe working environment.

Crossover between the two definitions of indirect discrimination

Although the definition of indirect discrimination was introduced to meet the EC Race Directive and does not apply to grounds of colour or nationality, in practice, a criterion that disadvantaged someone because of his or her colour would also be likely to disadvantage that person because of her or his race or ethnic or national origins.

Wider scope of provision, criterion and practice

The concept of 'provision, criterion or practice', introduced to comply with the EC Race Directive, is broader and less restrictive than the concept of 'requirement or condition' in the original definition of indirect discrimination in the RRA. The concept of 'provision, criterion or practice' covers the full breadth of formal and informal practices in employment.

Victimisation

For a claim of victimisation under the RRA to succeed, you have to show that you have been or would have been treated less favourably, on racial grounds, than others in similar circumstances and that the treatment was a result of your action in relation to allegations or proceedings under the RRA.

Acting in good faith

In order to make a complaint of victimisation, your original complaint must have been made in good faith (that is, you perceive it to be genuine and warranted).[46]

Harassment

The definition of what is intimidating, hostile, degrading, humiliating or offensive is both subjective and objective. The subjective element relates to your perception of treatment as harassment. The objective element consists of an employment tribunal having regard to not only to your perception of the treatment as harassment, but also whether the effect that it had on you can be considered reasonable. This test applies unless it is admitted that the conduct was intentionally hostile. The effect of this test is that an employment tribunal could decide that you were oversensitive and had unreasonably taken offence.

Harassment on grounds of colour or nationality involves less favourable treatment and may constitute unlawful direct discrimination. Therefore, this will normally be dealt with within the framework of direct discrimination.

Colour and racial harassment

While the statutory definition of harassment in the RRA applies only to grounds of race or ethnic or national origins, and not to those of colour and nationality, in cases where abuse is overtly directed at a person's skin colour, employment tribunals and courts may interpret 'race' broadly, to include colour.

Nationality and racial harassment

Offensive behaviour in relation to a person's nationality may also be regarded as harassment on the grounds of that person's actual or perceived national origins, and would therefore be covered by the statutory definition of harassment in the RRA.

Single incident

It is possible for a single incident, for example a racist joke, to be taken as sufficient to cause you to feel harassed.

Race relations questionnaire[47]

What is a race relations questionnaire?

The race relations questionnaire, also known as the RR65 form, provides an opportunity for you put relevant questions to your employer about your complaint of racial discrimination.

The purpose of the questionnaire is to find out more about how your employer thinks they have treated you. It can help you and your adviser to decide if you should take your case to an employment tribunal. The responses provided may assist you if you do make a claim, as the form may be used as evidence. It may be the first step towards going to an employment tribunal or it may solve the problem without any further action.

If you decide to take a case to an employment tribunal, the race relations questionnaire can help you to present your case more effectively. This is because:

- the questions and replies can show what is accepted or denied, and what the main issues in dispute are
- your employer will usually send any documents requested on the form, which you can then use if you take the case forward
- the replies to the form can help you decide how strong your case is
- the questions and replies can be used for cross-examination or comparison with what is said at the hearing

- the employment tribunal can use the information in reaching a decision. This can be very important as cases of discrimination can often be difficult to prove

Employer's failure to respond

Your employer does not have to complete the questionnaire, but failure to respond or any unclear answers may count against them at a subsequent employment tribunal.[48] This may include a finding of racial discrimination in your favour.

Time limits to serve the questionnaire

You need to send the form to your employer within three months of the most recent incident you are complaining about or if you have applied to an employment tribunal, you need to send the form within 21 days.[49] After 21 days, the questionnaire can only be sent to the employer with the authorisation of the employment tribunal, if a satisfactory reason for the delay has been given.[50]

You may also be entitled to send an additional questionnaire to your employer for acts of discrimination that occurred after the original act of discrimination.

Completing the questionnaire

Attached to the form, you will find guidance on completing it, including definitions of discrimination. You will need two copies of the form, one to send to your employer and one to keep.

For further advice on how to use the race relations questionnaire, and examples, please see: http://www.cre.gov.uk/legal/rr65_how.html

Supporting evidence in a racial discrimination case

The type of evidence necessary to support your complaint will depend on the type of discrimination and the unlawful act, as well as the finer details of what actually happened. For further details, see the section on tribunals, pages 488-533.

You may be able to use one or more of the following sources of evidence.

Comparator

In cases alleging direct racial discrimination (which includes segregation) the way a person has been treated should be compared with the way a person from a different racial group has been, or would be, treated in the same or similar circumstances.[51]

Employment tribunals have recognised that it may not always be possible to compare the alleged treatment with the treatment of an actual other person, and that a hypothetical comparison might have to be made with a person from a different racial group in a similar situation. The question to be asked is 'how would a person from a different racial group be treated, in circumstances that are not identical, but not too dissimilar?'

Employment code of practice

The RRA gives the CRE the power to issue codes of practice in the field of employment, and to give such practical guidance as it sees fit to eliminate discrimination and promote equality of opportunity.[52] The CRE's Statutory Code of Practice on Racial Equality in Employment came into force on 6 April 2006.[53]

The statutory code does not impose any legal obligations on employers but can be used in evidence in legal proceedings brought under the RRA, especially if it has not been followed by the employer. Employment tribunals must take account of any part of the code that might be relevant to a question arising during the proceedings.[54]

Employer's explanation

It is important to establish early on the employer's explanation for the complaint in question.

It is important to identify inconsistencies between the employer's explanation of what happened and witness statements, relevant documents or other sources of identified information.

Other acts of discrimination

Every complaint that is registered with the employment tribunal could form part of the claim against your employer. However, complaints that are not lodged with an employment tribunal (perhaps owing to time limits not being met) could be used to support the complaint in question.

You may also be able to identify other complaints from other current or previous employees, relating to racial discrimination, which could support your complaint. This is particularly effective if no investigation took place or remedial action was taken in regard to these other complaints.

Equal opportunities policies

It is important to demonstrate that the employer does not have an equal opportunities policy, or that the employer does have one but that it is not implemented in any meaningful way.

You may want to use the race relations questionnaire as a means to collect some of this information.

Statistics

Statistical evidence may help demonstrate the culture of the organisation, or treatment of other racial groups, as well as your own. These statistics could relate to:

- where certain racial groups are employed in shift patterns
- recruitment and appointment rates (including promotion) at certain points of the recruitment cycle, broken down by racial group
- types of grievances and disciplinary actions that have arisen, and their outcomes, at the organisation, broken down by racial group

If your employer does not collect such information, you may want to bring to the employment tribunal's attention non-compliance with the recommendations of the Statutory Code of Practice on Racial Equality in Employment.[55]

With particular reference to indirect discrimination, it would be important to collect statistical data that demonstrates that certain groups are less well served because of certain requirements, conditions, provision, criteria or practices.

Witness statements

You may want to request statements from any person who may have some first-hand information that supports your complaint, such as:

- staff who witnessed the behaviour complained of
- colleagues who may have been pressured into carrying out certain instructions that are discriminatory and are willing to say so
- staff who have a general awareness of the employer's behaviour towards certain racial groups

Information, advice and assistance

You should take any opportunities available to you:

- to obtain further information, advice and assistance about your rights
- to discuss the detail of your complaint
- to explore how to progress your complaint
- to determine the level of assistance the relevant body can provide you with

Various agencies can give you advice about your complaint. In some cases, they may also be able to give you legal assistance and help you to bring your case before an employment tribunal. You should make sure that the adviser is qualified in race discrimination casework.

Advice agencies

You can get advice about your complaint from:

Trade unions

Trade unions represent their members in the workplace (see page 399). If you are in a trade union, they can advise you. Other than your subscription as a member, there should be no charge for this service.

Advice services

A racial equality council, Citizens Advice Bureau office, law centre or another local advice service may be of assistance.

Many of these organisations are community-based and their services provided free of charge. However, you may want to ensure that this is the case when contacting them. For contact details refer to your local phone book.

Solicitors

Solicitors can also be a source of advice and support. For contact details of local solicitors, please see your local phone book.

You may be charged for this service. If you are on a low income you may be entitled to free legal advice through the legal help scheme. But this will only be available for initial advice about your complaint and not for representation at the employment tribunal.

It is also possible that your household contents insurance policies may include general legal advice.

A few law firms now provide a 'no win, no fee' service. In other words, you only have to pay for the service if you win the complaint of racial discrimination. See page 521 for general advice on 'no win, no fee'.

Preparing for a meeting with your adviser

Prior to the meeting, make a careful, detailed record of the incident where you believe racial discrimination took place. Note the names of possible witnesses and, if you can, ask them to make a record of what happened. It may also be helpful to collect any other documents (such as letters, wage slips, or appraisal reports) that may support your complaint.

If you are asked by the adviser to provide any of the above documents, you should provide a photocopy of these. You may want to use 'recorded delivery' when posting documents in case they are lost. Do ensure that you keep originals safe and secure.

Agreeing a course of action with the adviser

The adviser is supposed to act on you behalf. There should therefore be agreement as to how the complaint should be progressed. If you do not agree with the course of action proposed by the adviser or you lose confidence in their ability to progress the complaint, you should take steps to resolve the issues that are affecting the relationship or seek alternative advice.

If you have a weak complaint

When an adviser provides you with his or her view of the complaint, it is just that, their view. You can, if you choose to, seek a second opinion.

You should remember that the advice will be based on the level of evidence required to prove that the racial discrimination took place. It is important to consider the nature and extent of your evidence. This evidence is the only basis on which an employment tribunal will uphold your complaint.

The Commission for Racial Equality

What is the CRE?

The CRE is the leading organisation working to eliminate racial discrimination and harassment in Great Britain, and to promote equal opportunities and good relations between people from different ethnic and racial backgrounds. It is the only body with the statutory power to help enforce the Race Relations Act 1976 (RRA).

The CRE has statutory duties, responsibilities, and powers under the RRA.

Its three main duties are to:

- to work towards the elimination of racial discrimination and harassment
- to promote equality of opportunity and good relations between different racial groups

- to monitor the way the RRA is working and to recommend ways in which it can be improved[56]

The CRE's legal powers

As well as issuing statutory codes of practice, and other guidance, to help employers and providers of services in the public, private and voluntary sectors to develop fair policies and practices, the CRE can also conduct formal investigations of organisations and sectors where there is evidence that racial discrimination may have occurred.[57]

The CRE is the only body with the power to take legal action against organisations or individuals who instruct or put pressure on others to discriminate, or who publish discriminatory advertisements, and complaints should be referred to the CRE directly. See page 598 for contact details.

Discriminatory advertisements[58]

It is unlawful to publish, or to be responsible for publishing, any advertisement that indicates, or may reasonably be understood to indicate, an intention to discriminate, even if the act of discrimination were lawful.

The definition of advertisement is very wide and includes any form of advertisement or notice, whether public or not. For example, internal circulars or newsletters announcing staff vacancies, emails, displays on noticeboards or shop windows, and job advertisements, banners and pop-up windows on websites.[59]

Pressure to discriminate[60]

It is unlawful to induce, or attempt to induce, a person to discriminate against, or harass, someone on racial grounds. The pressure may amount to no more than persuasion, and need not necessarily involve a benefit or loss. Nor does the pressure have to be applied directly if it is applied in such a way that the other person is likely to hear of it. It is unlawful regardless of the consequences: for example even if the person who was put under pressure does not go on to commit an act of discrimination.

Instructions to discriminate[61]

It is unlawful for a person who has authority over another person, or whose wishes that person normally follows, to instruct him or her to discriminate against, or harass, someone on racial grounds.

CRE assistance

The CRE has a duty to consider all applications for legal advice and assistance from people who think they might have been discriminated against or harassed for reasons of race, colour, nationality (including citizenship), or ethnic or national origins.[62]

The CRE can only consider your application for assistance if your complaint falls within the scope of the RRA.

All applicants to the CRE receive some advice about their complaint, but only a small proportion receives legal representation.

The CRE applies strict criteria when deciding which cases to support. Cases are more likely to be supported if they:

- test a point of law
- are too complex for an individual to deal with on their own
- deserve any other special consideration[63]

If you wish to apply for CRE assistance, you should:

- contact your nearest CRE office (see page 598) or
- complete an application form that can be downloaded from http://www.cre.gov.uk/ap4astfm.pdf

You should give the CRE as much notice as possible of your complaint.

Note: Your complaint to the employment tribunal must be lodged in accordance with the deadlines fixed by the RRA (not the CRE) and applying to the CRE does not affect the employment tribunal deadline. The deadline is three months, less one day, from the date of the incident you are complaining about, unless the statutory dispute resolution procedures apply – in which case the deadline is automatically extended to six months.

Note: The CRE's services are free of charge.

Notification of assistance

Decisions on all applications are made by a committee of CRE Commissioners, which meets regularly: normally every six weeks. Decisions by the committee are final.

If the CRE is unable to offer advice and assistance or legal representation, you will be given a reason for this. Remember, you can always take your complaint to the employment tribunal without CRE assistance and support.

Further information

The CRE's website, www.cre.gov.uk, includes a catalogue of current CRE publications, including codes of practice, guidance documents, information about race relations, about the CRE's local, regional, national and international work, and about good practice in the field of racial equality. It also provides legal advice, explaining individuals' rights under the law, and what organisations must do to comply with the Race Relations Act.

Endnotes

[1] Attorney General's Reference (No 4 of 2004); R v D [2005] EWCA Crim 889, & R v Rogers [2005] EWCA Crim 2863

[2] Race Relations Act 1976 s 3

[3] CRE v Dutton [1989] IRLR 8

[4] O'Leary v Allied Domecq, unreported (2000) Central London County Court

[5] Seide v Gillette Industries [1980] IRLR 427

[6] Mandla v Dowell Lee [1983] IRLR 210, HL

[7] Nyazi v Rymans Limited, (1998) EAT/6/88

[8] Dawkins v department of the environment (1993) 49 EOR 377 and [1993] IRLR

[9] For example an employment appeal tribunal found in 1996 that a group of Asian Muslims suffered indirect racial discrimination because they were less able to comply with their employers' new summer working arrangements, given that Eid then fell during the summer months. The discrimination was racial due to the relatively high rates of non-compliance with these arrangements among workers from the Asian Indian sub-continent who also happened to be Muslims. Walker v Hussain Walker [1986] ICR 291 (EAT)

[10] Race Relations Act 1976 s 1 (1) (a)

[11] Race Relations Act 1976 s 1 (2)

[12] Please note that unlawful segregation may require a conscious act or practice by the employer to keep apart people of different racial groups (FTATU v Modgill [1980] IRLR 142)

[13] Race Relations Act 1976 s 1(1A) & 1(1)(b)

[14] Race Relations Act 1976 s 2

[15] Race Relations Act 1976 s 3A(1) & (2)

[16] For a complete overview, see the CRE's Statutory Code of Practice on Racial Equality in Employment, pages 56-57

[17] Asylum seekers are permitted to volunteer

[18] All v Woolston Hall Leisure Ltd [2000] EWCA Civ 170 (23 May 2000) available at: http://www.bailii.org/ew/cases/EWCA/Civ/2000/170.html

Vakante v Addey Stanhope School [2004] EWCA Civ 1065

Leighton v Michael [1995] ICR 1091

[19] See 26 in the preamble to the Council Directive 2000/43/EC of 29 June 2000 implementing the principle of equal treatment between persons irrespective of racial or ethnic origin, 'the Racial Equality Directive'

[20] Race Relations Act 1976 s 4 & 4A

[21] Race Relations Act 1976 s 27A

[22] Race Relations Act 1976 s 32 & 33

[23] Race Relations Act 1976 s 33

[24] Race Relations Act 1976 s 11

[25] Benefits, facilities or services may include training facilities, welfare and insurance schemes, entertainment and social events, being involved in negotiations and advice, representation and assistance in grievance, disciplinary or dismissal procedures

[26] Race Relations Act 1976 s 14 & s 29.

[27] Race Relations Act 1976 s 4(3)

[28] Race Relations Act 1976 s 35 & s 37 & s 38

[29] For further information, see the CRE's Statutory Code of Practice on Racial Equality in Employment, pages 89-90

[30] Race Relations Act 1976 s 42

[31] Race Relations Act 1976 s 6

[32] Race Relations Act 1976 s 4A & s 5

[33] For further information, see the CRE's Statutory Code of Practice on Racial Equality in Employment, pages 91–92

[34] Race Relations Act 1976 s 9

[35] The CRE is currently working towards reviewing this provision of the Race Relations Act 1976

[36] Race Relations Act 1976 s 65

[37] Race Relations Act 1976 s 68(1)(a)

[38] Race Relations Act 1976 s 54

[39] Race Relations Act 1976 s 68

[40] Race Relations Act 1976 s 68(6)

[41] Race Relations Act s 56

[42] Race Relations Act 1976 s 54 A

[43] Wong v Igen Ltd and others [2005] EWCA Civ 142

[44] See King v The Great Britain-China Centre [1992] ICR 516 and Glasgow City Council v Zafar [1998] ICR 120 for the approach to be followed in cases relating to the racial grounds of colour and/or nationality. The main difference between the burden of proof in cases of racial grounds of colour and nationality, as compared to cases on the racial grounds of race, ethnic or national origins, lies in to what extent employment tribunals or county or sheriff courts are bound to make findings of unlawful racial discrimination. In the latter instance, in circumstances where the applicant has established facts from which inferences of unlawful racial discrimination can be drawn and in the absence of an adequate explanation from the respondent, the employment tribunal or the county or sheriff courts will be bound to uphold the applicant's case; whereas in the former instance the tribunal or court will not be so bound to uphold the applicant's allegations

[45] Showboat Entertainment Centre Ltd v Owens [1984] IRLR 7

[46] Race Relations Act 1976 s 2(2)

[47] Race Relations Act 1976 s 65

[48] Race Relations Act 1976 s 65 (2) (b)

[49] Race Relations (questionnaire and Replies) Order 1977 SI No. 842

[50] 1977 SI No. 842 art 5(b)

[51] Race Relations Act 1976 s 3 (4)
[52] Race Relations Act 1976 s 47
[53] This code replaces the 'Code of Practice from the Elimination of Racial Discrimination and the Promotion of Equality of Opportunity in Employment', which came into force on 1 April 1984
[54] Race Relations Act 1976 s 47 (10)
[55] Statutory Code of Practice on Racial Equality in Employment, page 24, paragraph 3.25
[56] Race Relations Act 1976 s 43
[57] Race Relations Act 1976 s 48
[58] Race Relations Act 1976 s 29
[59] The RRA allows a small number of limited exceptions, where the advertisement refers to a situation where discrimination is not unlawful; for example, a lawful positive action training measure or a genuine occupational qualification. The advertisement should make it clear that the employer is making use of the exception
[60] Race Relations Act 1976 s 31
[61] Race Relations Act 1976 s 30
[62] Race Relations Act 1976 s 66
[63] Race Relations Act 1976 s 66 (1)

15 Maternity rights and benefits

Liz Carney

Introduction

This chapter will look mainly at maternity rights and family rights. It also defines sex discrimination and harassment. Many of the procedures for complaining about sex discrimination and sexual harassment, advice about collecting evidence, the burden of proof and time limits for making a claim to an employment tribunal are covered in the section on tribunals.

Rights and benefits

Ante-natal appointments[1]

You have the right not to be unreasonably refused time off from work to receive ante-natal care. As part of this right, you are allowed paid time off work to attend an ante-natal appointment (including any necessary travel time).

The employer can request that the mother provide an appointment card or other confirmation of the appointment, from a doctor or midwife. This duty (to provide a card or written confirmation) only applies to the second and any subsequent ante-natal appointment.

If there is evidence that the appointment could have been attended at a less inconvenient time to the employer, that may justify the employer refusing time off, but if the appointment time is the only one the doctor or midwife have available then it should be permitted.

If you want to make a claim to an employment tribunal for being unreasonably refused time off, or for not being paid for time off, your claim must be made within three months of the date of the ante-natal appointment.[2] If you receive compensation, it will be awarded for either the loss of pay for the time that would have been taken off, or for loss of pay if the time was allowed to be taken, but not paid for.

You may also be able to make a sex discrimination claim for less favourable treatment for a pregnancy-related reason.

Maternity leave[3]

If you are pregnant and an employee (see page 379) you have the right to 26 weeks' maternity leave. This is known as ordinary maternity leave (OML). There is a compulsory period of two weeks' maternity leave starting on the day of the birth.

If you are a pregnant employee who has been continuously employed by your employer for 26 weeks, up to the end of the 15th week before the expected week of childbirth (the 'qualifying week'), you have the right to 26 weeks of additional maternity leave (AML).[4]

OML can start at any time from the beginning of the 11th week before the expected week of childbirth. The latest it can start is the day of the birth.

If you are absent from work with a pregnancy-related sickness during the last four weeks before the expected week of childbirth, your leave is triggered automatically.

Notice requirements

You must notify your employer, during or before the 15th week before the expected week of childbirth, of the following:

- the fact that you are pregnant
- the expected date of childbirth (The MAT B1 certificate from the midwife will have the expected date of delivery)

- the date you wish to start maternity leave

If a baby is born prematurely you must notify the employer as soon as is reasonably practicable and inform the employer of the date you gave birth. The midwife or doctor can complete the MAT B1 showing the expected and actual date of birth.

Within 28 days of receiving notification, your employer must notify you of the date you are due to return to work at the end of maternity leave. An employer must assume that if you are entitled to additional maternity leave (AML), you will take the full twelve months' leave.

Once you have given initial notification, the start date of maternity leave can be varied by giving the employer 28 days' notice before the date varied or the new date (whichever is earlier) or, if this is not possible, as soon as is reasonably practicable.

If you want to return to work early you must give the employer 28 days' notice of your intention to return early.

Rights during maternity leave

You have a number of rights regarding:

- terms and conditions of employment
- leave
- pregnancy-related disadvantages

The benefits of your terms and conditions of employment, except pay, should continue during your maternity leave.

You should be able to take your accrued annual leave before or after maternity leave. The law is unclear as to whether a woman continues to accrue her 20 days' annual leave during AML, but there is currently an appeal to the House of Lords on a case related to people off on long term sick leave being able to accrue their holiday entitlement, which may have bearing on this issue.[5]

A woman must not be subject to any disadvantages or detriments for a pregnancy-related reason. Any company-related bonuses, for instance, must be paid.[6]

Any employee performance-related bonuses must be paid as a minimum for the two week compulsory maternity leave period.[7]

Pay rises during maternity leave must also be paid.

Any dismissal for reasons connected to pregnancy, childbirth, or taking or seeking to take maternity leave will be automatically deemed to be unfair dismissal.[8] This may constitute unlawful sex discrimination and no comparison with a man (the normal comparator – see page 497) will be needed.

If you are a pregnant employee or on maternity leave you must be given written reasons for dismissal automatically, without the requirement that you have to ask for them.[9]

While on maternity leave, you must be kept informed of any vacancies that arise, so you can apply for them if you wish. If the employer fails to make you aware of any vacancy, it may be deemed a detriment and unlawful sex discrimination.[10]

Right to return to work

You have the right to return to your original job after OML, on terms and conditions no less favourable.

You have the right to return to your original job after AML, or if that is not available, to a job that is both suitable and appropriate and on terms and conditions no less favourable.

Redundancy

If you are selected for redundancy on the grounds of pregnancy, childbirth, or taking (or seeking to take) maternity leave, your dismissal will automatically be deemed unfair.

In a redundancy situation, if you are on maternity leave, you must be given priority over other employees at risk of redundancy and offered any suitable alternative vacancy first.

Risk assessments

An employer who employs women of childbearing age, or women who have recently given birth or are breast-feeding, must carry out a general risk assessment, to see that there are no health and safety risks to the woman (both employees and self-employed women are covered by this obligation).[11]

If you are pregnant and give your employer written notification that you are pregnant, your employer must also carry out a further health and safety risk assessment specific to you and your job

Note: this applies to employees and self-employed women.

A failure to carry out a risk assessment and notify the woman of the results may be unlawful sex discrimination.

Where a risk assessment indicates there are risks, the employer must try to remove the risks, or find the woman a safe suitable alternative job, on no less favourable terms and conditions including pay, for as long as the risk continues. If no safe alternative work is available, the employer must suspend her on full pay.[12]

Note: the requirement to pay during suspension from work only applies to employees. It may however be unlawful sex discrimination not to pay as it may be deemed a detriment.

A claim should be made to the employment tribunal within three months, minus one day, of being suspended without pay, or without first having been offered suitable alternative work.

Statutory maternity pay

If you are a pregnant employee who has been continuously employed for 26 weeks (ending with the 15th week before the expected week of childbirth – the 'qualifying week') you are entitled to 26 weeks' maternity pay from your employer during OML.

To qualify for SMP you must have earned on average at least £82 if your baby was born on or before 15 July 2006 or £84 if your baby is due on or after 16 July 2006, over the eight weeks up to and including the qualifying week. You must give your employer 28 days' notice of the date you want SMP to start.

The first six weeks' pay are paid at 90% of average weekly earnings, assessed over the eight-week period up to the qualifying week. The remaining 20 weeks are paid at £106 a week. If your average earnings are below £106 per week, then all 26 weeks are paid at 90% of average weekly earnings.

Maternity Allowance

If you are an employee who does not qualify for SMP, you should make a claim for Maternity Allowance on Form MA 1, obtainable from any Jobcentre Plus office.

Maternity Allowance is paid to women who do not qualify for statutory maternity pay, for example because they are classed as self-employed or their earnings fall below the lower earnings limit.

You will qualify for Maternity Allowance if you have earned at least £30 a week for 26 weeks out of 66 weeks, ending on the week before the expected week of childbirth. The 26 weeks need not be continuous or with the same employer.

Proof of earnings, preferably payslips, needs to be sent with the claim form.

Maternity Allowance is paid at a flat rate of £106 for 26 weeks or if earnings are low at 90% of average weekly earnings.

It is a good idea to keep a calendar, diary or list of dates during pregnancy and copies of any letters sent to or received from the employer. It is also important to keep all wage slips.

Time off to care for dependants[13]

As an employee, you can take a reasonable amount of time off work to deal with any necessary emergency when:

- a dependant falls ill, or is injured
- you have to make arrangements for the care of an ill or injured dependant

- you have to make arrangements for the care of a dependant due to the disruption or ending of arrangements of care
- you have to make arrangements for care when a dependent child is unwell whilst attending school
- you have to make arrangements following the death of a dependant[14]

Note: a 'dependant' does not include employees, tenants, lodgers, or boarders

Who is a dependant?

A dependant is one of the following:

- a child
- a spouse or partner
- a parent
- a person living in the same household
- someone who reasonably relies on you for assistance when falling ill.

You must inform the employer of the reason for the absence as soon as possible and unless you are unable to, you must tell the employer how long you intend to be absent.

The right to unpaid time off work

The right to unpaid time off is for unforeseen events and not for recurrent illness. The unpaid time off is allowed, not to provide care, but to make arrangements for the provision of care.

A claim can be made to an employment tribunal within three months, minus one day, of the refusal of time off and compensation may be awarded.[15]

If you are dismissed for taking time off in an emergency you may be able to claim unfair dismissal and/or indirect sex discrimination.

Parental leave[16]

You have the right to take up to 13 weeks unpaid leave from work to care for a child.

To qualify for the right, you must:

- have at least one year's continuous service of employment with the employer
- have responsibility for a child under the age of five or under 18 if the child is disabled

Each parent has the right to take up to 13 weeks' leave for each child, and if twins are born, leave is doubled to 26 weeks.

The leave can only be taken in minimum blocks of one week. A maximum of four weeks' leave can be taken in any one year.

You must give the employer 21 days' notice of taking the leave, and you must state the expected week of childbirth (where parental leave is requested for the birth of a child) and the start and end dates of the leave to be taken.

The employer can request written confirmation of your responsibility for the child, the child's date of birth or evidence of the child's disability.

You can make a complaint to an employment tribunal within three months, minus one day.[17]

Paternity leave and pay[18]

As an employee, you have the right to two weeks' paid paternity leave, following the birth of a child.

To qualify you must have worked continuously for 26 weeks, ending within the 15th week, before the expected week of childbirth. If you have a contractual right to paternity leave or pay, you can take whichever is the most favourable, but not both.

The two weeks' leave must be taken within 56 days of the birth of the child. The leave can only be taken in blocks of one week or two weeks, but not individual days.

You do not have to be the biological parent and you may be a man or a woman, but you must be living with the mother and bringing up the child within an enduring family relationship. The leave must be to care for the child or to support the mother.

To qualify for the right, you must earn at least £82 if your baby was born on or before 15 July 2006 or £84 if your baby is due on or after 16 July 2006. A week's paternity pay is the lesser of £106 or 90% of your average weekly earnings.

You must give your employer notice of your intention to take paternity leave within or before the 15th week before the expected week of childbirth, or if this is not practicable (for instance if the baby is born prematurely) as soon as is reasonably practicable.

When giving the employer notice of your intention to take paternity leave, you must state the expected week of childbirth, when you will be starting leave and whether you will be taking one or two weeks' leave.

If the employer requests it, you must provide the notice in writing and include how you satisfy the conditions of entitlement.[19]

You can claim (within three months, minus one day) if you have suffered a detriment by taking or seeking to take paternity leave[20] or if you are dismissed for taking or seeking to take paternity leave.[21]

Flexible working[22]

As an employee, you have the right to request a change to your hours, times and place of work.

To qualify for the right, you must:

- have responsibility for a child under the age of 6, or 18 if disabled
- make an application for flexible working in writing to the employer

This application must state:

- that it is a request for flexible working
- the change required
- the date on which the change is to take place

- that you are responsible for a child
- the impact of the required change on the business
- how any impact might be dealt with (e.g. swapping shifts with colleagues, giving extra hours to a colleague etc)
- that you wish to be accompanied by a companion to the meeting with the employer

Within 28 days of receiving the written application, the employer must set up a meeting with the employee. You have the right to be accompanied at the meeting by another employee working for the same employer. All meetings must be held at a date and time convenient to both parties.

Within 14 days of the meeting, the employer must give you a decision on the application to work flexibly. (Note: only one application for flexible working can be made a year.) If the employer refuses, the decision:

- must be in writing
- must state the grounds for refusing the request to work flexibly
- must be dated
- must set out an appeal procedure

The employer can make a decision refusing the request to work flexibly on the following grounds:

- the burden of extra cost
- inability to meet customer demand
- inability to re-organise the work amongst existing staff, or recruit extra staff
- a detrimental impact on quality or performance
- insufficiency of work
- planned structural changes

If you appeal, it must be within 14 days of receiving the decision, and you must request an appeal in writing, stating the grounds for the appeal and dating the request. The employer must hold an appeal meeting within 14 days of receiving the appeal request.

If you are refused, the employer must give you a dated, written decision, within 14 days of the appeal meeting, giving the grounds for a refusal.

Complaint to an employment tribunal can be made because of the employer's failure to follow the correct procedure, or because the employer's decision was based on incorrect facts. It must be made within three months, minus one day, of the appeal decision,[23] and compensation of up to eight weeks' pay can be awarded. A claim may also be made for indirect sex discrimination.

Sex discrimination and work

Who is covered?

Protection from discrimination and harassment in employment is enshrined in the Sex Discrimination Act 1975. It is wider than employment protection under the Employment Rights Act 1996 because it uses a broader definition of employment. 'Employment' under the act is defined as:

'a contract of service, or apprenticeship, or a contract to personally execute any work or labour.'[24]

In addition, contract workers[25] and agency workers are protected under the Sex Discrimination Act. It is unlawful for an employment agency to discriminate against a woman in the terms on which it offers to provide services, by deliberately omitting to provide services or by subjecting her to harassment.[26]

What is discrimination?

Direct discrimination

'This is when a person discriminates against a woman if on the grounds of her sex she/he treats her less favourably than she/he treats or would treat a man',[27] for example, by giving a job to a man because the employer believes the woman is not as strong as the man, or that she will take time off to have children.

Indirect discrimination

'This is when an employer applies a provision, criterion or practice which he/she applies or would apply equally to a man but which puts or would put women at a disadvantage when compared with a man, which puts her at that disadvantage, and which he cannot show to be a proportionate means of achieving a legitimate aim.'[28] An example would be an employer having a policy that applies equally to men and women, of dismissing people for taking more than two absences for any reason, but which puts women at a disadvantage because women are more likely to have to take time off to make arrangements when children are sick.

Pregnancy

It is also unlawful sex discrimination to treat a woman less favourably on the grounds of her pregnancy, or because she is taking or seeking to take maternity leave.[29]

Victimisation

It is unlawful to treat a person less favourably for bringing proceedings under the Sex Discrimination Act (SDA), for giving evidence or information in connection with proceedings brought by anyone else, or on the basis that the discriminator knows or suspects someone has done or intends to do any of the above.[30]

Harassment

Harassment occurs if a person:

- subjects a woman to harassment if, on the grounds of her sex, he/she engages in unwanted conduct that has the purpose or effect of violating her dignity, or creating an intimidating, hostile, degrading, humiliating or offensive environment for her
- engages in unwanted verbal, non-verbal or physical conduct of a sexual nature with the purpose or effect of violating a woman's dignity, or creating an intimidating, hostile, degrading, humiliating or offensive environment for her

- on the grounds of a woman rejecting or not submitting to any of the above unwanted conduct, treats her less favourably than she/he would have if she had not rejected or had submitted to, the conduct.

The unwanted conduct is regarded as having the above effect if, in the perception of the complainant, it could reasonably be considered as having that effect.[31]

It is unlawful to discriminate against a woman in the arrangements made for offering employment, i.e. in the advert, interview and selection process for a job. It is also unlawful to discriminate in the terms of employment offered and to refuse or deliberately not offer her employment.

It is unlawful to discriminate against a woman in the provision or offering of promotion, training, transfer and any other benefits, facilities or services, or by refusing to afford her access to them.

For more information, see the Employment Tribunals section, on page 488.

Endnotes

[1] Employment Rights Act 1996 s 55 & s 56

[2] Employment Rights Act 1996 s 57

[3] Employment Rights Act 1996 s 71 - s 75
Maternity & Parental Leave Regulations 1999
Maternity & Parental Leave Regulations etc. 2002

[4] The expected week of childbirth is the week starting on a Sunday that includes the date on which the birth is expected

[5] IRC v Ainsworth [2005] IRLR 465, CA

[6] Employment Rights Act 1996 s 47 C

[7] Hoyland v Asda [2005] IRLR 438, EAT

[8] Employment Rights Act 1996 s 99

[9] Employment Rights Act 1996 s 92 (4)

[10] Visa v Paul [2004] IRLR 42, EAT

[11] Health & Safety at Work Act 1974
Management of Health & Safety at Work Regulations 1999, Reg 3 & Reg 16

[12] Employment Rights Act 1996 s 66

[13] Employment Rights Act 1996 s 57 A

[14] Employment Rights Act 1996 s 57 A (c)

[15] Employment Rights Act 1996 s 57 B

[16] Employment Rights Act 1996 s 76
Maternity & Parental Leave Regulations 1999

[17] Employment Rights Act 1996 s 80

[18] Employment Rights Act 1996 s 80A - 80E
Paternity & Adoption Leave Regulations 2002

[19] Small employers can recover (or seek advance payment of) 100% of the cost of statutory paternity pay from the Inland Revenue

[20] Employment Rights Act 1996 s 47 C

[21] Employment Rights Act 1996 s 99

[22] Employment Rights Act 1996 s 80
Flexible Working (Procedural Requirements) Regulations 2002

[23] Employment Rights Act 1996 s 80 (H)

[24] Sex Discrimination Act 1975, s 82

[25] Sex Discrimination Act 1975, s 9

[26] Sex Discrimination Act 1975 s 15

[27] Sex Discrimination Act 1975 s 1 (2) (a)

[28] Sex Discrimination Act 1975 s 1 (2) (b)

[29] Sex Discrimination Act 1975 s 3 (a)

[30] Sex Discrimination Act 1975 s 4

[31] Sex Discrimination Act 1975 s 4 (a)

16 Renting in the private sector

Slickston De Alyn

Introduction

This section provides a summary of the rights of those newcomers renting from an employer in the private sector. It also briefly covers rights when renting from a private sector landlord.

The housing market in the United Kingdom is divided into private and public sector housing. Legislation in the UK places responsibilities on landlords in both sectors. Some newcomers looking for work in the United Kingdom may find that an offer for employment includes the provision of accommodation for which rent will need to be paid. This will usually be provided under private sector housing law.[1]

The law is complex regarding your rights when you rent accommodation in the private sector. To be properly protected you must ensure that you have a tenancy agreement.

Tenancy agreements

A tenancy agreement is a contract between a landlord and a tenant. This sets out the terms and conditions of the tenancy and tenancy agreements. This can be agreed either verbally or in writing.[2] The majority of landlords give their tenants a tenancy agreement in writing.

If you do not have a written tenancy agreement, a verbal agreement between you and your landlord still counts as a tenancy agreement. However, you should try and get a tenancy agreement in writing.

Note: Your rights also depend on the type of accommodation you are living in and when you moved in.

Before moving into any rented accommodation provided, you should make sure that you understand the terms of the tenancy. If you are not clear about the information in your agreement, ask your landlord to confirm. Where the agreement is discussed verbally, it is always a good idea to confirm the length of the agreement and details of any other terms which might apply to the tenancy agreement.

The following are the 'key points' you need in the tenancy agreement:

- the amount of rent payable and when it should be paid
- whether you will be able to leave before the tenancy has ended
- whether the property is furnished, and if so, what furniture will be provided
- whether you are able to keep pets at the property
- whether you are able to have lodgers or to sublet
- the notice period and whether you can give notice to your landlord/ employer and obtain your own accommodation at a later date

Different types of tenancy

The law recognises several different types of tenancy, each with their own rules. In practice, this means that you must seek legal advice to determine which kind of tenancy you have. However, most tenancies will fall into the following categories[3]:

- occupier (tenant) with basic protection (If your employer is your landlord, this is the most likely category)
- assured shorthold tenant
- assured tenant
- protected tenant

There are some tenancies which are subject to special rules. These include tenancies where you are renting from an employer. In general, tenants renting from an employer will fall under the category of tenants with basic protection.

Occupier (tenant) with basic protection

If your employer provides you with accommodation as part of an offer of employment you will probably be classed as a tenant with basic protection. Tenants that usually fall within this category are those with:

- a 'company' let (where a company holds the tenancy and provides accommodation for you as a member of staff)
- accommodation provided by your employer in order for you to carry out your job. If you occupy accommodation because of your job (for example, a launderette assistant or a caretaker) you may not necessarily have to give up the accommodation if you leave the job
- a student let granted by an educational institution
- accommodation provided by the Crown or a government department
- accommodation provided by some housing co-operatives

Right to stay: occupiers (tenants) with basic protection

If you are renting from your employer you will have to agree the term of the period of occupation.[4] As a tenant with basic protection, if you do not move out when your landlord has given you notice to quit and the notice period has expired, your landlord has to go to court for a possession order. This will normally be granted.

If the tenancy is for a specified fixed term (for example, it is agreed that it lasts for 6 months or a year), your landlord does not have to give you notice to quit at the end of that term.

Your landlord still has, however, to apply for a possession order to evict you.[5] They can only apply once the fixed term has ended.

Rent: occupiers (tenants) with basic protection

As an occupier with basic protection you must pay the rent which you agreed with your landlord when you moved into the accommodation. You cannot apply to the rent officer or to the rent assessment committee to have the rent reduced. If your landlord wants to increase the rent you could try and negotiate. If you refuse to pay the increase this could lead to your landlord evicting you.

If you are employed by the landlord, and if you default on your rent, in some cases the landlord may:

- make deductions from your wages to cover arrears
- make deductions to cover damage

Note: This may not be legal. Whether this is legal or not will depend on your contract of employment. Unless this is specifically allowed, then your employer would be making unlawful deduction of wages and you could appeal to an industrial tribunal.

Your rights once your contract of employment has ended

Your employer has the same rights as any other landlord and this means that once your contract of employment has ended or even during your contract of employment, unless there is a specific provision preventing your eviction, your landlord can apply for mandatory or discretionary eviction.

Eviction

Mandatory eviction[6]

There are a number of reasons why you could face mandatory eviction:

- the owner of the house wishes to come back and live in the property
- the owner has gone bankrupt and the house is being repossessed
- you are more than two months in arrears with your rent
- you refuse or delay vital maintenance work to the building

Discretionary eviction[7]

A landlord can ask the court to decide if eviction is necessary if:

- you have broken the terms of your contract (i.e. significantly damaged the property)
- you are consistently late in paying the rent
- you lied about yourself to get the place
- you are unemployed or have lost your job (in cases where having a job was a condition of the contract)

Note: If these conditions do not apply and your landlord tries to evict you, you can seek civil or criminal remedy.

A victim of unlawful eviction and harassment has a number of criminal and civil remedies to call upon. Criminal proceedings can be brought by your local council. However, these sometimes take a long time. Delays of several months are not uncommon. But if successful, your landlord may be fined and you could receive compensation (known as damages) to recover any quantifiable loss or personal injury you might have suffered.[8]

However, for many people such remedies are too little too late. Generally, criminal courts cannot compensate you for your distress and suffering.

Therefore, concerned tenants may also apply to the civil courts for an injunction (an order of the court). County court judges have the power to order a landlord to re-admit an evicted tenant. They can also make orders restraining any future harassment, intimidation or eviction a landlord might be planning. Failure to comply with the terms of an injunction may result in your landlord being imprisoned. Injunctions can also be granted very quickly. Tenants can be restored to their homes within 24 hours of first seeking legal advice. Moreover, civil judges can order the landlord to pay their tenant compensation for any distress and shock suffered. Generally, civil damages are greater than criminal damages.

Note: The Housing Act 2004 introduces several reforms to protect the most vulnerable tenants, tackling antisocial behaviour and protecting deposits.[9] This Act also introduces the Residential Property Tribunal to arbitrate in disputes.

Note: The law provides protections for you as a tenant but there may be other obligations placed upon you through your contract of employment which may affect your rights.

The landlord's general responsibilities[10]

By law, your landlord has a number of responsibilities for repairs, including repairing and keeping in working order:

- the structure and exterior of the premises, including drains, gutters and external pipes
- the water and gas pipes and electric wiring (including, for example, taps and sockets)
- the basins, sinks, baths and toilets
- fixed heaters (for example, gas fires) and water heaters (but not gas or electric cookers)

Your landlord has these duties by law, no matter what is written in the tenancy agreement.

Note: If you ask your landlord to do these repairs they may attempt to regain possession of the property or not renew the agreement when it expires. Before attempting to use this general right to repairs you should consult an experienced adviser.

Au pairs and individual care workers

If you are an au pair or an individual care worker and you are resident in the family home, you will have fewer rights to occupancy.

If you are in this situation and you are having difficulties, contact the local Citizens Advice Bureau or another source of independent and reputable advice.

Caravan sites, farms, agricultural land or holding

If you live on the agricultural land or farm of your employer (in a caravan or other forms of housing) you are entitled to certain minimum standards.

If you live on a commercial caravan site that is not owned by your employer (for example it might be owned by an agent) then this site must be licensed. Your local council is responsible for checking licences and the owner of the site must deliver services according to the terms of the licence.

If you are in this situation and you are having difficulties, contact the local Citizens Advice Bureau or another source of advice, to help you interpret the terms of the licence to ensure the minimum standards you are entitled to are being met.

Houses of Multiple Occupation (HMO)

If you are living in a house that you share with others, you may be living in a House of Multiple Occupation (HMO). HMOs increasingly require licences. For example, shared houses over three stories (floors) high with five or more people forming two households must have a licence from April 6 2006.

Note: Other types of houses are classed as HMOs and there are three types of licensing.

If you are living in a HMO, then there are certain minimum standards that must be met. These include, among others, fire precaution regulations. If you are in this situation and you have concerns over minimum standards, contact the local Citizen's Advice Bureau or another source of independent and reputable advice.

Endnotes

[1] Rent Act 1977; Protection from Eviction Act 1977 s 3; Housing Act 1988 s 8, 20 – 21; Landlord and Tenant Act 1985

[2] Housing Act 1988, Case Law

[3] Most tenants do not live with their landlord. They have a 'non-resident' landlord. If such a tenancy began before 1989, it is usually either:
- a protected tenancy or
- a statutory tenancy

This means that as long as you pay your rent and act reasonably, it is very difficult for a landlord to evict you. However, if the tenancy began after 1989, it is usually either:
- an assured shorthold tenancy or
- an assured tenancy

The former (assured shorthold tenancies) are short-term lets of not less than six months. At the end of this period, your landlord has an absolute right to repossession, although he may choose to let you stay longer

Assured tenancies offer tenants greater protection. When the tenancy ends, landlords do not have an automatic right to repossession. Landlords must give a good reason for repossession. In most cases, assured tenants are removed only if they have built up substantial rent arrears (normally two to three months) or are damaging property The law was changed in 1997. After that date, the law presumes that new tenancies created are assured shorthold tenancies. In practice, this means that new tenants have little security. After six months, the landlord has a right to repossession, provided that he complies with all the necessary requirements. However, tenancies granted before this date remain subject to their own rules. In those circumstances, there is much a tenant can do to defend an action for repossession

[4] Housing Act 1988; Housing Act 1985; Housing Act 1988; Landlord and Tenant Act 1985

[5] Rent Act 1977; Protection from Eviction Act 1977 s 3; Housing Act 1988 s 8, 20 - 21

[6] Protection from Eviction Act 1977; Housing Act 1988; Landlord and Tenant Act 1985

[7] Protection from Eviction Act 1977; Housing Act 1988; Landlord and Tenant Act 1985

[8] Powers of Criminal Courts Act 1973 s 35; Protection from Eviction Act 1977; s 1(3A); Criminal Law Act 1977 s 6(1); Housing Act 1988 s 27; Protection from Harassment Act 1997 s 2 - 5, 7

[9] The Housing Act 2004

[10] Public Health Act 1961 s 17; Defective Premises Act 1972 s 4; Landlord and Tenant Act 1985 s 1, 11, 17, 48; Housing Act 1985 s 190, 604, 606; Housing Act 1988 s 116; Environmental Protection Act 1990 s 79 - 80, 82

17 Employment tribunals

Amar Dhudwar, Working Lives Research Institute

Introduction

This chapter aims to guide you through the process of bringing a tribunal claim. This process is quite complex. We have broken down the information into the various stages and topics to make it easier to follow. We explain the law and procedures, as well as give guidance on how to get on with each stage. This chapter should be read in conjunction with the chapters on 'Employment Rights' and 'Racial Discrimination'.

Glossary of key terms

Claimant

The 'claimant' is the individual bringing the claim in the employment tribunal.

Comparator

A 'comparator' is typically your 'equivalent' in the workplace. It may be a hypothetical person. If you are a part-time worker, a comparator will also be a part-time worker. If you are bringing a sex discrimination claim, your comparator is likely to be a member of the opposite sex. A more detailed description can be found on page 497.

Direct discrimination

Direct discrimination is where a person is or would be treated less favourably than another on the grounds of their gender, race, disability, religion or belief, sexual orientation, marital status or gender reassignment.

Dispute resolution procedures

Dispute resolution procedures are the grievance procedures that all employers, including small businesses, must have.

Employee

An 'employee' works for an employer under a contract of employment or apprenticeship. This may exclude, for example, agency workers and contractors. An employee differs from a worker (although the distinction is not a clear one).

Grievance

A 'grievance' is defined as 'a complaint taken by an employee about action which her or his employer has taken or is contemplating taking in relation to her or him'.

Indirect discrimination

Indirect discrimination occurs where the effect of a provision, criterion or practice imposed by an employer puts members of a group at a particular disadvantage in comparison with other groups.

Party or parties

The individuals or organisations involved in the claim are known as the 'parties' to the proceedings.

Respondent

The 'respondent' is the individual or organisation against whom the claim is brought.

Questionnaire procedure

The questionnaire procedure is intended to help individuals to obtain information from their employers about the alleged discriminatory treatment in order to decide whether or not to make a claim to a tribunal; or if a claim has been made, to assist in gathering evidence for their case.

Worker

A 'worker' works for an employer, but under a contract for services, similar to self-employment. A worker differs from an employee (although the distinction is not a clear one).

For definitions of part-time worker, fixed term employee, home worker, or agency worker, see pages 494-497.

The employment tribunal system

By far the most commonly used intervention in employment disputes is individual legal action in the employment tribunals. These tribunals are not part of the court system and have separate rules of procedure, as set out in the Employment Tribunals Act 1996 and the Employment Tribunals (Constitution and Rules of Procedure) Regulations 2004.1 These rules apply to employment tribunals in England, Scotland and Wales. In Northern Ireland, employment law is essentially the same as in England, Scotland and Wales, although claims are dealt with by the industrial tribunals and fair employment tribunals.

A tribunal panel generally consists of three members – a chairperson and two lay members. The person in charge of the hearing, the chairperson, will be legally qualified as a solicitor/barrister with at least seven years' experience.[2] The two lay members will have practical knowledge and experience of industrial relations. For each tribunal hearing, lay members are appointed from two separate panels of employer and employee representatives. A chairperson can deal with some matters sitting alone, and in some cases s/he can sit with just one lay member, subject to the agreement of both parties. Employment tribunals have the power to award compensation, introduce equal pay clauses and, in some cases, order your reinstatement or re-engagement.

As a result of changes introduced under the Employment Act 2002, which came into force from 1 October 2004, you cannot make a claim to an employment tribunal unless you have complied with the grievance procedures which all employers (there is no exception for small businesses) must have in place. Both employers and employees (not workers) must follow these procedures.

Note: If you are an employee and fail to follow the procedures, you cannot make a claim. See page 410 for the grievance procedures.

The statutory grievance procedures

Since October 2004 all employers must now have minimum procedures for resolving grievances, disciplinary action and dismissal. A failure to follow these procedures, where they apply, may impact upon the eventual outcome of your case.

Unless you follow these procedures, you will no longer, as a general rule, be able to make a claim to an employment tribunal. Failure to comply with the statutory dispute resolution procedures by either party can result in an increase or reduction of your award by between 10% and 50% at the discretion of the tribunal.

These new minimum procedures apply only to employees but not to other workers who supply services to employers, for instance freelancers or subcontractors.

If the dispute resolution procedures prove unsuccessful in resolving your grievance, you can pursue a claim in an employment tribunal. If the tribunal makes an error of law or the judgment was one which no reasonable tribunal could have reached, then you can appeal to the employment appeal tribunal. From there a further appeal can be made to the Court of Appeal and finally to the House of Lords.

As tribunals are open to the public it can be useful to get an early look at what a tribunal is like and find out what happens at a hearing. You can find details of your local tribunal office on the employment tribunal website: http://www.employmenttribunals.gov.uk

Human Rights Act and employment law

The Human Rights Act 1998 (HRA) came into force in October 2000 and incorporates into law certain rights and freedoms as set out in the European Convention on Human Rights (ECHR).

Many of these rights may protect you as a worker within the workplace. If you work in the public sector, you may be able to rely on the HRA to challenge your employer's actions where they have violated your human rights. The HRA will have no direct relevance if you work for a private sector employer, unless the private business provides services for a public authority.

However, it will be relatively unusual for a major HRA rights issue to arise within the workplace. Since many provisions of the HRA are reflected in employment law, you can rely on these rights to protect you, irrespective of whether you work in the public or private sector, rather than claim a breach of your human rights. Even so, the HRA must be taken into account by courts and tribunals when interpreting employment law. For further information on employment rights, see page 370.

What kind of claims can I bring?

The jurisdiction of employment tribunals extends to cover a vast number of complex areas. There are now over 70 different types of complaint, for example discrimination on the grounds of race, sex, disability, religion and belief, sexual orientation and age, unfair and constructive dismissal, equal pay, harassment and victimisation, unauthorised deductions from wages and redundancy pay.

Almost all tribunal claims are brought by an employee or worker (the claimant) against their employer (the respondent). The procedure for taking claims to employment tribunals is more or less the same, irrespective of the type of claim you are bringing. However, whether you are eligible to bring a certain type of claim will depend upon whether you are an 'employee' or a 'worker' – as some statutory rights apply only to employees, while others apply more widely to workers.

'Types' of worker

Employees or Workers?

An employee is defined as an individual who works under a contract of employment or Apprenticeship.[3] A worker also works for an employer, but is likely to work under a contract for services, which is more like self-employment. A contract for services is where a person or an organisation is under an obligation to perform some work or service for another person or organisation, without creating an employment relationship.

The distinction between an employee and a worker is not always clear, as there have been cases where self-employed workers have been considered to be employees because all or most of their work is for the same employer. In distinguishing an 'employee' from a 'worker', the tribunal will look to many factors within the four broad areas, as outlined below, to determine those who work under a contract of employment and those who work under a contract for services. Those who are able to satisfy the following tests, are considered to be 'employees':

- the control test – the degree of control exercised over the individual, in particular whether the employer can tell an individual what to do and how to do it
- the test for 'mutuality of obligations' – is there an obligation for the employer to provide work and is the individual obliged to accept the work given?
- the economic reality test –
- is the person in business on their own account?
- does the individual take a risk of loss or profit?
- do they provide their own equipment?
- and are they paid a regular wage?
- the organisational test – whether the individual is sufficiently integrated into the organisation to be regarded a part of the employer's organisation

For more information on whether you are a worker or employee see the employment rights section, page 379.

Part-time workers

There is no general definition of full-time or part-time workers in terms of number of hours worked.[4] As these definitions will vary from profession to profession, depending on the standard working week in any particular part of the economy, they are generally determined by the custom and practice of the employer.

But, in general, a part-time worker can be identified as an individual working less than full contractual hours or less than the standard working week. This would include workers who have no fixed hours at all (like a 'zero-hours contract')[5] and work on an 'as and when required' basis. For statistical purposes, part-time workers are counted as those working 30 hours or fewer.

As a part-time worker you have the right to 'no less favourable treatment' than full-time workers. This includes:

- the right to paid leave
- the right to the same pension arrangements as full-time workers
- the right to other contractual benefits

These rights are only limited by the fact that entitlement might be calculated on a pro rata basis.

If you are a part-time worker who is also an employee, you can bring a claim for unfair dismissal under specified circumstances of victimisation, for which no qualifying period is needed.[6]

Where claims are brought, the comparator must be a full-time worker who is employed under the same type of contract and employed to perform the same or broadly similar work.

Fixed term employees

The Fixed Term Employees (Prevention of Less Favourable Treatment) Regulations 2002[7] define a 'fixed-term employee'[8] as a person with a contract of employment which is due to end when :

- a specified date is reached or
- a specified event does or does not happen or
- a specified task has been completed[9]

These regulations only apply to fixed-term employees who have an employment contract with the employer they work for. They do not cover agency workers who have a contract with an outside company, apprentices, or students and other trainees on work experience placements or temporary work schemes. Examples of fixed-term employees would include:

- employees with fixed-term contracts to cover maternity or paternity leave or, as is common in the charity sector, contracts subject to continued funding
- employees doing work of a seasonal or casual nature whose contracts end once demand or the peak season is over, such as agricultural labourers or shop assistants
- employees whose contract expires when a specific task is completed, such as running a training course or working on a particular project

As a fixed-term employee you are protected by most statutory rights and you have the right to no less favourable treatment than comparable permanent employees with regard to the overall employment package.

The right to no less favourable treatment extends to any qualifying periods that may exist for employment benefits and opportunities for training and permanent employment.

You are also protected against disadvantages which are not imposed on permanent employees, for example where fixed-term employees are dismissed or selected for redundancy, purely because they are temporary employees, or where permanent staff are given better promotion opportunities than fixed-term staff.[10] Where less favourable treatment occurs, you have the right to ask your employer for a written statement explaining the difference in treatment. Your employer has 21 days to produce the statement and the explanation can be used as evidence at a tribunal hearing.

Some employment rights are dependent upon length of service. Because temporary workers usually have shorter periods of employment, you may lose out on protection against unfair dismissal, which only applies to employees who have worked for at least a year. However if you are dismissed for claiming your statutory rights under the regulations, you can bring a dismissal claim irrespective of whether you have worked for at least a year or if you are over the normal retirement age. For full details on what employment rights are available after certain periods, see page 382.

With regards to discrimination law, as a temporary employee you have the same protection against discrimination on the grounds of pregnancy and maternity as permanent employees. Therefore you cannot be dismissed, refused renewal of your contract or refused employment for these reasons.

You can also challenge the discriminatory impact of an employer's policies or practices, provided such less favourable treatment is on the grounds of your temporary employee status. For example, where an organisation has decided to make redundancies and decides to dismiss those employees on fixed-term contracts first, such a decision may have a more significant discriminatory impact on women than on men.

Agency workers

If you are employed through an agency, your employment status will depend entirely on your contract. Given that most agency work is offered on an 'as and when' basis and you are not required to take work if you do not wish to, it is unlikely that agency workers will be able to imply a contractual relationship and claim they are employed by their agency.

As an agency worker, you will be protected by core statutory rights such as the right to the national minimum wage, discrimination laws and health and safety regulations. For more information, see page 380.

Home workers

There are often difficulties as to whether a home worker is an employee and therefore protected by the full range of statutory employment rights or a worker with more limited rights. Although in some cases home workers have been considered as employees, other cases have struggled to identify mutual obligations or employer control to achieve employee status. For more information, see page 416.

Discrimination

Direct Discrimination

The key issue in direct discrimination is that you have been treated less favourably because of a protected characteristic (for example your gender, race or religious belief) than another has been or would be treated.

Comparator

That 'other' is referred to as your comparator and the exact identity of the comparator will depend on the grounds of discrimination. The comparator does not have to be an actual person; a hypothetical comparator can be used – the important issue is that it has to be someone who is in the same or a similar position to you (for example a job applicant) except for the fact that she or he is not a member of your protected class.

The following list provides an indication of who the comparator should be for each ground of discrimination:

- race – someone of a different racial group
- gender – a member of the opposite sex
- disability – a non-disabled person but with all the relevant skills and abilities
- religion and belief – a person of a different religion or belief
- sexual orientation – a person of a different sexual orientation
- age – this definition does not require a comparator

Test of less favourable treatment

There is no need to prove that your employer intended to discriminate[11] against you – the test is whether you would have received the less favourable treatment, had it not been for your protected characteristic. There is no defence available to an employer in a case of direct discrimination.

But what amounts to 'less favourable treatment'? Such treatment can include:

- setting different interview questions
- asking only women about their domestic or childcare commitments
- asking intrusive questions of workers thought to be gay
- paying different redundancy pay to women
- using racist name calling or allowing it to continue without disciplinary action
- using word of mouth recruitment

Indirect discrimination

Indirect discrimination is less obvious than direct discrimination. The difference between the two is that direct discrimination requires proof of different treatment between the applicant and the comparator, whereas indirect discrimination demands proof that the same provision, criterion or practice was applied, with the effect of disadvantaging one particular group more than other groups.

- to prove indirect discrimination, four questions need to be asked:
- did the employer apply a provision, criterion or practice?
- did it put members of the same relevant group at a particular disadvantage in comparison with other groups?
- did the provision, criterion or practice disadvantage you?
- can the employer justify the provision, criterion or practice as having a legitimate business objective?

The reference to 'a provision, criterion or practice' covers the full breadth of formal and informal practices in employment. It includes a range of human resources practices and informal work practices as well as contractual rules. As the claimant, you will need to work out and define the provision, criterion or practice applied. The questionnaire procedure can be very useful in identifying what provisions, criteria or practices have been applied if they are not explicit.

However, the tricky part of proving indirect discrimination is in demonstrating a particular disadvantage. So what kind of evidence could you use? With the necessity of comparing groups, statistical evidence can show how particular groups are disadvantaged by certain practices, along with evidence from experts or other witnesses. But even if you can show that indirect discrimination has occurred, your employer will have the opportunity to justify the provision, criterion or practice by showing that it is a 'proportionate means of achieving a legitimate aim' (that there is a good objective business reason for doing it).

Victimisation

To take legal action against your employer for discrimination or to assist others to do so is never an easy course of action. Many individuals may fear they will be singled out for using their workplace complaints procedure or exercising their legal rights. To ensure that people are not deterred from bringing discrimination claims or giving evidence or information on behalf of another employee through fear of a reprisal, all of the anti-discrimination legislation considered here prohibits 'victimisation'.

To bring a claim under the victimisation provisions, you will need to show that your employer has treated you less favourably for performing one of the following protected acts:

- bringing proceedings against your employer
- giving evidence or information in connection with proceedings
- otherwise doing anything else under or by reference to the relevant (discrimination) statute
- making an allegation of discrimination under or by reference to the relevant (discrimination) statute

WORKING IN THE UK: NEWCOMER'S HANDBOOK *2ND EDITION*

Many claims of victimisation turn upon the reason or motivation for the employer's action. You will not be not required to prove that the alleged discriminator intended to victimise you by reason of your doing a protected act. But it will be necessary to establish some causal link between the performing of the protected act and the less favourable treatment you received.

In claiming victimisation you will need to compare yourself with someone else (actual or hypothetical) who has not made a discrimination claim to demonstrate how your treatment was, or would be, less favourable.

Harassment

To bring a case of harassment, you will need to show that you have been subject to unwanted conduct on the basis of a protected characteristic (such as race, disability, sexual orientation) which has the purpose or effect of:

- violating your dignity
- creating an intimidating, hostile, degrading, humiliating or offensive environment for you

This test for harassment applies to disability, colour, ethnic or national origin, race, religion or belief and sexual orientation. Since October 2005, the Sex Discrimination Act has contained a prohibition of harassment (analogous to the provision outlined above) and sexual harassment – unwanted physical, verbal or non-verbal conduct of a sexual nature.

The harassment does not have to be intentional. Once you have made it clear that the conduct is unwanted and unwelcome, it can be considered harassment. The extent to which you feel the harassment has violated your dignity and created an offensive workplace environment is essentially a subjective test and you should expect to give evidence about the impact the harassment has had on your life. If relevant, medical and psychiatric evidence can be useful.

Given the nature of some harassment offences, there may be no witnesses to support your claim. Where this is the case and the harassment has been persistent over a period of time, and internal grievance procedures have proved inadequate, it can be useful to keep a diary of the incidents/behaviour to support your claim at tribunal.

While many cases of harassment may stretch over a period of time, a one-off act, providing it is serious, may also amount to harassment.

Discrimination law

The UK has developed a body of discrimination law that is made up of different acts and regulations, each outlawing less favourable treatment on specific grounds:

- race, colour, ethnic or national origins (Race Relations Act 1976)[12]
- equal pay (Equal Pay Act 1970)[13]
- sex and marital status (Sex Discrimination Act 1975)[14]
- pregnancy (Employment Rights Act 1996)[15] (see page 466 for more details)
- disability (Disability Discrimination Act 1995)[16]
- religion or belief (Employment Equality (Religion & Belief) Regulations 2003)[17]
- sexual orientation (Employment Equality (Sexual Orientation) Regulations 2003)[18] and
- age (Employment Equality (Age) Regulations 2006)[19]

All of these protected grounds have in common the concepts of direct and indirect discrimination, with the exception of the disability discrimination that instead provides for a duty to make reasonable adjustments and a duty not to treat a disabled person less favourably, in addition to victimisation and harassment.

The Equal Pay Act 1970 (EqPA) operates differently. It incorporates an equality clause into a person's contract of employment if they can show they have been paid less, or otherwise received less favourable terms and conditions of employment, than a person of the opposite sex where both were doing:

- like work
- work rated as equivalent
- work of equal value

Who can claim discrimination?

The term 'employee' is used throughout, but there is a broad interpretation of 'employment' so that discrimination laws apply to employees and workers (including job applicants) contract and agency workers, office holders, members of the police force, self-employed persons and members of the armed forces.

There are no maximum age limits and no requirement for a minimum number of days' or weeks' service before these provisions provide protection – you are protected from when you first apply for a job or day one of your employment.

You are protected in all aspects of employment including:

- recruitment
- selection
- transfer
- opportunities for training and promotion
- pay and benefits
- redundancy
- dismissal
- terms and conditions of work

The scope of protection is not dependent on a current employment relationship. If you have left your job, you can still make a claim of discrimination or victimisation against your former employer.

The Equal Pay Act 1970 (EqPA) protects all workers and applies to full-time and part-time workers, whether permanent or temporary, and irrespective of the age or length of service of the worker. See also page 512 on unfair dismissal.

Types of unlawful discrimination

Race

The Race Relations Act 1976 (RRA) makes it unlawful to discriminate on racial grounds. The RRA applies to anyone discriminated against on the basis of their race, ethnic or national origins, colour or nationality, and so applies equally to white people and ethnic minorities.

What is meant by 'racial grounds'?

The working definition of 'racial grounds' and 'racial group' refers to race, colour, nationality and ethnic or national origins. You can be a member of more than one racial group, and you can fall into a particular racial group either by birth or by adopting and following the customs of the group, provided you consider yourself a member and are accepted as such. When lodging a tribunal application, you can make a claim on the basis of all the protected grounds.

According to case law Sikhs, Jews, Romany Gypsies and Irish Travellers are recognised as racial groups for the purposes of the RRA. However religious groups are not specifically protected under the RRA. On this basis Muslims, Hindus and Rastafarians have not been accepted as racial groups. To rectify this anomaly, the Employment Equality (Religion & Belief) Regulations 2003 specifically address discrimination in employment and the area of vocational training on the grounds of religion and belief. For more on race discrimination, please see pages 424-465.

Gender and marital status

The Sex Discrimination Act 1975 (SDA) makes it unlawful to discriminate on the grounds of sex. The Act covers employment and vocational training, as well as education and the provision of goods and services This section only deals with discrimination in employment. The SDA is frequently thought to only prohibit discrimination against women However its terms apply equally to men and women.

The protection against discrimination on the ground of 'marital status' only applies if you are married. If you are a lone parent, you may be protected through the indirect discrimination provisions of the SDA, or on the basis that single parenthood constitutes 'family status'.

It is unlawful sex discrimination to treat a woman less favourably because she is pregnant. See page 466 for further details.

Disability

The approach of the Disability Discrimination Act 1995 (DDA) differs significantly from that of other discrimination legislation. Unlike race and sex discrimination laws which apply the right to equal treatment to everyone, protection under the DDA is only afforded to disabled persons. Instead of the twin concepts of direct and indirect discrimination found in the RRA and SDA, the DDA provides for direct discrimination, discrimination arising from a failure to make reasonable adjustments, and disability-related discrimination.

What is the meaning of 'disability'?

To be protected under the Act, you will need to show that you fall within the definition of a disabled person. According to the DDA, this means you will need show you have a physical or mental impairment which has a substantial and long-term adverse effect on your ability to carry out normal day-to-day activities.[20] If you have suffered from a disability in the past you are still protected against discrimination, even if you have recovered from the condition or if the effect of the impairment has lessened.

Physical impairment

The DDA does not define the term 'physical impairment'. But guidance on the meaning of disability has made clear that it includes sensory impairments, such as those affecting sight or hearing, and severe disfigurements,[21] such as scars, birthmarks, limb or postural deformations and diseases of the skin.

The following have also been found to come within the meaning of physical impairment:

- asthma
- back pain
- bulimia
- carpal tunnel syndrome
- chronic fatigue syndrome
- diabetes
- emphysema

Mental impairment

A mental illness or impairment must be one that affects the memory or the ability to concentrate, if it is to fall within the definition of a disability. A mental impairment can include learning difficulties, such as autism, and psychiatric and psychological impairments. If the mental impairment results from a mental illness, there is no longer a requirement to establish that it is 'clinically well-recognised'. Instead, you will now have to show that the mental illness has lasted (or will last) for at least 12 months and have a 'substantial' impact on day-to-day activities. The change has brought mental illnesses into line with other impairments and made the symptoms and effects of the complaint more important than its cause or origin.

The following have been found to come within the meaning of 'mental impairment':

- schizophrenia
- manic depression or anxiety
- severe and extended depressive psychoses
- dyslexia
- post-traumatic stress disorder
- autism

Substantial and long-term adverse effect

The term 'substantial' is not defined in the Act. According to the supplementary guidance, for the impairment to be considered substantial, it must be 'more than a minor or trivial'[22] one. In assessing whether the effect of the condition is substantial and more than 'minor or trivial' the tribunal will examine the extent to which you are affected by the impairment. Factors taken into account by the tribunal include:

- the time taken to carry out an activity compared with someone who does not have the impairment
- the way in which the activity is carried out in comparison with someone who does not have the impairment
- the cumulative effects of an impairment – the effect of your impairment to carry out each day-to-day activity may be minor, but the combined effect may be substantial
- the effect of the impairment on your behaviour – you may fall outside the definition if you can change your behaviour to carry out day-to-day activities
- the effect of the environment on your ability to carry out day-to-day activities – such as the time of day or night, temperature or whether you are tired or under stress

You do not lose the right to protection against discrimination if you are able to control or correct your disability. The tribunal must consider the effect your disability would have without the use of medication or aids and the actual effects after medication or other corrective aids.

An impairment has a long-term effect, and so amounts to a disability under the DDA, if one of the following is true:

- it has lasted for at least 12 months
- it is likely to last at least 12 months
- it is likely to last for the rest of your lifetime (if that is less than 12 months)

If you are in remission, the tribunal should also take into consideration the likelihood of the condition or effect recurring.[23]

Normal day-to-day activities

The reference to 'normal day-to-day activities' means those activities that are 'normal' for most people in their everyday lives, such as using cutlery, taking a bath, cooking etc. It does not refer to work-related activities, and sporting activities are specifically excluded. However, a tribunal may consider work-related activities if these exacerbate the effect of the impairment.

According to the DDA, your impairment amounts to a disability only if it affects your ability to carry out one of these normal day-to-day activities:

- difficulty with mobility, such as climbing the stairs or using public transport
- difficulty with manual dexterity, such as using a pen or a keyboard
- difficulty with physical coordination, such as being able to feed yourself or wash yourself
- inability to control continence
- difficulty in lifting, carrying or moving everyday objects
- difficulty with speech, hearing or eyesight
- difficulty with memory or ability to concentrate, learn or understand, such as understanding instructions
- difficulty in assessing the risk of physical danger

Progressive conditions

You are protected by the DDA if you have certain 'progressive conditions', such as cancer, multiple sclerosis, muscular dystrophy or infection with HIV.[24] These are treated as a disability from the date the diagnosis is made and are considered to have a substantial adverse effect from the moment they start to have an effect on your ability to carry out day-to-day activities.

Disability-related discrimination[25]

The Disability Discrimination Act makes it unlawful for an employer to treat you less favourably than someone else for a reason relating to your disability. The distinction between disability-related and direct discrimination is a fine one. Where direct disability discrimination would focus on the fact of the disability itself, with disability-related discrimination the focus is specifically on consequences of the disability. The term 'for reasons relating to' is much broader than the concept of direct discrimination and will cover situations which fall out of 'direct discrimination'.

Disability-related discrimination is now the only type of discrimination that can be justified. The justification or the reason for the discrimination has to be 'material and substantial'.

The duty to make reasonable adjustments

At the heart of the DDA is the requirement for employers to carry out reasonable adjustments[26] to accommodate the effects of a person's disabilities so as to enable disabled people to compete and perform on a more level playing field with able-bodied people. The duty arises when the 'provisions, criteria or practices' or the 'physical features' of the workplace put a disabled job applicant or existing worker at a substantial disadvantage in comparison with a non-disabled person.

Unlike less favourable treatment the duty only applies when the employer knows or reasonably ought to have known of the disability. The supplementary guidance gives examples of reasonable steps that employers might have to take including:

- making adjustments to premises
- allocating some of the disabled person's duties to another person
- redeploying the disabled person to fill an existing vacancy
- altering the disabled person's working hours
- assigning the disabled person to a different place of work or training
- allowing the person to be absent during working hours for rehabilitation, assessment or treatment
- giving or arranging for training or mentoring
- acquiring or modifying equipment, instructions or manuals
- modifying procedures for testing or assessment

- providing a reader or interpreter
- providing supervision or other support

Sick pay and access to health services

For further information on Statutory Sick Pay, for a range of health and disability-related benefits and for information on accessing the NHS, see pages 140-156.

Religion and belief

The Employment Equality (Religion & Belief) Regulations 2003 make it as unlawful to discriminate or harass on the grounds of adhering to a particular religion or holding a particular belief as it is to discriminate against a person for not adhering to a specific religion or belief.

It is also unlawful to discriminate on the grounds of perceived religion and belief – if you are discriminated against because you are thought to be a Muslim, you can still use the law even if you do not belong to that faith group.

What constitutes a religion or belief?

You are protected against discrimination on the grounds of your religion, religious belief, or similar philosophical belief.[27] There is no statutory definition of 'religion or belief'. The DTI's explanatory notes[28] suggest that the term 'religion' would include those religions widely recognised in this country (such as Christianity, Islam, Hinduism, Judaism, Buddhism, Sikhism, Rastafarianism, Baha'ism, Zoroastrianism and Jainism) and the sects within a religion (such as the Catholic and Protestant branches of the Christian Church).

The regulations cover not just members of organised religious groups, but anyone who holds a religious or similar philosophical belief. According to the ACAS Code of Practice, tribunals will need to consider a number of factors when deciding what is a religion or similar belief. These could include looking at whether there is collective worship, a clear belief system, or a profound belief affecting the way of life or view of the world.

The definition is likely to extend beyond the better-known religions and faiths and include beliefs such as paganism and humanism, as well as fringe cults. The regulations cover those without religious beliefs, but do not cover political beliefs.

Sexual orientation

The Employment Equality (Sexual Orientation) Regulations 2003 make it unlawful to discriminate in the workplace on the grounds of sexual orientation. The regulations provide protection on the basis of sexual orientation towards:

- persons of the same sex (lesbian and gay workers)
- persons of the opposite sex (heterosexual workers)
- persons of the same sex and of the opposite sex (bisexual workers)

The regulations do not provide protection for transsexual people, as there are specific regulations[29] that prohibit discrimination against transsexual workers.

The regulations also protect workers on the basis of perceived sexual orientation. So if you are discriminated against because you are mistakenly thought to be gay, lesbian or bisexual, then you also have the right to pursue a claim of unlawful discrimination or harassment on grounds of sexual orientation.

Importantly, there are two particular exceptions in the regulations which have been the subject of strong criticism from trade unions and other interested groups. Although the regulations apply to most employment benefits, they do not cover benefits which depend on being married. This means that if you are in a same-sex relationship and have yet to register your partnership through the Civil Partnership Act, you will not be treated in the same way as married couples in relation to all benefits, such as with survivors' benefits under pension schemes.

Age

The Employment Equality (Age) Regulations 2006 make it unlawful to discriminate on the basis of age. Unlike other discrimination legislation, the regulations allow the employer a limited defence of direct age discrimination in 'exceptional circumstances'.

An employer wanting to introduce an age-related provision will have to show that the reason for it falls within a list of specific objectives and that the means were both proportionate and necessary in the circumstances.

The list of specific aims would include:

- health and safety reasons
- facilitation of employment planning
- particular training requirements for a post
- encouraging or rewarding loyalty
- the need for a reasonable period of employment before retirement[30]

At the moment there is no national mandatory retirement age, though many people retire at the age when they are eligible to receive their state pension. There have been proposals that a statutory default retirement age of 65 will be introduced, after which employers could oblige their employees to retire.

Starting work and employer's duties to check documents

It is illegal for employers to employ someone who does not have permission to work in this country. The onus is on employers to ask all prospective employees for one of a number of documents to verify their eligibility for employment. When you start work you will be asked to produce one or more of a number of documents.

See page 318 for further information.

Equal pay

The Equal Pay Act 1970 (EqPA) covers all terms and conditions of employment[31] between men and women.

If you wish to claim that you have been paid less on the ground of your race, disability, religion, sexual orientation or age, you will need to prove (under the relevant legislation) that there has been either direct or indirect discrimination. This will be more difficult than proving under the EqPA that you have been treated less favourably with regard to a particular contractual term for work that is equal or similar to that of a suitable comparator.

Under the EqPA you are entitled to equal pay and equal terms and conditions in circumstances where you are able to show that you are employed to do:

- work of the same or a broadly similar nature, known as 'like work'[32]
- work which has been rated as equivalent under a valid job evaluation scheme[33]
- work which is of equal value[34] to that of someone of the opposite sex in the same employment as you

Remember that there is an obligation on employers to provide every employee with a written statement of the terms and conditions of employment within two months of starting work.[35] See page 376 for further information on employment rights.

What is 'like work'?

In deciding whether you are employed on 'like work', the tribunal will first ask whether the job you do is the same as, or broadly similar to, that of the comparator. As the wording suggests, there is no need to show that the jobs are absolutely identical. So long as there are no differences of any practical importance in the terms and conditions of employment, trivial differences will not rule out an equal pay comparison.

The focus should be on what you and the comparator actually do in practice on a day-to-day basis, and not what the job description may indicate.[36]

What is 'work rated as equivalent'?

You are entitled to claim equal pay if you are doing a job which has been 'rated as equivalent' to that of the comparator under a valid job evaluation scheme (JES).

A JES is a technique for comparing the demands of jobs within an organisation, in order to develop a rank order of jobs, usually as the basis for a grading and pay structure. The 'demands' of various jobs are broken down into a number of factors (such as skills, responsibility, physical and mental requirements) and points are awarded for each factor on a predetermined scale.

There is no legal obligation for employers to carry out a JES; however, where one has been carried out, you are entitled to rely on it to gain equal pay.

What is work of 'equal value'?

To claim 'equal value', you must be employed on work which in terms of the demands made on you (such as effort, skill and decision) is of equal value to that of a wo/man in the same employment. In choosing the comparator, it is possible to compare yourself with an individual (of the opposite sex) doing a completely different job – such as comparing clerical with manual jobs as well as jobs in different grades within each sector. For example, in one claim, a canteen cook chose to compare herself with three skilled craftsmen – a painter, a joiner and a thermal insulation engineer.[37]

Some claims will not succeed in certain circumstances, as it maybe lawful to pay workers different rates to reflect their different qualifications, though on a day-to-day basis they may appear to perform similar tasks. Workers may also be paid differently on account of their job performance, so long as the assessment is based on their actual work, not their work potential.[38]

Comparator

The EqPA states that you and your comparator must be working in the same employment – you must be employed at the same establishment or at different establishments covered by common terms and conditions.[39] The comparator must be an actual person of the opposite sex (as the EqPA does not allow a hypothetical comparator) who is working in 'like work', 'work rated as equivalent' or work of 'equal value' in the same employment at the same time.[40] It is for you, not the tribunal, to choose a comparator of the opposite sex.

It can be beneficial to compare yourself with a few employees, as this may increase your chance of being awarded equal pay. But to find even one comparator can be difficult, especially if you work in a large or a non-unionised workplace, because of a lack of information about other employees' pay and terms and conditions. In these circumstances the questionnaire procedure can be useful to gain information about earnings and hours, analysed according to sex.

Remedies

If you are successful in your claim, then your contract is deemed to include an equality clause from the date of the tribunal application. The equality clause is the technique used by the EqPA to bring about future equal pay and has the effect of changing the less favourable terms to provide equivalence with your comparator. This means that you are entitled to the same pay and/or other benefits as your comparator. You may also be entitled to back pay, with accrued interest.

Unfair dismissal

If you consider you have been unfairly dismissed, you can complain to an employment tribunal. But to be able to bring a complaint of unfair dismissal, you must first satisfy a number of qualifying conditions:

- you must have been employed as an employee[41]
- you must have had been employed for not less than one year at the time of the dismissal

- you must have not reached the retiring age for your position, or the statutory retiring age of 65
- your employment must have been within the territorial scope of the UK

Before the tribunal moves on to the question of whether the dismissal was fair or unfair, they must be satisfied that you have been dismissed in accordance with Section 95 of the Employment Rights Act 1996. According to Section 95, you are treated as having been dismissed only if one of the following three events occurs:

- your employer terminates your contract (with or without notice)
- your employer fails to renew your fixed-term contract
- you terminate your contract, with or without notice, because of your employer's conduct (also known as 'constructive dismissal')

Your employer is under a statutory obligation to provide a written statement of the reasons for dismissal within 14 days of your requesting such a statement.[42] If your employer unreasonably fails to provide a written statement, you have the right to complain to an employment tribunal.

What does not count as dismissal? The following are some examples of what will not count as dismissal:

- if you resign without any pressure from your employer or leave by mutual agreement
- you are suspended on full pay
- your employer withdraws a job offer before you start work
- your circumstances change and you can no longer continue to work for your employer (known as frustration of contract)
- you are laid off or put on short-time working and your contract allows for this, and then you claim redundancy

Once you have determined that you have been dismissed within the meaning of Section 95, the tribunal will then move on to the question of whether or not the dismissal was fair. At this stage, the tribunal will then examine the reasons for dismissal and establish the reasonableness of the employer's conduct. In deciding whether your employer acted reasonably in dismissing you, the tribunal will consider, amongst other factors, whether the employer followed the appropriate grievance and disciplinary procedures.

Automatically unfair dismissals

Some dismissals are automatically unfair. You do not need one year's service with your employer to claim unfair dismissal if the dismissal is related to, for example:

- race, gender or disability discrimination
- pregnancy or maternity discrimination
- union membership or activities
- health and safety
- enforcing a statutory right

Proving discrimination

Evidence

It is virtually impossible to find direct evidence of discrimination, since employers rarely admit to discriminatory intentions and more often than not the evidence will simply not exist. Therefore it will be necessary for you to present evidence that allows the tribunal to determine whether discrimination has taken place from the key facts of your case.

Statistics

The importance of statistical evidence is reinforced by the codes of practice issued by the Commission for Racial Equality (CRE), the Equal Opportunities Commission (EOC) and the Disability Rights Commission (DRC), all of which recommend that employers should carry out regular monitoring of their staff profile as part of their equal opportunities policies, in order to measure the effects of employment and promotion decisions and to see to how far imbalances exist between jobs and grades. The Employment Equality Regulations on religion and belief and sexual orientation do not require the collection of such data.

Therefore collecting statistical evidence of an imbalance between different job grades or groups, broken down by racial group, gender or disability within an employer's workforce, can be used to establish a pattern in the treatment of a particular group or to indicate of areas of discrimination.[43] However, gaining access to such information is not always easy. You should use the questionnaire procedure, which is available for all claims of discrimination as well as apply to the tribunal for 'discovery and inspection' of documents that are relevant to your case.

Discrimination questionnaires

The discrimination questionnaire is a good way of obtaining information and evidence for your case. The information, statistics and documents gathered from the questionnaire can be used as evidence in the tribunal hearing, in particular for cross-examination of witnesses. This evidence may influence the tribunal's final decision. For further information on the race relations questionnaire, see page 453.

If you have yet to submit your claim to the employment tribunal, on the ET1 claim form, you have three months less one day from the date of discrimination to present the questionnaire to your employer. If you have already submitted the ET1 form, then the questionnaire must be sent to your employer within 21 days from the date that the ET1 was lodged with the tribunal.

If your employer fails to reply to the questionnaire within a reasonable period of time,[44] or responds in an evasive or ambiguous way without reasonable excuse, it is open to the tribunal at the hearing to draw an adverse inference from this failure or insufficient response. This adverse inference may be that the respondent has discriminated against the claimant.

Further particulars, documents and written answers to questions

In addition to the discrimination questionnaire, you can also use other information-gathering procedures in order to prepare your case for hearing or a settlement. These procedures will allow you to decide which facts are agreed or disputed, identify useful witnesses for the case and allow you to focus on the forthcoming hearing. In many cases the information uncovered can be a key factor in early settlement of the case.

A request for further particulars can be used to clarify a vague response, gather more information about certain facts or ask questions that have not previously been answered by the employer on the ET3 form or the questionnaire. The ET3 form asks your employer whether they intend to defend the claim, and if so on what grounds.

A request for documents should be used when the respondent holds documentary evidence that will assist your case.

A request for written answers to questions will be similar to a request for further particulars; however you can ask a much wider range of questions.

Witnesses

You can invite witnesses to the hearing to give relevant evidence. If your witnesses are unwilling to attend, you can ask the tribunal to issue a witness order to summon them to attend the hearing. You must apply to the tribunal in writing well in advance of the hearing.

Codes of practice

All the equality commissions have issued statutory codes of practice, which provide practical guidance on conduct in particular areas. Breach of a code of practice does not give rise to a right to take an employer to an employment tribunal. However, compliance or non-compliance with these codes is admissible as evidence in a tribunal hearing and may influence the eventual outcome of the hearing.

Burden of proof

The same burden of proof is applied across all the areas of possible discrimination. Once you have made out a potential case of discrimination (prima facie case), the burden then shifts to the employer to provide a plausible explanation for the unfair treatment.45 If the employer fails, then the tribunal must find that unlawful discrimination has occurred.

You must prove your case on the balance of probabilities. This means you must identify facts from which a tribunal could conclude that there has been unlawful discrimination, in the absence of an adequate explanation. If you fail to prove such facts you will fail in your claim.

The outcome of the case will usually depend on what inferences the tribunal can draw from the facts of the case.

These can include the inference that an employer has committed a discriminatory act if:

- they fail to reply
- they provide evasive or unequivocal answers to a questionnaire
- they have failed to comply with the relevant code of practice

At this stage, if you are able to prove facts from which the tribunal could infer that you have been treated less favourably on a protected ground, the tribunal will then turn to the respondent to explain and justify any difference in treatment. To discharge that burden it is necessary for the respondent to prove, on the balance of probabilities, that the treatment was in no sense whatsoever on a protected ground.

A tribunal will expect cogent evidence to discharge that burden of proof. In particular, the tribunal will examine carefully explanations for failure to deal with the questionnaire procedure and/or code of practice. If the employer is unable to provide a satisfactory explanation for the less favourable treatment, then the tribunal will infer discrimination.[46]

Do I need a lawyer or representative?

There is no requirement for you to attend a hearing with a solicitor or other professional. You are free to represent yourself. But given the complexity of this area of law and the likelihood that your employer will be represented, it is advisable to have at least consulted an appropriate organisation or individual before you make a claim to the employment tribunal and before you attend a tribunal hearing.

Many applicants and respondents put their own cases to the tribunal although some choose to have a representative who may be a lawyer, trade union official, representative of an employers' organisation, or simply a friend or colleague.

Where can I get legal advice and assistance?

There are a number of organisations that provide free legal advice and representation in employment tribunals. See the Further Information chapter, page 556 for more details.

Public funding

There is no public legal funding (formerly known as legal aid) available for representation at employment tribunals in England and Wales, except occasionally for very complex cases; although basic preliminary advice can sometimes be sought under the Community Legal Service Scheme. This provides a short session with a solicitor or adviser to talk through any legal issue on a preliminary basis, for example to help with filling in the claim form (ET1). If you are eligible this will depend on your income. You can find out more from the Community Legal Service Scheme website: http://www.clsdirect.org.uk or by calling 0845 345 4335.

Legal aid may be available for an appeal to the employment appeal tribunal, depending on your financial circumstances.

Equality commissions

You may also be able to get advice and assistance with legal representation from the Equal Opportunities Commission (EOC), the Commission for Racial Equality (CRE) or the Disability Rights Commission (DRC). All of these commissions have websites, which contain detailed advisory publications for individuals. Increasingly, these commissions only provide further support and assistance with legal representation in cases that test a point of law, are too complex for you to deal with on your own or which deserve some other special consideration.

Trade unions and the voluntary sector

If you are a member of a trade union, you may be entitled to free legal advice and representation as a benefit of your membership. However, unions will have their own criteria for assessing whether a claim has a reasonable prospect of success.

There are various kinds of voluntary sector advice agencies that may be able to offer free advice and/or representation. Your local law centre or Citizens Advice Bureau can help you by providing free specialist advice, but getting assistance with representation at the hearing may be difficult. Some of the larger charities can advise and sometimes represent you in employment-related cases. See Further Information chapter, page 556 for more details.

Solicitors and legal advice

Some solicitors are part of local referral schemes and are able to offer a free or low-cost initial interview whether you qualify for funding or not. You can check the directory on www.clsdirect.org.uk for solicitors in your area and then check under 'charging' to see whether they offer this service.[47]

Some solicitors are willing to conduct claims on a 'no win, no fee' basis. This means that if you lose your case, there are no fees or costs payable to your solicitor, and if you win your case, the solicitor's fees will come out of your compensation. However, the likelihood a solicitor will accept your case on this basis will depend upon the strength of your case and your chances of success.

For a full range of services to contact, see the further information, especially regarding 'Legal Advice', see page 578.

How do I make a claim to an employment tribunal?

Before making a claim to an employment tribunal, you must ensure you have complied with the dispute resolution procedures (if applicable).[48] (See page 410.)

The Employment Tribunals (Constitution and Rules of Procedure) Regulations 2004 set out amended tribunal procedures, including new requirements for submitting claims. From October 2005, all claims must be on form ET1.

You can get the form from a job centre, ACAS, your union, a local advice agency or the regional or national employment tribunal offices. The form can also be downloaded from the employment tribunal website: http://www.ets.gov.uk

Your claim cannot be accepted unless it meets certain conditions. By law you must provide:

- your name and address
- the name and address of the respondent
- the details of your complaint
- whether or not you were an employee of the respondent

Unless you provide this information, your application will not be accepted. Once the form is completed you can submit it online through the ETS website or send it to the appropriate employment tribunal office.

Time limits

The normal time limit for more or less all tribunal claims is three months, less one day, from the date of the incident you are bringing a claim about (such as the date you were dismissed or not appointed for a job or promotion).

However, since the introduction of the new dispute resolution rules, the three-month time limit for employment tribunal cases will automatically be extended to six months where the rules apply, in order to allow you and your employer time to resolve the dispute. These grievance procedures will apply if you intend to bring a claim for one of the following:

- race, sex and disability discrimination in employment
- sexual orientation discrimination in employment
- religion and belief orientation discrimination in employment
- equal pay
- redundancy payments
- unauthorised deductions and payments
- breach of contract arising or outstanding on dismissal
- breach of working time regulations
- inducements or detriments relating to trade union membership or activities
- inducements relating to collective bargaining
- detriment in relation to union recognition rights
- detriment in employment
- detriment in relation to national minimum wage
- detriment relating to european works councils

A tribunal claim for equal pay has a time limit of six months from the end of the relevant employment if you have left the employment, but can be brought at any time while you are still working in the job. If you have worked on a series of short-term contracts, the tribunal can aggregate these, providing there is an underlying stable employment relationship, so that the six-month period runs from the end of the last contract.

The time limit for claiming redundancy payment is six months from when the employment contract was terminated. But this is only in relation to redundancy payment, as claims for unfair dismissal – for instance, because the selection criteria for redundancy was unfair – are subject to the standard three-month time limit.

It is not always easy to know when an act or failure has occurred, especially in cases where the act or failure to act continues over a period of time. In these circumstances, the time limit is considered to start from the date of the last of these acts or failures.

What happens if I miss the deadline?

The time limits for making a claim are strictly enforced and it is unlikely your application will be accepted should you miss the deadline. However, in limited circumstances tribunals do have discretion to extend the time limits.

In all discrimination cases (on grounds of sex, race, disability, religion and belief, sexual orientation, as a part-time worker or being on a fixed-term contract) a tribunal can grant an extension of the time limit if it would be 'just and equitable' to do so.[49] This is a wider discretion than in non-discrimination cases such as unfair dismissal claims, where a tribunal will only accept a late claim if it was not 'reasonably practicable' to issue the claim in time.

The tribunal has no discretion to extend the time limit in equal pay claims, although there are some instances in which the time limit may be modified, such as when the employer has concealed relevant facts or where the claimant is under a disability.

What happens after I have submitted my claim?[50]

Once you have submitted your claim form to the local tribunal office, copies of the completed application form are then sent to your employer, along with a response form (ET3) on which they must provide certain information and say whether they resist (do not agree with) your claim and, if so, why.

Once your employer has received the response form, he or she has 28 days to respond. If she or he fails to reply or provide the necessary information, a default judgment can be issued. A default judgment allows a tribunal chairperson to make a decision about your claim without your having to go to a hearing.

In most cases, a copy of your claim will also be sent to ACAS. This is the independent conciliation service. They will try to help you and your employer to reach an agreed settlement if that is what you want to do.[51] You may be told that your claim has been given a fixed period for conciliation by ACAS. This means that you and your employer must use this period to try to reach an agreed settlement. If you do not reach a settlement by the end of this period, your claim will then proceed to a tribunal hearing. However, if you do not wish to negotiate a settlement using ACAS, then the fixed period will end as soon as they are informed, and then your case will be heard.

Once the employer's response has been accepted, the next stage will involve preparing the 'agreed bundle' of documents and statements to be used at the hearing and calling witnesses. In preparing for the hearing, either side can make a written request for additional information from the other. If your employer does not provide the information you have requested, you should write to the tribunal as soon as possible, enclosing a copy of your written request, and ask the tribunal to issue an order. If witnesses are important to your case, but will not come to the hearing freely, you can ask for a witness order to make them attend.

In some cases there will be issues that need to be dealt with before the full hearing. Previously these would have been dealt with through a directions hearing or a preliminary hearing, but new rules have introduced case management discussion meetings and pre-hearing reviews and specified the issues that can be decided at them.

What is a case management discussion?[52]

After you have lodged your claim and received a copy of the respondent's response form, you should expect to receive a letter from the tribunal within the next two to three weeks inviting you to attend a case management discussion (CMD). This is an informal hearing to discuss how the case will be dealt with, what the procedure will be for preparing for the full or main hearing and to clarify the issues in dispute which the tribunal will need to decide on at the full hearing.

The sorts of issues the chairperson will want to discuss at the CMD include:

- clarifying the issues involved in the case and which of those issues are in dispute

- which documents you and the respondent will be relying on
- the witnesses you and the respondent are likely to call
- deciding the date and length of the main hearing
- discussing the need for medical reports or expert witnesses

The CMD is heard by a chairperson sitting alone. If you are legally represented, it is possible for a CMD to take place by telephone.

It is important to note that the CMD will not consider the merits of your case (that is, whether you should win or lose). Therefore you are not required to present documents or take any of your witnesses with you to the CMD.

What is a pre-hearing review?[53]

All preliminary hearings are now called pre-hearing reviews (PHR). These are interim hearings, which consider the preliminary issues of the case, although in some instances they may proceed to decide aspects of the case, or even dispose of the case altogether. They are usually heard by the chairperson alone.

The kinds of things the chairperson will want to discuss at the PHR include:

- whether you are an employee for the purposes of the relevant legislation
- whether the claim was submitted within the required time limits
- whether it would be 'just and equitable' to consider an out-of-time claim

In a PHR both sides must explain the basis of their case. You or the respondent can be required to pay a deposit where the chairperson believes the claim or the response has little prospect of success but is still arguable or defendable. The deposit, which can be up to £500, is usually refunded after the hearing or it can be offset against any order for costs.

The chairperson can also decide whether to 'strike out' a claim or a response that is 'scandalous, vexatious or has no reasonable prospect of success', or which has been conducted in a 'scandalous, unreasonable or vexatious manner'.

If the tribunal decides against you or the respondent on any point, that part of the case ends there.

What happens at the main hearing?[54]

If the complaint is not settled or withdrawn at an earlier stage, it proceeds to a full hearing where the tribunal panel will decide any outstanding procedural issues, and make a final ruling on your claim.

Before going into the hearing, a tribunal clerk will explain the procedure to you, discuss with you the number of witnesses you have and collect any additional or new documents you may have brought for the tribunal. You should tell the clerk if you or any of your witnesses have any special needs or concerns. At the hearing, tribunal panels try to keep the proceedings as simple and informal as possible and the chairperson will assist you and the respondent in putting your case over as fully as possible as the hearing proceeds.

At the beginning of a hearing, the chairperson and lay members will introduce themselves and will normally set out the format of the hearing. There are no rules as to which side starts first, but generally in an unfair dismissal case the respondent will give evidence and call any witnesses first, while in a discrimination case you will normally be first to give evidence followed by any witnesses.

Both sides are then given the opportunity to ask, and be asked, questions by the other side ('cross-examination'). You and the respondent can then give further evidence to clarify matters which came up when being asked questions by the other side ('re-examination'). Finally, the tribunal panel may also ask questions of you and the employer or the witnesses.

Once all the evidence has been heard, the tribunal usually announces its decision and the reasons for it on the same day.

A written decision is also sent to the parties, generally within three to six weeks.

However, a tribunal may decide to reserve judgment, usually in complicated cases or if there is insufficient time to consider its judgment, in which case you will receive the decision and the reasons for it in writing at a later date. If you are successful, the tribunal will normally deal with the issue of compensation or other remedies at the hearing.

Remedies

If you are successful in your case, the tribunal can make an unlimited award of compensation for:

- injury to feelings (not applicable to claims for unfair dismissal)
- loss of earnings
- loss of future earnings
- loss of benefits such as pension, company car, health insurance
- personal injury

You can also ask for aggravated damages if your employer behaved in a high-handed, malicious, insulting or oppressive way that worsened the injury to feelings.

The size of the injury to feelings award will reflect the length of time over which the discrimination occurred as well as the seriousness of the act. It has been suggested that injury to feelings awards should be a minimum of £500 and a maximum of £25,000. Awards above or below these limits should only be made in exceptional circumstances.[55]

In 2004-05, the median award in unfair dismissal cases was £3,476 and in race discrimination claims, £6,699. For sex discrimination claims the median award was £6,235 and disability discrimination awards were £7,500.

A tribunal can also make a recommendation for the employer to take certain actions to reduce or avoid the impact of the discrimination on you if you are still working for the employer.

Costs

Costs are not usually awarded in unsuccessful tribunal claims. However, a tribunal has the power to award up to £10,000 costs where it finds that the claim or the defence was misconceived and had no reasonable prospect of success; or where someone has acted frivolously, vexatiously, abusively, disruptively or otherwise unreasonably in bringing, defending or conducting a case.

A wasted costs order can be made against a representative who has caused another party, including their own client, to incur costs through their 'improper, unreasonable or negligent act or omission'. This only applies where the representative has charged for their services. The rules do not specify a limit on the amount of a wasted costs order.

A tribunal can also make the respondent pay you for the time you or your representative have spent preparing for your case. This is called a preparation costs order. The tribunal can only make this order if you have not incurred legal costs. This means that it will only be made if you have run the case yourself or have been represented by a not-for-profit or voluntary organisation. The rate at present is set at £25 per hour.

How do I appeal to the employment appeal tribunal?

The first stage of an appeal is to the employment appeal tribunal (EAT). Decisions from the EAT can be appealed to the court of appeal (CA). An appeal cannot be brought simply because you are unhappy with the original decision and feel that a different tribunal would reach a different, more favourable, decision.

The EAT can hear appeals from employment tribunals on questions of law only. There is no appeal on a question of fact, unless the tribunal's finding was one which no reasonable tribunal could have come to, on the evidence. An appeal can only brought on the following grounds:

- error of law – if a tribunal has wrongly interpreted the law, has not asked the right legal questions or has failed to follow a binding case authority

- perversity – if it can be shown that no reasonable tribunal would have come to the decision taken based on the evidence presented
- conduct of the hearing – bias or apparent bias and improper conduct by the tribunal are all grounds for appeal
- unreasonable delay – if the tribunal has taken too long to reach its decision, and that delay has resulted in an error, there can be grounds for appeal

An appeal must be lodged within 42 days of the date that the judgment or the written reasons were sent to you and the respondent.

You must enclose copies of the claim and response forms and the written judgment with the notice of appeal.

Endnotes

[1] SI 2004/1861

[2] House of Commons (2003), Employment Tribunals, Research Paper 03/87, London: House of Commons Library

[3] Employment Rights Act 1996, s 230(1), (2)

[4] The Part-Time Workers (Prevention of Less Favourable Treatment) Regulations 2000 does not provide a definition in terms of hours worked

[5] Case C-313/02 Wippel v Peek & Cloppenburg GmbH & Co KG [2005] IRLR 211

[6] Part-Time Workers Regulations 2000, reg 7

[7] Available at: http://www.opsi.gov.uk/si/si2002/20022034.htm (last accessed 18 May 2006)

[8] The Fixed-term Employees (Prevention of Less Favourable Treatment) Regulations 2002, s1(2)

[9] Further guidance has been issued by the DTI: http://www.dti.gov.uk/employment/employment-legislation/employment-guidance/page18475.html

[10] http://www.dti.gov.uk/employment/employment-legislation/employment-guidance/page18475.html

[11] The irrelevance of motive was established in two decisions of the House of Lords: R v Birmingham City Council, ex p EOC [1989] IRLR 173 and James v Eastleigh Borough Council [1990] IRLR 288

[12] Refer to Section on 'Race Discrimination'

[13] Further guidance on the Equal Pay Act 1970 is available from the Equal Opportunities Commission: http://www.eoc.org.uk

[14] An overview of the Sex Discrimination Act 1975 is available at: http://www.eoc.org.uk/Default.aspx?page=15497&lang=en (last accessed 18 May 2006)

[15] The full text of the Employment Rights Act 1996 is available at: http://www.opsi.gov.uk/acts/acts1996/1996018.htm (last accessed 18 May 2006)

[16] The full text of the Disability Discrimination Act 1995 is available at: http://www.opsi.gov.uk/acts/acts1995/1995050.htm (last accessed 18 May 2006)

[17] The full text of the Employment Equality (Religion & Belief) Regulations 2003 is available at: http://www.opsi.gov.uk/si/si2003/20031660.htm (last accessed 18 May 2006)

[18] The full text of the Employment Equality (Sexual Orientation) Regulations 2003 is available at: http://www.opsi.gov.uk/si/si2003/20031661.htm (last accessed 18 May 2006)

[19] A copy of the draft Regulations is available at: http://www.opsi.gov.uk/si/si2006/draft/ukdsi_0110742664_en.pdf (last accessed 18 May 2006)

[20] Disability Discrimination Act 1995, s 1(1)

[21] Disability Discrimination Act 1995, Sch 1, para 3; SI 1996/1455 (excluding tattoos and piercings); Disability Guidance, Part II, paras A16-A17

[22] Paras A1-A10 of the Disability Guidance, Part II, outline factors which may have a bearing on the meaning of 'substantial' : these include the time taken to carry out an activity, the way in which an activity is carried out, the cumulative effects of an impairment, the modification by the person of his or her behaviour, and the effects of the working environment

[23] Greenwood v British Airways plc [1999] IRLR 600

[24] Disability Discrimination Act 2005

[25] Disability Discrimination Act 1995, s 3A(1)

[26] Disability Discrimination Act 1995, s 3A(2)

[27] Employment Equality (Religion & Belief) Regulations 2003, reg 2(1)

[28] DTI (2003) Explanatory Notes for the Employment Equality (Sexual Orientation) Regulations 2003 and the Employment Equality (Religion and Belief) Regulations 2003, DTI: London, at para 11

[29] The full text of the Sex Discrimination (Gender Reassignment) Regulations 1999 is available at:
http://www.opsi.gov.uk/si/si1999/19991102.htm (last accessed 18 May 2006)

[30] TUC (2005) Guide to Equality Law, London

[31] This includes basic pay, performance-related bonuses, sick pay benefits, redundancy payments (contractual and statutory) unfair dismissal compensation, holiday entitlement, shift and overtime rates, hours of work, as well as non-contractual benefits such as company cars and luncheon vouchers

[32] Equal Pay Act 1970, s 1(4)

[33] Equal Pay Act 1970, s 1(5)

[34] Equal Pay Act 1970, s 1(2)(c)

[35] Employment Rights Act 1996, s 1

[36] E Coomes (Holdings) Ltd v Shields [1978] IRLR 263, CA

[37] Hayward v Cammell Laird Shipbuilders Ltd [1987] IRLR 186 CA; [1988] IRLR 257 HL

[38] Brunnhofer v Bank der Osterreichischen Postsparkasse [2001] IRLR 571

[39] British Coal Corporation v Smith [1996] IRLR 404, 410: 'the terms and conditions do not have to be identical'; it was enough if they were 'substantially comparable' (Lord Slynn)

[40] Equal Pay Act 1970, s 1(2) and (6)

[41] Employment Rights Act 1996, ss 95(1), 230(1). An 'employee' is an individual who has entered into, works or has worked under a contract of employment. A contract of employment is a contract of service or apprenticeship. Therefore those who are not employees, for example an independent contractor or free-lance agent, cannot normally complain of unfair dismissal

[42] Employment Rights Act 1996, 92(2)

[43] West Midlands Passenger Transport Executive v Singh [1988] ICR 614, 619

[44] SDA 1975, s 74(2)(b); RRA 1976 s 65(2)(b)

[45] Burden of Proof Directive (Council Directive 97/80/EC)

[46] Barton v Investec Securities Ltd. [2003] ICR 1205. In Igen Ltd and Ors v Wong [2005] the Court of Appeal clarified the application of the burden of proof in discrimination cases. The judgment makes amendments to the guidance issued by the EAT in Barton, and sets out the revised guidance in an annexe

[47] Legal Services Commission (2005) A Practical Guide to Community Legal Service Funding, LSC: London

[48] Refer to 'What happens when something goes wrong?'

[49] Sex Discrimination Act s 76(5); Race Relations Act s 68(6)

[50] Further information is available at: http://www.employmenttribunals.gov.uk/the_hearing.asp#What_will_happen_at_the_hearing

[51] See page 443 for further information on ACAS's role in mediation

[52] Employment Tribunals Service (2005) The hearing: Guidance for claimants and respondents, ETS: London
Available at: http://www.employmenttribunals.gov.uk/pdfs/english/The_hearing.pdf (last accessed 18 May 2006)

[53] Employment Tribunals Service (2005) The hearing: Guidance for claimants and respondents, ETS: London
Available at: http://www.employmenttribunals.gov.uk/pdfs/english/The_hearing.pdf (last accessed 18 May 2006)

[54] Employment Tribunals Service (2005) The hearing: Guidance for claimants and respondents, ETS: London
Available at: http://www.employmenttribunals.gov.uk/pdfs/english/The_hearing.pdf (last accessed 18 May 2006)
(last accessed 18 May 2006)

[55] Orthet v Vince-Cain [2004] IRLR 85

18 How can I send money to another country?

Andrea Winkelmann-Gleed, Working Lives Research Institute

What are remittances?

Remittances are defined as any transfers of funds from immigrants or migrants (who are also referred to as newcomers), to their relatives or friends in their country of origin.

Remittances have become an increasingly important feature of modern economic life and they are now recognised as a significant source of global development finance[1] providing external funding to developing countries. See http://www.livelihoods.org/hot_topics/migration/remittancesindex.html#1 for more information.

It is generally thought that remittances sent by individuals contribute substantially to development aid through their contribution to local livelihoods and alleviating poverty, particularly as money is passed directly between trusted individuals.[2] The Department for International Development (DFID) states that remittances can therefore have an even greater impact on people on low incomes, and can better assist them to improve their livelihoods and take advantage of opportunities. They provide much sought-after foreign exchange to recipient countries, while supplementing the domestic incomes of millions of poor families across the world.

For you, and for many other newcomers, an advantage of working in the UK is the ability to send money back home to friends and family in your country of origin.[3] Current research shows that the amounts people send back home vary from regular transfers of anything from a few up to several hundred pounds, to occasional gifts for special occasions. All estimates for annual remittances from the UK are based on assumptions and thus are subject to enormous margins of error. Figures vary from £500 million to £3.5 billion with more realistic estimates of combined formal and informal transfers probably being anything between US$200 and US$300 per person per annum.[4]

How can I send remittances?

Money transfers can be made through credit unions, UK high street banks, building societies, the post office or through Money Transfer Businesses (MTBs), also called Money Transfer Operators (MTOs).

Business strategies for banks and post offices are very different from those of MTOs. For the latter it is the core of the business whereas banks and post offices offer a wide range of products. Banks in the UK have typically overlooked remittances as a business, but are now recognising the opportunities. In developing countries banks are actively becoming involved by acting as agents to MTOs.

ATMs and debit cards have recently been added to the available remittance transfer products. However, this option seems limited to certain countries, particularly the US and Mexico.[5]

It can be difficult for some newcomers to set up a full UK banking account and some banks charge high fees for money transfers.[6] This has led to high level dialogue between banks, money transfer companies and other stakeholders on ways to reduce costs and improve access to low-income senders and recipients.

There are a number of less formal MTOs and, since June 2002, all money service businesses in the UK are required to register their business to comply with the law and become part of the legal system of money transfers. While this may have driven out small and inefficient businesses, there remains limited control over the level of services provided and 'informal' or 'alternative' remittance systems prevail. The UK government has recently financed a survey to help users to compare money transfer services and choose options that are appropriate for specific situations.[7]

DFID has set up remittance country partnerships with Nigeria, Bangladesh and Ghana. These partnerships will include a range of measures to remove impediments to remittance flows, improve access (and the terms of that access) in these countries to remittances and other financial services, and strengthen the capacity of the financial sector to provide efficient and widespread transfer payment services. More information is available here: http://www.sendmoneyhome.org/Contents/about%20dfid.html

The transfer process

To give you an idea of the process of transfers the example of Western Union (which is widely accessible in the UK) has been chosen. However, you should choose the option that is most appropriate to you. Western Union allows you to make transfers either online, by visiting one of their agents or on the phone. Western Union offers the world's largest money transfer network for sending and receiving money with over 170,000 agent locations. Information on Western Union is easily available at their offices or through their website (http://www.westernunion.co.uk/homePage.asp) which provides a wide variety of information, including news, practical advice, stock quotes and discussion.

Online transfers

Step 1: enter receiver information
Whom are you sending to? How much are you sending? And where will the receiver pick it up? Registered users enter a user name and password, and automatically skip ahead to Step 3.

Step 2: enter personal information and register
In order for Western Union to provide you with better service and faster transactions in the future, new users are required to register before completing a transaction.

Step 3: select additional services
Choose any of the available services to include with your money transfer. Services available depend on the pick-up location.

Step 4: review amount, charges and enter payment information
If necessary, modify the information where appropriate. Once you're ready, enter your credit card or debit card information.

Step 5: review your order
If necessary, modify the information where appropriate. Before submitting the payment, please read and agree to the terms and conditions regarding this service.

Step 6: your receipt
Upon approval of your payment information, your transaction will be sent. You are given a receipt containing a Money Transfer Control Number (MTCN) confirming the transaction.

Once the money has been transferred, the receiver may pick up the funds. At any time after completing your transaction, you can return to westernunion.co.uk and click on order status to find out if the funds have been picked up or not.

Transfer through an agent office

(A list of your nearest agent office is available on the 'send money here' website)

Step 1: complete form

Complete the 'to send money' form, including:

your and your receiver's first and last name (as shown on identification)

- the city and country to which the money is being **sent**
- the sterling amount you wish to send
- any additional services requested (subject to availability)

Step 2: identify yourself

Identify yourself (you may be required to present two forms of identification):

- for amounts from £600 to £1999.99: one form of primary identification verifying the full name
- for amounts from £600 to £1999.99, where no primary ID is presented: one form of primary identification verifying the full name (Birth Certificate, etc) and one form of non-primary identification verifying the current/permanent address (Utility Bill, a letter from a hostel manager confirming temporary residence, etc)
- for transactions from £2000 and above: one form of identification verifying the full name and one form of identification verifying the current/permanent address. The same document must not be used to verify both name and address

Step 3: present payment
Give the clerk the money you want to send plus the transaction fee.

Step 4: collect the receipt from the clerk
Be sure to save the receipt with your Money Transfer Control Number (MTCN) and share the MTCN with the receiver. The receiver may use this number to collect the funds, however, it is not mandatory for the receiver to collect funds.

Step 5: check status
To obtain the status of your money transfer, you can check the order status online or call 0800 833 833.

Transfer over the phone

Step 1: Call FEXCO, Western Union's representative in the United Kingdom

From the UK, call the freephone number 0800 833 833 (24hrs a day). Transactions initiated outside the UK will not be accepted.

Step 2: give your information
Give the operator the receiver's information and amount you want to send.

Step 3: give your payment information

- give the operator your UK based Visa®, MasterCard®, Switch® or Solo® credit or debit card number to complete the transaction
- please note, credit or debit card transactions cannot be made from mobile or public telephones
- some credit or debit card transactions may take longer to verify and require Western Union to call the sender back
- additional fees may apply for telephone money transfers
- the operator will verify your information and give you a Money Transfer Control Number (MTCN).

Step 4: obtain your Money Transfer Control Number (MTCN)
Be sure to write down the MTCN and share it with the receiver. The receiver may use this number to pick up funds, but it is not required. You will also need this number to track the status of your transaction.

Step 5: check the status
To track the status of your transaction, you can check the Order Status online or call 0800 833 833 to speak with a customer service representative.

Choosing a service

If you want to send money home or to another country, there is a range of money transfer products and services to choose from. Some offer convenience, others a low price, and others speed or security. Some may be more appropriate to migrants as they do not have the same level of documentation requirements. The following distinguishes between Credit Unions, UK high street banks, UK building societies and Money Transfer Operators.

Credit unions

Credit unions are financial co-operatives owned and controlled by their members. Each credit union is managed and controlled by a volunteer board of directors.

There are similar safeguards with credit unions to those with banks and building societies. They are regulated by the Financial Services Authority, audited annually, and are members of the Financial Services Compensation Scheme.

Crucially for newcomers, credit unions enjoy slightly different identification requirements for opening accounts. Credit unions are permitted to accept a letter from a responsible person in the absence of traditional identification.

Credit unions are different in each local area. You need to ask yourself two questions:

- is there a credit union in my local area?
- does it have a facility to remit money abroad (This is typically a partnership agreement between the credit union and a money transfer operator)? For example, credit unions in Southwark, Edmonton and Rochdale have such a facility

To locate a credit union and find out whether they operate remittances, see the credit union search facility on the Association of British Credit Unions Limited website www.abcul.coop or call their helpline on 0161 832 3694.

Banks and Building Societies

High street banks and building societies offer a wide range of financial services and remittances are only a small section of their business. In order to use their services for a money transfer you are required to have an account with them. The following are the main high street banks and building societies in the UK, and you will find branches in most high streets in reasonably sized towns:

- Abbey
- Alliance & Leicester
- Barclays
- Citibank
- Halifax Bank of Scotland (HBOS)

- Co-operative Bank
- HSBC
- Nationwide
- Lloyds TSB
- NatWest
- Royal Bank of Scotland (RBS)
- Standard Chartered

If you have not been in the UK for long it can be difficult to open an account or you may not be offered all banking services but rather just a basic banking account. You will generally need to provide identification in the form of two items of documentation. This can require evidence of earnings, such as pay slips or copies of utility bills in addition to passports and personal ID. Depending on your working and living arrangements it can be difficult to provide such documentation and you may have to address this with your employer.

How your employer can help

If you are working without receiving a pay slip you should speak to your employer or the agency you work for and try to obtain a detailed break-down of your pay as well as any deductions (for tax and National Insurance, travel to and from work or any other work-related expenses) made from that pay. If you are living in accommodation that is provided with your job or that you rent through an agency or share with others, you may not have access to utility bills. Even if you have the right documents, it may not be straightforward to open a bank account. You may find that some of the building societies are more accommodating. In any case it is worth mentioning this to your employer and asking for assistance in form of a letter explaining that you are in employment and legally resident in the UK. You can then take the letter of support from your employer with you in addition to the two forms of identity.

The following is a selection of country-specific banks with branches in the UK. Some of them offer advice on their websites for specific money transfers and it is worth checking out what services and rates a country's main banks are offering and if they have a branch in the UK:

- Bangladesh – Sonali Bank
- China – Bank of China (Hong Kong) Ltd, Canara Bank, Shanghai Commercial Bank
- Ghana – Ghana International Bank, Express Funds
- India – Bank of Baroda, Bank of India, ICICI Bank, State Bank of India, Remit2India
- Kenya – Bank of Baroda
- Nigeria – Equity Bank

These may be a safe option for transfers to main cities where branches are present or if the recipient has an account. However, you have to check out the fees carefully as banks are generally more expensive than money transfer operators.

Post offices

The UK post office offers the MoneyGram® international money transfer service that enables you to quickly send and receive cash domestically or internationally, without the need for a bank account or credit card. Money can be sent to more than 84,000 locations in around 170 countries (see below). MoneyGram® is available at over 2,300 selected post office branches across the UK. To find the most convenient branch for you, telephone 08457 22 33 44.

MoneyGram® securely transfers sums of up to £6,999 around the world in 10 minutes at competitive prices. For example, a £200 transfer to Jamaica would cost £9.99, while a £300 transfer to Belarus would cost £24. Costs increase depending on the amount you send, and standard rates range between £12 for a transfer of £100 and £140 for transfers of £4000. There are however cheaper rates for some countries such as Brazil, China and the Caribbean.

For more details see the Post Office website:
http://www.postoffice.co.uk/portal/po

Remittance service providers also called Money Transfer Operators (MTOs)

These are some of the numerous money transfer operators. By listing certain providers and leaving out others no recommendation or critique of their services is implied. Some provide only country-specific services or offer much more competitive rates to certain countries compared to others. The following is not an exclusive list.

- Cash 2 India – provides money transfer services to India via debit account, credit card, PayPal or bank account from anywhere in the world
- Cashmo – money transfer service from Europe to Africa
- Chequepoint – the company has more than 73 wholly owned branches worldwide and access to many other branch networks through correspondent banking relationships.
- First Remit – offers international money transfers
- Global Currency Solutions – Specialises in bank to bank remittances for amounts over £1000. Typical clients are businesses, business owners and individuals making large one-off payments in foreign currency
- iKobo – offers money transfer services to anywhere in the world
- Instamoney – money transfer specialists, working in 60 countries
- Interchange – specialists in foreign currency exchange
- RapidRemit – online service that allows money transfers to India and Pakistan
- Moneybookers – large worldwide money transfer network
- Moneycorp – UK-based foreign exchange specialists
- MoneyGram – large worldwide money transfer network with over 75,000 agent locations worldwide
- MoneyTT International – offers money transfer services to China
- Onlinefx – international money transfer service
- Paypal – an online money transfer system
- Sendwise – money transfer system to India

- Senvia Money Services – international money transfer specialists
- Travelex – global foreign exchange specialists
- WebMoney Transfer – internet payment system allowing instant secure payments worldwide

This is not a full list and others can be listed by typing 'money transfer' into an online search engine – you will also find individuals' experiences with certain services listed. However, as always with using the internet please be careful what kind of information you give away and make sure you are only sending money through official, secure sites if you choose online transfers (look out for 'https', confirming a secure site).

While all the service providers listed above form part of the formal system, there are also informal, non-registered service providers. These include shop owners, travel agents, import-export traders, trusted friends and other individuals. Generally the informal service providers are used where there is no banking system (for example in post-conflict situations) or where the banks are weak and mistrusted. Informal providers may also be more appropriate when accessing rural areas in countries with a banking system limited to urban centres. Thus the general process of sending remittances has to start with an analysis of the finance system in the receiving country.

How do I choose a provider?

All banks offer electronic transfer services and most also offer bank drafts, credit unions offer a range of services while some money transfer companies primarily offer cash transfers.

As individual circumstances vary, you will have to decide for yourself which channels offer the best services for sending remittances. Your choice will depend on a range of factors and the following questions may help you to make your choice:

- which country would you like to send money to and to which location within that country? If it is a small rural location your options are more limited than in a capital city
- how large is the amount you would like to send?

- do you want to make frequent transfers or are they irregular or just one-offs?
- do you have a full banking account? If so, does your bank have branches in the country you want to send money to?
- do you have a PC? If so you may find it easier to compare service providers
  There are also a number of internet sites listing experiences with money transfer operators and banks, such as for example the following sites:
  http://www.reviewcentre.com/reviews85163.html
  http://www.italymag.co.uk/forums/archive/index.php?t-1836.html
- do you trust online banking to transfer your money online?
- what experiences have your friends and family had with certain providers?
- do you prefer the safety of speaking to someone face-to-face in an agency? Do you want the money to reach its destination quickly or can you wait a few days?
- what level of risk are you prepared to take? Would you trust an individual you do not know?

How much will it cost?

The cost of sending money transfers varies greatly from 2.5% (already quite high) to as much as 40% for sending £100. Fees for sending £500 range from £4 to £40, giving lower percentage costs of between 0.8% and 8%. This is as a result of fixed charges being higher for small transfers. Moreover a few banks and building societies set minimum fees and the post office fees increase depending on the amount you send with special rates to certain countries.

Overall fees are not just based on the country of destination or the amount sent, but also on the service provider used. Banks and building societies tend to be more expensive on low-value transfers and banks often focus on higher value customers who hold an account with them. MTOs tend to offer lower rates for small remittances and may also offer more convenient opening hours. It is worth checking out country-specific services, as these can be cheap, convenient and appropriate to the needs of certain customers. Particular MTOs offer particularly low charges to certain countries, such as First Remit, Chequepoint and Travelex for small remittances sent to Ghana or Nigeria.

MTOs tend to guarantee the exchange rate, but not the amount paid to the recipient as this can be subject to further charges added at the recipient's end.

How long does it take?

Transfers through banks vary from 2 to 10 days with an average of 5 days, depending on transfer mechanisms and processes. MTOs are quicker and it can take as little as 24 hours for a transfer through an MTO with some being conducted within 10 minutes.

Other contacts that you may find useful

The DFID website provides downloads of translated leaflets with Bangladesh, China and India country pages - in Bengali, simplified Chinese, Hindi and Gujarati. Leaflets providing information on money transfers to each country are available, and 500,000 leaflets will be printed and widely distributed. They are also available from www.sendmoneyhome.org or by calling PBI on 020 7332 6277.

The project is hoping to expand the number of countries covered from six to as many as twenty-two with the new ones being Afghanistan, Albania, Brazil, Ethiopia, Jamaica, Mozambique, Nepal, Pakistan, Rwanda, Senegal, Sierra Leone, Somalia, Sri Lanka, Tanzania, Turkey, Uganda, Ukraine and Zambia.

Furthermore the website indicates on a monthly basis the exchange rates offered by individual providers, and the final amount to be collected by the recipient in local currency, though it has to be noted that most providers cannot guarantee this amount, due to possible fees and fluctuation of exchange rates at the recipient's end. This means it will be possible to see which providers are consistently offering best value for money.

How can I complain if transfers go wrong?

If your transfer does not reach the recipient you should in the first instance contact the service provider you have used – and you may decide to pay more for the transfer in order to have some assurance that the operator offers some refund if things go wrong.

Larger service providers, such as Western Union, offer some compensation or a refund service (following written request). This is set out on the back of their transfer forms if you use one of their branches.

If something goes wrong and the money transfer company you used is unable to resolve the problem to your satisfaction, you should contact the Financial Ombudsman for help:

Financial Ombudsman Service
South Quay Plaza
183 Marsh Wall
London E14 9SR

Consumer helpline: 0845 080 1800
020 7964 1000 (switchboard) +44 (0)20 7964 1000 (from outside the UK)
Fax: 020 7964 1001 (main fax)
complaint.info@financial-ombudsman.org.uk

Endnotes

[1] HM Government (2005) The UK's contribution to achieving the Millennium Development Goals. 01/05 produced for HM Government by GWS Group, pp43-44

[2] Chimhowu, A., Piesse, J. and Pinder, C. (2004) The impact of remittances. Enterprise Impact News. EDIAIS. Issue 29, April 2004

[3] Blackwell, M. and Seddon, D. (2004) Informal Remittances from the UK, values, flows and mechanisms. A report to DFID. Norwich: Overseas Development Group

[4] Sriskandarajah, D. (2005) Migration and Development, a new research and policy agenda. World Economics. 6 (2) April-June 2005

[5] Sander, C. (2003) Migrant Remittances to Developing Countries. Prepared for DFID by Bannock Consulting, June 2003. http://64.233.183.104/search?q=cache:9ll3lvLr5zAJ:www.bannock.co.uk/PDF/Remittances.pdf+remittances+from+uk&hl=en&ie=UTF-8

[6] McKay, S. and Winkelmann-Gleed, A. (2005) Migrant Workers in the East of England, project report for the East of England Development Agency, Cambridge. London: Working Lives Research Institute, London Metropolitan University. 4. August 2005

[7] DFID (2005) 31. March 2005 Sending money home? A survey of remittance products and services in the United Kingdom. London: DFID

How can I send money to another country?

19 How do I become a UK citizen?

Chris Taylor, NIACE

What are the benefits of having UK citizenship?

You can apply for a British passport and use this to travel. Even if you are already a citizen of another country, you may wish to apply for British citizenship because it may give you more freedom to travel. For example, certain countries may require visas if you use your original passport so you could use your British passport instead.

With British citizenship you can work anywhere in the EEC. See page 25 for details of EEC countries.

You can also stand for election as a local councillor, Member of Parliament (MP) or Member of the European Parliament (MEP) and you can vote in a local election, general election or European election (Commonwealth citizens and Irish citizens have all these rights anyway, EU citizens can vote – and stand as candidates – in local or European elections only).

There is no restriction on a British national being a citizen of another country as well. So, you do not need to give up any other nationality when you become a UK citizen. Many other countries, however, do not allow dual nationality.

How do I become naturalised?

There are some key requirements:

- you have to be over 18
- you have to have lived in the UK for five years and you must not have been away from the country for more than 90 days in the last year or for more than 450 days in the last five years
- you have to have 'be of good character' i.e. have a clean police record
- you have to pass the citizenship test or complete an ESOL with citizenship course and get a qualification in speaking and listening

If you are married to a UK citizen, you have to have lived in the UK for three years and must not have been out of the country for more than 270 days in those three years.

You also have to pay a fee to apply.

How long do I have to be in the UK before applying?

You have to be in the UK for five years before applying for citizenship or three years if you are married to, or the civil partner of, a UK citizen.[1]

What is the citizenship test?

If you are applying for naturalisation, you need to prove your knowledge of life in the UK as well as your English language ability. There are two ways in which you can do this. Most people will take a test. If your English language skills are already at or above ESOL Entry 3 you can take a test called the 'life in the UK Test'.

If you are not sure what your level of language is, you should work through the tutorial on the Life in the UK Test website www.lifeintheuktest.gov.uk. If you can't understand the tutorial, then you probably need to enrol on an ESOL with citizenship course.

For more information on ESOL, see the relevant section, on pages 284-292.

You can take the test on a computer at one of the life in the UK Test centres in the UK. You can find where the test centres are from the www.lifeintheuktest.gov.uk website or by calling 0800 154245. There are currently 100 test centres in the UK.

The test consists of 24 multiple choice questions based on the information in chapters 2, 3 and 4 of the handbook 'Life in the United Kingdom: A Journey to Citizenship'.

45 minutes are allowed for the test, but most people will be able to complete it in much less.

You can take the test as many times as you like.

The handbook is available from The Stationery Office and is priced at £9.99. The book can also be ordered online from: http://www.tso.co.uk/bookshop.

Further details about the test are on www.lifeintheuktest.gov.uk. This website also contains a full list of centres where you can take the test. Or you can call the Life in the UK Test helpline on 0800 015 4245.

If you pass this test you will not need to produce additional proof of your knowledge of English.

What do I need to take with me to the test?

You will need to take your passport or photographic driving licence with you.

Alternatively, you can take a passport size photo of yourself, signed on the back by a professional person who knows you. The photo will then be signed by a member the test centre staff and forwarded to the Home Office.

How much does it cost?

The test will cost you £34 and you will be told the result on the day. You will get a pass notification letter. It needs to be kept safe and to be attached to the completed citizenship application form when you send it to the Home Office. The test centre will also notify the Home Office of all results electronically.

Do I have to do a test?

If your English language level is at or above ESOL Entry 3 you take the citizenship test. Passing the test will mean you have also met the language requirements for naturalisation. No other proof of language proficiency will be required.

If your English is below ESOL Entry 3 you must take an ESOL qualification, at the right level for you, in speaking and listening. In England, this is a Skills for Life ESOL qualification in speaking and listening at Entry 1, Entry 2 or Entry 3. In Scotland, this is 2 ESOL Units at Access Level under the Scottish Credit and Qualifications Framework approved by the Scottish Qualifications Authority. You have to study for this qualification in an ESOL class using a citizenship context. You can find a course at your local college or adult education centre and the course should be free.

Do I have to take a complete ESOL qualification?

No, you do not have to take or complete the ESOL qualification but you do have to take a qualification in speaking and listening. This can be a unit towards the full qualification or a full qualification. You will also need a letter from your college showing that your ESOL qualification has been gained through study of ESOL in a citizenship context.

How long must I study ESOL for citizenship?

There is no fixed time. Your ESOL course needs to be long enough for you to achieve the qualification.

How long can I 'bank' a qualification? Can I apply for citizenship later?

At present there are no time restrictions so you can 'bank' the qualifications.

Exemptions

You don't have to take the test or follow an ESOL and citizenship course if:

- you are over 65
- you have a long term health condition
- you have a cognitive learning difficulty
- you have a physical disability which would prevent you from going to an ESOL class or taking the test

The citizenship ceremony

To become a citizen, you must attend a citizenship ceremony and take an oath and pledge to the United Kingdom. The Home Office will write to invite you to a ceremony if your application is successful. They will send the wording of the oath and pledge and the phone number and address of the local authority. Then you contact the local authority to book the ceremony.

Citizenship ceremonies are normally organised by:

- local councils in England, Scotland and Wales
- the Northern Ireland Office

When you arrive at the ceremony, there is usually a group of other new citizens. The registrar will host the ceremony. You show your invitation and you receive a card with the words you have to say. After a welcome speech, the registrar invites you to take the oath or the affirmation. You can choose to take an oath:

'I swear by Almighty God ...'

Or you can choose the affirmation:

'I do solemnly and sincerely affirm ...'

After the oath or affirmation, you take the citizenship pledge. Then you receive your citizenship certificate and an information pack. After the citizenship ceremony your local authority will tell the Home Office that you've attended and then you can apply for a British passport.

What does it mean for my family?

Children can't be included in your naturalisation certificate but they can be considered for registration as British citizens too. When you complete the application form, you can give your children's details too.

Children who are part of a family application also receive invitations to the citizenship ceremony but they don't take the oath. At the ceremony, they will simply get their citizenship certificates. Parents receive the certificates of children who can't attend.

Will it make a difference to my current citizenship?

You may, as a naturalised British citizen, lose your existing nationality. This depends on the law of the other country. UK citizens can hold dual nationality.

Endnotes

[1] http://www.ind.homeoffice.gov.uk

20 Further information for advisers and advocates

Gavan Curley and STAR

Introduction

This section outlines further information that may be useful for advisers and advocates in finding help related to the handbook subject areas – typically guidance and advice relating to aspects of employment, training and financial support.

What's available depends on where you are in the UK. Typically services provide free and impartial information and advice, in person, via the internet or over the telephone. There may be specialist advisers who work in or travel to a particular neighbourhood and offer advice in local premises such as community centres and village halls. It's important when facilitating access to a service that that you find out if the service is free, and also establish if it is necessary to book an appointment to see someone, or you can just drop in. Opening times will also vary, so it's important to make sure these are known in advance.

The kind of functions offered by organisations may include research resources or statistics, a particular support service in accessing training or employment, charitable support in the area of education and employment, or networks of support to assist refugees and asylum seekers in these areas. They may offer specific legal advice for a particular issue or help newcomers access services that they are entitled to.

Many specialist training and employment organisations have developed an expertise in delivering a range of services to new migrants and especially to refugees. Mainstream advice organisations, such as Citizens Advice Bureaux, also offer valuable resources in a variety of areas, and can be a good place to start: the national website of Citizens Advice (www.adviceguide.org.uk) lists Citizens Advice offices in the UK and offers some advice and information. Many Citizens Advice offices provide a phone and drop-in service at different times of the week, so again it is worth checking opening times in advance.

A useful starting point is Information, Advice and Guidance partnerships. In England, specialist advice services are usually part of an Information, Advice and Guidance (IAG) partnership – a group of organisations working together to ensure that people get the best possible help. A local IAG partnership will be able to provide information about the help available in a particular area. At the moment each area has its own identity. Work is currently under way to develop one recognisable national brand. So wherever you are in England sources of help should soon be more obvious than they are currently. In the meantime local IAG partnerships have done lots of work to promote their services locally. If you haven't come across any information, your local Learning and Skills Council (LSC) should be able to tell you who to contact. The Learndirect advice line is an alternative resource worth trying.

Information Access Points (IAPs) are another useful starting point. An IAP is a place where adults can get information, advice and support on learning, training, courses and jobs. Here those seeking information can talk in confidence to trained and experienced advisers. These advisers will also be able to offer advice on funding, childcare and other related issues. They are situated across the country, and many are to be found within community and voluntary organisations.

There may well be lots of support out there that you're not aware of. This section of the handbook should provide a useful starting point, but it's important to look at as many options as possible when giving advice.

The focus of this section, and book, is national, but for each geographical area, there are general principles you can follow, particular 'gateway' agencies that will provide access to local services and advice, and techniques universally applicable to do with search methods. Major organisations covering a region or country of the UK have also been included. While the resources here generally focus on universally targeted support services, many smaller refugee community organisations will be specific to a certain area, nationality, ethnic or religious group.

The chapter is divided into two alphabetical lists: firstly, of common queries or subject areas likely to be of interest to those seeking work, training or financial support; and secondly, of organisations that may be relevant to the provision of advice and support to newcomers. There will obviously be some cross-over between the lists, but we have tried to avoid excessive duplication. If you do not find an entry corresponding to your exact query, try to think laterally about what it is you are after, and which organisation might then be the most suitable to approach.

The sources referred to relate to the overall themes and the structure is as follows:

A-Z of common queries:
- broad themes include immigration status and advice, citizenship, gender and race equality, education and training, employment programmes, employment rights, and benefits

A-Z of organisations:
- groups who are concerned with refugees, asylum seekers, migrant workers, and students
- national, or overarching, organisations whose activities will be of interest to the above
- where available, a contact address, phone number (including helpline if applicable), email address and website are provided. There is also a brief description of the nature of the organisation, and the relevant advice or services offered

While every effort has been made to ensure that the information is as accurate as possible, details of organisations and projects can change at any time. Local Citizens Advice Offices should keep up-to-date records of organisations' contact details and status.

There are in addition a number of useful sources of guidance and advice focusing on specific areas of interest. For example:

- The Child Poverty Action Group (CPAG) handbook Migration and Social Security (2002) is the leading guide to migrant entitlement and social security benefits. CPAG also publishes the Welfare Benefits and Tax Credits Handbook
- The Joint Council for the Welfare of Immigrants (JCWI) have recently published (2006) their Immigration, Nationality and Refugee Law Handbook, which is the leading source on immigration and nationality issues
- *Inclusion* have published the Welfare to Work Handbook Second Edition (2004), edited by Will Somerville and Chris Brace, which provides guidance on a range of welfare to work programmes and adult training and education
- The Immigration Law Practitioners' Association's (ILPA) guidance on asylum appeals and on the asylum system provides an excellent overview of the asylum process
- The Refugee Council's Information Services survival kit also keeps practitioners and advocates up to date with the latest in the refugee field
- CARA's (Council for Assisting Refugee Academics) Higher Education Pathways: A Handbook for the Refugee Community in the UK (2005) covers courses and sources of funding for refugees in higher education
- LORECA's (London Refugee Economic Action) Directory (2005) on Employment, Training and Enterprise lists a huge number of organisations across London
- The Disability Alliance publishes the Disability Rights Handbook and *Inclusion* publishes the Disability and Carers Handbook (2004),

edited by Neil Bateman and Will Somerville, for further information on disability issues
- Shelter and the Chartered Institute of Housing publish the Guide to Housing Benefit and Council Tax Benefit.

Note: It is of the utmost importance that newcomers receive the correct advice. This is particularly true of legal advice. If legal advice is required seek an independent and reputable source.

A-Z of common issues and queries and how to tackle them

Advice
(See also Legal advice)

Many new migrants, refugees and asylum seekers have skills and experience, but they face barriers in using these and need support, advice and training to fulfil their potential.

It is important newcomers speak with a trained adviser who can look at the specific case and situation:

Information and advice:

- 'mainstreaming vocational guidance for refugees, asylum-seekers and migrants' is the multi-lingual site of a European partnership which aims to meet the needs of vocational guidance advisers, counsellors and all others who support refugees, asylum-seekers and migrants in their efforts to prepare for education and work in their new countries. The site includes a large number of links to relevant organisations and papers and guidance available in this area: www.gla.ac.uk/rg/index.htm
- NICEC (the National Institute for Careers Education and Counselling) have produced a briefing, 'Employment and Training Advice for Refugees: What Works?': www.gla.ac.uk/rg/eproso06.pdf
- AdviceNow: www.advicenow.org.uk is part of the Advice Service Alliance (the coordinating body for independent advice services in the

UK). This website provides independent law and rights advice, and links to legal service providers.
- AdviceKit: www.advicekit.info provides advice on services in Manchester
- The Refugee Council One Stop Service advice lines are:
    - Brixton (phone calls only): 020 7346 6777
    - Birmingham (phone calls only): 0121 622 1515
    - Leeds (phone calls only): 0113 386 2210
- For non-asylum advice, there is the London advice services alliance (LASA): www.lasa.org.uk. Their advice line provides social security information and welfare benefits advice to advisers within the UK (not just London). The LASA advice line is open on Tuesdays, Wednesdays and Fridays between 10.30am and 12.30pm on 020 7247 1735 or you can email: info@lasa.org.uk
- For a list of Citizens Advice Bureaux (CAB) across the UK, see the National Association of Citizens Advice Bureaux (NACAB) website: www.adviceguide.org.uk/nacab/plsql/nacab.homepage
- Community Legal Service Direct: www.clsdirect.org.uk runs a national helpline (0845 345 4 345) offering free advice about benefits, tax credits, housing, employment, education or debt problems
- The UK Advice Finder: www.advicefinder.org.uk is a directory of advice providers in the UK – including advice agencies that work with asylum and immigration issues. Registration necessary.
- Another free online source is: www.findsupport.co.uk – a directory of self-help and support groups in the UK
- The Learning and Skills Council (LSC) has prepared a guide to engaging refugees and asylum seekers: http://senet.lsc.gov.uk/guide2/hardrefugee/index.cfm
- Other One-Stop-Service charities include:
    - Refugee Arrivals Project www.refugee-arrivals.org.uk
    - Refugee Action www.refugee-action.org.uk
    - Migrant Helpline www.migranthelpline.org.uk
- For information on the latest developments for EU nationals see www.asylumsupport.org.uk

Asylum appeals

If an initial asylum claim is rejected, applicants are entitled to an appeal. For more about statistics and research on appeals go to:

- www.icar.org.uk to resources, then statistics and then 'UK appeals process'
- www.amnesty.org.uk to reports and 'Get it right: how Home Office decision making fails refugees'

If you are an adviser to an asylum seeker who is looking for legal advice, please see entries in the 'Legal Advice' section.

Asylum process

Information on the asylum and appeals process:

- see the Home Office 'applying for asylum' section: www.ind.homeoffice.gov.uk
- JCWI (Joint Council for the Welfare of Immigrants) website: www.jcwi.org.uk/resources/briefings/briefdec2000.html
- Community Legal Service Direct have produced a factsheet on asylum: www.clsdirect.org.uk/legalhelp/leaflet08.jsp?lang=en

Making asylum claims:

- Upon arrival in the UK, the asylum claim is made to an immigration officer at the airport, port or station. For more on modes of entry go to www.icar.org.uk to resources then signposts
- In-country applications are made in person to the Home Office Immigration and Nationality Directorate (IND) at Lunar House, 60 Wellesley Road, Croydon CR9 2BY

If a claim is rejected:

- an applicant can appeal
- an applicant may be granted either Humanitarian Protection (HP) or Discretionary Leave (DL) under Human Rights legislation

- the claim may fail but an applicant cannot be deported under Article 3 of the European Convention on Human Rights
- the applicant may be deported (see deportation)

Banking and bank accounts

A basic bank account has been created following consultation with those working on social exclusion and in preparation for changes in benefits payments from Jobcentre Plus. The basic bank account does not have an overdraft facility, but will accept direct debits and payments such as salary cheques.

The Immigration Status Document issued by the Home Office has recently been accepted by the British Bankers Association as an acceptable form of establishing identity, and has been included in the guidance sent to banks. This should be introduced across all banks by September 2006. For more information on bank accounts, see page 365.

Benefits

Advice

Jobcentre Plus offices are a point of contact for benefits for people of working age. Identity documentation and financial records are usually needed to proceed with claims. Those having problems receiving benefits should contact their local Law Centre, Citizens Advice Office, or seek independent advice. Citizens Advice offices or the local law centres will provide expertise in benefit assessment and in advising on claims.

Information

- Coventry Law Centre has a list of useful benefit leaflets relevant to migrants: http://www.covlaw.org.uk/immigration/leaflets.html
- The Department for Work and Pensions (DWP) provides printable online claim forms at their website: http://www.dwp.gov.uk/resourcecentre/claim_forms.asp. The decision maker's guide is the DWP's internal guidance for staff on how to deal with benefit claims. It is available at DWP offices and on their website at: www.dwp.gov.uk/publications/dwp/dmg/. There are a number of other internal

DWP guidance manuals, including guidance on disability, guidance to doctors about incapacity for work, and the Social Fund, that are also available on the DWP's website. Those who do not have access to the Internet or prefer not to use it can make an appointment to view such documents at a local Jobcentre Plus office.

- There are several Acts of Parliament governing social security and a large number of regulations which also have the force of law. The legislation has been greatly amended and you can find details on the DWP website at: www.dwp.gov.uk/advisers/docs/lawvols/bluevol/index.asp. They may also be available in hard copy at a good public library or you can ask to see them at a DWP office (who may know them as the Blue Volumes).

Childcare/children/unaccompanied minors
(See also SureStart)

Advice
If a person is looking for childcare facilities for a refugee or asylum seeking child, they should call their local authority for details of subsidised childcare facilities. If a person has children, they may be entitled to certain benefits or tax credits (see pages 156 and 170). The Refugee Council Children's Panel also has an advice and information line: 020 7582 4947.

Information

- Refer to the Government programme for children SureStart, that runs a public enquiry unit: 0870 0002288: www.surestart.gov.uk
- For information on the rights and entitlements of unaccompanied asylum seeking minors, including what happens when they turn 18, see: http://www.refugeecouncil.org.uk/infocentre/entit/entit_children.htm
- Save the Children has many useful resources: http://www.savethechildren.org.uk
- The Children's Legal Centre runs a refugee and asylum seeking children project: www.childrenslegalcentre.com/Templates/Internal.asp?NodeID=90033 which works to help non-immigration specialist

professionals working with asylum seeking and refugee children find out about this group of children's rights and entitlements.

Citizenship

Advice
New Government regulations on gaining naturalisation came into force on 1 November 2005, and a number of sources provide guidance and advice in this area.

Information
- www.lifeintheuktest.gov.uk: useful preparation for those applying for naturalisation as a British citizen
- see also the Advisory Board on Naturalisation and Integration (ABNI) on: www.abni.org.uk
- NIACE, together with LLU+, have produced a 'citizenship materials for ESOL learners pack' to help ESOL teachers develop learners' knowledge of life in the UK, help them become more active citizens and to support applications for citizenship: www.niace.org.uk/projects/esolcitizenship
- The Learning and Skills Council (LSC) has produced a factsheet 'delivering skills for life' on the English language learning provisions: http://readingroom.lsc.gov.uk/lsc/2005/funding/providers/delivering-skills-for-life-factsheet-7-2005.pdf

Community organisations
- There are over 500 refugee community organisations (RCOs) in England. To find out which organisations work in your area, you can contact a member of the Community Development Team at the Refugee Council on 020 78203070

Compulsory school age
- in England and Wales a person is no longer of compulsory school age after the last Friday of June of the school year in which their 16th birthday occurs

- in Scotland pupils whose 16th birthday falls between 1 March and 30 September may not leave before the 31 May of that year. Pupils aged 16 on or between 1 October and the last day of February may not leave until the start of the Christmas holidays in that school year
- in Northern Ireland a person is no longer of compulsory school age after the 30th June of the school year in which their 16th birthday occurs

Conflict

Advice

In the field of community conflict and conflict resolution, a major source of expertise lies with Neighbourhood Renewal Advisers (NRAs). The Neighbourhood Renewal Unit (NRU) at DCLG has developed a pool of NRAs with expertise in conflict resolution who can be deployed to areas and programmes as and when conflicts arise. The NRU works to promote mainstream community cohesion and conflict resolution within neighbourhood renewal policies and programmes. To receive advice from an NRA, contact your local Government Office.

In addition, the Local Government Association has produced 'community cohesion: an action guide': http://www.lga.gov.uk/Documents/Publication/communitycohesionactionguide.pdf. The CRE's safe communities initiative produced 'defeating organised racial hatred – an information pack' in March 2006: http://www.cre.gov.uk/Defeating_organised_racial_hatred.pdf

Information

For reports on wider conflict issues see:

- report 'fleeing the fighting: how conflict drives the search for asylum' www.amnesty.org.uk
- asylum rights has a specialist sub-group working on asylum and conflict. Contact them on 020 7820 3056 or info@asylumrights.org www.asylumrights.org

- good links page to useful websites on conflict: www.asylumsupport.info

Data
See 'Statistics'.

Disabilities

Advice
There are very few resources or services that specifically target new migrants, refugees or asylum seekers with disabilities. You should contact mainstream service charities that work with disabilities like the Royal National Institute for the Blind: www.rnib.org.uk

Information
- City Lit Centre for Deaf People has a course in London for deaf people new to the UK. For more information contact them on 020 7383 7624
- DIAL UK: www.dialuk.info provides a number of information factsheets for those with disabilities. It is the national organisation for the network of Disability Information and Advice Line services
- The Disability Alliance: www.disabilityalliance.org provides information on social security benefits for disabled people
- RADAR: www.radar.org.uk campaign for better lifestyles for disabled people and their families

Education

(See also Studying)

Advice

– Accessing education (entitlements) for those under 16 years old

While all children are entitled to education and to free school meals, other types of benefits, like uniform grants, and the legislative policy that outlines the parameters of the entitlement differ according to the system the person is under. Find out more information at: http://www.qca.org.uk/9997.html

– Accessing education (entitlements) for those over 16 years old

If the student is over 16, the head of the school or college can choose whether or not to accept the student, depending on the person's level of education. For more information: http://www.childrenslegalcentre.com

More generally, Learndirect: www.learndirect-advice.co.uk provide information on what is available in different parts of the country. An adviser can be contacted for free on 0800 100 900 for England, Northern Ireland and Wales, or 0808 100 9000 for Scotland.

Information

- The Council for Assisting Refugee Academics (CARA): www.academic-refugees.org and RETAS: www.education-action.org have produced a handbook specifically aimed at refugees seeking to further their education
- The Educational Grants Advisory Service: www.egas-online.org.uk support for learning: www.support4learning.org.uk/money and Hotcourses: www.hotcourses.co.uk provide more information on financial assistance
- The Student Awards Agency Scotland (SAAS) is the body responsible for handling student funding in Scotland, including fees and loans applications, and information on eligibility. Tel: 0845 111 1711 email address: saas.geu@scotland.gsi.gov.uk

- for asylum seekers with children of school age in Manchester there is a free booklet from Manchester EMAS: http://www.manchester.gov.uk/education/emas
- Refugee Education Email Network (REFED): www.groups.yahoo.com/group/refed also provides support for teachers and other professionals working with young refugees and asylum seekers, allowing them to share information and discuss practice
- Save the Children provide education resources: supporter.care@savethechildren.org.uk
- Africa Educational Trust (AET): www.africaeducationaltrust.org Tel: 020 7836 5075/7940 offers educational advice to refugees with an African background, and some financial support for study. You can email them at info@africaeducationaltrust.org

Elderly

Advice

Many refugee community organisations have programs for the elderly - local agencies will have further information.

Information

- Help the Aged is a national agency dedicated to serving the elderly: www.helptheaged.org.uk
- Age Concern works to promote the well-being of all older people and to help make later life a fulfilling and enjoyable experience. They produce over 40 comprehensive factsheets designed to answer many of the questions older people – or those advising them – may have. In England: www.ageconcern.org.uk and Scotland: www.ageconcernscotland.org.uk

Employment

Advice

Refugees

In some cases refugees' employment experience will have direct relevance to the present-day UK economy; in others the economy will have been so different that the job cannot be matched here (so the guidance task will be to look for transferable skills). However, refugee clients may have difficulty in describing their experience because of poor general language skills, or lack of specialist vocabulary, or incomplete understanding of the UK labour market. They need time to explore these issues, so it is important where possible to seek help from someone familiar with that occupational area. There can also be a challenge to convince employers of the benefits to them of considering recent refugees.

- check with your local Jobcentre Plus or Chamber of Commerce if there is a job brokering service for refugees near you. At a national level, the Employability Forum provides information for employers through research, conferences and materials: www.employabilityforum.co.uk
- The Refugee Council Training and Employment Section (TES) has a career's advice service for refugees and asylum seekers, including advice drop-in sessions: Monday – Friday 10 am to 12 pm. The TES Careers Advice Line is: 020 7346 6700.

Asylum seekers

Those who have not yet obtained refugee status are often restricted from employment or publicly-funded training (see page 72). Many of the agencies that help refugees also help asylum seekers.

Other migrants

There are also many migrants to the UK who are neither refugees nor asylum seekers. Individual specialist advice services may be open to these other migrants, depending on the conditions of their funding.

Information

- for further information and a range of leaflets on rights at work and on joining a union, visit the 'rights at work' section of the TUC website or contact the information line to be sent further details (0870 6004882)
- for more information, including more on skills, training, and qualifications, see the infocentre of the Refugee Council website

under training and employment. This page also includes information about the Refugee Doctors' Database (for more about refugee doctors see under Health)
- there is a useful report from the Department for Work and Pensions on refugees and employment at this address: http://www.dwp.gov.uk/publications/dwp/2003/wrl/main_rep.pdf
- TIGER (www.tiger.gov.uk) is a user-friendly guide through different aspects of UK employment law.
- The International Labour Organisation has work based information www.ilo.org
- a useful government website for jobs training, careers, childcare and voluntary work is: www.worktrain.gov.uk
- for Scotland, there is: Careers Scotland (0845 8 502 502) and: www.careers-scotland.org.uk
- the Connexions website has a searchable database of jobs www.connexions-direct.com/jobs4u for young people

Employment disputes

Advice
Anyone who is a member of a trade union is entitled to free legal advice and representation, and should approach their union representative before making a claim to a tribunal.

Information
- The TUC: www.tuc.org.uk (see A-Z listing) will have details of all affiliated unions. Some of the major ones are Unison: www.unison.org.uk, GMB: www.gmb.org.uk, Amicus: www.amicustheunion.org, TGWU: www.tgwu.org.uk
- working in the UK: your rights - is an advice leaflet from the TUC for people coming to work in the UK from the 8 new member countries of the European Union. It gives information on legal rights at work and is available in English, Hungarian, Estonian, Czech, Latvian, Slovak and Polish

- the Trading Standards department of your local council can also offer advice
- see also ACAS, which has a helpline dealing with employment questions: www.acas.org.uk and Tel 08457 474747

ESOL (English for Speakers of Other Languages)

Advice:

There is no central database of ESOL courses. The most effective way of finding provision is your local college.

Information

- Refugee Council Training and Education Service (TES) hotline at 020 7346 6700 has a list of ESOL courses in London
- contact the Refugee Education and Training Advisory Service (RETAS) at 020 7426 5800 for UK wide resources
- contact regional One-stop service offices for a listing of regional ESOL courses

Families

Family reunification

- anyone in this position should seek advice from a legal representative (see legal advice section) as requests to have family members join individuals in the UK are a legal matter
- the British Red Cross, on behalf of the UNHCR, helps refugee families (on low income) pay for the flights of close family members joining them in Britain from other countries: www.redcross.org.uk
- there is a website dealing with the reunification of families separated by the war in Iraq. Those visiting the website can register their own and relatives' names: www.familylinks.icrc.org

Family tracing/Family message service

- The British Red Cross provides a family tracing service, a family message service, and health and welfare reports for family members. The service is free (see British Red Cross)

Health

Advice

Like other UK residents, both refugees and persons with an outstanding application for refuge in the UK are entitled to use NHS services without charge.

Asylum seekers and refugees are often from very different cultures, may not understand the principles behind the UK health system, may not speak English, and may have complex healthcare requirements. It is important to take these factors into account when advising them.

Information

Accessing health services for refugees and asylum seekers

- signpost to the NHS Direct line (0845 46 47) where a qualified nurse can give advice about health inquiries (or will refer to a local GP if necessary). Translators are available if needed
- most local health authorities have interpreting services
- harpweb offers a useful internet 'portal' for asylum seekers and refugees: www.harpweb.org.uk

Accessing mental health services for refugees and asylum seekers

- The Refugee Council, together with the Medical Foundation for the Care of Victims of Torture, run the Breathing Space project, a mental well-being project for refugees and asylum seekers around the UK 020 7820 3072 www.refugeecouncil.org.uk/refugeecouncil/what/what008.htm
- The Refugee Therapy Centre's central purpose is to provide culturally sensitive psychotherapeutic help for children and families of recently arrived refugees who are having problems of adjustment www.refugeetherapy.org.uk 020 7272 2565
- useful website including bilingual health information, health briefings, maps, translated appointment cards, and country information is: www.mentalhealth.harpweb.org
- The Refugee Studies Centre has created a psychosocial training

module that details the mental health needs of refugees. It can be downloaded free at: http://www.forcedmigration.org/rfgexp

Note: The Medical Foundation and the Refugee Support Centre cannot take direct calls unless referred by an appointed agency, like Breathing Space's London-based Bi-cultural team, or a GP.

Entitlements/rights to health care

- see the 'access to health service' briefing on the Refugee Council website through infocentre, support and entitlement, and then health: www.refugeecouncil.org.uk
- see also the Department of Health website: www.doh.gov.uk/PolicyAndGuidance/International/AsylumSeekersAndRefugees/fs/en

Refugee health workers

- The Refugee Council has a doctor's database found in the 'training and employment' section of the website
- The Migrant and Community Refugee Forum have a career development project for overseas health professionals. They award up to £500 to refugee doctors and nurses to help them with examinations and books needed for verification and re-qualification (020 8964 4815)
- Southwark College's Medical English Unit provides language training for health professionals qualified overseas; help with job applications; ESOL and IT classes (020 7815 1500) www.southwark.ac.uk
- The Refugee and Overseas Qualified Doctors Programme (ROQDP) hosted by Institute of Health Sciences Education at Barts and the London, Queen Mary's School of Medicine and Dentistry, Queen Mary University of London provides training for doctors who have settled status in the UK and need to sit PLAB and gain limited registration with the GMC in order to practice in the UK. For more information see their website on: www.ichs.qmul.ac.uk/nhs/refugeedoctors/index.html

Translated health information

- Equip of NHS provides links to sites with translated health information: www.equip.nhs.uk/language.html

Harpweb (see above): www.harpweb.org.uk and Multikulti: www.multikulti.org.uk are also useful

Housing

Advice

For advice on housing options and rights for those not in NASS accommodation, contact Shelter 020 7505 4699 (info@shelter.org.uk) Shelter also has a free housing information website which has a database of organisations that provide advice: www.shelter.org.uk

Information

- Homeless London has a useful website for advisers on accessing services for homeless people in London: www.homelesslondon.org.uk
- HACT: www.hact.org.uk is a development agency that acts as a catalyst for change in the housing sector has produced a number of reports on refugee housing issues (020 7247 7800)
- PRAXIS: www.praxis.org.uk gives advice in areas of housing, in their hosting scheme and youth housing advice, as well as counselling (020 7729 7985)
- The Chartered Institute of Housing (CIH) is the professional body for people working in housing in the UK. It promotes the provision and management of good quality, affordable housing: www.cih.org
- The Housing Benefit Guidance Manual can be viewed at local authorities, who will hold a copy. It is also available on-line at www.dwp.gov.uk/housingbenefit/manuals/index.asp

Immigration

Advice

While there a large number of independent agencies offering advice and services around the area of immigration, some of the major organisations worth referring people to are the Immigration Advisory Service: www.iasuk.org, the Joint Council for the Welfare of Immigrants: www.jcwi.org.uk and the Refugee Legal Centre: www.refugee-legal-centre.org.uk. In general, if someone is looking for advice relating to a substantive asylum claim, application or variation of entry to the UK, nationality or citizenship application, admission to the UK under community law, removal or deportation from the UK, application for bail, or appeal or application for judicial review of any of the areas listed above, they will need to seek the advice of an immigration solicitor or registered immigration adviser. You can find a full list of regulated advisers in your local area on the: www.oisc.org.uk website by using the 'adviser finder' search engine.

Information

- There are a large number of immigration regulations, rules and guidance that can be found at: www.homeoffice.gov.uk and: www.ukvisas.gov.uk
- The Office of the Immigration Services Commissioner (OISC) website has a list of regulated advisers, in a large range of languages: www.oisc.org.uk. They also have a helpline (0845 000 0046)
- Direct people to their local law centre (see the Community Legal Service: www.justask.org.uk or their local CAB)
- Community Legal Service Direct have produced a factsheet on immigration: http://www.clsdirect.org.uk/legalhelp/leaflet21.jsp?lang=en
- The Legal Services Commission has produced a series of leaflets that give immigration information they can be downloaded free from www.legalservices.gov.uk or ordered from 0845 3000343. The topics covered include: permission needed to enter the UK, applying for permission to come to the UK, working in the UK, family reunification, naturalisation and more
- UKLGIG (the UK Lesbian and Gay Immigration Group may be useful: www.uklgig.org.uk

Integration

Advice

The government's integration strategy for refugees, Integration Matters, aims to develop the skills of refugees and help them into work (see also SUNRISE). The Refugee Council day centre team has links with the Besom Foundation, which will assist new refugees to settle into the community (painting/redecoration, furniture, bedding, etc). Referrals need to be made via the Day Centre team (020 7820 3000).

Information/policy/research

- a great deal of work has been done is the past few years on integration issues in the EU. For example, Refugeenet is the website of the EU Networks on Reception, Integration and Voluntary Repatriation of Refugees and is a source of information and ideas, including reports, relating to the Integration of Refugees in Europe. www.refugeenet.org
- The UK Government produced an integration strategy report 'Full and Equal Citizens' in 2000. In 2005, the strategy 'Integration Matters' was produced. This is available at: www.homeoffice.gov.uk/docs3/refugee_integration.html
- The Home Office is currently running a pilot scheme on providing caseworkers to refugees aiming to help them into education or employment, called SUNRISE (see also A-Z of organisations): http://www.ind.homeoffice.gov.uk/ind/en/home/laws___policy/refugee_integration0/sunrise__strategic0.html
- The Advisory Board on Naturalisation and Integration: www.abni.org.uk is an independent board established by the Home Office to advise and report on the understanding of language and civic structures requirements of the 2002 Nationality, Immigration and Asylum Act. The Board advises on ways in which existing language and citizenship education resources and support services might be developed, and on future development of study programmes.
- There is an introductory guide to resettlement available here: www.more.fi

International student queries

Advice / Information

- a useful resource is the UKCOSA (UK Council for International students) helpline (020 7354 5210) or at www.ukcosa.org.uk UKCOSA produce a number of useful factsheets on various issues for students from overseas. They cover most aspects of life, work and finance in the UK
- The National Union of Students (NUS) international students officer can be reached at: 020 7561 6500

Interpretation (see also Translation)

Advice/Information

- The Refugee Council One Stop Services offers interpreters for clients for all their services ranging from legal advice on benefits and immigration to counselling and health advice (see Refugee Council)
- Many local and health authorities have interpreters on their staff
- Languageline provides commercial interpreting and translation services specifically geared towards language-impeded situations in the public and commercial sectors of the United Kingdom: www.languageline.co.uk

Legal advice

Advice

For general legal advice, there are a number of commonly signposted agencies, which may be helpful if newcomers have a grievance about an employment issue, such as discrimination, harassment, malpractice, or an employment dispute (see also 'immigration' and 'advice'). Although there is no public legal funding (formerly known as legal aid) available for representation at employment tribunals in England and Wales, except occasionally for very complex cases, basic preliminary advice can sometimes be sought under the Community Legal Service Scheme.

Information

- Asylum Aid (020 7247 8741): www.asylumaid.org.uk
- The Bar Pro Bono Unit (BPBU): www.barprobono.org.uk can provide free assistance to applicants with short cases (up to three days) for no fee, particularly in those cases where no legal aid is available and individuals are unable to afford legal assistance. To gain assistance applicants must download and complete an application form available on their website
- Community Legal Service (CLS) also provides a comprehensive list of advisers dealing with immigration, nationality and asylum issues: http://www.clsdirect.org.uk (0845 345 4335)
- ECRE has produced a report on the availability of free and low cost legal assistance for asylum seekers across Europe: www.ecre.org
- Employment Tribunals: www.employmenttribunals.gov.uk is a useful source
- The Free Representation Unit (FRU): http://www.freerepresentationunit.org works on a similar basis as the BPBU in providing free representation, except they only accept referrals from agencies with whom they have links, mainly Citizens Advice Bureaux
- The Govan Law Centre: www.govanlc.com/advice.htm provides basic advice pages on Scots law
- Immigration Law Practitioners Association can provide information and assistance: www.ilpa.org.uk
- JCWI advice line (020 7251 8706) is available Tues & Thur 2.00 – 5.00 pm
- The Law Centres website lists those available in each area: www.lawcentres.org.uk
- The Law Society has some leaflets on basic legal matters (buying a home, making a will) that are translated: www.lawsociety.org.uk
- Liberty (National Council for Civil Liberties) has a free online advice guide to human rights and civil liberties in England and Wales: http://yourrights.org.uk. Liberty also has a telephone advice line (0845 1232307)
- The Office of the Immigration Services Commissioner (OISC) website

has a list of regulated advisers: www.oisc.gov.uk/adviser_finder/adviser_finder.stm. If a person wants to complain about any person giving immigration advice, including solicitors, barristers or legal executives, they should complain to the OISC
- Refugee Legal Centre can be called during office hours (020 7780 3200)

Legislation

Advice/Information

- ICAR's website has downloadable resources, including publications on 'UK Asylum law and process': www.icar.org.uk
- Her Majesty's Stationery Office: www.hmso.gov.uk site contains the full text of all Public and Local Acts of the UK Parliament, the Explanatory Notes to Public Acts, Statutory Instruments and Draft Statutory Instruments and Measures of the General Synod of the Church of England. In addition, from June 2004, the full text of the Explanatory Memorandum for Statutory Instruments laid before the UK Parliament are available from the Statutory Instruments pages
- For Scotland, there is also the Scottish Parliament website: www.scottish.parliament.uk. The website is available in several languages, and provides news from the Scottish Parliament

Libraries

Advice/Information

- A variety of information and services is available at local libraries, including information on work and learning opportunities. They will also often provide access to computers and the internet
- UK Public Libraries on the Web provides a full listing: http://dspace.dial.pipex.com/town/square/ac940/weblibs.html

Local Authorities

Advice

Local authorities work within the powers laid down under various Acts of Parliament. Their functions are far-reaching, covering such areas as education, waste management, community safety, environmental services, and social services. Some are mandatory, which means that the authority must do what is required by law. Others are discretionary, allowing an authority to provide services if it wishes. About two million people are employed by local authorities in the UK. The systems of government in the constituent countries of the UK, England, Scotland, Northern Ireland and Wales, differ. There is the added dimension of the devolved assemblies and legislatures. Many authorities will have dedicated teams offering services to refugees and asylum-seekers.

The Government information website Directgov provides a directory of authorities in the UK: www.direct.gov.uk/Dl1/Directories/LocalCouncils/fs/en

Information

- much information can be found at the LGA (Local Government Association) the representative body for local authorities: www.lga.gov.uk. The Local Government Information Unit is also helpful: www.lgiu.org.uk
- www.tagish.co.uk is an online directory that contains, amongst other resources, listings of all central and local government websites

Media

Advice/Information

- for facts behind the media myths, see Refugee Council press myths: http://www.refugeecouncil.org.uk/news/myths/myth001.htm
- The RAM project (Refugees, Asylum seekers and Mass media) promotes best practice in media representation of refugee and asylum issues. They also invite exiled journalists to participate in various projects: www.ramproject.org.uk
- a report by ICAR that is the result of several events organised to debate regional media coverage of refugee and asylum issues is available here: www.icar.org.uk/pdf/pubram001.pdf
- Presswise has an article on reporting on asylum and refugee issues

that is for journalists. It includes good practice guidelines for reporting on refugees and a myth buster section: www.presswise.org.uk
- Articles from round the world news on asylum issues can be found here: www.asylumsupport.info

Mentoring

Advice/Information

- information on mentoring is available from: www.mentorsforum.co.uk
- Refugee Resource, based in Oxford, are establishing a refugee mentoring scheme for adults from October 2006. For more information contact them at: info@refugeeresource.org (0845 458 0055)
- see also the Time Together scheme run by TimeBank (see A-Z of organisations) which matches refugees with mentors: www.timetogether.org.uk
- The Refugee Women's Association (RWA) runs a mentoring scheme tailored for refugee and asylum seeking women who are employed and who wish to become mentors. The objective is for the women to assist and support unemployed refugee women in their search for employment. For more information please contact Jasmina Dimitrejevic (020 7923 2412), or email jasmina@refugeewomen.org.uk RWA's contact details are Print House, 18 Ashwin Street, London E8 3DL email: info@refugeewomen.org
- The Refugee Education and Training Advisory Service (RETAS) runs a mentoring scheme for job-ready refugees which gives focused advice two days per week on how to find employment in a specific profession. Contact them at 14 Dufferin Street, London, EC1Y 8PD or on tel: 020 7426 5800 or 020 7426 5801 (an Advice Line is operated Tue/Thu 14:30 - 17:00) or via email at retas@education-action.org

Money transfers

Advice/Information

- sometimes also known as remittances, money transfers can be made through credit unions, UK high street banks, building societies, the Post Office or through Money Transfer Businesses (MTBs), also called Money Transfer Operators (MTOs)
- DFID (the Department for International Development) has set up remittance country partnerships with Nigeria, Bangladesh and Ghana. These partnerships will include a range of measures to remove impediments to remittance flows: http://www.sendmoneyhome.org/Contents/about%20dfid.html
- to locate a credit union and find out whether they operate remittances, see the credit union search facility on the Association of British Credit Unions Limited website: www.abcul.coop or call their helpline (0161 832 3694)
- The Post Office website: www.postoffice.co.uk/portal/po will have information about its MoneyGram® international money transfer service

NASS (National Asylum Support System)

For more about see: NASS www.refugeecouncil.org.uk/infocentre/entitlements/sentit001 or the Immigration and Nationality Directorate website: www.ind.homeoffice.gov.uk

New Deal

New Deal is a key part of the Government's strategy to get people off benefits and into work. It is delivered by Jobcentre Plus through its network of Jobcentre Plus offices around the country. New Deal gives unemployed people the opportunity to develop the skills and experience that employers want so that they can find lasting, worthwhile jobs. For more information call 0800 868 868, or check: http://www.newdeal.gov.uk

Public awareness materials

For basic information, myth-busting and factsheets on asylum seekers, who counts as a refugee, causes of flight etc, there are a number of resources:

- The Refugee Council has compiled some frequently asked questions: www.refugeecouncil.org.uk/infocentre/faqs/faqs001.htm and produced 'Credit to the Nation' a report on the positive contributions of refugees: www.refugeecouncil.org.uk/downloads/rc_reports/credit.pdf
- Forced Migration Review has some basic information on the global situation for displaced people on their website: www.fmreview.org
- UNHCR also has basic information and reports that can be accessed on their website: www.unhcr.ch
- Presswise has an article explaining the different types of migrants and answers to some myths about asylum seekers: www.presswise.org.uk
- a report by Oxfam and the Refugee Council 'Poverty and Asylum in UK' highlights some of the issues refugees and asylum seekers face in the UK: www.refugeecouncil.org.uk/publications/pub004
- The BBC has an asylum myth buster: http://news.bbc.co.uk/1/hi/uk/3074577.stm
- IPPR has produced a series of fact files, including 'Asylum in the UK': www.ippr.org.uk/ecomm/files/asylum_factfile_feb05.pdf 'EU Enlargement and Labour Migration': www.ippr.org.uk/ecomm/files/ipprFFEUenlarge1.pdf and 'Labour Migration to the UK': www.ippr.org.uk/ecomm/files/FFLabMigFINAL.pdf. These can be downloaded free from their website
- a 'test' that highlights the contributions refugees have made to UK society www.refugeechallenge.com
- The Guardian produced a useful report called 'Welcome to Britain' http://www.guardian.co.uk/Refugees_in_Britain
- you can see a MORI Poll on public opinion of refugees and asylum seekers at this site: www.mori.com/poll/refugee.shtml
- ICAR has a publications list on their website, under resources, then digest relevant publications. The list includes books, magazines, journals and states conclusions and availability of each: www.icar.org.uk

Racism/Race relations

Advice

The CRE (Commission for Racial Equality: www.cre.gov.uk) is the statutory body set up under the Race Relations Act 1976 to help eliminate racial discrimination, and promote equality of opportunity and good relations between people from different racial groups. It provides information, advice, guidance and legal assistance on matters concerning racial discrimination and racial equality. Its website will also provide links to the local services provided by Race Equality Councils.

Information:

- The Institute of Race Relations news network can be accessed here: www.irr.org.uk
- The Refugee Council has a leaflet (that is translated) for asylum seekers and refugees about racial harassment: http://www.refugeecouncil.org.uk/publications/pub002.htm#4
- The Home Office has a leaflet that discusses changes that are being made to the Race Relations Act 1976. It can be downloaded from the website: http://www.homeoffice.gov.uk/comrace/race/raceact/index.html

Refugees

Advice/Information

- The Refugee Council has an Information Line (020 7820 3085)
- They have produced a guide for advisers that work with refugees and asylum seekers (with versions for advisers in London, Yorkshire and Humberside, West Midlands and the Eastern region). It gives practical steps and advice on the most common issues that asylum seekers face. The free advice guide can be found on the website: http://www.refugeecouncil.org.uk/publications/pub016.htm
- ICAR (Information Centre about Asylum and Refugees in the UK): www.icar.org.uk is a helpful advice source
- Refugee Action provides advice and support to refugees and asylum

seekers, and the website has details of their many offices distributed across the country: www.refugee-action.org.uk
- RAGU (the Refugee Assessment and Guidance Unit) provide advice on refugee employment and provide training for advisers who are working with refugees and asylum seekers: www.londonmet.ac.uk/ragu/home.cfm

Refugee week

Refugee Week celebrates the economic and cultural contributions that refugees and asylum seekers make to the UK and promotes understanding of the reasons why people seek sanctuary. It usually takes place at the end of June with events all over the country kicking off with the 'Celebrating Sanctuary' festival in London: www.refugeeweek.org.uk. For 2006, this will take place from 19-26 June. International Refugee Day coincides with the week, falling on 20 June.

Rural Areas

Citizens Advice have produced a guide that looks at the strategies rural Citizens Advice Bureaux have employed to best serve their local migrant worker communities. 'Supporting migrant workers in rural areas' can be downloaded at: www.citizensadvice.org.uk/index/publications/assisting_migrant_workers.htm

Statistics

Advice

Precise statistics on the number of refugees in the UK are lacking – this is difficult because refugees were living in the UK before the Government began collecting statistics on them. Also, refugees are free to move and may no longer live in a specific area of the UK or may no longer be in the UK. There are however a number of sources of information that can provide a clearer picture of the national and international make-up and distribution of migrants, and the Home Office publishes quarterly figures detailing the numbers (and country of origin) of those claiming asylum.

Information

General statistical information requests

- Statistical summaries can be found on Refugee Council website: http://www.refugeecouncil.org.uk/infocentre/stats/stats007.htm

Home Office statistics can be accessed here: www.homeoffice.gov.uk/rds/immigration1.html

Country specific and international information

- if the information requested is about one of the top ten groups to seek asylum in the UK, then statistical information can be found in Refugee Council statistical summaries: www.refugeecouncil.org.uk
- fax the Home Office country information and policy unit (020 8760 3130) They will provide statistics by nationality, and detention statistics
- when looking for statistical information on region of origin this site is useful: www.unhcr.ch
- For EU statistics on asylum go to: www.ecre.org
- Organisation for Economic Co-operation and Development (OECD) has a section with statistics and reports on 'International Migration'
- International Labour Organization (ILO) has a useful International Labour Migration Database
- EUROSTAT also provide data on topics related to migration and asylum, in particular under the heading 'People in Europe'
- The Migration Information Source provides extensive migration statistics as well as a useful background context: www.migrationinformation.org

UK regional information

- The London Asylum Seekers Consortium (LASC) website has statistics on the number of asylum seekers supported by London boroughs: http://www.westminster.gov.uk/communityandliving/ethniccommunities/asylumseekers
- ICAR have a good statistics page about asylum in UK on their website: www.icar.org.uk

- The Refugee Studies Centre at Oxford: http://www.qeh.ox.ac.uk/rsp/ have more academic information
- Forced Migration Online offers a wide variety of online resources dealing with the issue of forced migration worldwide: http://www.forcedmigration.org

Student Organisations

Student Action for Refugees (STAR) is part of a national network of student groups called 'Interaction'. Other members are People and Planet (P&P), Amnesty, Oxfam, Student Partnerships Worldwide (SPW), Speak, Christian Aid, Student Christian Movement (SCM), Free Tibet campaign, National Union of Students (NUS), Medsin, Campaigns Against Arms Trade, One World Week and Student Assembly Against Racism (SAAR)

For guidelines on how to work with these groups on campus, please contact the STAR National Office (see www.star-network.org.uk)

Studying

For all aspects of studying at University, including advice leaflets on immigration status, finances, accommodation etc. see the UKCOSA website: www.ukcosa.org.uk

SUNRISE (Strategic Upgrade of National Refugee Integration Services)

SUNRISE is a key delivery mechanism for the Home Office's Refugee Integration strategy, Integration Matters, published on 9 March 2005. Under the proposed scheme, each new refugee who chooses to participate will work with a caseworker to manage the transition from asylum seeker to refugee. The caseworker will connect them with employment and education services and arrange volunteering and mentoring opportunities. It is being piloted in Leeds/Sheffield, Scotland, Manchester and London. Further information is available here: www.ind.homeoffice.gov.uk/ind/en/home/laws_policy/refugee_integration0/sunrise_strategic0.html. You can also contact them at 020 8760 8489 and monish.dutt2@homeoffice.gsi.gov.uk.

Sure Start

Sure Start website: www.surestart.gov.uk is at is a government programme which aims to achieve better outcomes for children, parents and communities by increasing the availability of childcare for all children, improving health, education and emotional development for young children and supporting parents, both as parents and in their aspirations towards employment.

For further information contact the Public Enquiry Unit (0870 0002288) and info.surestart@dfes.gsi.gov.uk

Trafficking

Advice

Thousands of women, men and children are trafficked annually to the UK for the purposes of sexual exploitation or forced labour. Traffickers often exert absolute control of their victims, making it extremely difficult for victims to escape and seek help. Victims of trafficking may require accommodation, legal as well as psychological assistance and protection. A number of organisations are involved in providing basic assistance to victims:

- Anti-Slavery International www.antislavery.org
- The Poppy Accommodation and Support Service provides housing, access to legal services and general support to up to 25 adult female victims of trafficking for sexual exploitation: http://www.poppy.ik.com/
- Asylum Aid provides free legal advice and representation to women trafficked into the UK: http://www.asylumaid.org.uk/index.htm
- Joint Council for the Welfare of Immigrants offers free legal advice on immigration, nationality and asylum matters: http://www.jcwi.org.uk
- The Medical Foundation for the Care of Victims of Torture provides care and rehabilitation for individuals and their families who have been subjected to torture and other forms of organised violence: http://www.torturecare.org.uk/

Information

- The Home Office has recently released (January 2006) a consultation document on trafficking that is looking to develop UK policy. It is called 'Tackling Human Trafficking – Consultation on Proposals for a UK Action Plan'
- Anti-Slavery International can provide useful information: www.antislavery.org
- The Home Office has put together a 'toolkit' for all agencies working with possible victims of trafficking: www.crimereduction.co.uk/toolkits/tp00.htm
- CARF (Campaign against Racism and Fascism) briefing 'How anti-trafficking initiatives criminalise refugees' is helpful: http://www.carf.demon.co.uk/feat50.html
- UNHCR has produced a number of reports, policy statements and guidance documents on trafficking: www.unhcr.ch

Translations (see also Interpretation)

Advice

Newcomers can find an approved translator through local community organisations, a One Stop Service or the Institute of Translation and Interpreting: www.iti.org.uk. There are many informative websites that include translated information for refugees and asylum seekers.

Information

- Refugee Council website includes translated briefings on topics relevant to asylum seekers and refugees such as racial harassment, information for people with refugee status or ELR, hard cases support etc: http://www.refugeecouncil.org.uk
- Multikulti: www.multikulti.org.uk provides regularly updated advice on immigration and asylum, welfare benefits, employment, housing, health and debt. Languages include Albanian, Arabic, Bengali, Chinese, Farsi, Gujarati, Somali, Spanish and Turkish.

Voluntary return

- A voluntary departure is where an asylum seeker withdraws their asylum claim before all appeal rights have been exhausted and wishes to leave the UK. In all cases they are asked to sign a disclaimer confirming that they wish to leave prior to the conclusion of their application
- if someone wants to leave voluntarily, they can contact: The Refugee Action Voluntary Return Project 'Choices' Manchester office: 0161 233 1200 or London office: 020 7654-7700 or the IOM London office: www.iomlondon.org (020 7233 0001) varp@iomlondon.org

Volunteering

Advice

There are no restrictions on asylum seekers participating in genuine voluntary work.

Information

- The National Centre for Volunteering: www.volunteering.org.uk produced 'The A-Z of volunteering and asylum: a handbook for managers' by Ruth Wilson, 2003, which is an excellent resource
- there is also the NCVO (National Council for Voluntary Organisations): http://www.ncvo-vol.org.uk/asp/search/ncvo/main.aspx?siteID=1 The NCVO is the umbrella body for the voluntary sector in England
- The Scottish Council for Voluntary Organisations (www.scvo.org.uk) is the national body representing the voluntary sector in Scotland. It aims 'to advance the values and shared interests of the voluntary sector by fostering co-operation, promoting best practice and delivering sustainable services'
- National Council for Voluntary Action (020 750 2490)
- Volunteer Development Scotland: www.vds.org.uk aim to support volunteers and voluntary organisations through training, by producing publications, and by establishing local Volunteer Centres (01786 479593)

- www.do-it.org.uk is a national database of volunteering opportunities and also contains information on volunteering
- Volunteering (England): www.volunteering.org.uk have lots of useful information. Regent's Wharf, 8 All Saints Street, London, N1 9RL (020 7520 8900)
- there is a volunteering coordinator at the Refugee Council
- Community Service Volunteers, 237 Pentonville Road, London N1 9NJ (020 7278 6601) can help with placements.
- SOVA (Supporting Others through Volunteer Action): www.sova.org.uk run a mentoring scheme for refugees in Wales, which aims to facilitate the successful integration of refugees into Welsh communities and to support them in securing independence (029 2049 5281)

Women

Advice

The needs of female refugees are different from those of male refugees, and they may require additional support to help them access services, gain employment, and integrate into UK society. They may well be caring for children, and a large number will have been the victims of sexual assault, and may, for example, be unaware that victims of rape can seek free professional advice and support in the UK. Accessing language classes can be a particular problem where childcare facilities are lacking.

Information

- Refugee Action have produced a useful report 'Is it safe here? Refugee women's experiences in the UK': http://www.refugee-action.org/researchreport.pdf
- ICAR have produced a navigation guide to women refugees and asylum seekers in the UK: www.icar.org.uk/?lid=2011
- The Refugee Women's Association: www.refugeewomen.org website provides information on women and employment (020 7923 2412)
- for advice and information on employment related issues contact Working Families on: office@workingfamilies.org.uk or see their

website: www.workingfamilies.org.uk. Their helpline phone number is 0800 013 0313
- Maternity Alliance is a charity dedicated to promoting the well-being of pregnant woman and their families that closed in December 2005. However, their publications can be purchased from the National Childbirth Trust charity: www.nctresources.co.uk (0870 112 1120) (office hours) shop@nctsales.co.uk
- Rights of Women have an advice line and downloadable information sheets and resources: www.rightsofwomen.org.uk
- for legal issues affecting refugee women, direct female refugees to the Refugee Women's Resource Project: 020 7247 7789 or the Refugee Women's Legal Group: www.rwlg.org.uk
- The Women's Aid website now has translated information about domestic violence: www.womensaid.org.uk
- The BBC website also has links and information about organisations which offer advice and support on domestic violence, aimed at ethnic minorities: http://www.bbc.co.uk/health/hh/links.shtml#ethnic.

A-Z of organisations

Advisory, Conciliation and Arbitration Service (ACAS)

Brandon House
180 Borough High Street
London
SE1 1LW

Tel: 020 7210 3613
Helpline: 08457 474747
www.acas.org.uk

ACAS is a public body that promotes good workplace relations. Their national helpline answers employment questions and provides general advice on rights at work for both employers and employees. The website gives details of their regional offices around the UK.

Adult Learning Project

Tollcross Community Education Centre
117 Fountainbridge
Edinburgh EH3 9QG

0131 221 5800
www.tollcross.edin.org/alp/index.html

The Adult Learning Project is based in Tollcross, Edinburgh, and runs a wide range of community learning courses. Where possible they will provide childcare and aim to keep any costs to a minimum.

Age Concern

Astral House
1268 London Road
London SW16 4ER

Free helpline: 0800 00 99 66
www.ageconcern.org.uk

Age Concern provides an information line that offers detailed information to older people and their families on a range of issues including benefits, care and housing. It is open 7 days a week from 8am - 7pm. They also produce over 40 comprehensive factsheets designed to answer many of the questions older people – or those advising them – may have. In Scotland, go to www.ageconcernscotland.org.uk

Asylum Support

Website that focuses on all matters that concern people seeking asylum, together with a directory of online resources relating to asylum and refugees, conflict, country data, court cases, deportation, detention, discrimination, funding, gender, government, human rights, human trafficking, law, media, migration, policy and studies. It also has a good selection of downloadable publications.

www.asylumsupport.info

Black and Ethnic Minorities Infrastructure in Scotland (BEMIS)

The Mansfield Traquair Centre
15 Mansfield Place
Edinburgh
EH3 6BB

0131 474 8045
www.bemis.org.uk

BEMIS aims to support organisations or individuals who may face discrimination on grounds of race, culture, colour, language, and faith. This support includes representation, dissemination of information, training opportunities, and the development of the black and minority ethnic voluntary sector throughout Scotland.

The Bridges Programme (Scotland)

27 Main Street
Bridgeton
Glasgow
G40 1QA

0141 554 5440
admin@bridgesprogrammes.org.uk
www.bridgesprogrammes.org.uk

A specialist agency that helps refugees and asylum seekers living in Glasgow gain meaningful work experience within their field of expertise. It is the only work shadow/work experience scheme for asylum seekers and refugees in Scotland. They also develop accreditation and up-skilling schemes, to help refugee professionals access sustainable jobs at the appropriate level.

British Council

0161 957 7755
general.enquiries@britishcouncil.org

The UK's international organisation for educational opportunities and cultural relations. There are regional offices around the UK, as well as in 110 countries worldwide.

British Red Cross

44 Moorfields
London
EC2Y 9AA

0870 170 7000
information@redcross.org.uk
www.redcross.org.uk

They offer practical and emotional assistance to vulnerable asylum seekers and refugees. Trained volunteers provide support to thousands of people every year, helping them to access local services and adjust to life in a new country. They also provide a comprehensive information pack for refugees in the UK, covering issues from health services to where to pray.

Child Poverty Action Group

94 White Lion Street
London
N1 9PF

020 7837 7979
staff@cpag.org.uk
www.childpoverty.org.uk/

Advice line (advice agencies only; Monday-Friday, 2pm-4pm)
020 7833 4627
advice@cpag.org.uk

CPAG promotes action for the relief, directly or indirectly, of poverty among children and families with children. They work to ensure that those on low incomes get their full entitlement to welfare benefits. In their campaigning and information work they seek to improve benefits and policies for low-income families, in order to eradicate the injustice of poverty.

ChildcareLink

Freephone 08000 96 02 96
www.childcarelink.gov.uk

ChildcareLink is funded by the Scottish Executive and the Department for Education and Skills, under the National Childcare Strategy. It aims to help people back to work by addressing the problem of finding childcare. The website provides a database of childcare opportunities, searchable by town or postcode. All childcare and early education providers in Scotland are regulated by the Care Commission.

Citizens Advice Bureaux (CAB)

Most towns will have a CAB. The Citizens Advice Bureau Service offers free, confidential, impartial and independent advice from nearly 3,400 locations including bureaux, GP surgeries, hospitals, colleges, prisons and courts.

Advice is available face-to-face and by telephone. Most bureaux offer home visits and some also provide email advice. They can help with problems at work, but also with a wide range of other problems such as debt, consumer issues, housing and immigration. You can find out your nearest CAB using the online search mechanism at www.citizensadvice.org.uk or from your local telephone directory.

They also provide the online 'Adviceguide' service (www.adviceguide.org.uk) that offers independent advice on your rights – practical, reliable, up-to-date information on a wide range of topics, including benefits, housing, employment and debt, consumer and legal issues; details of reliable sources of advice if you need more help; information in English, Welsh, Bengali, Gujarati, Punjabi, Urdu and Chinese; and useful fact-sheets to print off.

Commission for Racial Equality (CRE)
St Dunstan's House
201-211 Borough High Street
London
SE1 1GZ

info@cre.gov.uk
www.cre.gov.uk
London (head office): 020 7939 0000
Birmingham: 0121 710 3000
Manchester: 0161 835 5500

A statutory body set up under the Race Relations Act 1976 to help eliminate racial discrimination, and promote equality of opportunity and good relations between people from different racial groups. They provide information, advice, guidance and legal assistance on matters concerning racial discrimination and racial equality. Among other publications, the CRE has produced:

- Tackling Racial Harassment in Scotland: A caseworker's handbook (2001)

- Statutory Code of Practice on the Duty to Promote Race Equality (2002)

- Statutory Code of Practice On Racial Equality In Employment (2006)

Commission for Racial Equality (CRE Scotland)

Provides information, advice, guidance and legal assistance on matters concerning racial discrimination and racial equality, with special reference to Scotland.

www.cre.gov.uk
0131 524 2000

Commission for Racial Equality (CRE Wales)

Provides information, advice, guidance and legal assistance on matters concerning racial discrimination and racial equality, with special reference to Wales.

www.cre.gov.uk
02920 729200

Community Action Network – Enterprise & Employment for Refugees

3rd Floor, Downstream Building
1 London Bridge
London
SE1 9BG

020 7785 6226
canhq@can-online.org.uk
www.can-online.org.uk

Support for business and social enterprise start-up, including workshops and one-to-one advice and mentoring. Construction industry training and work placements. Funding for childcare. Access to business loans for people unable to access mainstream lending.

Community Legal Service (CLS)

Just Ask! Web Administrator
CLS Policy Team
1st Floor, 12 Roger Street
London
WC1N 2JL

Directory Helpline: 0845 608 1122
www.justask.org.uk

CLS has replaced the old Legal Aid Board in England and Wales. The CLS Directory provides details of all solicitors, advice agencies and information providers who hold or have committed to the CLS Quality Mark.

COMPAS

COMPAS (Centre on Migration, Policy and Society)
University of Oxford, 58 Banbury Road, Oxford, OX2 6QS

+44 (0) 1865 274711
info@compas.ox.ac.uk
www.compas.ox.ac.uk

The mission of the COMPAS is to provide a strategic, integrated approach to understanding contemporary and future migration dynamics across sending areas and receiving contexts in the UK and EU.

Connexions

www.connexions.gov.uk

The Connexions Service was set up to give all 13 to 19 year olds in England a better start in life. It provides them with integrated information, advice and guidance and helps with their personal development. Connexions aims to help young people take part in learning, achieve their full potential, and make a smooth transition to adult life. Services are drawn together in 'One Stop Shops', bringing together a range of services when and where people need them. For details of your local partnership please visit the Connexions website or contact the appropriate government office.

Council for Assisting Refugee Academics (CARA)

London South Bank University

Technopark
90 London Road
SE1 6LN

020 7021 0880
Info.cara@lsbu.ac.uk
www.academic-refugees.org

CARA helps refugees with academic backgrounds to re-establish their careers in the UK. CARA runs a small grants programme and an information and advice service.

Council for Ethnic Minority Voluntary Organisations (CEMVO)

Boardman House
64 Broadway
London
E15 1NG

020 8432 0410
enquiries@CEMVO.org.uk

National infrastructure networking organisation, providing services and support to minority ethnic voluntary sector organisations and communities. Has regional offices across the UK.

Council for International Education (UKCOSA)

UKCOSA: The Council for International Education
9-17 St Albans Place
London N1 0NX

Advice Line: 020 7107 9922
www.ukcosa.org.uk

UKCOSA provides advice and information about studying in the UK, including the educational rights and entitlements of refugees and asylum seekers. Information and advice to students is free.

Department for Communities and Local Government (DCLG)

Eland House
Bressenden Place
London
SW1E 5DU

Enquiry Helpdesk: 020 7944 4400 (open between 8.30am and 5.30pm Monday to Friday)
contactus@communities.gsi.gov.uk
www.communities.gov.uk

DCLG, created in May 2006, brings together for the first time responsibilities for local government, social exclusion and neighbourhood renewal (formerly under the Office of the Deputy Prime Minister) with new responsibilities for communities, race, faith, and equalities.

Department for Education and Skills (DfES)

www.dfes.gov.uk
Support line for students in higher education: 01325 392 822

Department of Trade and Industry (DTI)

www.dti.gov.uk/er
Enquiry Unit: 020 7215 5000

The department's Employment Relations website covers employment law and equality legislation, including religion or belief and sexual orientation.

Disability Rights Commission (DRC)

DRC Helpline
FREEPOST MID02164
Stratford-upon-Avon
CV37 9BR

www.drc-gb.org
08457 622 633
Textphone: 08457 622 644
(Operator available at any time between 8am and 8pm, Monday to Friday)

The DRC is an independent body established in April 2000 by Act of Parliament to stop discrimination and promote equality of opportunity for disabled people. It runs a national helpline – giving advice and information to disabled people, employers and service providers.

Education Action International

14 Dufferin Street
London
EC1Y 8PD
United Kingdom

Freephone number: 0800 389 6843
www.education-action.org

Education Action International works with people affected by conflict in their home countries and countries of refuge. They aim to support children and adults to achieve their potential through literacy, life-skills and employment training (see also RETAS).

Educational Grants Advisory Service (EGAS)

501-505 Kingsland Road
London
E8 4AU

020 7254 6251
egas.enquiry@fwa.org.uk
www.egas-online.org/fwa

EGAS helps individuals identify trusts for which they might be eligible. It also produces a guide to funding.

Employability Forum

2 Downstream
1 London Bridge
London
SE1 9BG

020 7785 6270
info@employabilityforum.co.uk
www.employabilityforum.co.uk

The Employability Forum is an independent organisation that promotes the employment of refugees and the integration of migrant workers in the UK.

It acts as a catalyst – working with the voluntary sector, employers and government, identifying the key issues and developing strategies for integrating refugees and migrants in the world of work.

Employment Agency Standards Inspectorate (EASI)

www.dti.gov.uk

If you work for an agency that is treating you badly and you think it might be breaking the law, you can report it to the government office that regulates agencies. Part of the Department of Trade and Industry, the EASI has a specific enquiry line: 0845 955 5105.

Employment Tribunal Service (ETS)

Enquiry line: 0845 795 9775
www.ets.gov.uk

Provides information about the role and functions of the employment tribunal service.

EntitledTo

http://www.entitledto.co.uk

EntitledTo provides free web-based calculators to help people work out their entitlement to benefits and tax credits. EntitledTo has been Sunday Times website of the week and was featured on BBC Radio 4's Moneybox programme. It does not however provide individuals with specific advice about their benefit or tax credit claim.

EQUAL

Equal Support Unit
ECOTEC Research and Consulting Ltd
Priestley House
12-26 Albert Street
Birmingham B4 7UD
United Kingdom

Helpline: 0121 616 3660
Information line: 0121 616 3661
equal@ecotec.co.uk

Funded through the European Social Fund, Equal is an initiative which tests and promotes new means of combating all forms of discrimination and inequalities in the labour market, both for those in work and for those seeking work, through transnational co-operation. Equal also includes action to help the social and vocational integration of asylum seekers.

Equal Opportunities Commission

Arndale House, Arndale Centre
Manchester
M4 3EQ
info@eoc.org.uk

Helpline: 0845 601 5901
www.eoc.gov.uk

The EOC works to eliminate sex discrimination in the UK, and provides advice and information via a free and confidential helpline. It provides information on legal rights, and what next steps can be taken, including advice on how to take a case to an employment tribunal or a court.

Equality Direct

Helpline: 0845 600 3444
www.equalitydirect.org.uk

This is a confidential advice service for businesses on equality. The website contains information about refugees and asylum seekers that includes definitions, employment rights and contact details for key organisations.

GHARWEG Advice, Training and Careers Centre

5 Westminster Bridge Road
London
SE1 7XW

020 7620 1430
gharweg@aol.com
www.gharweg.org.uk

Covers London. They have a one stop centre offering training, support and advice for African refugees and asylum seekers: on housing, immigration, employment, training, and welfare rights. Legal advice, careers, employment and training services; capacity building workshops for small organisations.

Glasgow Anti-Racist Alliance

30 Bell Street
Glasgow GL1 1LG

0141 572 1140
Mail@gara.org.uk

The Glasgow Anti Racist Alliance (GARA) is a multi-agency social inclusion partnership (SIP). It has been established to tackle the social exclusion of young people caused by racism in the city of Glasgow.

Guidance Council

Renaissance House
20 Princess Road West
Leicester
LE1 6TP

0870 774 3744
www.guidancecouncil.com

This is an independent campaigning body for career guidance in the UK. Provides links to guidance services.

ICAR (Information Centre about Asylum and Refugees in the UK):

School of Social Sciences
City University
Northampton Square
London
EC1V 0HB

020 7040 4596
icar@city.ac.uk
www.icar.org.uk

The Information Centre about Asylum and Refugees (ICAR) in the UK is an academic research and information organisation in the School of Social Sciences at City University, London. ICAR aims to raise the level of public debate and understanding of asylum in the UK context and to encourage evidence-based policy making.

Immigration Advisory Service (IAS)
County House
190 Great Dover Street
London
SE1 4YB

020 7967 1221/1330
Helpline: 020 7378 9191 (24 hours; 7 days)
advice@iasuk.org
www.iasuk.org

Free individual advice and representation throughout the UK. IAS undertakes all immigration and asylum work including tribunal and judicial review. Offices in Birmingham (Central and Sheldon), Cardiff, Glasgow, Hounslow (Ebury and Grove Road), Leeds, Liverpool, Central London, Manchester, Middlesborough, Norwich, Oakington and Sylhet, Bangladesh.

Immigration and Nationality Directorate (IND)
Lunar House
40 Wellesley Road
Croydon
CR9 2BY

General enquiries: 0870 606 7766
www.ind.homeoffice.gov.uk

Home Office department responsible for immigration control (website also contains information on the National Asylum Support Service – NASS – the Home Office department responsible for supporting asylum seekers; helpline – 0845 600 0184).

The Initiative

Adelphi Centre
12 Commercial Road
Glasgow G5 0PQ

Freephone 0800 027 2628 or Tel: 0141 420 3573, ext 243
www.the-initiative.or.uk
info@the-intiative.org.uk

Provides training and volunteering opportunities for refugees and asylum seekers.

International Organisation for Migration

IOM UK Office
21 Westminster Palace Gardens
Artillery Row
London
SW1P 1RR

+44 (0)20 7233 0001
Freephone: 0800 783 2332
www.iom.int (UK Office: www.iomlondon.org)

Information: info@iomlondon.org
Return and Reintegration: VARRP@iomlondon.org
AVRIM - Return of Irregular Migrants: avrim@iomlondon.org

Specialist information and sites on a range of asylum issues from voluntary return to migration health issues. London office visiting times 10 am–1pm and 2pm–4:30pm Monday to Friday. No appointment is necessary.

Institute for Public Policy Research (IPPR)

30 - 32 Southampton Street, London WC2E 7RA

+44 (0) 20 7470 6100
www.ippr.org.uk

Think tank that conducts research on migration, equality and citizenship, statistics on asylum. Migration fact files and public opinion on asylum.

Jobcentre Plus

http://www.jobcentreplus.gov.uk
Refugee Operational Policy Team: 0114 259 6220

Jobcentre Plus is an Executive Agency of the Department for Work and Pensions. Launched in April 2002, Jobcentre Plus brought together the Employment Service and parts of the Benefits Agency that delivered services to working age people (see also New Deal). The website provides links to local offices' addresses and phone numbers, which provide advice on finding a job and applying for benefits. They also provide the Jobseeker Direct helpline on 0845 60 60 234.

Jobcentre Plus has adopted a Refugee Operational Framework, which focuses on partnership working with refugee organisations and other partners. It is also developing a customer services leaflet aimed specifically at refugees.

Joint Council for the Welfare Of Immigrants (JCWI)

115 Old Street
London EC1V 9RT

+44 02 (0) 7251 8708
info@jcwi.org.uk
www.jcwi.org.uk

JCWI provides free advice and casework, training courses, and a range of publications. For specific queries on immigration, refugee or nationality issues there is an advice line: 020 7251 8706 (Tuesday and Thursday 2-5pm). They do not operate a drop-in advice service.

Language Line

11-21 Northdown Street
London
N1 9BN

Translation service: 0800 169 2879
Office: 020 7520 1430
www.languageline.co.uk

A 24-hour interpreting service offering access to interpreters in more than 100 languages over the telephone. Public and voluntary services can subscribe to this service. They also provide translation for documents.

Language and Learning Literacy Unit (LLU+)

London South Bank University
103 Borough Road
London
SE1 0AA

020 7815 6290
lluplus@lsbu.ac.uk
www.lsbu.ac.uk/lluplus/

LLU+ is a consultancy and professional development centre for staff working in the areas of literacy, numeracy, dyslexia, family learning and ESOL (English for Speakers of Other Languages). They also offer a course for front-line workers dealing with refugees – 'Refugee Awareness for the Workplace'.

Learndirect

http://www.learndirect.co.uk/

At Learndirect you can find hundreds of specially created online courses in computers, office skills and self development, designed so that you can learn at a time, place and pace to suit your needs. Information on their network of over 2000 Learndirect centres to help with local learning needs can be found on the website.

See also Learndirect Scotland, who operate around 500 learning centres as well as a database of courses throughout Scotland. Advice is also available on funding and on choosing a course (www.learndirectscotland.com; Freephone 0800 917 8000).

Learning and Skills Council (LSC)

Cheylesmore House
Quinton Road
Coventry CV1 2WT

0845 019 4170
www.lsc.gov.uk

The Learning and Skills Council (LSC) is responsible for funding and planning education and training for over-16-year-olds in England.

LINKnet Mentoring

LINKnet Mentoring
31 Guthrie Street
Edinburgh
EH1 1JG

0131 225 6284
enquiries@linknetmentoring.com
www.linknetmentoring.com

A voluntary organisation operating in the areas of Edinburgh, Lothian, Fife, and the Borders. Support is offered for academic, career, and personal development, and is aimed at visible minority ethnic people.

LORECA (London Refugee Economic Action)

020 7089 2735
loreca@osw.org.uk
www.loreca.org.uk

LORECA is a pan-London project that supports refugees to enter employment, training and enterprise.

Medical Foundation for the Care of Victims of Torture

111 Isledon Road
Islington
London
N7 7JW

020 7697 7777
www.torturecare.org.uk

The Medical Foundation provides training on working with survivors of torture and organised violence. Available to voluntary organisations, refugee community organisations and statutory agencies. Branches in the North West, North East and Scotland.

Migrant and Refugees Community Forum (MRCF)

2 Thorpe Close
London
W10 5XL

020 8964 4815
info@mrcf.org.uk
www.mrcf.org.uk

Provides grants to health professionals (refugees, asylum seekers and other overseas medical professionals) undertaking training programmes or exams leading towards registration with professional bodies, including costs of preparation of exams.

Migrant Helpline

The Rendezvous Building, Eastern Docks
Freight Services Approach Road
Dover, Kent
CT16 1JA

Tel: 01304 203 977
www.migranthelpline.org.uk

45 Friends Road
Croydon
Surrey
CR0 1ED

Tel: 020 8774 0002

The organisation, partly funded by the National Asylum Support Service (NASS), is one of six agencies providing assistance and support for asylum seekers and refugees entering and living in the UK. Migrant Helpline runs induction services in Kent and Croydon for newly arrived asylum seekers. The organisation also provides a network of One Stop Services throughout Kent and East Sussex. In addition they run a series of programmes designed to help asylum seekers and refugees integrate fully into the community. Such initiatives are designed to help these people obtain employment, become proficient in English, find suitable housing, secure education for children, etc.

Migrants Qualifications Project

Public Liaison Unit
London Development Agency
Devon House
58-60 St Katharine's Way
London
E1W 1JX

020 7954 4500
www.lda.gov.uk/server/show/ConWebDoc.499

This is a pan-London project that will enhance the employment opportunities of 2000 migrants in key sectors of the London economy (e.g. medical, engineering, construction, etc). It identifies the transferable skills and qualifications of migrant workers and supports them to fulfil their potential in the employment market. It is supported by, among others, the LDA, the five London LSCs and the Government Office for London (GOL).

Migrants Resource Centre

24 Churton Street
London
SW1V 2LP

020 7834 2505/6650
info@migrantsresourcecentre.org.uk
www.migrantsresourcecentre.org.uk

Multi-lingual advice centre for migrants and refugees, giving advice on benefits and immigration issues; community education facilities with CD-roms and website learning of ESOL and IT skills; conversational English workshops.

Multikulti

Website (www.multikulti.org.uk) provides information, advice, guidance and learning materials in a number of community languages, focusing on the following areas of welfare law – debt, employment, health, housing, immigration and welfare benefits.

National Association of Citizens Advice Bureaux (NACAB)

See Citizens Advice Bureaux.

National Institute of Adult Continuing Education (NIACE)

Renaissance House
20 Princess Road West
Leicester
LE1 6TP
United Kingdom

0116 204 4200/4201
enquiries@niace.org.uk
www.niace.org.uk

NIACE is the national, independent organisation in England and Wales that represents and advances the interests of all adult learners and potential learners – especially those who have benefited least from education and training. NIACE has significant experience of working with refugees and asylum seekers in these areas.

National Institute for Careers Education and Counselling (NICEC)

NICEC
Sheraton House
Castle Park
Cambridge,
CB3 0AX

01223 460277
enquiries@crac.org.uk

NICEC is a network organisation initiated and sponsored by CRAC. It conducts applied research and development work related to guidance in educational institutions and in work and community settings. Its aim is to develop theory, inform policy and enhance practice through staff development, organisation development, curriculum development, consultancy and research.

National Academic Recognition Information Centre (NARIC)

Qualifications & Skills Division
UK NARIC
Oriel House
Oriel Road
Cheltenham
Glos GL50 1XP

0870 990 4088
info@naric.org.uk
www.naric.org.uk

NARIC is the UK's official information provider on the comparability of international qualifications from over 180 countries worldwide.

Neil Bateman Associates

www.neilbateman.co.uk

Provide training and advice specialising in social policy and welfare rights issues.

New Vision

An online publication by refugees for refugees. It informs the refugee community on current developments and issues related to immigration, education, employment, health, culture, society etc. Reflects the views and interests of socially excluded and marginalized refugees and asylum-seekers and tells their unheard stories.

www.newvision.org.uk

North of England Refugee Service (NERS)

2 Jesmond Road
Newcastle
NE2 4PQ

0191 245 7311
info@refugee.org.uk
www.refugee.org.uk

Offers information and advice on higher education. Also makes referrals to institutions and educational service providers.

Northern Ireland Council for Ethnic Minorities (NICEM)

3rd Floor, Ascot House
24-31 Shaftesbury Square
Belfast
BT2 7DB

028 9023 8645
info@nicem.org.uk
www.nicem.org.uk

Serves all ethnic minorities in Northern Ireland, including refugees and asylum seekers.

Positive Action in Housing

98 West George Street
Glasgow G2 1PJ

0141 353 2220
home@paih.org
www.piah.org

An ethnic minority led charity. It aims to enable access to quality, affordable housing, free from fear of racial harassment and abuse.

PRAXIS

Pott Street
London
E2 0EF

020 7729 7985
admin@praxls.org.uk
www.praxis.org.uk

Provides information, advice and financial assistance for education, training and employment. Makes referrals to other organisations. Also runs general education courses and specific courses for health professionals and interpreters.

Prince's Trust

18 Park Square East
London
NW1 4LH

0800 842842
info@princes-trust.org.uk
www.princes-trust.org.uk

Range of services aimed at young people (aged 18-30) including educational underachievers, refugees and asylum seekers, unemployed, in/leaving care. Careers advice; volunteering and work placements; mentor support; small funding awards for community projects and to help access education, training and work. Training in basic skills; money management and personal development.

Racial Equality Councils (RECs)

A listing of Racial Equality Councils can be found at: www.cre.gov.uk/about/recs.html (check the website or the phone book to find your nearest REC)

Local organisations, set up to help promote equality of opportunity, tackle racial discrimination and promote good race relations. RECs are jointly funded by local authorities and the CRE.

Refugee Access

Refugee Access Project
Yorkshire and Humberside Regional Consortium for Asylum Seekers and Refugees
Phoenix House, 4th Floor
3 South Parade
Leeds
LS1 5QX

0113 214 3942
refugee.access@leeds.gov.uk
www.refugeeaccess.info

This is the website for asylum seekers, refugees and agencies working in Yorkshire, Humberside and the Liverpool area. It is a regional project to record skills and prepare refugees and asylum seekers for employment. It provides skilled refugees with a detailed employment portfolio to help them get jobs appropriate to their level of qualifications and also to help deal with local skills shortages.

Refugee Action

The Old Fire Station
150 Waterloo Road
London SE1 8SB

020 7654 7700
www.refugee-action.org.uk

Refugee Action has over 20 years' experience in the reception, resettlement, development and integration of asylum seekers and refugees in the UK. They provide advice and support, and the website has details of their many offices distributed across the country.

Refugee Assessment and Guidance Unit (RAGU)

The Learning Centre
236-250 Holloway Road
London N7 6PP

020 7753 5044
ragu@londonmet.ac.uk
http://www.londonmet.ac.uk/ragu/home.cfm

The Refugee Assessment and Guidance Unit was set up to improve the employment prospects of refugees and asylum seekers with higher level education or professional qualifications from their own countries. They also provide training for advisers who are working with refugees and asylum seekers.

Refugee Council

240-250 Ferndale Road
London SW9 8BB
T 020 7346 6700
info@refugeecouncil.org.uk
www.refugeecouncil.org.uk

Learning and Integration Unit (LIU)
3-9 Bondway
London SW8 1SJ
T 020 7840 4488
training@refugeecouncil.org.uk

London Advice line: 020 7346 6777
Yorkshire & Humberside Advice line: 0113 386 2210
West Midlands Advice line: 0121 6221515
Eastern region Advice line: 01473 297 900

The Refugee Council is the largest national organisation in the UK working with asylum seekers and refugees. Their work includes: giving advice and support to asylum seekers and refugees to help them rebuild their lives working with refugee community organisations, helping them grow and serve their communities caring for unaccompanied refugee children to help them feel safe and supported in the UK offering training and employment courses to enable asylum seekers and refugees to use their skills and qualifications campaigning and lobbying for refugees' voices to be heard in the UK and abroad keeping them high on the political agenda and discussed in the media and producing authoritative information on refugee issues worldwide, including reports, statistics and analysis.

Refugee Legal Centre

153-157 Commercial Road
London E1 2DA

020 7780 3200
www.refugee-legal-centre.org.uk

An independent, not-for-profit organisation providing legal advice and representation for those seeking protection under international and national Human Rights Asylum law.

Refugees Arrivals Project (RAP)

41b Cross Lances Road
Middlesex
TW3 2AD

020 8607 6888
rap@refugee-arrivals.org.uk

Independent advice service on access to NASS support, health, education and legal matters for refugees, asylum seekers, their relatives and friends. Covers the airports at Heathrow, Gatwick, Stansted, Luton and London City. Emergency accommodation, while waiting for NASS decision.

Refugees into Jobs (RIJ)

North West London Refugee Employment and Training Agency
3-7 Carlton Avenue East
Wembley
Middlesex
HA9 8UA

020 8908 4433
info@rij.dircon.co.uk
www.brent.gov.uk

RIJ assists refugees in West London through providing a range of services from advice and guidance through to the provision of grants for necessary training and support once in work.

Relocation Advisory Service

Phone (from UK): 0845 602 0297
Phone (from overseas): +44 141 248 2808
info@scotlandistheplace.com
www.scotlandistheplace.com

Established under the Fresh Talent Initiative, RAS aims to be a 'One Stop Shop' for questions relating to your move to Scotland, including work permits, accommodation, and becoming a student.

Resource Information Service

Bramah House
65-71 Bermondsey Street
London SE1 3XF

020 7939 0641
www.ris.org.uk

A specialist information charity - leading provider in the UK of directories, websites and information systems about services for people in need.

RETAS (Refugee Education and Training Advisory Service)

General Line: 020 7426 5800

RETAS is a division of Education Action International. RETAS supports the social and economic development of refugees and asylum seekers in the UK and at a European level by facilitating their access to education, employment and training opportunities and unlocking their potential both as individuals and members of the community.

RETAS offers information, advice and guidance on education, training and employment for refugees. Their drop-in advice service is free and open to asylum seekers and refugees (aged 16+) who need advice, guidance, advocacy or information on all aspects of education, training and employment. In addition, they offer special services for health professionals. Through their outreach service they assist marginalised refugees, including women, refugees with disabilities and young refugees.

RETAS Telephone Advice Line is open one afternoon per week. It is available for refugees and asylum seekers and it covers advice on education, training, government and other funding schemes in the UK. The advice line is open on Thursdays from 2.30-5.00pm on 020 7426 5801. Online advice will be available shortly.

Refugee Net

www.refugeenet.org

Refugee Net is the website of the EU Network on reception, integration and voluntary repatriation of refugees. It is a source of information and ideas related to the integration of refugees in Europe. It maintains a database on projects and organisations which provide services to refugees.

Refugees Online

www.refugeesonline.org.uk
info@refugeesonline.org.uk

Offers free training courses in website production and online journalism to refugees and asylum seekers in the UK who have experience of writing professionally.

Refugee Resource

3 Collins Street
Oxford
OX1 1XS

0845 458 0055
info@refugeeresource.org

Run a work placement and recruitment programme for refugees.

Refugee Support Centre

47 South Lambeth Road
London
SW8 1RH

020 7820 3606

Counselling/psychotherapy to refugees and asylum seekers. Training, support and information to health care, Social Services and community workers on the psycho-social needs of refugees. Addressing the unmet mental health needs of especially vulnerable groups, such as elderly refugees and children.

Refugee Womens Association (RWA)

Print House
18 Ashwin Street
London
E8 3DL

020 7923 2412
info@refugeewomen.org

The RWA runs a mentoring scheme tailored for refugee and asylum seeking women who are employed and who wish to become mentors. The objective is for the women to assist and support unemployed refugee women in their search for employment.

Roma Support Group

PO Box 23610
London
E7 0XB

020 7511 0822
roma@supportgroup.freeserve.co.uk
www.romasupportgroup.org.uk

Services for Roma refugees and migrants: befriending, language support and advocacy to assist people in accessing services; education support for children and young people.

The Ruth Hayman Trust

PO Box 17685
London
N6 6WD

trustee@ruthhaymantrust.com
www.ruthhaymantrust.com

Provides small grants to help adults living in the UK who have English as their second language to take up education and training. Awards are up to £200, but refugees have found this fund especially useful.

The Scottish Council for Minorities (SCM)

19 Iona Street,
Edinburgh,
EH6 8SP

0131 555 0030
www.scmonline.net

SCM aims to promote social inclusion for minorities and disadvantaged groups. It is active in the voluntary sector, enabling refugees and asylum seekers to access volunteering and employment opportunities.

Scottish Refugee Council

5 Cadogan Square (170 Blythswood Court)
Glasgow
G2 7PH

0141 248 9799
www.scottishrefugeecouncil.org.uk

Provides advice, information and assistance to asylum seekers and refugees living in Scotland. They also have specialist services in areas such as housing and welfare, education and employment, family reunion, women's issues, community development, the media and the arts.

Skillnet

Norton Park
57 Albion Road
Edinburgh
EH7 5QY

0131 475 2451
skillnet@btinternet.com
www.skillnetedinburgh.org.uk

An Edinburgh and Lothian based organisation which aims to support minorities in obtaining employment and education opportunities.

SOVA (Supporting Others through Volunteer Action)

1st Floor Chichester House
37 Brixton Road
London
SW9 6DZ

020 7793 0404
mail@sova.org.uk

SOVA works to strengthen communities by involving local volunteers in promoting social inclusion and reducing crime. SOVA is the leading national volunteer mentoring organisation working in the Criminal Justice System in England and Wales.

STAR (Student Action for Refugees)

3 Bondway
London
SW8 1SJ

www.star-network.org.uk

STAR is a unique organisation giving university students and young people the opportunity to:

- learn about and raise awareness of refugee issues in innovative ways

- support refugees in a practical way in their local communities through volunteering and
- campaign with and for the rights of refugees everywhere

The STAR network is made up of university based student groups, young people (16-18 year olds) involved in the STAR Youth Programme and Friends of STAR.

Time Together

TimeBank
The Mezzanine
Elizabeth House
39 York Road
London
SE1 7NQ

020 7401 5420
f.hammond@timebank.org.uk

Time Together is a scheme which matches refugees with mentors in the UK.

Trades Union Congress (TUC)

Congress House
Great Russell Street
London
WC1B 3LS

020 7636 4030
www.tuc.org.uk

Know your rights information line: 0870 600 4882

As the representative body for unions in the UK, the TUC campaigns for a fair deal at work and for social justice at home and abroad. For further information and a range of leaflets on rights at work and on joining a union, visit the 'Rights at Work' section of the TUC website or contact the information line to be sent further details.

Scottish Trades Union Congress (STUC)

0141 337 8100
www.stuc.org.uk

STUC represents around 630,000 working people in Scotland, the members of 46 affiliated trade unions. STUC's purpose is to coordinate, develop and articulate the views and policies of the trade union movement in Scotland, and to promote trade unionism, equality and social justice, the creation and maintenance of high quality jobs, and effective public services.

Wales Trades Union Congress (Wales TUC)

029 2034 7010
www.wtuc.org.uk

Wales TUC represents just under half a million working people in Wales, the members of 50 affiliated trade unions. Wales TUC is an integral part of the TUC, and campaigns to ensure that the TUC's role is undertaken effectively in Wales.

UK Advice Finder

www.advicefinder.org.uk

A comprehensive source of accurate information on organisations providing help and advice to the public.

UK Lesbian and Gay Immigration Group (UKLGIG)

c/o Gay.com

22/23 Carnaby Street
London W1F 9SE

020 7734 6168 (admin)
Helpline: 020 7734 3705 (12pm - 5pm Mondays and Fridays excluding bank holidays)
info@uklgig.org.uk
www.uklgig.org.uk

UKLGIG is a national lobbying and campaigning organisation working for legal equality for lesbians and gay men. UKLGIG is also a support and campaign group for lesbians and gay couples with immigration problems which they would not face if they were heterosexual. It also arranges for exchanges of information, provides a support network and advises on and supports applications to the Home Office.

UK Parliament

www.parliament.uk

The website includes an archive, publication list, and has a very good information service email/enquiry email.

UKCOSA (The Council for International Education)

9-17 St Albans Place
London N1 0NX

Telephone (not for advice) - from outside the UK: +44 20 7288 4330
www.ukcosa.org.uk

UKCOSA provides advice and information to international students studying in the UK and to staff who work with them. All UK universities and most colleges of further and higher education with international students are members of UKCOSA, which also receives funding from the UK Government's Department for Education and Skills. Information and advice to students is free. Note that UKCOSA does not offer a drop-in advice service to personal callers. International students seeking advice must consult the Student Advice pages. UKCOSA have also produced the leaflet, 'sources of funding for international students'.

Umbrella Bodies Forum

www.askNCVO.org.uk/umbrellas

A free searchable database containing all the contact details and information about the activities of over 80 national umbrella and resource bodies.

United Nations High Commissioner for Refugees - UK (UNHCR)

Millbank Tower
21/24 Millbank
London
SW1P 4QP

020 7828 9191
gbrlopmi@unhcr.ch
www.unhcr.org.uk

Contains information about supporting refugees worldwide. The London office covers the UK and Ireland and is involved in asylum policy issues, refugee law training and raising awareness of refugee issues.

UNHCR Evaluation and Policy Analysis Unit

http://www.unhcr.ch/cgi-bin/texis/vtx/research

Contains latest research on issues related to the work of UNHCR and the welfare of displaced people.

Volunteering (England)

Regent's Wharf
8 All Saints Street
London
N1 9RL

020 7520 8900
www.volunteering.org.uk

Volunteering England works to promote volunteering as a powerful force for change, both for those who volunteer and for the wider community. The web site offers a range of resources for anyone who works with or manages volunteers, as well as those who want to volunteer.

Welsh Refugee Council

Phoenix House
389 Newport Road
Cardiff
CF24 1TP

029 2048 9800
Email: info@welshrefugeecouncil.org
www.welshrefugeecouncil.org

Provides advice, information and assistance to asylum seekers and refugees living in Wales.

Working Lives Research Institute (WLI)

Working Lives Research Institute
London Metropolitan University
31 Jewry St
London
EC3N 2EY

(0) 20 7320 3042
workinglives@londonmet.ac.uk
www.workinglives.org

The Institute undertakes socially committed academic and applied research into all aspects of working lives, emphasising equality and social justice, and working for and in partnership with trade unions.

World Refugee

Up-to-date news about refugees and asylum seekers from around the world with a good archive.

www.worldrefugee.com

Further information for advisers and advocates

21 Benefit rates

Benefit rates 2006-2007

Asylum Seekers: Essential Living Needs[1]
(From 10 April 2006)

	£
Qualifying couple	63.07
Lone Parent, aged 18+	40.22
Single person, aged 18-24	31.85
Single person, aged 25+	40.22
Single person, aged 16-17 (except qualifying couples)	34.60
Single person, aged under 16	45.58

Means Tested Benefits (weekly)

For a full list of benefits, which are uprated annually in April of each year, see www.rightsnet.org

The website also has an easy to read and downloadable 'poster' of all the latest benefits. For this year (2006-2007) it can be downloaded from:

http://www.rightsnet.org.uk/pdfs/lasa_rates_poster_2006_2007.pdf

---

[1] The Asylum Support (Amendment) Regulations 2006

Income Support and income-based Jobseeker's Allowance £

Single person, under 18	Lower rate	34.60
	Higher rate	45.50
Single person, aged 18-24		45.50
Single person, aged 25 +		57.45
Lone parent, aged under 18	Lower rate	34.60
	Higher rate	45.50
Lone parent, aged 18 +		57.45
Couple, both under 18		34.60/45.50/68.65
Couple, one under 18		45.50/57.45/90.10
Couple, both aged 18 +		90.10
Dependent children		45.58

Premiums

Carer	26.35
Disability, single person	24.50
Disability, couple	34.95
Disabled child	45.08
Enhanced Disability, single person / lone parent	11.95
Enhanced Disability, couple	17.25
Family	16.25
Pensioner, single (JSA only)	56.60
Pensioner, couple	83.95
Severe Disability, per qualifying person	46.75

Housing Benefit & Council Tax Benefit

As for Income Support / income-based JSA or Pension Credit, except for:

Personal Allowances	£
Single person, aged under 18 (n/a for Council Tax Benefit)	45.50
Single person, aged 65 +	131.95
Couple, one or both aged 65 +	197.65

Tax Credits

Working Tax Credit (annual rates)

Basic element	1665
Couple / lone parent	1640
30 hours element	680
Disability element	2225
Severe disability element	945
50 + return to work, 16-29 hours	1140
50 + return to work, 30 + hours	1705
Childcare costs, one child (up to 80% of)	175 (per week)
Childcare costs, two children (up to 80% of)	300 (per week)

Child Tax Credit (annual rates)

Family element	545
Baby addition	545
Child element	1765
Disabled child	2350
Severely disabled child	945

Pension Credit £

Minimum Guarantee

Single	114.05
Couple	174.05

Additional amounts

Severe Disability (per person)	46.75
Carer	26.35

Non Means Tested Benefits

Attendance Allowance	Lower rate	41.65
	Higher rate	62.25

Bereavement Benefits[2]

Bereavement Allowance	Aged 45-54	25.28-78.35
	55-Pension	84.25
Widowed Parent's Allowance		84.25
Bereavement Payment (lump sum)		2000.00

Carer's Allowance

Carer's Allowance	46.95

Child Benefit

Only / eldest child	17.45
Lone parent rate	17.55
Other children	11.70

---

[2] Widow's Pension & Widowed mother's Allowance paid at same rates

Disability Living Allowance £

Care component	Lower rate	16.50
	Middle rate	41.65
	Higher rate	62.25
Mobility component	Lower rate	16.50
	Higher rate	43.45

Incapacity Benefit

Short term (under pension age)	Lower rate	59.20
	Higher rate	70.05
	Long term	78.50
Long term, age addition	Aged under 35	16.50
	Aged 35 – 44	8.25
Long term invalidity allowance[3]	Lower rate	5.30
	Middle rate	10.60
	Higher rate	16.50

Industrial Injuries Disablement Benefit

(Variable depending on % disablement)

Under 18	15.58 – 77.90
Under 18 with dependants	25.42 – 127.10
Aged 18 +	25.42 – 127.10

Jobseeker's Allowance

Under 18	34.60
Aged 18-24	45.50
Aged 25 +	57.45

---

[3] Only payable for transitionally protected IBLT cases

Maternity Allowance £

Standard rate 108.85

Severe Disablement Allowance[4]

Severe Disablement Allowance		47.45
Age addition	Aged under 40	16.50
	Aged 40-49	10.60
	Aged 50-59	5.30

Statutory Maternity, Paternity & Adoption Pay
108.85

Statutory Sick Pay
70.05

National Minimum Wage

(Per Hour)	October 2005	October 2006
Aged 22+	£5.05	£5.35
Aged 18-21 or in approved training	£4.25	£4.45
Aged 16-18	£3.00	£3.30

[4] Severe Disablement Allowance ceased to be available for new customers from April 2001

22 Biographies

Authors

Alison Balchin

Alison Balchin is an Employment Rights Officer at the TUC. Her responsibilities include developing TUC policy on individual employment rights, in particular issues affecting 'atypical' workers. She also covers the Human Rights Act and civil liberties in the workplace, including data protection and freedom of information issues, monitoring and surveillance at work. Alison has considerable policy development and advisory experience in the field of employment rights. Previous employment includes Centre for Labour Market Studies (Leicester University), Low Pay Units, the British Medical Association (BMA) and the Association of Teachers and Lecturers (ATL).

Neil Bateman

Neil Bateman is a writer, trainer and consultant who specialises in welfare rights and social policy issues.

He has established and managed a local authority welfare rights service, been an established policy adviser to the Local Government Association and his written work has been extensively published. He is also a contributor to other *Inclusion* handbooks. More information is available at www.neilbateman.co.uk

Bee Brooke

Bee Brooke graduated from Cambridge University in 2004 with a degree in Philosophy. After graduating she worked at *Inclusion* and has carried out qualitative and quantitative research in a range of fields, including learning and skills, youth inclusion, and in particular, welfare to work. She contributed to the 'Evaluation of StepUP: Final Report', published by the Department of Work and Pensions. Bee is now pursuing a career in NHS management.

Liz Carney

Liz Carney began her career as an employment law advisor, representing Leicester's homeworkers, mainly black and minority women involved in the hosiery trade. In 1996, Liz became a Welfare Rights Officer for Leicester Social Services department. In 2005, after qualifying as a solicitor (in public childcare proceedings, representing parents) Liz joined Leicester City Council's Discrimination Action Project, representing women from Pakistani, Bangladeshi and Somali communities. She currently undertakes casework in all areas of discrimination in employment.

Council for Assisting Refugee Academics (CARA)

CARA helps refugees with academic backgrounds to re-establish their careers in the UK. CARA runs a small grants programme and an information and advice service. Sinead O'Gorman was responsible for putting together the chapters from CARA.

Gavan Curley

Gavan Curley is a freelance writer and researcher with several years' governmental experience in the fields of race relations, the integration of migrants and community cohesion.

He has also worked for a number of years in the not-for-profit sector, as well as running advice surgeries for an Inner-London Member of Parliament. He has accreditation from the National Council for the Training of Journalists.

Slickston De Alyn

Slickston De Alyn is an independent advisor on a range of social policy issues. Slickston has provided representation for community groups and those with special status (including refugee and asylum seekers) on a range of housing issues. He has worked in policy across government and is a community advocate providing independent advice to community groups in London. He has a Degree in Social Policy and a Master's in Policy Analysis.

Amar Dhudwar

Amar is a Research Fellow at the Working Lives Research Institute (WLRI), currently working on an ESF-HE funded project comparing the labour market discrimination experiences of refugees and ethnic minority workers.

Prior to joining WLRI, Amar worked as a Project Researcher at Croydon Council, as a research intern at the Institute for Public Policy Research (IPPR) and as RAXEN project officer at the Commission for Racial Equality (CRE). She also completed work on a major research project for the Department for Constitutional Affairs on 'Tribunals for Diverse Users' at University College, London.

Alex Doyle

Alex Doyle works for *Inclusion* and has contributed to a range of research projects on learning and employment for excluded groups. This has included performing and analysing qualitative research on transitions into employment for homeless people and quantitative analysis on job brokerage and employment support. She graduated from Liverpool University in 2005 with a degree in Mathematics and Psychology.

James Lee

James Lee is the Mainstream Policy Adviser for Employment and Training at the Refugee Council. He has been working with refugees and asylum seekers for over six years. He trained initially in post-compulsory education teaching in the UK and then overseas. He also has a Master's degree in Political Philosophy from the University of York. Before taking up his present position, he worked with asylum seekers and refugees in Yorkshire and Humberside. This included a secondment from the Refugee Council to Leeds Metropolitan University as part of the Aimhigher funded Refugees into Higher Education Partnership.

Philomena de Lima

Philomena de Lima works as Researcher/Development Officer with the UHI PolicyWeb located at the University of the Highlands and Islands – Millennium Institute. She recently completed a study on migrant workers in the Highlands and Islands of Scotland in collaboration with Ionad Nàiseanta na h-Imrich, and is currently leading a multidisciplinary team on a similar study in Grampian (Scotland). She has authored a number of publications on ethnic minorities. Among her most recent publications is An Inclusive Scotland? The Scottish Executive and Racial Equality in G. Mooney and G. Scott (eds) Exploring Social Policy in the 'New' Scotland, published by the Policy Press.

Sean Moley

Dr Sean Moley worked for eight years as a secondary school science and ICT teacher before obtaining a PhD in Psychology in 2004 from the University of Reading. Prior to working at *Inclusion* he worked as a project manager on a workplace basic skills programme and he now specialises in research and consultancy in the field of learning and skills.

Graham O'Neill

Graham O'Neill has worked on race equality issues since 1999, joining the CRE in 2002. At the CRE, Graham has investigated numerous individual and collective complaints of racial discrimination and has worked on legal policy issues, most notably the Race Equality Duty and the Discrimination Law Review.

Ranjit Singh Rana

Ranjit Singh Rana joined the Commission for Racial Equality in 2001, in the role of Policy Officer and then Public Policy Team Manager. He is currently the Senior Policy Officer on Employment. His responsibilities include developing CRE policy in employment; taking an active role in advising, monitoring and in ensuring compliance with the Race Relations Act 1976; and developing and sustaining the CRE's public relations across central government and national and local agencies.

He has been actively involved in the race equality field since the early 1990s. Much of the work was progressed in a personal and professional capacity: the latter pursued through the Racial Equality Council movement in several roles, which include Race Discrimination Caseworker and Director.

Beryl Randall

Beryl Randall is Project Manager at the Employability Forum, which she joined in 2001. Her work includes identifying good practice in migrant and refugee employment. Former employment was with Reed-in-Partnership, where she worked on New Deal programmes and Employment Zones.

Beryl contributed to the first edition of the Newcomer's Handbook and is currently a graduate member of the Chartered Institute of Personal Development (CIPD).

Parnesh Sharma

Parnesh Sharma is a doctoral student in the Faculty of Law, Oxford University; he holds an M.Phil from Cambridge and a M.A. from the University of British Columbia in Canada. He is currently on sabbatical leave from the Immigration and Refugee Board of Canada.

Parnesh is also the Associate Research Director at the Centre for International Health and Human Rights Studies. Previously published works include the book: Aboriginal Fishing Rights: Law, Courts, Politics – a case study of the fight over a billion-dollar industry which has pitted the Government of Canada against its aboriginal peoples; the book, published in 1998, is still in print and is a recommended textbook for university-level courses.

Will Somerville (Editor)

Will Somerville edited the first edition of this handbook, published as the Newcomer's Handbook (2004) ISBN: 1-870563-68-9. He has edited four other welfare rights guides, including two editions of the Welfare to Work Handbook. He has also published in the Journal of Local Economy, the Industrial Relations Services Employment Review, the British Institute for Human Rights and Working Brief.

Will is currently the Senior Policy Officer at the Commission for Racial Equality (CRE). He was previously a Policy and Research Manager at *Inclusion*, a policy analyst at the Strategy Unit in the Cabinet Office and a researcher at the Institute for Public Policy Research (ippr). He has managed projects for government and the voluntary and private sectors, including the Department for Work and Pensions, the European Union, the Anglo-German Foundation, Brent and Hackney Local Authorities and UNISON.

Helen Sunderland

Helen Sunderland is Head of the ESOL Division at LLU+ (formerly the London Language and Literacy Unit) at London South Bank University, where she works in teacher education, project development and consultancy. She has over 20 years experience of teaching adults, including working with parents on how to help their children with literacy.

Her current projects include the citizenship materials for ESOL learners with its associated teacher training programme (with NIACE) and the Skills for Life Quality Initiative (with CfBT and other partners), where LLU+ is producing materials for teacher trainers. Helen has collaborated on several publications for LLU+, including Friends Families and Folktales, Writing Works, The Teachers' Video, Dyslexia and the Bilingual Learner, and is currently working on a guide for teachers called Teaching Basic Literacy to ESOL Learners.

Chris Taylor

Chris Taylor is a Development Officer at NIACE. She has 25 years experience in the teaching and managing of literacy, language and numeracy programmes for adult learners. She leads the Citizenship Materials for ESOL learners project.

From 1998 to 2001 she worked at the Refugee Council. During this time she was member of the REEF group at DfEE, the Basic Skills Agency Advisory Committee and the DfEE working group on ESOL in response to the Moser Report.

Rob Whelton

Rob Whelton is a consultant researcher associated with the University of the Highlands and Islands – Millennium Institute. He has worked with the UHI PolicyWeb and Ionad Nàiseanta na h-Imrich (National Centre for Migration Studies) and specialises in contemporary migration issues. He holds a Batchelor of Laws degree from the University of Aberdeen. For more information see www.robwhelton.co.uk

Andrea Winkelmann-Gleed

Dr Andrea Winkelmann-Gleed is working as Research Fellow for the Working Lives Research Institute (http://www.workinglives.org/staff_awg.html)). She has recently completed a project on migrant working in the East of England and is currently coordinating an ESF-funded, 2-year project investigating creative approaches to workforce ageing (CAWA).

Her PhD research investigated the integration of migrant nurses and some findings are published as a book: Migrant Nurses: motivation, integration, contribution (2006) ISBN-13-978-1-84619-007-X. Radcliffe Medical Press, Oxford.

Partners

Centre for Economic & Social Inclusion

Inclusion are an independent not-for-profit organisation dedicated to tackling disadvantage and promoting social justice. They offer research and policy services, tailored consultancy and bespoke and in-house training, running a wide range of conferences and events. Their key areas of social policy expertise are welfare to work, learning and skills, regeneration, homelessness, criminal justice and social exclusion.

Commission for Racial Equality (CRE)

A statutory body set up under the Race Relations Act 1976 to help eliminate racial discrimination, and promote equality of opportunity and good relations between people from different racial groups. The CRE provides information, advice, guidance and legal assistance on matters concerning racial discrimination and racial equality.

Council for Assisting Refugee Academics (CARA)

CARA helps refugees with academic backgrounds to re-establish their careers in the UK. CARA runs a small grants programme and an information and advice service. CARA publishes the Higher Education Pathways: A Handbook for the Refugee Community in the UK.

Employability Forum

The Employability Forum is an independent organisation that promotes the employment of refugees and the integration of migrant workers in the UK. It acts as a catalyst – working with the voluntary sector, employers and government, identifying the key issues and developing strategies for integrating refugees and migrants in the world of work.

Joint Council for the Welfare of Immigrants (JCWI)

JCWI provides free advice and assistance for new immigrants and for the settled community wishing to be reunited with their families. It is an independent organisation that has never sought nor accepted central government funds. JCWI provides free advice and casework, training courses, and a range of publications relating to immigration, refugee or nationality issues. JCWI publishes the Immigration, Nationality and Refugee Law Handbook 2006.

LLU+ at London South Bank University

LLU+ is a consultancy and professional development centre for staff working in the areas of literacy, numeracy, dyslexia, family learning and ESOL (English for Speakers of Other Languages). LLU+ also offers a course for front-line workers dealing with refugees called 'Refugee Awareness for the Workplace'.

National Institute for Adult Continuing Education (NIACE)

NIACE is the national, independent organisation in England and Wales that represents and advances the interests of all adult learners and potential learners – especially those who have benefited least from education and training. NIACE has significant experience of working with refugees and asylum seekers in these areas.

Neil Bateman Associates

Neil Bateman Associates provide training and advice specialising in social policy and welfare rights issues.

Refugee Council

The Refugee Council is the largest national organisation in the UK working with asylum seekers and refugees. Their work includes giving advice and support to asylum seekers and refugees to help them rebuild their lives, working with refugee community organisations, offering training and employment courses to enable asylum seekers and refugees to use their skills and qualifications, campaigning and lobbying for refugees' voices to be heard, and producing information on refugee issues worldwide, including reports, statistics and analysis.

STAR

STAR is an organisation made up of student-based groups comprised of university students and young people. STAR raises awareness of refugee issues in innovative ways, supports refugees in a practical way in their local communities through volunteering, and campaigns with and for the rights of refugees.

Trades Union Council (TUC)

As the representative body for unions in the UK, the TUC campaigns for a fair deal at work and for social justice at home and abroad. It also provides information and a range of leaflets on rights. This information is also available at the 'rights at work' section of the TUC website or via an information line.

Working Lives Research Institute (WLRI) at London Metropolitan University

The Institute undertakes socially committed academic and applied research into all aspects of working lives, emphasising equality and social justice, and working for and in partnership with trade unions.

23 Abbreviations

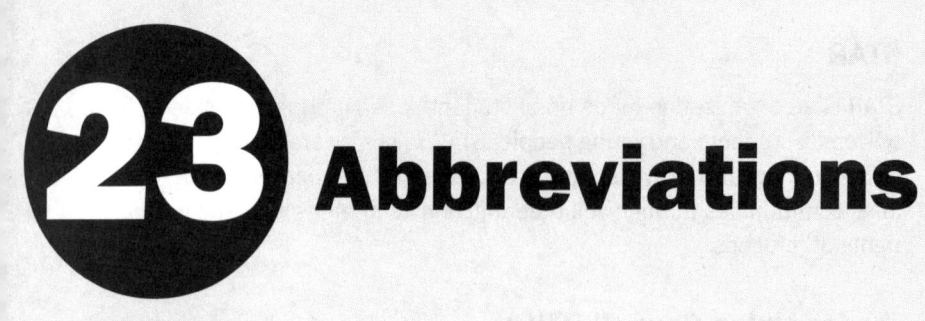

A8	Eight of the new states which have joined the EU – Czech Republic, Estonia, Hungary, Latvia, Lithuania, Poland, Slovakia, Slovenia
AA	Attendance Allowance
AA	Advanced Apprenticeship
ACAS	Advisory Conciliation and Arbitration Service
ACL	Adult and Community Learning
ADF	Adviser Discretion Fund
AIR	Asylum Interview Record
ALU	Asylum Liaison Unit (liaises with ports)
AML	Additional Maternity Leave
APEL	Assessment of Prior Experiential Learning
APIs	Asylum Policy Instructions
ARC	Application Registration Card
ASU	Asylum Screening Unit
AT	Action Team
BB	Bereavement Benefit
BET	Basic Employability Training
BoND	Building on New Deal
CA	Carer's Allowance
CAB	Citizens Advice Bureau
CARA	Council for Assisting Refugee Academics
CB	Child Benefit
CDL	Career Development Loan
CIPU	Country Information and Policy Unit

CIS	Construction Industry Scheme
CMD	Case Management Discussion
CPAG	Child Poverty Action Group
CRE	Commission for Racial Equality
CTB	Council Tax Benefit
CTC	Child Tax Credit
CV	Curriculum Vitae
DDA	Disability Discrimination Act
dep.	Dependant
DfFES	Department for Education and Skills
DFID	Department for International Development
DHP	Discretionary Housing Payment
DL	Discretionary Leave
DLA	Disability Living Allowance
DM	Decision Maker
DMA	Decision Making and Appeals
DMG	Decision Maker's Guide
DRC	Disability Rights Commission
DTI	Department of Trade and Industry
DWP	Department for Work and Pensions
e2e	Entry to Employment
EAL	English as an Additional Language
ECHR	European Convention on Human Rights
ECO	Entry Clearance Officer
ECSMA	European Convention on Social and Medical Assistance
ECtHR	European Court of Human Rights
EEA	European Economic Area
EEC	European Economic Community
EFL	English as a Foreign Language
EGAS	Educational Grants Advisory Service
ELB	Education and Library Board (Northern Ireland)

ELE	Exceptional Leave to Enter
ELR	Exceptional Leave to Remain
EMA	Education Maintenance Allowance
EOC	Equal Opportunities Commission
EqPA	Equal Pay Act
ESF	European Social Fund
ESOL	English for Speakers of Other Languages
ETFO	Environment Task Force Option
ETO	Education and Training Opportunity
ETP	Employer Training Pilot
ETS	Employment Tribunals Service
EU	European Union
EZ	Employment Zone
FCO	Foreign and Commonwealth Office
FE	Further Education
FTET	Full Time Education or Training
GLA	Gangmasters Licensing Authority
GP	General Practitioner
HB	Housing Benefit
HEI	Higher Educational Institution
HNC	Higher National Certificate
HND	Higher National Diploma
HO	Home Office
HP	Humanitarian Protection
HRA	Human Rights Act
HRT	Habitual Residence Test
HSE	Health and Safety Executive
HSWA	Health and Safety at Work Act
IAA	Immigration Appellate Authorities
IAP	Intensive Activity Period
IAS	Immigration Advisory Service

IB	Incapacity Benefit
ibJSA	Income-based Jobseeker's Allowance
ICD	Integrated Casework Directorate
IDIs	Immigration Directorate Instructions
IELTS	International English Language Testing System
ILM	Intermediate Labour Market
ILPA	Immigration Law Practitioners' Association
ILR	Indefinite Leave to Remain
IND	Immigration and Nationality Directorate
IS	Income Support
ISD	Immigration Status Document
JCWI	Joint Council for the Welfare of Immigrants
JES	Job Evaluation Scheme
JMA	Jobseeker Mandatory Activity
JR	Judicial Review
JSA	Jobseeker's Allowance
JSAg	Jobseeker's Agreement
LA	Local Authority
LEA	Local Education Authority
LEC	Local Enterprise Company (Scotland)
LFI	Learning Focused Interview
LLU+	Language and Learning Unit at South Bank University
LMS	Labour Market System
LORECA	London Refugee Economic Action
LOT	Longer Occupational Training
LPWSP	Lone Parent Work Search Premium
LSC	Learning and Skills Council
LTA	Leave to Appeal
LTE	Leave to Enter
MA	Modern Apprenticeship
MEP	Member of the European Parliament

MIC	Music Industry Consultant
MOLP	Music Open Learning Provider
MP	Member of Parliament
MTB	Money Transfer Business
MTCN	Money Transfer Control Number
MTO	Money Transfer Operator
NARIC	National Academic Recognition Information Centre
NASS	National Asylum Support Service
ND25 Plus	New Deal for 25 Plus
ND50 Plus	New Deal for 50 Plus
NDDP	New Deal for Disabled People
NDfM	New Deal for Musicians
NDLP	New Deal for Lone Parents
NDM	New Deal for Musicians
NDP	New Deal for Partners
NDYP	New Deal for Young People
NETP	National Employer Training Programme
NHS	National Health Service
NI	National Insurance
NIACE	National Institute of Adult Continuing Education
NIC	National Insurance Contribution
NICEC	National Institute for Careers Education and Counselling
NINO	National Insurance Number
NMW	National Minimum Wage
NRP	see UK NRP
NVQ	National Vocational Qualification
OISC	Office of the Immigration Services Commissioner
OML	Ordinary Maternity Leave
OSAT	On-Site Assessment and Training
OSS	One Stop Service

OU	Open University
p2w	progress2work
PC	Pension Credit
PHR	Pre-Hearing Review
PILON	Pay in Lieu of Notice
PLAB	Professional and Linguistic Assessment Board
PO	Presenting Officer
PRC	Police registration certificate
PSIC	Person subject to Immigration Control
RAGU	Refugee Assessment and Guidance Unit
RCO	Refugee Community Organisation
RETAS	Refugee Education and Training Advisory Service
RFRL	Reasons for refusal letter
RLC	Refugee Legal Centre
RLE	Refusal of Leave to Enter
RRA	Race Relations Act
RWA	Refugee Women's Association
SAAS	Student Awards Agency for Scotland
SAL	Standard Acknowledgement Letter
SCQ	Self-completion questionnaire
SDA	Severe Disability Allowance
SDA	Sex Discrimination Act
SEF	Statement of Evidence Form
SEGS	Science and Engineering Graduates Scheme
SEP	Self Employment Provision
SJFT	Short Job Focused Training
SLC	Student Loans Company
SMP	Statutory Maternity Pay
SoS	Secretary of State
SOVA	Supporting Others through Volunteer Action
SPP	Statutory Paternity Pay

SSC	Sector Skills Council
SSP	Statutory Sick Pay
SVQ	Scottish Vocational Qualification
T/A	Temporary admission
TCU	Third Country Unit
TD/ T.Doc	Travel Document
TfW	Training for Work
TUC	Trades Union Congress
UCAS	Universities and Colleges Admissions Service
UK	United Kingdom
UK NRP	UK National Reference Point (for Vocational Qualifications)
UKCOSA	UK Council for International Education
UKRP	UK Residence Permit
UN	United Nations
UNHCR	United Nations High Commissioner for Refugees
VAF	Visa Application Form
VSO	Voluntary Sector Option
WBL	Work Based Learning
WBLA	Work Based Learning for Adults
WFI	Work-Focused Interview
WTC	Working Tax Credit

Abbreviations

24 Index

16-17 year olds	194, 205-6, 209-11, 231
18-21 year olds	345, 349, 389, 637
25 and over (See New Deal for 25+)	
50 and over (See New Deal for 50+)	
A-Z queries	560-93
A-Z organisations	593-630
A8 countries	26
A8 nationals – social security benefits	119, 124-5
Abbreviations	648-654
ACAS (Advisory Conciliation and Arbitration Service)	444-7, 593
Accession states	21
Accidents at work	404
Accommodation	387, 480-7
Action Teams (ATs)	263-5
Adult and community learning centres (ACL)	284-5
Advice agencies	458-460
Adviser Discretion Fund (ADF)	184-5
Agency workers	413-497
Agreeing a course of action with your adviser	459-460
Appeals	
Benefits	179-81
Employment	529
Immigration	64-7

NARIC	330
Application forms	
Work permit	24
Student visa	58
Travel documents	79
Jobs	295-301
Application Registration Card (ARC)	321
Changes	73
Applying for assistance	458-9
Applying for work	295-301
Apprenticeship	211-214
Recognition	327
ARC (See Application Registration Card)	
Assessment of Prior (Experiential) Learning (APEL/APL)	334
Asylum	70-76
Asylum Casework Directorate (ACD)	72
Asylum Screening Unit (ASU)	70
Asylum seekers	70-76
Attendance Allowance	146-148
Authors' biographies	638-45
Au pairs	47-49
Availability for work	130-2
Bank accounts	365-7, 563
Bank holidays	398-9
Benefit Agency (see Jobcentre Plus)	
Benefit appeals	179-81
Benefit decisions	178-182
Benefit entitlement	111-2
Benefit rates table	632-7
Benefit Run Ons	182-3
Benefits	108-191

Benefits – immigration restrictions	113-129, 194
Bereavement Benefit	635
Better Employability Training (BET)	196
Budgeting loans	177
Building on New Deal (BoND)	278-279
Bullying	404-406
Burden of proof	449, 518-519
Car insurance	369
Career Development Loan (CDL)	99
Carer's Allowance	154-155
Carers	154-155
Challenges (see appeals)	
Change of circumstances	181
Change of status	29-30
Checks before starting work	430-1
Child Benefit	156-8
Child Tax Credit	170-3
Citizens Advice Bureau	597-8
Citizenship	85, 550-5
Citizenship ceremony	554
Citizenship test	553
Claiming asylum	70-71
Claiming benefits	112-4
Commission for Racial Equality	438, 460, 520, 585, 598-9
Community care grants	177
Complaint of racial discrimination	439-448
Connexions/Careers Service	600
Contracts	
Employment	313, 378-9, 385, 407, 408, 410
Work trial	347
Housing	480-2

Contribution-Based Jobseeker's Allowance	129-133
Council Tax Benefit	161-163
Course tutor	287
Covering letters	297-298
CRE (See Commission for Racial Equality)	
Credit union	540
CV	296, 335
Deductions from pay	386-388
Dentist	42-43, 154-155
Direct discrimination	427-428
Disabilities	151-153, 567
Disability Living Allowance	148-151, 636
Disciplinary procedures	409-410
Discretionary Leave (DL)	20, 70-71, 72
Discrimination	400-1, 407-8, 424-465
Discrimination at work	433-465
Discriminatory Advertisements	436
Dismissal	514-516
Dismissal rights	514-516
DL (see Discretionary Leave)	
Doctor	42-43, 154-155
Documentation	318-325
Documents	320-2, 376-8, 511
Domestic workers	45-6
Driving licences	368-9
EAL (See English Language)	
Education Maintenance Allowance (EMA)	208-211
EFL (See English Language)	
ELR (See Exceptional Leave to Remain)	
Employee	379-388
Employer Training Pilots (ETPs)	215-217
Employment	220-283

Employment appeal tribunal	529-30
Employment for training in skills to be used outside Great Britain	439
Employment placements	343-344
Employment programmes	220-283
Employment rights	370-423
Employment Service (see Jobcentre Plus)	
Employment status – employee (See employee)	
Employment status – worker (See worker)	
Employment tribunals	288-533
Employment Zone (EZ)	266-271
English for Speakers of Other Languages (ESOL)	284-292
English language	83, 95, 284-292, 338, 553
Entitlement – benefits	111-112
Entitlement – health care	154-155
Entry clearance	28, 32, 48
Entry to Employment (e2e)	205-209
Equal opportunities monitoring	298
Equal pay	512-6
ESOL (See English for Speakers of Other Languages)	
Europe	21
European Economic Area (EEA)	25
European Union (EU)	21, 118
Evidence in a case of racial discrimination	449-459
Exceptional Leave to Remain (ELR)	21, 117
Exceptions to unlawful racial discrimination	388-9
Family amnesty	77
Finding work	294-311
Fresh Talent	53
Funeral costs	172-5
Further Education	192-195
Further information for advisers	556-60

Gangmasters Licensing Agency	414-6
Gateway Protection Programme	77
Gender discrimination	497, 503
Genuine Occupational Qualification	439
Genuine Occupational Requirement	439
Global Agreement on Trade in Services (GATS)	36
Grievance procedures	410-1, 489-91, 522-3
Habitual residence	123, 124
Harassment	404-8, 430, 452-3, 477-8, 500-1
Health	140-5, 573-5, 154-5
Health and Safety	401-4, 406-7
Higher Education	92-107
Highly Skilled Migrant Programme (HSMP)	52
Holiday Entitlement	398-99
Homeworkers	516-8
Housing	575 580-7
Housing Benefit	158-9
Humanitarian Protection (HP)	20, 70, 76, 321-2
Husband (see Spouse)	
IELTS (See International English Language Testing System)	
Illegal work	28-9, 32, 264, 375, 420-2, 432-3, 511-2
Illegal workers (see Irregular Migrants)	
Illness, work related	151-3
ILR (see Indefinite Leave to Remain)	
Immigration and Nationality Directorate (IND)	607-8
Immigration rules	24-69
Immigration status	19-20, 24-33
Immigration Status Document (ISD)	321
Incapacity	141
Incapacity Benefit (IB)	140-3, 271-3, 636

Income	301-3
Income Support	133-7, 633
Income-Based Jobseeker's Allowance (ibJSA)	633
IND (See Immigration and Nationality Directorate)	
Indefinite Leave to Remain (ILR)	20-1, 62-3, 76
Indirect Discrimination	428-9, 450-1, 476, 489, 498-9
Induction	314-5, 357-8
Innovators	52
Insurance	369
International English Language Testing System (IELTS)	83, 95
Internships	36
Interpreters – social security	112, 290
Interpreting	578, 610
Interview process	305-311
Irregular migrants	319
Investors	50-1
Job applications	295-301
Job Grant	183-4
Jobcentre Plus	193, 609
Jobs (see employment)	
Jobseeker Mandatory Activity	273-4
Jobseeker's Agreement	131
Jobseeker's Allowance (JSA)	637, 129-33
Jobseeker's Direction	201
Language support	288-9
Learndirect	202-5, 610-1
Learning and Skills Council	611
Learning Focused Interview	231
Leave (see Holiday Entitlement)	
Legal rights	378-393
LinkUP	277

Longer Occupational Training (LOT)	197
Maternity benefits	467-71
Maternity rights	467-79
Mediation	443-6
Mentoring	342-3, 582
Midwives	62
Migrant workers	370-423, 425-6
Minister of religion	39-40
Missionary	39-40
Modern Apprenticeships	211-4
Money transfer	535-548, 583
Money transfer operator	535-548, 583
Mortgages – help with cost of	162-3
NARIC (See National Academic Recognition Information Centre)	
NASS (See National Asylum Support Service)	
National Academic Recognition Information Centre	327-30
National Asylum Support Service (NASS)	71-2, 77, 79-80
National Curriculum	284
National Employer Training Programme (NETP)	215-7
National Health Service (NHS)	109, 154-5, 362, 572
National Institute of Adult Continuing Education (NIACE)	614, 644
National Insurance	362-4, 376-7
National Insurance Number (NINO)	362-4, 376-7
National Minimum Wage (NMW)	388-390
National security	439
National Vocational Qualification (NVQ)	211-5, 335
Naturalisation	550-5
New accession states	21
Newcomers	19
New Deal	220-1, 232-262
New Deal 25 Plus	244-51

New Deal 50 Plus	251-5
New Deal for Disabled People	260-2
New Deal for Lone Parents	255-60
New Deal for Musicians	240-4
New Deal for Partners	255-60
New Deal for Young People	232-40
NHS (See National Health Service)	
Nurses	62
NVQ (See National Vocational Qualification)	
Occupier with basic protection	482-3
One Stop Service (OSS)	71, 561-2
Ordinarily resident	22, 170
Overpayments	169
Overseas domestic workers	45-6
Pathways to Work	271-2
Parental leave	381, 384, 396-7, 472-3
Parents	393-7, 255-60
Partners	227, 255-6
Passport	320-3, 550, 554
Paternity leave	395-7, 473-4
Pay	394-9, 412, 419, 470-6
Pension	110-2, 118, 135, 511
Pension Credit	137-9
Permit-free employment	38
Person subject to immigration control	20-1
PLAB (See Professional and Linguistic Assessment Board)	
Placements	343-4
Police raids	421-2
Portfolios	333-5
Positive action	439
Pregnancy	487-71, 477

Private households	418-9, 438
Probationary periods	313-4
Professional and Linguistic Assessment Board (PLAB)	38
Professional bodies	331-333
Programme Centres	199-202
Progress2work	274-6
Proving discrimination	449-50, 498, 518
Public funds	21, 118
Public holidays	398-9
Qualifications	326-35, 431-2
Race relations questionnaire	441, 453-4
Racial discrimination	424-65
Racial grounds	426, 433, 503
Reciprocal agreements	119-20, 126
Recruitment process	303-4
Redundancy	408-12
References	304-5, 341, 344, 357
Refugee	21, 76-87, 92-107, 321
Refugee Assessment and Guidance Unit (RAGU)	84, 586, 619
Refugee Action	562, 586, 591, 618
Refugee Council	619, 646
Refugee Education and Training Advisory Service (RETAS)	621
Religious or Faith Groups	426-7
Remedies	448, 514, 528
Remittances	534-549
Rent – help with cost of	158-61
Right to reside	22, 120-2
Right to work	31, 72-3, 320-5, 420-1
Rights	370-423
Rights for working parents	392-7
Salary guide	302-3

Sanctions	238, 270
Science and Engineering Graduates Scheme (SEGS)	46-7
Scotland	81, 290-2
Scottish Refugee Council	624
Scottish Vocational Qualification (SVQ)	210
Seafarers	419
Seamen recruited overseas	439
Seasonal agricultural worker	43-4
Seasonal Agricultural Workers Scheme (SAWS)	43-4
Section 4	71, 75
Sector Based Schemes (SBS)	420
Segregation	427-8
Self-employment	197, 243-4, 249, 253, 315-6
Sending money home	534-549
Setting up a business	51, 315-6
Sex discrimination	476-9, 503-4
Shop workers	388
Short Job Focused Training (SJFT)	197
Sickness	132, 140, 143-5, 382, 384, 393, 408, 509, 637
Sick Pay	132, 140, 143-5, 382, 384, 393, 408, 509, 637
SJFT (See Short Job Focussed Training)	
Skills for Life	203, 205
Social Fund	173-7
Social Security	108-190
Social Security appeals	108-114, 177-181
Social Security office (see Jobcentre Plus)	
Speculative applications	301
Spouse	93, 472
Starting work	312-6
Statements	457

Status	19-20, 28-30, 32-3, 379-81
Statutory Sick Pay	143-5, 393, 637
Student	58-61, 92-107
Student nurse	29, 33
Student support	93, 96
Studying	588
SUNRISE	80, 81, 588-9
Supporting evidence in a case of racial discrimination	454-6
SVQ (See Scottish Vocational Qualification)	
Tax	301-3, 369, 380, 390-1
Tax code	363-5, 391
Tax Credits	108, 164-73, 181, 254, 634
Teachers	38, 43-4, 287
Temporary admission	20, 73
Tenancy agreements	480-7
Time limits for assistance	70-1, 522-4
Trade Union	399-400, 435-6, 457, 521
Trade Union membership	399-400
Trainer	287
Training	42, 73-4, 82, 192-218
Training and Work Experience Scheme (TWES)	36
Training for Work (TfW)	195-7
Translating	289-90, 578, 590, 228-9
Translation assistance	289-90
Travel document	322, 78-9
Travel to interview	348-51
Tribunals	446-8, 488-533
UCAS (See Universities and Colleges Admissions Service)	
UK citizenship	550-5

UK Council for International Students	579, 601, 628
UKCOSA (See)	
UN convention travel document	322
Unable to work	121-3, 133-4, 140, 144-5, 167, 222
Undocumented workers	420-1
Unfair dismissal	514-21
Universities and Colleges Admissions Service (UCAS)	104-5
University courses	102-5
Unlawful racial discrimination	433-8
Variation of leave	319
Victimisation	429-30, 452, 477, 499-80,
Visa	29, 31
Volunteering	336-343, 352-3, 432, 591-2, 629
Wales	85, 592, 599, 627
Welsh Refugee Council	630
Who can work in Britain?	371-5
Wife (see Spouse)	
Work Based Learning for Adults (WBLA)	195-9
Work culture	362-9
Work experience	250-1, 336-51
Work Focused Interviews	137, 226-232
Work permit	31, 34-7, 419-20
Work placements	343-4, 353-60
Worker's registration document	376-8
Work trials	344-8
Worker	379-81, 388, 413
Working holiday maker	49-50
Working in private households	418-9
Working parents' rights	393-99

Working tax credit	164-9, 634
Working time rights	397-9
Written statements	49-11, 381, 383-5, 409-11, 417, 441, 443, 498, 512, 515
Young people	232-40

WORKING IN THE UK: NEWCOMER'S HANDBOOK *2ND EDITION*

Notes

WORKING IN THE UK: NEWCOMER'S HANDBOOK *2ND EDITION*